Incredible Memories

Incredible Memories

Anne Aitken -John

Copyright ©2019 Anne John-Aitken
All rights reserved. No part of this book may be reproduced, stored in a retrieval system or transmitted in any form or by any means, electronic, mechanical, photocopying, recording or otherwise, without the prior permission of the author.

Published by Red Feather Publishing

Cover: Silk scarf designed by Bernadette Aitken

ISBN: 978-0-9942845-2-5

Dedicated to my five children and six grandchildren. Hope you enjoy reading tales of my younger days. I have enjoyed living my life and tried to grasp as many experiences as possible, or those which presented themselves.

Life is as beautiful as one wants it to be. Far too short to fit all one's ambitions. So I will enjoy it while I can and while it includes my wonderful family.

Your loving Mum, Nonna.

Contents

Book I
'29 to '47 1
Chapter 1
FIRST YEARS 4
Chapter 2
JAMAICA '38 36
Chapter 3
ANECDOTES OF YOUNGER DAYS 59
Chapter 4
JAMAICA '39 70
Chapter 5
EVACUEES ARRIVE IN JAMAICA 78
Chapter 6
MY SIXTEENTH YEAR 87
Book II
Leaving Jamaica 91
Chapter 7
APRIL 1947 TO JULY 1968 93
Chapter 8
EDGBASTON 98
Chapter 9
MOVING ON 104
Chapter 10
I JOIN THE NAVY 109
Chapter 11
H.M.S. MERCURY 115
Chapter 12
FIRST TASTE OF A REAL GALLEY 119

Chapter 13
PROMOTION 124

Chapter 14
H.M.S. GAMECOCK, BRAMCOTE 129

Chapter 15
JOCK, TOM IN MY LIFE 136

Chapter 16
I MEET TOM'S FAMILY..140

Chapter 17
FURTHER PROMOTION 143

Chapter 18
TOM AND I BECOME ENGAGED 147

Chapter 19
COURSES BEFORE DEMOB 149

Chapter 20
WE MOVE ON..151

Chapter 21
THE START OF MARRIED LIFE 154

Chapter 22
OUR FIRST CHILD 158

Chapter 23
RETURN TO DELAMERE RD 164

Chapter 24
FLY TO MALTA...165

Chapter 25
MOVE TO SHENVAL 174

Chapter 26
MOVE TO CANNICH 179

Chapter 27
AN EVENTFUL YEAR...182

Chapter 28
VISITORS WE HAD WHILE IN CANNICH 187
Chapter 29
OUR STAY AT WOODLEY 190
Chapter 30
KETTERING OUR NEW HOME 193
Chapter 31
ALISON'S ARRIVAL 196
Chapter 32
VISITORS 200
Chapter 33
MORE ABOUT LIFE IN KETTERING 203
Chapter 34
PLANS TO EMIGRATE 207
Chapter 35
THE START OF A NEW LIFE 210
Chapter 36
MY DREAM -THE AUSTRALIAN TRIP 219
Chapter 37
ON THE MOVE 228
Chapter 38
THE FLOODS CAME 233
Chapter 39
FREAK WET SEASON 240
Chapter 40
A VISIT TO EXMOUTH GULF 247
Chapter 41
TROPICS AT LAST 252
Chapter 42
MAJOR BREAK-DOWN 259
Chapter 43
FINAL DAYS WITH THE GIRLS 263

Chapter 44
FITZROY CROSSING TO KATHERINE 266
Chapter 45
KATHERINE TO DARWIN 270
Chapter 46
DARWIN TO KATHERINE 273
Chapter 47
LONG HAUL TO ALICE 280
Chapter 48
ALICE SPRINGS AND WESTERN COUNTRYSIDE 284
Chapter 49
ALICE SPRINGS VISITS 288
Chapter 50
EAST OF ALICE 292
Chapter 51
SOUTH TO ULURU 294
Chapter 52
OODNADATTA TRACK & FURTHER SOUTH 298
Chapter 53
SOUTH AUSTRALIA 302
Chapter 54
VICTORIA AND BEYOND 305
Chapter 55
TASMANIA 309
Chapter 56
NEW SOUTH WALES 312
Chapter 57
NEW ZEALAND 317
Chapter 58
SYDNEY 327

Chapter 59
WEST OF SYDNEY 330
Chapter 60
QUEENSLAND.. 338
Chapter 61
THE FINAL LEG 359
Chapter 62
AROUND THE WORLD ON A SHOESTRING 379
Chapter 63
BOONDARABI, MOORA 414
Chapter 64
JAMAICA RE-UNION 1984... 431
Chapter 65
UK BY CAR 436
Chapter 66
LONE TRIP AROUND THE WORLD....................................... 445
Chapter 67
LASTLY 450
ACKNOWLEDGEMENTS 451
APPENDIX 1... 453

Book I

'29 to '47

Haiti the land of my birth
Mountains full of mahogany
Port au Prince the city I was born
The natives as black as ebony
Their nature as beautiful as
The quiet seas at dawn.
Creole and French their language
Voodoo mixed with Christianity their religion.

At three months I was taken to Santo Domingo
To experience a fierce cyclone
Then shipped out to Curacao
Away from a city which no longer existed
From the heavy rain and winds that raged
On to Halifax, Canada in the cold north
To join a ship, the Atlantic to cross
For a short stay in England, equanimity.

Then to return once more to my birthplace
And spend happy, exhilarating years
With the people I grew to love and embrace.
Then once more return to England on leave
Three months, meeting relatives, a different environment
Where the grass is so green, the weather so wet
Only one language to contend with
And everyone looked so white.
An experience, in my mind quite set.

Incredible Memories

Returning to spend a memorable year in Haiti
At five, then moved to Puerto Rico
Spanish speaking, rich in warmth and music
To start my schooling in a new 'lingo'
The island not very hilly, full of beautiful beaches
Two special years spent in this memorable 'isle'
Then we sailed across the vast Atlantic
Two weeks of great fun on board.
Returning once more to the shores of England.

By seven, to appreciate, much more the countryside
Full of elegant buildings, some ancient Castles
Cowslips along the roads, fields full of red poppies
Cows and sheep in the meadows or on commons

Snow, slush, slippery ice, galosh's and wellington boots
Fog, Scotch-mist, damp, cold and a warm wood fire
Smoky, smelly, sooty chimneys, black shiny coal
Cold bedrooms, eiderdowns, warm dressing-gowns, hot water bottles
To stay six months, English measles leave me cripple.

A very exciting boat trip, and back to the West Indies
The sunshine and warmth to be my cure.
While on the ship, a huge iceberg we did sight
Singularly brilliant, beautiful, dangerous to be near
Sailed to Bermuda, 'umpteen' small islands
Unusual shapes, appearing to be floating on the sea
Ultra marine waters with white sandy beaches
A sight of great beauty, hardly a car did we see
Transport was by buggy, surrey or cart.

Arriving in Kingston, Jamaica, berthing at a long pier
Called the 'island of rivers' attractive mountains
Populated by many charming nationalities
Negroes, East Indians, Chinese, South Americans, Europeans
All thriving in this wonderful climate, unaware of differences
Even the poor seemed content and happy with their lot
Their rhythmic bodies, their music enveloping their lives
Happiness and joy of living became very contagious
Here to spend many happy years of my life
Despite a long war and deprivation
To complete my thorough education.
Before sailing once more, on a banana boat

'29 to '47

To cross the great Atlantic still fraught with danger
Ferocious, stormy seas and still an odd mine to miss
Arriving in England to be saddened by the after math of war
Complete streets demolished by Hitler's bombing raids
Street after street, massive bomb craters
Shells of houses full of uncanny pink flowers
Which managed to grow even out of the walls
It took many a year to clear, rebuild, and hide the devastation
But the spirit of the British was never crushed
They had won through in spite overwhelming odds.

                        By Anne John Aitken

Chapter 1

FIRST YEARS

In relating certain parts of my life to the family and friends, they made me realize that I have had quite a full one. I am writing it because I have been asked to relate parts of my travels through my life, what could be called, possibly unusual and I hope of some interest to whomever shall read it. So, with some trepidation I have been persuaded to write. I was born in Port au Prince, Haiti, in the West Indies or greater Caribbean Islands. When I was four or five, I was taken and shown where this big event took place. The building I can remember quite well. We arrived at a large car park. When I got out of my father's car I was confronted by a huge double-storied, white building. There were several men and women walking in the car park in white uniforms and some in army uniforms. It was an American Army Hospital.

My father Basil Joseph John (1903-1974) was born in Satara, India. Satara was a town about 100 miles out of Bombay. My mother was born in Valparaiso, Chile. My father's mother was Irish and his father was of Greek-Armenian descent. My mother's mother was Chilean of Spanish-English descent; my mother's father was a Scot. How much more Scottish could one be with a surname like Burns. I remember well his quiet Scottish accent. In the 18th and 19th century many Europeans settled in South America. My grandmother's maiden name was Swinburn; she was companion to my grandfather's first wife who I believe died in childbirth. My grandfather later married my grandmother.

I was born on the 14th of October 1929 in an American Army Hospital. A little bundle of very mixed I D's! Registered as a British Subject by my father the day I was born, I had a dual birth certificate. One written in French which meant by their law I was Haitian. At the age of twenty-one I could pay them US $200 to relinquish that right. I have been told that should I return to Haiti, I would be imprisoned. I have not found out whether this is fact and would not return just in case. The other birth certificate was in

FIRST YEARS

English with the stamp of the British Consulate. This gave me the right to hold a British passport. I had a brother, David, 14 months older than me. As children we travelled on either parent's passport. Mostly on our mother's.

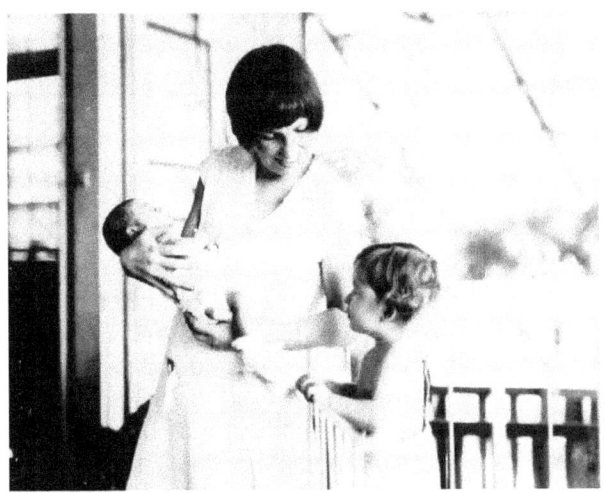

Self (1 month old), Mummy and David 16 months, Haiti 1929

Mummy, self (1 year old) and David (2 ½ years old) 1931

When I was 3 months old my parents were moved to Santo Domingo, now the Dominican Republic, with the Shell Oil Company, the company my father worked for. We went wherever he was transferred. We were in Santo Domingo until I was one, or more correctly 11 months old. The island was hit by a terrible cyclone. We lived out of the city. Now called Ciudad Trujillo, named after a ruthless dictator who ran the country while we were

Incredible Memories

there. The city was completely demolished, except I was told, the Canadian Bank. This survived because someone had left all the windows open on the top floor and the wind howled through. Thousands lost their lives that day. Some said, many more lost their lives at the hands of "El Presidente" as he used this as an excuse to bump off the opposition. Our house was almost completely demolished. And so began my exciting life or rather varied life. At that time my father was away on a business trip, had it not been for our gardener we might not have survived.

Our house was raised on bricks forming pillars at certain points under the house to support it. These were about a metre high. The only solid part of the house were the concrete floors of the bathroom and the kitchen. The cyclone hit with great force and was upon us quicker than expected. David, my brother, was saved just before a cupboard fell on him. Juan, our gardener had seen which way the cyclone was coming and had taken us under the house to the side of the concrete floor furthermost from that direction. There we stayed until the winds passed. Then he and my mother went out to see what they could salvage in the way of food and clothing. Tulia our nurse stayed with David and me. My mother and Juan were met by total devastation. The coconut plantation next door had about six trees left standing, three of these were topless. The hedge down the side of our driveway had completely disappeared as had the roof of our house and all but two of our walls. My mother insisted Juan go home and see that his family and wife were all right, he had four children. This was after they had rescued what food they could find plus some water which they had to boil so I could have a feed. Once he had seen his family were safe with relations he returned to look after us. He was so loyal to us and truly loved us as his own.

He had no sooner returned than we were hit again by strong winds. Juan hurriedly moved us around to the other side of the concrete block till the wind quieted. We lived in these conditions for three days before anyone could get to us. At this time my father had been sent to the other half of the country, Haiti. This was a terrible time for my father as he did not know if we had survived. Our first visitor was Mr. Mantibo from the Shell office who had walked all the way to try and find us. The devastation was such that it was extremely difficult to find the right direction. The landscape was so changed.

He told my mother about the total destruction in the city. He was so relieved to see we were all alive and unharmed. He left us with a few cans of food he had brought. During the day someone brought us some water, which was fairly expensive. It had to be boiled before we could drink it. We camped out for three days during which we could see a huge pall of smoke. The government had all the bodies burnt They had all available labour set to clean up all the streets and clear away debris.

FIRST YEARS

My father arrived a few days later and were we glad to see him. We gathered our remaining belongings and were taken to the Port where a ship was waiting to evacuate us. This must have been a very difficult time for my mother; besides the ordeal of the cyclone, she had lost a lot of her precious belongings, among them books she had been given by her father.

We were being sent to England. First, we had to go to Curacao to get a boat as none left the Dominican Republic for England. It was where I first got a liking to the smell of oil and gasoline (petrol). When I was a bit older, I learnt that Curacao was a small island off the East coast of South America. Curacao was where the Dutch Shell Oil Company had a big oil refinery.

Trip to England.

It was not long before we were put on a ship bound for England, via Halifax, Canada.

When we reached England, we went to stay with my mother's parents in a huge house in Darlaston Road Wimbledon. This is where I became more independent. While in the back garden with my grandfather Burns, to his great delight, I let go of his knee and took my first steps. Well, apparently after that there was no holding me. I didn't want anyone to hold my hand "thank you very much", I could do it myself and did. Up and down the path I went with my mother, nurse and grandmother following with outstretched hands, which I refused. Every time I fell, "I could get up myself" and did. My mother recalled I had such a determined look on my face and then when I succeeded a large grin, which told all. I'd look around for applause and would promptly fall again.

I revisited the house in 1983 while on a trip to England. The owner kindly invited me in and took me through to the back garden, after I had told him my grandparents used to own the house many years before. It was a strange feeling. While standing looking down the back garden a fox crossed and disappeared through a hole in the back fence. It was a funny sensation standing there. I had a feeling the garden had not changed much in all those years. High hedges all around to hide one from ones neighbours. A path running down the left side of the garden with a well-kept lawn taking up the rest of the garden. Lacking in the colour of flowers. The only colour was in the different shades of green in the trees, shrubs, hedge and lawn. There was a garden bench near the path but I doubted it was the same one my grandfather had sat on. The path was the same one I had taken my first steps along. How many thousands steps I have taken since? I have climbed an 8,000 ft. mountain, hitchhiked around New Zealand, Tasmania and parts of the U.S.A and Canada, but more of that later.

My First Memory

My first real memory was of us living in Haiti when I was about two and a half or three. It was a new and exciting house and my mother had a little baby. This was my sister Pat, she had been born in Santo Domingo. We had returned to Santo Domingo several months after the cyclone. The servants spoke this funny language, it was Creole, a mixture of African and French. I had been used to hearing Spanish spoken.

It did not take me very long to understand them. They were all so kind to David and me. We had this wonderfully big garden, it had a rough driveway, a bit hard on the knees, if one fell over. It ran down the right side of the house and garden, starting from the road at the front of our garden, with huge wooden gates. On the right a very high, well-kept hibiscus hedge, of many colours. I can remember some low-lying buildings. They were white, just at the back of the house, possibly the servants' quarters. At the other end of the driveway were some more gates, metal ones, but they were not as big as the front ones. Outside these gates was a dirt road that lead up to the mountains. On market days there used to be all the country people passing with donkeys, baskets on either side full of vegetables or meat. The women with baskets on their heads. They'd be singing or just chatting, but always seemed to be happy. I was happy at this house. I remember things like my mother making pumpkin pie and I'd be able to lick the bowl when she had finished. Actually, I think David and I had to take it in turns or share. Yummy stuff. My mother often made our ice cream too. Well she'd make the mixture and then our faithful gardener, Juan, (he must have come over to Haiti with us) would mix it. The contraption was a wooden drum with a handle at the side. The mixture was put into a metal container, fit with a lid on, then this went into the centre of the wooden drum, around this Juan would put some chipped ice mixed with salt. On the top of the container was a cogwheel attached to the lid and this was attached to the handle, which when turned would rotate the container. How long it took to turn the container I don't know, but the mixture in the container would eventually freeze and that was our ice cream. A softish, chocolate, coffee or vanilla ice cream was the finished product, a very popular treat.

The house was a double story colonial style house. It was white and believe it must have been made of concrete. There were wide verandahs halfway up each side of the house and across the front of the house. Several steps in a wide semi-circle lead up to the centre of the front verandah, the floor of which had black and white tiles. My parents often gave cocktail parties, to which David and I were not supposed to appear. Once when I opened a side door, slightly, to see what was going on, I was spotted by this gorgeous French lady called Madeline. She beckoned me. So being an innocent child thought it was quite all right as a grown-up was calling me. She sat me on her lap and started talking to me in French. She smelt of some delicious perfume and was dressed in a beautiful silk chiffon dress. She had three rows of beads around her neck.

While I was admiring these beads, I noticed a large mole on her chin, this reminded me of one I had on my tummy. As we had become such good friends, I thought I should show her my mole and lifted my frock to show her, we had something in common. I had not realized that everyone close to us had taken an interest in our conversation, probably because I was talking to her in French, which seemed strange to them, as I was English and only about four at the time. In fact, I spoke English, French and Creole. Everyone started to laugh. It broke the spell of my being so special to this lady. I shot off her lap and disappeared through the door.

Another time my parents had about six friends to dinner. They had their pre-dinner drinks out on the verandah and then went in to eat. David and I slipped out of the house and sat on the verandah pretending to be grown-ups. David emptied all the remains out of the glasses into one which he drank, though he did drink it slowly, we thought we were real big shots. I had a hand full of nuts and a few of those delicious little biscuits. Cheese mixed with ketchup, some cheese with sweet pickle on others, then there were some little red and white cocktail onions on sticks, with a little square of cheese on the end. Olives, black, green and some with red stuff in the middle. Didn't like them much!

By the time our nurse Tulia found us, David was sitting there giggling, quite intoxicated. I had eaten too much so was feeling a little bit "ick". Tulia took us off to bed and said she'd bring some milk up to us. By the time she returned David was sound asleep. We always liked these occasions as the gardener was dressed in a nice white suit and our nurse and the laundress were in black dresses with a pretty white apron on, that had lace around it. They had to serve at drinks and then at dinner. This meant that David and I could roam around, as long as we were quiet. We'd spy on the 'goings on'.

Incredible Memories

Pat held by Tulia, David in sailor suit, self in front at the Polly's gate, Haiti 1932

A Bit of Excitement

One day my sister Pat, then 2 years old, decided to take a walk by herself. This caused such an uproar. We were all running around calling "Pat!". Then someone noticed the back gate was open. My poor mother was so upset. Pat was very blonde and my mother thought she must have been kidnapped for a voodoo sacrifice. No one knew where to start looking. All the servants were calling out in Creole to all the neighbour's servants and to passers-by. No one had seen her. Then the German baker from up the hill arrived in his little green van. Who should be sitting in the front seat with him but "a smiling Pat"? She thought that was great fun.

The baker had found her wandering up the road while on his way home and had recognized her. At the same time my father arrived home from the office, my mother had phoned him when Pat went missing. I couldn't understand why everyone started crying. Neither could Pat, so she started to cry too. I think they put a chain on the gate after that, because I can remember David and I trying to climb over it one day because we couldn't open it.

By this time David had started Kindergarten at a friend's house down the road. Juan used to put us both on our donkey and lead it down to the house via the back road. We'd drop David off then I'd get to ride it back. Sometimes Juan would jump up behind me and that meant we could go a little faster. Which I loved. Then one day we were on our way down. I was sitting behind David with my arms around him when some little boys walking to school threw a stone and hit our donkey, she bucked and we both fell off. I fell on David's arm and broke it. For many a year he blamed me for breaking his arm.

On another occasion it was the beginning of the Mardi-Gras. There were a couple of American marines visiting us. David, Pat and I were dressed up in costumes and the American guys thought it was a good idea to use our front gates as the background to some photographs they wanted to take with us. To send to their folks back home. Pat refused to go to the gates and put on a real shindy. I was standing there when suddenly a hand reached through and grabbed me, a frightening experience. Then I knew why Pat didn't want to go there. There was a hole in the gate just about her eye level and she must have seen someone looking through the hole. There were a lot of people coming down from the hills for the three-day ceremonies before Lent.

Chico, Mummy, self, Pat and David, front wall of our house, Puerto Rico

Incredible Memories

Mardi Gras, Haiti 1934

Mummy, David, self and Pat on our donkey at the back gate of our house in Kenscoff, Haiti 1933

FIRST YEARS

Birthday Party

As a child I was rather shy and did not enjoy going to birthday parties, there always seemed to be heaps of children and grown-ups there. Half of whom I did not know. The food always very sickly and they always had jelly and Coca cola, which I disliked. I was always dished up with both and everyone would say "Eat up. it's nice" or "It's good for you". I did not agree and as parents did not stay with us, I felt I had no one to turn too to rescue me. Nearly always I ended up with a tummy ache, then I'd be dosed up with something called Castoria. A brown syrupy medicine, not unpleasant to take. When I look back my stomach-ache was probably caused by my dislike of parties and the stress I felt before arriving to the 'unknown". Strange how one's memory is triggered, we remember in detail such small events in our lives which were tantamount to some great episode.

At Lee's birthday party, David, self and Pat, 1935

On Leave

We went to England, on what they called leave, we did this every three years. It must have been 1934 when we went on our "leave". We stayed at a lovely country house in a village called Bairstead in Kent. I have since looked it up in an up to date map and it doesn't appear to exist. I expect like so many beautiful quiet country villages it has been gobbled up and made into a housing estate and now has a different name. But I still have a wonderful memory of it.

I don't recall much of the inside of the house, but it had a lovely verandah, quite wide and it was grey. It looked out onto a beautiful lawn and garden. Across the lane that ran up the side of this garden, David and I discovered some disused chicken pens. They were big enough to crawl into. There were nesting boxes and higher up a roosting bar. They had all been cleaned out. We found them marvelous hiding places. We could run from one to the other and pretend all sorts of wonderful games, like cowboys and Indians, hide and seek, we could hide from Nurse when she wanted us to go to bed. Being the summer, the evenings were light until very late. Not something we were used to in the West Indies, so it didn't feel like bedtime. The days always seemed to be bright and sunny.

My parents went off on a driving tour to Scotland for three weeks and left us with a nurse. I can picture what she looked like but her name deludes me. She was quite young and came from the village. She had a round face, blue eyes and big red cheeks. Her hair was black and was very neat with two pigtails at the back. Grannie Burns came down to stay with us. I absolutely adored her, she was such fun and I loved her Spanish accent .One cold morning she had us marching up and down the verandah smacking our hands against our thighs while we sang "The grand old Duke of York, he had ten thousand men. He marched them up to the top of the hill and then he marched them down again."

We had a visit from Granddaddy John, Aunt Enid and Aunt Teresa John. I think at that time our Aunt Teresa was still at school. Aunt Enid was my best-loved aunt, she was always laughing. The Aunts played all sorts of games with us. Chased us around the lawn and played hide and seek among the shrubs. Then we had a wonderful picnic tea.

Nurse lay out some rugs on the lawn, we children sat on them with a plate each in front of us. There were plates of cheese, tomato and lettuce sandwiches, all crusts removed and cut neatly in triangles, a plate of biscuits and a plate with slices of chocolate Swiss roll, my favorite. I particularly liked the crisp chocolate icing. The grown-ups sat around on deck chairs with a trolley full of plates with the same sort of things we were eating but they also had a pot of tea, a jug of hot water and a little jug of milk also some slices of lemon in a little glass dish. We thought it was very funny because the teapot had a puffy hat on with the spout and the handle sticking out. We had serviettes tucked down the front of us and the grown-ups had ones on their laps. I can't remember if they stayed overnight.

All I can remember is that we had great fun. We thought it was a marvelous idea having tea like that. We didn't do that in the West Indies. Everything seemed to taste so much nicer this way too. When my parents returned of course we were very excited to see them again but we couldn't wait to tell them what fun we had had while they were away.

Another occasion which springs to mind was a day we spent with Aunt Enid and Aunt Teresa at London zoo. I loved the monkeys. One thing Aunt Enid always related was, when the elephants came around, sort of chairs on their backs, David said he wanted to go on one but my Aunts said no to that. Don't think either wanted to go on them and they would have had to accompany David. He started to cry and nothing seemed to console him. So, I pipe up, "But he needs to." Which Enid thought was really funny, reminding me of it for many a year later.

Back to the West Indies

It was not long before we were on a boat returning to the West Indies. While on the trip David and I decided to explore. We thought it would be a good idea to climb under a lifeboat, lie on our tummies and look over the side of the ship to see what it looked like from that angle; the sea rushing past all bubbly, like foam. And we could see the portholes below us. Great fun. That is what some very frightened parents and stewards found. The look of fright on their faces was very memorable. One of the stewards lay on his stomach and got hold of our feet and pulled us back much to every one's relief. We saw no danger in what we had done but soon got told what could have happened. There was my mother in tears. My father, I think was ready to give us a good spanking, but instead gave a big hug. Spoilt one of the exciting moments of my life! The captain was very relieved and also very understanding. He sat and talked to us about the sort of things we could and could not do while on his ship. He told us that each day one of the crew would take us to different parts of the ship and show us how things worked.

We got to see the foaming waters again from the stern of the ship. To our great excitement we were taken down into the noisy engine room. I liked the smell of it but not the noise. During the voyage we were treated like royalty. We had to say good- bye to all our new friends at the end of our journey.

Then we were back to Haiti. As we came down the gangplank we were met by friends and joy of joys our servants were there too. Immediately we started to talk Creole to them. We hadn't forgotten it. I was about five then. We moved to another house. Closer to the city of Port au Prince.

The house again was a Colonial style double story but wooden this time. At the back of the ground floor to the left of the house ran a long building with a verandah running the full length. Off this were the servant's quarters and the kitchen. In the back yard there was a circular, shallow, duck pond in which David learnt to swim. It was cleaned out of course and filled with clean water before we were allowed in. Further down the garden we had duck pens and chicken pens and at a higher level we had pigeon houses. Then to the right of this there was a large enclosure, probably about 15 ft. high, made of corrugated tin, painted green and maroon. There was a door leading into it. Of course, one day, David and I found this open so we decided to investigate. It would be an exciting place to explore. We went up a flight of steps and at the top, guess what, a lovely big swimming pool. We knew the grown-ups used to go in there and have lots of fun but we were never allowed. To this day I don't know if David fell in or he thought he could swim in it, like the duck pond. But in he went, when I saw he was in trouble, or maybe just swimming under the water like he used to in the pond I didn't wait to find out I just started screaming my lungs out. Joseph our gardener come handy man, arrived and fished David out. Of course, we got a good telling off and we never went in there again. They made sure of that. They kept the door locked.

Joseph lived at the bottom of the garden. David and I used to visit him quite often, he seemed to like our company. When he wasn't working for my parents, he was a cobbler. He made all our very comfortable leather sandals, mend shoes and showed David and me all the various tools. He used to get us to stand on a piece of brown paper and draw around our feet, I remember this was rather ticklish. This gave him an idea of our foot size. He had a sewing machine too, which we were not allowed near. The little building he lived and worked in was a double story wooden building with a tin roof. He worked on the ground floor, one room, and he lived upstairs. Also, one room. The rooms were fairly large though. He also kept pigeons.

We still had Juan, and a nice old cook, Monique. She was a dear and just loved us; in fact she used to spoil us with little tit bits from the kitchen. We also had a young nurse; I don't know what happened to Tulia. I think she must have gone back to Santo Domingo. One night my parents were out to dinner and my mother asked the nurse to stay in and look after us. She was to sleep in a bedroom in a sort of attic room. But when my parents returned, they found the nurse lying on the living room floor with a candle at her head and one down at her feet, and she was in a trance. My mother was terrified so she telephoned some friends and asked what she should do. She was told that it was some sort of Voodoo ritual. Better to leave her to come out of it.

Needless to say, when she came out of the trance she was fired. The Haitians practiced both Christianity and Voodoo. They were very simple, lovable people and they loved *us*. They thought what the Missionaries taught them was quite good but they kept their old beliefs too. They were very gentle with us and treated us like their own.

When Mardi-gras came around again much to my parent's horror, the locals decided to use the vacant land next door to us for their three-day celebrations. My mother was very upset by the thought of the noise for three days and nights. For a couple of days before this started David and I spent a lot of the time by our fence watching all the preparations.

They killed pigs and goats, which we witnessed. So we learnt how it was done. I watched in fascinated horror. After killing the animals, the blood was drained into bowls. This was part of their ritual. Everyone danced, sang, ate and drank for three days and nights and then fell in a sort of trance. Or maybe some of them were in a sort of trance the first day.

Friends of ours, very kindly, said they could put us up while all the festivities were going on. My mother, Pat and I stayed down in the Shell house near the installation with the McTagarts. He was the engineer down there. David and my father stayed in town with an American couple, The Graus. I loved when we visited them as Collie Graus used to make delicious waffles with maple syrup and oodles of melted butter. Makes my mouth water just thinking of the gooey brownies she used to make too. I have never tasted any that could compare.

While visiting one day I discovered on the wall out on the front verandah, a little white cap. When I lifted the cap there was a little copper coloured bit of metal inside. So I called David and showed him. I suggested he put his finger in and press the piece of metal, which he obediently did and ended up getting a terrible shock. It was an electrical socket to screw a plug into. I got into terrible trouble over that!

One day while my father and David came down to the McTagarts, David and I were playing on the lawn out front when my mother called out with a terrified voice that we were to run to the house as quickly as we could. When we got there, Mr McTagart shot an 8ft. snake. Boy were we lucky! After the celebrations and our exciting camping out we returned to the quiet life, back home.

Soon after my mother had another baby, Theresa. I enjoyed watching her being bathed. She was a very cuddly baby.

My father had a model T Ford, during his holiday. I recall him working under the bonnet. I don't ever remember my father getting his hands dirty and here he was with black grease all over them. He told David and I he was doing a "de-coke", whatever that was! There were engine parts all over the place, which we were not allowed to touch. David and I were fascinated and I loved the smell of the oil and petrol that my father used on a rag to clean his hands.

At this time Pat had a pet hen she used to cart around all over the place. Poor thing. It was quite a pretty looking hen with rusty and yellow coloured feathers, here and there brown and a few black and brown ones too. On looking back she probably found comfort in having a pet and companion as now there was a new baby in the house and our Mummy was very busy with it.

A Christmas Party

At Christmas time we all went up into the hills, to a place called Kans Kauf, to a Christmas party at some friend's house. We drove up a dirt road and then turned off to the right up a winding dirt driveway to the house. During the party I noticed, from their verandah, the Daddy of the house, walking down the driveway with a big suitcase. I thought this rather funny and mentioned it to my mother. She made some excuse and said not to worry about it. Not long after we heard "Ho Ho Ho" in a loud voice, there was Santa Clause coming up the driveway with a big red bag over his shoulder. We all received a present. I don't remember connecting the Daddy with Santa Clause because I was a little afraid to go and get my present from him.

One night I woke with a terrible earache. My mother put eardrops in and took me to the Doctors next day. He stuck a pointed thing with a light on the end of it into my ear. It was very painful, said he could see a lump and would syringe it out. Boy was that painful, I nearly hit the ceiling. He then decided to try and get the object out with some tweezers. Eventually he pulled out a red bean, which I remembered I'd put in some days before, until then had forgotten about it. He gave me a big red lollypop because I had been so good but said it was not a good idea to put things down my ear.

David and I Playing

I remember this very long room downstairs. All along one side were cupboards; right up to the ceiling, at the end of these was a basin and mirror. Then a door leading out into the back yard. On the opposite side there were windows. We used to love watching my father shaving; this was the room he used. He had this floppy short brush, which he'd wet, then put it into a soap bowl, swish it around then put all this foamy stuff on his face. Then he would get a thing with a razor blade in and scrape it down his face, rinse it off in the basin of water and continue to do that until all the foam was off his face. Then he would scrape it up his face in the other direction, every now and then feeling his face with his hand. After all of that he would rinse his face, the little brush and the thing with the razor, pull the plug out and there was all these black specks all over the basin. It was fascinating watching, so one day David and I decided we would imitate him. We got all the gear out then took it in turns lathering our faces and shaving but we couldn't see anything coming off

FIRST YEARS

our faces so we decided to shave our eyebrows. Then we got out some scissors and gave each other a haircut. THEN we were caught.

Self and David 1933

Seaplane

I recall when six years old, being told we were leaving our island home for another. The exciting part of this was that we were going by flying boat.

We arrived down at the harbour, walked along a long pier and there was an airplane sitting in the water. Where was the boat I thought? We were ushered down a few steps, through a door into the plane. I was very confused. Maybe this plane would take us to the flying boat. But how would it land on the boat? How big was the boat going to be? All these questions raced across my mind.

Then a huge roar, a terrible noise and slight shuddering, then movement. We were traveling at such a speed. The water rushing past the port hole windows. Oops, my stomach suddenly moved up into my throat. We were air borne. The windows had droplets of water scudding across them and then cleared, I could see. As we turned, the town full of houses beneath us. I hoped we would not fall, it looked as though we may. Everything just seemed completely impossible.

I was soon distracted by the sight out of my window. There were massive wads of cotton wool all around us. Next, we were inside one of these objects, the windows had droplets on them again. They formed patterns of little river-lets running from the front to the back, and at great speed. Then they disappeared completely

Before I knew it, we were out in the clear blue sky again and the windows were denuded of water, they sparkled in the sunlight. With all this excitement I forgot to think about the flying boat. We were given orange juice, which didn't taste like orange juice, and a crayon book and crayons. Looking out of the window was much more interesting.

It seemed no time at all when my tummy and my ears started to feel uncomfortable again. We were given chewing gum and told to chew it as we were going down. What a splash!! We moved along in the water and stopped at another pier, we were in Santo Domingo, I was told, just dropping some passengers off.

Not long after we were chewing gum again as we took off into the sky once more. We were all given sandwiches and a pineapple drink. That didn't taste like pineapples either. We flew in and out of clouds, then all of a sudden, the plane dropped. My stomach came right up into my mouth and I had to swallow hard. I had a bit of an earache. This voice kept on coming from somewhere telling us what was going on, it told us that we were soon to land at San Juan, Puerto Rico. This is where we got off, this is where our new home was going to be.

I felt very sad that we were not going further in the plane. We were all helped out onto a rather narrow pier. Pat didn't want to walk along it, as you could see the water lapping underneath, making a slurping sound because the plane landing had roughed up the water between the planks. So, Daddy had to carry her. We were met by someone from the Shell company, who Daddy seemed to know and were whisked off to our new home.

San Juan

We were driven, it seemed hundreds of miles, to our house. Friends of ours had rented a house they hoped would suit our family. I was so tired I don't remember much. But the next day I woke and looked out of the window, we were right by the blue sea.

My parent's friends, the Patersons, sent their chauffeur over to pick us up for lunch at their house. I was still finding things a bit strange, especially as the language was different. They spoke Spanish and not Creole or French. During the afternoon, we children were taken for a drive while the grown-ups caught up with the latest news, what had happened since the last time they had met. When that was, I do not know.

The first Spanish words I learnt were *agua*, water, and *guagua*, bus. Must have been Puerto Rican, as bus is *autobus* in Spanish. Within a couple of weeks David and I were speaking Spanish.

FIRST YEARS

Next thing we knew we were starting school. A new experience for me. Don't know that I liked the idea very much, but I didn't have much choice. We were taken in to be introduced and to be enrolled. The building seemed massive, the classrooms enormous and quite overwhelming, but at least to start with David and I were to be in the same class. My mother would take us into the City by bus and then after school come back by '*guagua*' to collect us. We did all our lessons in Spanish and were being taught by nuns. Our nun was Sister Alba. A big lady and she seemed quite amused by us or was it the way we spoke Spanish? Anyway, she wasn't as frightening as I first thought.

We had one English class a week where we all had to read one sentence over and over again and then say what it was in Spanish. David and I had an advantage over the others, being able to speak English. After a term, David was put into another class, probably because he was older than me and doing very well with Spanish.

Some of the children lived quite close to the school, they would go home for lunch. I remember having a green lunch tin. My favourite lunch was Heinz sandwich spread. It has never tasted as good as it did in those days. I've tried it several times in all the other countries we've been to. It does not compare! One day some of the children came back from lunch and told Sr. Alba that one of the boys was not coming back. He had fallen down some stairs and been taken to hospital. We later heard he had died. We were trooped off to the church next door to pray for him.

I looked forward to the weekends, it became a weekly visit to the Paterson's. On Sunday we went to church. After lunch we had a siesta and then go over to the Paterson's. Sometimes we went for a swim at the country club before lunch if we attended an early Mass. While my parents played monopoly, the chauffeur took us children for a drive and then to this little ice cream place. It was a round building the shape of an igloo with a serving counter in the middle at the front. We'd all get an "Eskimo Pie", an ice cream on a central round stick, the shape of an igloo, vanilla ice cream covered in dark chocolate.

Our house seemed a very big one to me. Turning into a driveway, to the left of the house. Out the front of the house were two big raised ponds with fish and waterlilies, on either side of the front path. We entered the house through a fly screen door into a long front verandah, from there you went into a large room. To the right of this room, but sort of to the back of it was the dining area. There was a well-polished oval mahogany table with six chairs, there were two pieces under the table that could be added to extend it. I can't remember what sort of furniture was in the big room, but I do remember that there were some French doors going out of the dining area, facing the ocean. Opposite the dining room were the stairs, to the right of the stairs was a short passage leading to the garage. At the bottom of the stairs if you looked to the right was a door into a sort of pantry, then the kitchen. In the pantry there was a large water filter and our icebox. I remember this because when we came home from school our old cook would pour us a big glass of cold milk which we would have with some cookies. I used to have two glasses of milk if I could. Lovely stuff with thick cream on the top.

Halfway up the stairs was a small landing, to the right, over the garage was a bedroom in which Teresa slept, if my parents were going out in the evening, our nurse Conchita used to sleep there. At the top of the stairs, to the left was David's bedroom. Practically right opposite the stairs, my parents very large bedroom, this had French doors going out on to a long balcony. To the right of my parents' room was another fairly big room in which Pat and I slept. There were two windows which opened out onto the balcony. My bed was along the wall the windows were in. My parents' bedroom overlooked the ocean.

One day while I was looking through some drawers in an alcove just outside David's room, I found this most beautiful green silk purse. I had never seen anything like it before. There were flowers in the material, the same colour green, but they were sort of raised. The edge, where the bag opened and where the clasp was, were gold and it had a gold carrying chain. When I opened it, there was money inside; nickels, dimes, quarters and dollars. My imagination ran away with me and I thought I had found a treasure trove. This was my little secret. I took a dime and hid it under my pillow, put the bag carefully back and covered it with the scarf that had been on it when I found it.

The next day when I went to school, I took the dime. Now I could buy the little packet that had a pink chewy sweet in it that all the other children were buying. I didn't like the sweet very much but I wanted the packet to cut the front and back out which were pictures of playing cards. The only thing was that I could only buy them after school from a lady who sat under a tree on the sidewalk, just in front of the church. So this meant I had to hang back when my mother came to pick us up from school and then run to catch up to my mother and David. They didn't seem to miss me as David always took my mother's hand and would start telling her all that went on in school that day. This little exercise happened for several days. Then one day there were a lot more children in the queue in front of me and my mother retraced her steps and caught me buying the packet. Of course, she wanted to know where I got the money from. I told her I had found a treasure bag. So when we got home, very reluctantly, I showed her where the treasure was. She told me it was hers and she had noticed little bits of money were going missing and she had blamed the servants but because it was such small amounts, she did nothing about it. Bang went my treasure trove and I think, my belief in fairies.

Our house was right on the beach. We were not allowed to go down to the water on our own as we couldn't swim. David and I made friends with Buddy and Marjorie Willsey, two American kids who lived down the road. After our parents met, we were allowed to go and play at their place and they'd come over to ours. Or go over the wall and play on the beach digging holes and filling them with water, which we fetched by the bucketful from our garden hose. We'd build sandcastles, hills and roadways and pretend all sorts of games

At the weekends and sometimes during the week, while our parents played tennis, we would go to the Country Club where they had a big swimming pool. My father taught us how to swim. Holding me on my back he'd say "now kick your legs" then he let me go. I moved along a bit and then I realized he wasn't holding me. Needless to say, I panicked and sank. He hauled me out spluttering and objecting. Wasn't much I could do as I was too far from the side of the pool. After I calmed down. "Now we'll do it again only this time keep kicking and I'll walk along beside you."

It wasn't long before David and I were little water babes. We used to play on the beach with other children in the neighbourhood and we used to all look after each other. There was a boy called Tito, quite a bit older than us. He said his father asked him to look after us. I think he was 14 years old. Tito had many siblings, a brother older than him and seven younger. They built a house nearly opposite to us. While the house was being built David and I would go over to watch the proceedings. One day when the workers were doing the plastering of the walls, one of the workers let me climb up on the scaffolding next to him and he showed me how it was done. He even let me have a go. After that I always took an interest in any buildings going on.

What a wonderful two years we spent in Puerto Rico. Tito taught us how to fish, how to make kites and climb coconut trees. Life was all together very full and exciting. There were Buddy and Marjorie Willsey, Jerry, can't remember his surname, all American army kids, Tito, a Puerto Rican, from a family of nine.

One of probably, the most dangerous days in my life, was when Jerry went into his father's work shed and brought a bullet out to show us. His father used to make his own bullets for practice shooting. Jerry explained all about bullets to us. We thought he was very clever. "Come down to the gate and I'll show you something." So David and I followed him. Jerry had also brought a hammer with him. He put the bullet on the ground and held it with his thumb and index finger. "Now if I hit it hard with the hammer right where that little dot is in the middle of the bullet it will make a big bang." We squatted down beside him and he hit the bullet. It went off with a big bang all right and blew his thumb off. We were all splattered with blood. His mother and one of the servants ran out to see what had happened. His mother became hysterical, David and I just stood there in horror. The maid asked if we knew where the thumb was. That was the first we knew it was missing. David and I took off home as fast as our legs would take us. Later my father explained what could have happened if the bullet had gone sideways and hit one of us. Needless to say, we were not allowed to go and play with Jerry again. They never did find his thumb. His father was very nice about the whole thing and assured my parents that his shed would be locked hence forth.

Then there was Juanita, our marvellous old cook, her daughter was our nurse. Conchita mostly looked after Teresa and Pat. Her son, who was our age, probably more David's age than mine, well he used to come and spend the day during weekends and school holidays. His name was Leo, if I remember correctly. He used to play with us. I remember we used to play cowboys and Indians around the garden. He was not allowed to leave the garden, something to do with his father. He was an ex-policeman or detective having been singled out by some "baddies" and beaten up, I also remember hearing someone saying he had been shot in the head. This left him with brain damage or something so was out of the force. He used to turn up at times and our mother used to call us in and tell us we were not allowed to talk to him. But I did once and he talked in a funny way, I couldn't understand him very well. And I remember he held his left arm in an odd way, and he had a big scar on his face. Which made him a little scary.

Conchita didn't like to have her son out of her sight. His Abuela, grandmother, was very strict with him. If she thought he was being naughty, she'd whack him on his legs with a cane. He used to get a whack if he called her Abuelita, little grandmother, until I said to her one day that she was an Abuelita because she was so small and she thought that was funny. He didn't get whacked after that and we started calling her Abuelita to tease her. We must have been pretty cheeky. David used to sing out at breakfast time, *"Abuelita dame pan negro con mantequilla y marmelada por favor."* Give me brown bread with butter and marmalade please. He only said Abuelita sometimes when he wanted to tease her and our parents were not around.

We had a little lamb given to us, it was black, light orangey brown and white, very unusual colour, and we called him Sam. He had to be tethered so he didn't run away. We loved playing with him, as he did with us. He grew very quickly and luckily had no horns, he loved butting me probably because I was a little tubby. When we got off the school bus and got to our street, I never knew which gateway he was hiding in, waiting for me to run past. Then I would hear him running towards me and I'd take off in top gear, my school satchel firmly across my bottom in case he caught up with me. He more often than not did. I tried every means of evasion. One day I got to the front door, opened the fly-screen door and ran in but the fly door didn't shut in time and he got in. Both of us were a bit surprised, then I thought if I run upstairs, he wouldn't be able to follow me. Wrong. He clattered up the stairs after me, around the landing and up the next flight of stairs and into my bedroom. I jumped on my bed and he did too. He thought this was the best game he had ever played. Then I went out the window on to the balcony but luckily he did not follow me, I think he was distracted by the noise of someone coming up the stairs. My mother would have Sam tethered on a short rope when she left to pick us up from school, but somehow he would manage to get loose by the time the bus arrived. I must have looked a very funny sight tearing up the road with a naughty sheep after me. Apparently, he would run then jump in the air and do a bit of a prance then take off after me again. I never saw this as I was too busy in full flight in terror of him butting me. It hurt. Even without horns his head was very hard. As he got bigger and stronger my parents thought it better to get rid of him. Juanita said they would take him and that was the last time we saw old Sam.

One day Tito suggested we walk along the beach to Punta Maria and do some fishing. We took a container of water and some sandwiches as this was going to be a long walk and a bit of 'an explore'. Tito said we would probably get hungry. We also took a small frying pan and some oil. We all had string and some bent pins as our fishing hooks, with these we hoped to be catching our lunch.

When we arrived at Punta Maria we were tired and thirsty. There was a lovely little pool of clear green-blue water, we all dumped what we had been carrying and went and sat in the water. Much to our surprise the water was quite warm. The pool was surrounded by some flat rocks and had some very small hermit crabs on them enjoying the sunshine. They soon disappeared when we entered the water. The walk along the beach had been quite exciting. All along the beach there had been coconut trees and another tree with dark green shiny leaves, which had a little fruit on, like an almond, which Tito said we could eat. They tasted a bit bitter. On the way we found some coconuts that had fallen off the tree and Tito smashed them on a rock until there was a slit then we sucked the water out. Then he smashed the whole thing and we ate the white flesh inside. One was quite green and the inside was just a sort of jelly substance, very sweet and delicious. We saw crabs scurry down into their holes. Tito showed us how we could, with a long piece of grass, tease the crabs to come out again, but they were not big enough to eat. So we just played around with them for a while.

After we had cooled down, we decided to try our luck at fishing. We threw our lines in with a bit of crust stuck on the end of the pin. And guess what some little sprats appeared and started to nibble at the crusts. Then Tito showed us how to pull the line in very quickly and jerk it over our shoulder. I know no one is going to believe us but we did catch some very small fish. Then he showed us that if we stood very quietly in the water and sprinkled some crumbs around us the fish would come in around us, By holding our hand in the water, when the fish came around we could also, if we were very nimble, scoop a fish or two out in our hand and throw them on to the beach. When we felt we'd caught enough Tito washed the sand off the fish, lit a fire and fried the fish until they were very crisp, and I mean crisp, then we ate them bones and all and were they *delicioso*, in English delicious. They went down very well with our sandwiches.

One of the most exciting times I had was when David, Tito and I decided that we would swim out to the reef. We had no idea how far out it was, but it didn't look too far. Goodness knows how far out it was, but it was far. We kept on stopping and lying on our backs and floating and resting then we'd swim some more. When we got to the reef, David was the first there and he climbed on to the reef and stepped right on to a sea urchin. When he looked around, he saw the reef covered with them so dived straight back into the water. We were exhausted but knew we would have to swim back. To step on a sea urchin is a very painful experience, David stuck his foot out of the water and Tito tried to get the barb out. Then we decided to float for a while and start our journey back, we knew it would be a slow and tiring swim. When we were what we thought was halfway back, we noticed all the people were out of the water and shouting. There was a small rowing boat coming towards us. And then we saw them, a row of shark fins between us and the shore. One of us remembered someone having said that if we saw a shark to splash like mad and make a big noise, so we did, tired as we were. This huge black man called Tom, I think because he came from the small island called St. Thomas, arrived and hauled us into his boat and made for shore. Everyone on shore cheered madly, we just tried to get our breath back.

We knew Tom from before, he was always hanging around the beach and we became quite good friends. He was not very friendly when we got back, boy did he tell us off, both in English and in Spanish. We sure kept our guardian angels busy, maybe Tom was an angel.

Another thing I remember well about Puerto Rico were the beautiful seashells we could collect along the beach or up on the rocks. But when we looked for them on the rocks, we had to be careful we didn't get nipped by the little hermit crabs. The wife of the manager of Libby's Can Foods, a lovely American lady with gorgeous long golden coloured hair, beautiful kind blue eyes and a very quiet voice, showed me several ways to use these shells. They lived opposite us in a big sandy coloured house. This lady taught me to make some very small beautiful ladies with hooped skirts and fancy hats by building four small shells on top of each other, gluing each as I went, then gluing another shell which fitted into a hole at the top of the shells making the skirt. This shell looked like a big busted lady with a very slim waist. Then with tweezers she'd break off a slither of another shell and I'd glue these to the sides of the body shell, up where the shoulders would be. When these had stuck, I'd find another pink coloured shell that was more a rounded shape, this I stuck on to the body to be the head. To make sure this stayed in place I had to lay the whole thing down and lay two matchsticks on either side of the shell to keep it in the position I wanted it to be. Sometimes I'd make it so the head was tipped forward as if the lady was looking down. When this was firmly stuck, I'd find a shell the shape like the Shell Company sign, this would be the hat. Some of the shells that we used for the head were sometimes black or a sort of purple colour so instead of a hat we'd put a shell upside down and fill it with tiny little shells or chips of shell and make it look like a basket full of fruit and vegetables. On the faces we'd mark in eyes, nostrils, and a mouth. On one of the arms sometimes I'd hang a little long, pointed shaped shell that looked like a closed parasol. To keep all the different shaped shells separate and easy to find I stuck a lot in match boxes. The boxes stuck together to look like a small chest of drawers, then popped the smaller shells into them.

David and I used to make model airplanes out of balsa strips which we cut to lengths and pinned to a plan and then put a drop of glue to each joint. When we had made sides, top and bottom we glued them in position then made the wings and tail. The nose was a solid piece of balsa shaped like the nose of a plane, with a hole in. We'd attach the propeller with a hooked wire to which we'd put a rubber band attached to another hook in the tail. Then we'd cover the whole thing with a fine tissue paper. When stuck and dry we'd paint some dope, I think it was called, all over the plane. This hardened the paper and also made it very smooth. After all that we'd wind the propeller up and let it go. Quite often they flew.

And more often than not too they would crash into something and bang would go all our hard work.

We used to make kites in more or less the same way. We would tie together the spines of a coconut leaf in the form of a cross, then tie string to the tips so that we ended up with a sort of diamond shape then we would stretch tissue paper to the edges but leave a gap just above the cross piece. Then we'd tie string from the top to the outer points and at the centre of the kite and join them in equal lengths and to this we tied the lead string which we would hold to fly the kite. We would then make a tail from another piece of string tied to the bottom of the kite. On this at intervals we would tie short strips of rag. Then we'd test it for balance before painting dope on the tissue paper to strengthen it. Then off down to the beach to fly it. To start it off we'd run down the beach with the kite behind us letting out the string slowly. Sometimes the kite would just go around and around and dive into the sand and we'd feel very disappointed but with a little adjustment to the weight of the tail it would take off at our next trial. We would see how high we could get the kite to go and try to make it do all sorts of things like dive and then go up again or just swoop from side to side. Sometimes there would be bigger boys down on the beach with their kites but they would have razor-blades tied to the tails of their kites and they would come along and try to cut our kites free, we lost a few kites like that My father made a huge box kite and we took it down to the beach and flew it. Then he handed me the cord and it just lifted me straight off my feet. That was exciting too. My father grabbed me before I really took off.

Then there was the time a small tidal wave hit our garden stonewall and flattened it. It flowed right through the house and down our street. The garden wall must have softened the blow as is didn't do any damage to the house walls and only shifted the furniture around a bit. I remember at a certain time of the year we used to get some very big waves that used to crash nearly halfway up the beach. We would run down to meet these before they actually smashed onto the beach and dive through them, then swim like mad before the water came back down the beach because if you got caught in it the force would suck you under and toss you around under the water. Not a pleasant experience. Had it happen to me a couple of times, you think you are never going to come up again. We would swim out and wait until the next wave was coming in but make sure there wasn't another following to closely. Then we would follow it in and run up the beach and keep running so that when it was rushing down back into the sea it didn't take you with it and tumble you under the water. Our guardian angels sure had their hands full with us.

FIRST YEARS

Puerto Rico is where David and I first learnt to smoke. My father bought Lucky Strike or Camel cigarettes by the carton, this he kept in the top part of his clothes cupboard. On the left of the cupboard there was a door and a hanging section, on the right another door and inside four or five drawers, which we pulled out and used as steps, above them a shelf. At the back was a mirror. This frightened the hell out of me the first time I climbed up. It was on this shelf that he kept his cigarettes. Also on that shelf we found a packet of what looked like chocolate chewing gum. What a stroke of luck we could chew some gum after we had a smoke. Little did we know that these were laxatives, I don't have to tell you what happened to us. We helped ourselves to a packet of cigarettes, the poor servants got blamed for that too until we got caught.

My father came home for lunch, unless he had a business lunch, whatever that was, then after lunch, he would have a siesta returning to the office about 2 p.m. While he was having his siesta, we got onto the car and used the cigarette lighter to light up our cigarettes. We sat in the back seat with our feet up on the backs of the front seats pretending we were grown-up. Of course, the car was full of smoke. When Daddy came out what a surprise or shock, here were two little naughties smoking their heads off. He had to go to the office but he said that when he got home he would make us smoke a whole packet and that would make us sick and we would never want to smoke again. It didn't work. I expect I could write a book just on our stay in Puerto Rico so many exciting things happened while we were there.

When I was seven years old, David must have been eight, we made our First Holy Communion. For this we had to have special instructions, on how to go to confession and how to receive the body and blood of Christ. But of course, it was just a wafer and we didn't have anything to drink. And we had to be very careful we didn't touch the wafer with our teeth after it was put on our tongue. We were not allowed to chew it, we must just swallow it down. I just hoped my mouth was not too dry. While we were being instructed, we were shown all these photos of little children who had been so good and had died and gone straight to heaven because they 'had been so good'. The alternative we were taught was that we would go somewhere called purgatory where we would have to atone for being naughty. Of course we could go to confession and tell the priest all our naughty things and if he forgave us and we said all the prayers he gave us to say then we would be all right if we were sorry for what we had done, then we could go to communion. Frightening stuff.

My mother made me a beautiful long white dress, with a long net veil, a little bag that hung on my wrist, made of the same material my dress was made of, lined with white satin. I had a small prayer book in this. It had been my mother's when she made her First Communion. I did try very hard to be like all the children we had been told about, but it was very hard especially when some of the things the grown-ups told us were naughty didn't seem to be naughty to me, They were just exciting and fun. Anyway, I couldn't have been that bad because the priest always used to say, "that's a good girl, now go and say 3 hail Mary's and pray for me." I used to wonder why I had to pray for him, but I never asked anyone.

1st Holy Communion, Puerto Rico 1936

The final day arrived with all the little girls dressed in their white dresses and the boys in their white shirts and trousers with a ribbon tied in a bow around their arm, also carrying their books and rosaries. They walked down one side of the aisle and we walked down the other side. I felt so good that day. And for many a year after that we were taken to mass every Sunday and on special feast days. We were trouped off to confession every Friday when we were at school and by my mother, every Saturday during the school holidays. We were taught how to pray the rosary. We prayed in the morning when we got up, we prayed before our classes started, before our meals and after our meals at school and also before we were let out of class at the end of the day. That was so we would have a safe journey home and if we didn't make it, well then we were safely saved from that terrible place called Hell.

At that young age I never felt I needed to fear 'that' as I didn't really understand what they were talking about; "venial sin and mortal sin". Just as well or I would have been scared out of my wits.

One thing I do know is that I have a guardian angel or maybe two because I've been in some situations that without an angel, I'd have been in real strife. These stories, though I don't remember them in any detail, meant a lot to me. I did think of them and suppose because of the way they were told to us they did have some influence on my life. We were given holy cards with pictures of these good children with prayers on the backs which we used as markers in our prayer books. I do remember one little boy he was about ten years old, and in the picture he was lying on his death bed, he was a lovely looking boy, he had his hands clasped together on his stomach with a set of rosary beads in them. He had been very ill and because he had accepted all his sufferings as the will of God and so he had died a peaceful death. Of course, I knew nothing about illness or how one died so just sort of thought he must have had a very bad stomach-ache or something and then sort of went to sleep and didn't wake up again.

At this young stage of my life I had only seen one dead person and that was a body, or part of a body that had been washed up on the beach. David and I had seen a big crowd up the beach so we ran to see what was going on. A man in the crowd got hold of David and me and told us in a very kind way what had happened and that he thought we should run along home. I don't know what he said but I know what I saw was not very pleasant but it did not have a bad effect on me, I just took it as part of life, nobody else seemed to be making a big deal about it, a few were crossing themselves, but then people were always doing that in Puerto Rico. They did it before they got on a bus, some did it as they were leaving their houses, going into church and out of church, so I just accepted it all as part of mine and their lives. And so we moved on to something else, no big deal.

There was one time when I was very frightened. We went to visit some friends, for afternoon tea I think, there were two boys and a girl in the family but they were older than us so they really didn't want to play with us. The house seemed very dark and I remember did not have a very good feel about it. We were in this big room and there seemed to be very heavy green curtains on all the windows as well as separating the room in two. I was standing next to my mother's chair when all of a sudden, I spotted a small alligator sliding across the room. Well, I just screamed, and I wasn't a screamy sort of child, jumped onto a settee, which was the highest point I could see. The older boy came out from behind the curtain laughing his head off and told everyone that it was only a stuffed one and he had tied a length of black cotton on to the nose and slowly pulled it across the room to make it look real. I was not impressed and I don't think my mother was either. I don't remember visiting them again.

We had some Puerto Rican friends called Lee and I remember being taken to visit the grandparents who lived in a huge house. In the garden they had this enormous sort of palm tree, at the base of each leaf, against the main trunk was shaped like a massive cup in which was water, we scooped some out and drank it and it was so sweet, nearly like coconut water. The house was one of the most beautiful colonial houses I have ever visited and it had a very exciting rambling garden with all sort of exotic plants and trees, pathways leading through all of this. I remember thinking "I hope we are going to be here for a long, long time, I don't really want to go home." Down the back garden they had a cute little monkey. It had a collar around its neck, from this there was a lead like a dog's lead, this was attached to a wire stretched between two trees. The monkey could run up and down this. We were allowed to give it a banana, but not allowed to touch it, in case it bit us.

One day I looked across the road to Tito's house and saw his aunts, mother and our nurse sitting under a tree so ran over to join them. They were very busy combing a couple of Tito's sister's hair. Every now and then they would grab something and squash it between their thumbnails. Conchita told me not to get too near as they had nits and she didn't want me to catch them as my mother would be very angry. She was anyway when I told her where I had been and what I'd seen!

Our two year stay in Puerto Rico went very quickly, then it was time to go on leave again. We boarded a small steamer which was to take us to the island of St. Thomas to then connect with a ship going to England. It wasn't until we were on board and getting ready for bed, as it was late evening, that I realized my father was not coming with us. For some reason, he was to join us at a later date. I was terribly upset at this. I thought that I would never see him again. We said goodbye to him and were taken down into our cabin. The porthole of our cabin was just level with where my father was standing and I remember waving to him and as the ship moved off, he looked so lonely. The figure of him standing there got smaller and smaller, and then the ship turned and I could no longer see him. All around us was water and it was getting dark. As we sailed out of the harbour, we passed some large stone walled forts. These had been built during the years when the Spaniards occupied Puerto Rico. While living on the Island we had been taken to explore the fort. Now I was seeing it at a different angle.

We were woken early the next morning, after breakfast we went up on deck only to see we were nearly docked. St Thomas was a very small island, to the East of Puerto Rico, and not that far as it only took us overnight to get there. It was a very beautiful island. They spoke English there. There were not many cars, here everyone travelled in horse or mule drawn carriages or carts. We were taken to a grand Hotel with tiled floors. As you entered there was this massive stone staircase, or so it seemed to me. These led up to a wide balcony which went right around the first floor, all the bedrooms went off from this. On the balcony were cane chairs and sofas with tables in front of them, a few people sitting around drinking coffee and reading newspapers, or just sitting as though they were waiting for something. I remember feeling very shy as we walked past them all as we followed the porter who was taking our luggage to our rooms. Some turned and glanced at us as we went past, very few smiled.

In the middle of the morning, a man from the Shell Company came and picked us up and took us for a tour around the island, in a horse drawn carriage. Everything looked so fresh and clean and very green, with beautiful flowering trees. Poinciana, plumbagoes, and beautiful hedges of some shrub with yellow and red leaves or green and red, or just red leaves, and other hedges were in all the lovely colours you get in the prickly bougainvillea. Very exciting, sitting high up in an open carriage as the horse trotted along, going slowly up hill and then at a quick trot as we went downhill.

The next day when we woke up and looked down from our bedroom porch, we saw there were a lot of market stalls set up. The steward told us that a big American tourist ship was due in that day. I remember my mother was not very impressed and she remarked "oh, have we got to put up with loud American tourists all day?" And they were loud too. It certainly was a very noisy day. A lot of them came into the hotel to buy drinks and to eat. The vendors in the market were calling out their wares and the tourists were calling out to each other. But I must say looking down from the verandah it was a very colourful picture.

The day after we boarded a Danish ship which was to take us to England. We were all in a large cabin with our own bathroom. But I remember in the evenings we were taken to another bathroom where a stewardess took over and ran our baths and just about cooked me the first time the water was so hot. She was a very stern, large, lady who was quite terrifying. The next night I refused to go and have a bath with her. I told my mother the bath was too hot and she was very rough so my mother stayed and supervised testing the water before I would get in, and I said I could wash myself except my back.

Incredible Memories

David and I of course roamed the ship and made new friends especially with the crew. We watched one sailor painting the side of the ship as we sailed along. He was sitting on a plank held by some ropes over the side of the ship. We hung over the rails watching him. When he pulled himself up and stood on the deck, he was huge, blond and I thought one of the best-looking men I had ever seen.

We were taken up to the part of the ship where they had the big steering wheel. We were told it was called the bridge. It didn't look like a bridge to me. They also had the hooter up there and we were allowed to pull the string that set off the fog horn when we were going through a foggy patch, we had to count slowly to four and then pull, this was to warn any other ships that might be in the vicinity that we were there. The bridge was an exciting place to be. There were always at least three of the crew there at a time and we got told why they did this or that. And just next to the bridge was another small room where there was a guy with a funny looking ruler with a pencil on the end of it which he moved on a map. He told us he was working out where we were, I knew where we were. We were in the middle of the ocean and at times it looked very rough. Big huge waves and the ship went up and down in them. Sometimes when we were down all you saw was a big mountain of water. Then we would be right up in the air. Or so it seemed. When it was like this we were not allowed out on deck.

At mealtimes a steward would walk up and down the passages between the cabins donging the dinner gong. One day one of the stewards gave us the donger, showed us how to do it and we walked around donging the gong, it was great fun and we felt so important. Each table had their special steward, ours was a big stout man with dark hair combed flat on his head and he wore glasses. He mostly seemed to be smiling but if any of us didn't eat all our meal he would get this sad look on his face, so we would take another mouthful and he would smile again, he used to give us extra fruit to take to the cabin with us.

During the first months of the war, which was only 2 years later we heard the Germans sank that ship. We were very sad to hear the news and prayed for the captain and the crew. All were lost and we could not understand why as it was a Danish ship and they were neutral.

I remember the delicious fruit we had for dessert and at breakfast. All from California. Peaches twice the size of a tennis ball. And juicy, big oranges with California printed in blue on their skins. Fresh fruit and vegetables were scarce in Puerto Rico, we always seemed to have canned food there. Those were the days of Popeye the sailor man and I thought canned spinach was delicious, Popeye ate it by the can full. And small carrots too I remember a day when this oblong, white vegetable dish, with rows of these carrots was on the table just by my left arm; I demolished the lot. Then my mother realized she had ordered them and asked the maid. I sheepishly owned up to having eaten them. No wonder I was a little tub of a thing, that Sam liked to butt.

David and I created a manhunt or rather a child-hunt one day on the ship. We hadn't been seen by anyone for what must have been a long time, David and I were having fun. When found we were both up in one of the lifeboats.

We were at sea for two weeks but it didn't seem that long. The last night on board the Captain usually had a fancy-dress party and dinner for the adult passengers. David and I were wandering around the ship to see what sort of costumes people were wearing when there was a big commotion. This American young lady, traveling with her parents, to celebrate her 21st birthday, had stepped on a needle and it had gone right into her foot. The father was carrying her and calling for a steward to take him to the ship's doctor. Never heard the end of that story but it was exciting while it lasted. Not long after that the stewardess caught up with us and told us our baths were ready and we were to be quick and get ready for bed. Some people have all the fun.

The next day people were still celebrating and some men were a little the worse for wear. We were all excited because when we went up on deck after breakfast, we could see the coast of England in the distance. We were leaving the Atlantic Ocean and going into the Irish sea with the coast of England on our right. It took us the good part of the day to go up the coast and then into the mouth of the Severn. About an hour before we got to the mouth, the ship stopped and a tug boat pulled up alongside of us and a man in uniform came on board, he was the Pilot we were told, the customs also boarded and the engines started up again and we were on our way. We had at last arrived in English waters. We would soon be seeing our relatives again. I know my mother was very excited at the thought of meeting up with her brothers and sisters. David and I were excited because we were about to start some more exciting things in our lives.

Chapter 2

JAMAICA '38

The Island of the Rivers

We arrived on a beautiful day, the waters were very calm as we sailed up the harbour. And what a Beautiful harbour it was. On our right was a narrow strip of land, at the end of which was the famous Port Royal, where the pirates of old used to meet to store their ill-gotten goods. The harbour was formed by a massive earthquake, the centre sank leaving this wonderful natural waterway. The ship turned right into the main part of the harbour. To our left lay the capital of Jamaica, the city of Kingston.

After the delay in docking manoeuvres and customs clearance we disembarked onto a very noisy wharf. I was carried down a very wobbly gang plank to terra firma. The Heiser's chauffeur drove us from the docks to 10 Belmont Avenue, Cross Roads. This house was the Heiser's; the family was holidaying in their native land, Germany.

I don't remember much about the inside of the house but we had to go up several steps to get onto the "L" shaped verandah, which lead to the front door. There was a huge bay window to the left, my parent's bedroom. The verandah was sheltered from the winds and sun by a very thick vine. The driveway ran in a semi-circle to the front and then out again to a gate right on the corner of the property.

To the right of the house was a huge lawn area, well it seemed huge to me anyway. A high hibiscus hedge of several colours hid the road. At the back of the house, from the back door, there was a path leading to the garage and servants' quarters. On one side of the path was a vegetable garden and on the other side were chicken pens. To get to the garage there was a gate, which was always kept shut. At that end of the lawn there was an enormous mango tree and below the tree there was a garden bench. In the mornings I used to hop to this bench and my mother would leave me with a book, crayoning book and some crayons and a drink. One morning while I was sitting outside, three "John Crows" landed in front of me. I had never seen one of these birds before. They were black with a bald, red head and neck. The neck was a brighter red. They were a type of vulture. One of them hissed at me. I was terrified especially as I couldn't run away. You can imagine the scream I let out, it's a wonder they didn't lose *all* their feathers. People came running from all directions. Of course, the vultures flew off in fright from my screams and everyone running towards me.

I was quite hysterical and my mother thought I was exaggerating when I tried to tell her about these terrible looking birds. The gardener laughed and said, "Dem's John Crows, Miss Anne, no fe worry." That was all right for him to say. I had felt quite helpless. I think it was from that experience that I decided I was going to walk again. And quickly. With determination I would hold on to things and walk slowly around them. It was summer holidays so that gave me two months of practice What with my stubbornness to conquer this disability and going swimming often, I was soon on my feet again, able to play with the others in my family and with friends.

My mother would go with the gardener down to the markets in Kingston at the weekends. That was where everyone got their fresh vegetables, eggs and meat. They brought a live hen home one week, to fatten it up to kill. The gardener said that hens tasted better than roosters. Well, we kids fell in love with 'Henny Penny', as we called her. She was a real character; she kept getting out of the pen but would always go back. Then came the dreaded day when she was to get the chop. Well we couldn't find Henny Penny anywhere. Finally, we found her down in a corner, left of the front steps and when the gardener picked her up, she laid an egg. There on the ground were another couple of eggs, so we said, "You can't kill her now!" She received a reprieve. Out of all the eggs she laid she produced one little light brown hen who we called 'Little Red Hen', and did she turn out to be a bossy little thing too. Henny Penny was a mixture of greys and light browns. She was a pretty little thing and a very good mother.

A Visit to King's House

In those days everyone had calling cards. Soon after we arrived in Jamaica, I remember being driven to Government House to leave our calling card. There was a day during the year when all new British subjects were invited to a Garden Party to meet the Governor, his wife and family. There were two very smartly dressed Policemen on guard duty on the gates and two more at the front door. The colonial dress uniform for the police was a white jacket with polished brass buttons and a wide black shiny belt, white pith helmets with the police badge on the front. They sometimes wore bright red trousers with a gold stripe down the side, and sometimes navy-blue trousers, below these, huge, black shiny boots.

We drove slowly up the driveway, which was lined with palm trees at intervals and in between there were the lower growing lignum vitae tree. Translated means "wood of life." When in flower it had a delicate blue flower, pale green leaves and a blotchy bark. At the front of the building one of the policemen came forward and opened the car doors for us. My father said we were there to leave our calling cards; we were led up the front steps into a large hallway. In the middle facing us was a small table with a well-polished silver platter, this is where you put the card, and beside it was a visitor's book, which my parents signed, adding all the children's names. Then we left. Quite exciting for a little girl of eight. Still couldn't get used to the idea that everyone spoke English, as none of the other West Indian islands we had lived on was English the native tongue. Well that is if you could call it English. The natives had a lovely way of expressing themselves, it took a little getting used to, but it wasn't long before I picked up the "quashi" Jamaican accent and way of speaking.

School

Pat and I were enrolled as students at the Immaculate Conception Convent School, to start the new term in September. Just before we arrived in Jamaica the school, down in Kingston, had been burnt to the ground. So the school was moved up to the convent on Old Hope Road, just up the road from Cross Roads.

A huge hall had been divided into four classrooms by folding doors that went from the high ceiling to the floor. In inclement weather the doors were folded back and the hall was used for assembly. Normally we just lined up, in our classes, just below the high verandah that ran around the South side of the Convent. The nuns looked down on the rows, they could easily spot anyone talking or misbehaving. Occasionally the headmistress would pick out one of the senior girls to read a particular passage from the Gospel or Epistle of the day. We would say our "before school" prayers and sing a hymn and the national anthem, which in those days was "God save the King". King George VI was reigning at that time; in fact he had not been king for very long. His brother the Prince of Wales had just abdicated to marry an American, Mrs. Simpson. So the

Duke of York was next in line, and became King. The 1t Friday of each month we said the whole rosary. So altogether the assembly took quite a long time. Then we'd all be marched off to our classes with some marching music being played over a speaker. Sometimes the record was a little scratchy.

Our uniforms were white dresses with a light blue tie. I wore brown socks because my sports house was St. Francis. Pat wore blue socks for her house, which was "Immaculata". We wore straw hats with a blue band. These were called "Jippy Jappy" hats!!The nuns, who belonged to the Order of St. Francis, wore long brown habits with black veils. Under the veil they wore a white face piece which had a stiff bit that fitted very tightly above their eyebrows, then a softer bit around their face, under the chin, down under a highly starched bib. The whole thing tied at the back of their head, under their long veil. We always hoped the wind would blow their veils up so we could see the colour of their hair, which was cut short, usually like a man's short back and sides. Around their wastes they wore a white cord tied at the left side and from this cord they had the Rosary, with very large beads and a heavy cross. These used to rattle as the nuns walked along so we could hear them coming. Some used to wrap their beads in their habits so we couldn't hear them coming! Most wore sandals but shoes if they were going out. They must have been very hot in those habits. From under the bib there was a thinner brown piece of material hanging down to below their waste. A lot of the nuns used to walk along with their hands clasped under this. Most of the nuns were American; The Mother House was in Boston if I remember correctly. There were a few Jamaican nuns too, and a couple of Chinese nuns. Mostly very young.

When we started school, we seemed to attract a lot of attention. Maybe Pat and I looked like little Chinese dolls as we both had fringes cut straight across our foreheads; the length was just to the bottom of our ears and cut straight around the back. I think at that time we were the only English girls too. Some of the boarders, who mainly came from South America, were interested because they heard we spoke Spanish. I felt very shy talking it, as I hadn't spoken it for six months. I didn't enjoy all this attention. Had I not been so shy I probably would have continued to speak Spanish fluently as there were always girls from South America the entire time I went to that convent. Then later when the war was on, we had a lot of Gibraltarian girls. They were evacuated out to Jamaica, and they also spoke Spanish.

The classes were Co-ed until the age of ten. Pat and I were the only white children other than three Americans. The American Consuls two daughters and the son. Betty the middle one was in my class. I think their surname was Watson. The school was made up of Jamaicans of mixed descent, African, mainly the Eastern countries like Nigeria, East Indians, Chinese, mainly from Canton. There were many of mixed nationalities. Then the South Americans came from Panama, Columbia, Venezuela and Costa Rica. I remember having a terrific crush on a Costa Rican girl; she was so beautiful and very '*simpatica*'. She was a prefect and about seven years my senior. I first noticed her when it was her turn to stand up on the verandah with the nuns at morning assembly. I later got to know her and even though I thought so much about her I cannot recall her name. I even chose her to stand proxy at my Confirmation.

The first year I was there my school subjects included Latin, Geometry and Algebra, all new subjects to me. Latin, I found fairly easy, Geometry interesting but Algebra a bit complicated. I found English very hard especially the grammar and the spelling. English Literature, another subject I found interesting and quite fun depending on what books we were working on. Nearly every year of my schooling we did one of Shakespeare's plays plus probably something like Silas Marner or Heidi when we were about 10 years old. I loved Botany, Hygiene and Physiology, Geography; History was all right I suppose depending on what part of History it was. We seemed to do a lot of American history and of course West Indian, which was more to my liking, especially when it was to do with Columbus discoveries and the pirate days. English History seemed to be endless with so many Kings and Queens to remember. As I got older, I wished I had paid more attention to what I had been taught.

At the end of my first year I started to take more interest in sport. My leg was much stronger and I entered into long jump, hurdles and relay racing. Much to every one's surprise, in the first school sports day; I came first in the 75yards hurdles. It was probably because I could hear my Father's voice coming out of the spectators. He was yelling, "Come on 'our fat'". Whether I wanted to finish the race quickly to please my father or so people wouldn't know what he affectionately called me I am not quite sure. I can't recall feeling offended at him calling me "Our Fat". I remember him telling me a tale of an incident in India which involved his Father. It was at a Club where there was a gentleman who claimed he could make up a rhyme on the spot if someone gave him a couple of names. My Grandfather chose Sanacarib and Johosafat. The result was:

'Of the lean Sanacarib
You could easy crack a rib
Not so Johosafat
Because he was so fat.'

I thought that pretty good and felt fat was good and tough, so that was all right. My father was a sensitive and very affectionate man and I knew he wasn't making fun of me for being a little tubby. The first year in Jamaica went very quickly. After a few months living at Belmont Ave. my parents found a suitable house. Number 20 Hope Road Half-Way-Tree. It was a nice single-story house, surrounded by shady trees, a very big garden. It was probably about half an acre; it had chicken pens down behind the garage. I remember it had a central room in which there was a piano. The owners had left the piano for us to look after. The rest of the furniture was ours, which had been sent over from Puerto Rico.

At 20 Hope Rd, Half-Way-Tree, Jamaica 1938

Pat's and my bedroom had French doors onto the front verandah. To the left were two big walk-in robes, a door led to the central room and next to that a door into a small corridor which led to my parent's and Teresa's bedrooms. Halfway to their rooms on the right was the bathroom. The verandah was **L** shaped at the left end of the verandah there was another set of French doors, which led into the sitting room.

Incredible Memories

In the tropics it was hardly ever used as such, this led into the dining room and also into the central room. They both opened into a large back verandah, which was enclosed by latticework. On the left of the back porch and down a few steps which led to a long porch which in turn led to the kitchen and then the servants' quarters and back garden. I can't quite recall where David's room was when he came out from England for school holidays. I think he slept in the sitting room which was not often used.

The front verandah ran right across the front of the house and down the right side, with wide concrete steps half-way down the verandah leading to the driveway. There was a thick vine enclosing the corner of the verandah, this area was used as an entertaining area.

My father and mother sitting on side steps of 20 Hope Road, Pat on my right, Bunty (Teresa) on my left

We bought a green parrot when on a trip into the hills. He was very bright and soon learned to talk. Our gardener fed it chili peppers he said that helped them to talk quickly. We had him in a cage on the corner of the verandah. Once he got used to us, we could let him out and he'd fly up and down the verandah and play hide and seek with our cat around the legs of the chairs. He soon picked up things like "Stop it Pat", "Mummy I want breakfast", "Bye Daddy", when my father drove off to work. Also "Where's Andy? I'm thirsty", and several other things. He would fly onto our shoulders or fingers so we could scratch his head, which he loved, when we stopped, he would say" Scratch Polly." Unfortunately, we forgot to shut his cage door one night and the next-door cat had him for dinner. We were very upset about that and the cat was no 1 enemy after that.

Our parents bought us a donkey from the charcoal man. He used to come around with a donkey cart, loaded with bags of charcoal, as we cooked on a wood and charcoal stove. Or rather the cook did.

We called the donkey Rose Bud. She was a brown donkey and very gentle. My mother would sit Pat and I up on her back and we'd go for an afternoon walk. We found out in a couple of months that Frank had wanted to sell Rose Bud because she was pregnant and therefore wouldn't be able to pull his cart in her condition. Soon after a little grey cubby appeared on the scene. He was adorable, so now we had two donkeys. Most people had a dog of sorts to prevent burglaries. A friend who was leaving Jamaica had a 4-year-old Alsatian, called "Solo", and he offered Solo to us. He was very good with children but had been taught to kill anything smaller than himself. The friends had lived on a sugar cane plantation. They had rats and mongooses on the property. The mongooses had got out of control as the number of snakes dwindled. As there weren't many snakes, they ate chickens, ducks and cats. My parents were a bit apprehensive at first as my mother was pregnant and she feared for the infant. Solo absolutely adored my mother. He was a marvellous watchdog. He never left the property even when the gates were left open. He was also very fond of us children; in fact he was very possessive. When the single guys from Shell came visiting, Solo had to be chained, as he didn't like them giving us "piggy backs" or to pick us up.

Our house was raised on concrete pillars as most of the houses were. I remember when we got home from school, Pat and I used to catch a tram from Cross Roads to Half Way Tree then wait for the down tram to pass on the double lines. Then our tram could continue and turn around into Hope Road with screeching wheels. The driver would stop right outside our house once he got to know us; they were nearly always the same drivers at the time we got off school. We would go in the house very quietly as my mother would be having a 'siesta', hurriedly change out of our uniforms and duck under the house. There we had hidden a packet of cigarettes, a box of matches and a tube of Colgate toothpaste, which we used to disguise the smell of cigarettes.

On one particular day we discovered we had run out of cigarettes. I suddenly remembered that the captain off one of the Shell tankers had given my father a few cigars, the real big Churchill kind of cigars; our father was not a cigar smoker. They were kept in a silver cigar box on a table in the sitting room. I volunteered to go and fetch a couple. When I opened the box there were only two left but I felt sure they would not be missed as they had been there for a very long time. Down I went, bit the end off and stuck a matchstick in the end as I had observed done. I felt very knowledgeable and quite grown up. We lit up and sat there puffing away. Pat was some ways through hers when she said she felt a bit sick, I continued to smoke mine then felt a bit sick too, so we decided to go inside and run a cold bath. I was sure that would make us feel better.

My mother came through while we were wallowing around, ducking our heads under the water. We must have looked a bit green as my mother asked if we felt all right. Pat said she was feeling sick. We were told to get out of the bath and get into bed. Our mother then dosed us with Castoria, a brown syrupy mixture, not unpleasant to take, a children's recipe for upset tummies. Had our temperatures taken, that was normal. We were both glad to stay quietly in bed.

This episode did not put paid to our smoking. But we decided cigars were not for us. Even "jack ass rope" was better. Jackass rope was what the natives smoked. It was cured tobacco leaves rolled together forming a long rope. The vendor would then roll a length of it as one would ordinary rope and carry it over their shoulder. They would cut whatever length one wanted with a very sharp knife. A 'penny worth' usually did us for a spell, which would have measured about one inch.

What one did was chop off a wee bit, chop it up, roll it in your hand and either put it into a pipe or onto a cigarette paper. If we didn't have cigarette paper, we just used a bit of brown paper. A square of that hard toilet paper did just as well. That was the only type of toilet paper we could get during the war years anyway. After rolling the tobacco into which ever paper, we licked along the edge to hold it all together, but if you didn't use enough spit the cigarette would start to unravel and we'd lose some of the tobacco halfway through smoking it.

My parents allowed me to have piano lessons as we had the piano. I loved playing and did very well. Unfortunately,. I played some tunes by ear, like 'Boogie Woogie', which my mother did not approve of. Though my mother, who had a beautiful soprano voice, had used the piano to practice her scales, when we moved house she used this as an excuse to discontinue my lessons. My teacher was very disappointed, (as I was), she even offered that I could go and practice at her home. My mother went and practiced at a friend's house. She often sang over the local Radio Station and at various concerts, much to my embarrassment until in my teens, when I appreciated her lovely voice. It was so different to crooning.

Langley Mountain Stay

In 1939 David came out for his long school holidays. I thought he was terribly brave coming all that way by himself. He looked different and so much more grown up though he was only eleven.

The weather at this time of year was very hot and humid; we were taken up into the mountains for a month where it was cooler. We stayed on a coffee and banana plantation called "Langley". It was owned by Robbie and Helen Gillies, about a sixteen mile drive up through beautiful countryside up in the Blue Mountain range. Half the journey there was on bitumen road then we'd turn off onto a dirt road. When we got to Langley, we had to turn right through a cut away in a small hill to a wonderful valley. Through the cut away and to the left running up the hill were two small cottages, one behind the other but some distance apart. To the right there was a path leading to the original "Great House." The slaves had burned this down about 1857, there was only the stone outline left and it was a bit overgrown. The locals said there was a "dupee", (ghost) there so they avoided going near it especially at night.

Leaving that scene, we drove on down a winding narrow road, over a bridge, which took you down through the valley, after about a mile we arrived at a huge stone building. It was a long building; originally it had housed the slaves. On the ground floor there was the machinery to weigh and bag the coffee beans and also to store the beans. The top floor was made of local timbers; the roof had massive eighteen-inch square beams going across on top of the stonewalls from one side to the other

There was a flight of wooden steps running up the outside of the building, which led into the end of the building used for storage. A lift system, manually worked, to bring the bags of coffee up for storage. These bags were only carted down to Kingston when a ship was due, which then took them to Europe. This room was used and opened up on payday; all the workers came up when their name was called. They were paid three pence farthing for each bunch of bananas carried down the hillside and laid in neat rows at the entrance to the property they were then loaded on to trucks and driven to Kingston.

On paydays Robbie had rows of florins and half crowns in a money tray. I used to swap old Victorian and sometimes older coins for modern ones and so started my coin collection. I lost most of these when I left home to join the Navy. They mysteriously disappeared from my belongings. I suspect my youngest brother swapped them at school!

Getting back to the old building. On both sides of the building there were large wooden windows that opened outwards, when shut they were held shut by a wooden bar. The far side of the building looked down on to a river, which joined another river beyond the building. So there was always the lovely sound of running water.

The storage room was separated from the rest of the building by a heavy wooden door. From this door the upper level of the building probably measured at least one hundred yards by fifty-foot wide and had been made into Robbie and Helen's home. A ten-foot wide corridor ran down the left side into a very large area, which was the dining room and the living room, both quite separate. There were two forty by twenty-foot bedrooms to the right. A bathroom that had a door into the corridor and one into the third bedroom, that was Robbie and Helen's bedroom, then came the kitchen.

In the bedrooms were huge double beds, single beds and a cot in each. The Gillies' used to let these rooms to families like ours once they had got to know us. For many years we stayed there until our family grew to eight then we had one of the cottages.

From the dining area there was a set of concrete steps leading down to the driveway. Below the living area there were more storage rooms and around the end of the building a small bedroom where Naisey the cook slept when needed to cook for family and guests.

On the other side of the driveway were huge flat concrete areas with drainage at each corner and a dome shaped storeroom at the far end. These were tiered. Two were next to each other and three steps up from the driveway. On the next tier there were three next to each other. Beyond them was a building that housed an engine, generator and a big water wheel that worked at night to produce electricity and also charged several batteries. These batteries were used during the day to supply current to the shortwave radio and sometimes for a light on a dark stormy day.

Old Mr. Gillies had built a thirty-foot wall across one of the rivers to dam the water during the day. We used to swim in this when it was full. It took about half the morning to fill. Boy was it cold when we first jumped in but it seemed warmer as we swam up and down. Then we'd climb out onto the dam wall and have a rest before diving in again. When the dam was over-flowing, we had to be careful as we walked along the wall, it would be a long way to fall if we lost our footing, the wall was only about two and a half foot wide. At the far end of the wall there was a gateway that prevented the water from running along an aqueduct, this ran along the hillside about a mile down to the powerhouse. Just on sunset the gate was opened and the water ran down to the big wheel, which had buckets all around it. When they filled with water it turned the wheel and kept the generator going. The water then ran down a pipe back into the river. There was usually enough water to keep the lights going until about eleven at night, after that we used flashlights or kerosene lamps. Then first thing in the morning someone would run up and close the dam gates. While doing that we'd slip down and get a few freshwater lobsters from under the rocks and maybe a cocoa root from along the bank. We ate these and yams instead of potatoes. In fact, I don't remember ever seeing a potato while in Jamaica.

The cottages always had other families staying in them, so we always had other boys and girls to swim with. One year there was a family called Scoggins staying, they had two French evacuees, a boy and a girl, visiting with them. One day we all decided to try and walk up the river to see where it started, we had been told it started on the property.

Off we went, we took food with us. Walking about two miles up the path passed the dam before we joined the river. The river was full of massive boulders, some we had to climb over. Every now and again we'd come to a waterfall, we'd climb up the side of it. When we got hot, we'd go for a dip in one of the pools below a waterfall. Our cloths would dry off with the heat of the day. We never got to the head of the river that day as we had to give ourselves sufficient time to return before dark as it would be very dark walking through the last two miles through the forest. It wasn't so easy climbing down the side of the waterfalls.

As we got nearer to home, we came to a very good swimming hole, which we had swum in on the way up. We decided to go skinny-dipping. We girls went behind the rocks to get undressed, the boys were already in the water so they had to look the other way until we got into the water. We swam around for about ten minutes. The water was freezing cold when we got in, but we soon got used to it. The boys were very good; they teased us several times and said they'd come after us. I don't think any of them were game to come anywhere near us. They were put on trust to turn their backs while we got out and dived behind the rocks. We soon were dry again. On our trek home it was still very warm. What a lovely day we had all had, the other families dropped us off at the 'big house' and then they had to walk up the hill to the cottages but promised to come back after the evening meal. When the younger members of the family had gone to bed, we teenagers sat around in the dark, the only light was moon light, and told ghost stories about what we had been told happened on the property. As you can imagine when it was time to say good night, we at the great house were very happy we didn't have the long walk back to the cottages. We heard the next day that a couple of the boys had walked on ahead and frightened the others as they passed by.

Another day we decided to walk to the head of the river via a little-used track. This was a lot quicker. On the way up we saw many lovely plant specimens. Ginger lilies taller than any of us, so lush they looked as if one could eat them. The path crossed the river at several points. We found a huge flycatcher by the side of one of these crossings and spent some time there watching insects landing on the lip of the flowers. They snapped shut and we could hear the buzzing as it tried to escape, then silence.

There was another plant that had an upside-down flower, nearly transparent when the sun was behind it. The insect would climb up into the flower, which incidentally smelt pretty horrible, then when it got into the neck of the flower there was a sticky liquid which seemed to paralyse the fly. It was then sort of dissolved, and that was lunch!

We watched all sorts of insects and water spiders plus heard frogs but did not see any. Each crossing was unique in what it had to offer us visually, in sound and scent. We'd test each other to see who could find the most of some sort of interest. The older ones of us who had maybe learnt something about a plant or insect would enlighten the younger ones.

As we got nearer to the summit and the head of the river, the river narrowed. Then at last there it was, beautiful clear, sweet water pouring out of the hillside down a very high rocky escarpment. We couldn't see any way up the side of the waterfall. By continuing up the path, using a machete to clear parts of the path as we went, we finally reached the summit and walked above the waterfall. It was quite flat and we were able to walk a bit further back from the waterfall, we looked out for miles with Kingston in the distance. We must have been a couple of thousand feet above sea level.

What a glorious scene lay before us, it was quite breathtaking. The air was so fresh and pure, unpolluted. We all lay down on a grass patch and drank in the sight of the blue sky with a few white clouds floating by, listening to the birds. All agreed this was one of the most beautiful places we'd ever been to. What a wonderful spot to live. After having a drink and demolishing the sandwiches we'd brought it was time to think of our return journey. Reluctantly we made for the path but promised ourselves we would return one day with tents and camp overnight. This never happened. But I did return one day with Panchito one of Robbie's faithful dogs. Quite often Panchito and I would go off on our own exploring. He was a good companion, a good rat catcher too. He would always warn me of anyone or anything approaching. He'd run back to me, the hairs on the back of his neck would go up. I'd ask him to sit, which he did right on my feet. As the person approached, he'd growl following them with his eyes. Then I'd say, "come on", but he'd walk behind me for a while before running off ahead of me again. He was a white terrier. Blind in one eye, they thought from being spat at by a toad or it could have been from a vine that grew in the bush, which blinded a lot of animals.

Joining the Girl Guides

During my tenth year I joined the Girl Guides. The first test I had to pass was the Tenderfoot. For this I had to learn all the Guide rules and promises, I had to light a campfire using no more than two matches. This I passed quite easily, and then I could wear a uniform. I felt quite proud of myself and vowed I'd pass many more tests and get to be a captain of a company one day. This I never did but I did manage to pass many badges, I had no more room on my sleeves to sew them on. My father used to say that I would have to sew them on my bottom next. After being awarded the blue and white cords, I received the gold cords, then the Little House Emblem and finally was the first in the southern hemisphere to be awarded the Queen's Guide Award. My Girl Guide Captain Sister Emmanuel was so proud of me, she never let anyone forget it. For years after I left Jamaica she used to write to me with news of what was going on in the company and would send a newspaper clipping with my photo and a bit about my being the first Queen's Guide, what country I was living in and that I was now married with so many children. In 1947 I was chosen to represent Jamaica at the 1st World Jamboree that was being held in the USA. I was most unhappy that this could not happen as at that time the family were going to the UK on leave and my parents would not allow me to stay behind. Little did I know that my parents had decided to separate and only my father would be returning to the West Indies. I suppose thems the breaks.

Each year, during the summer holidays, Sister took us camping at Montego Bay. The nuns at the convent there allowed us to have their school hall. We slept on not too comfortable school benches; a few of us fell off these during the night but didn't like the idea of sleeping on the floor because of creepy crawlies. We had seen several cockroaches and knew there'd be scorpions and the like crawling around at night. We all had torches, essential as the loos were outside and some distance from the hall. Old fashioned type, hole in the ground.

The different patrols took it in turns cooking the meals; I didn't relish my turn, as I knew very little about cooking or preparing food, never having to do it as we had servants. Needless to say, I was soon taught how. On the day we had to do lunch we were not allowed to go to the beach, the highlight of my day. The beaches in Montego Bay were some of the most beautiful in Jamaica. The waters were usually calm, the sands fine and very white, and the water a clear turquoise colour. One did not have to swim out too far, stick your face in the water and open your eyes to observe the most colourful coral and sea anemones with a variety of fish swimming lazily around.

We were there for two weeks, I returned looking like an Indian. All the girls were lavishly smeared with coconut oil, the result we were cooked to a cinder, some of us suffered sunburn the first day so Sister poured vinegar over the burn spots! No wonder I have the skin I have these days. The last night camping we'd have a concert of sorts, some of the older girls made up some really humorous skits, Sister always sang, she had a beautiful voice. We'd have a special meal and a couple of the nuns were invited to share our evening with us. The company leader would make a speech and Sister would have several words to say.

We travelled to Montego Bay from Kingston by train. It took us eight hours to travel one hundred and eight miles. There were stations on the way but the train would stop for a group of people, sometimes only one person, along the way if they gave the driver enough time to stop. Not very hard as the train sure didn't travel very fast. The carriages were made up of two rows of slatted seats divided by a narrow aisle. Extremely uncomfortable and very hot in the middle of the day. Certainly not the sort of seats one could doze off in. Sister would book two carriages for all the Guides and just hope the train didn't get too crowded or we'd find as we did one year that we would be sharing with others. This year the train pulled up and a burly policeman got on and said the government department had priority over us and proceeded to bring on some manacled prisoners, about seven in number, plus a man in a straight jacket. Sister hurriedly doubled us up and the police handcuffed the prisoners to the arms of the seats, some had to sit in the aisle while the man in the straight jacket lay on the floor between the seats. I have never seen such wild eyes except in a frightened animal. Not an experience I would like to repeat. Needless to say, my parents were not very happy about the situation and needed a lot of persuasion the next year.

I returned to Jamaica in 1984 for a reunion of old girls and to celebrate Sister's 50th anniversary of being the person to introduce Guiding to the school and to being the captain of 21st St. Andrews Guide Company. What a reunion that was! To meet up with so many of my old school mates. I stayed with several families of present and past Guides. There was a big banquet with presentations of badges and of the most recent Queen's Guide Award. Of course, they were all very curious to see who this Anne John was that Sister was always talking about, much to my embarrassment.

It was sad also to see what had happened to my beloved Jamaica over the years. Where I remembered fresh green and clean areas were now dry, devoid of foliage, places dirty with goats roaming around eating the rubbish lying on the streets and crumbling sidewalks. Where there had been neat hedgerows up peoples' driveways, there was nothing. Gardens cleared of all shrubs and anything a thief could hide behind. Except high bougainvillea hedges to prevent a person climbing over into another property, too prickly to even attempt. But more of my visit in later pages.

Visiting Langley in 1940

When we were up visiting Langley in 1940 Helen, Naisey and my mother were large with child. Quite funny to see three very pregnant ladies in the kitchen preparing meals. The kitchen was not very big so at times they were busy trying to avoid each other's tummies.

That year, seven of us, we older boys and girls, there was Arthur, William and Virginia Scoggin, David, Pat and I and a French evacuee Tom, decided to take a hike up to see Uncle Bill. He wasn't a real uncle but everyone called him that even the adults.

My parents, Robbie and Helen had been up a few nights earlier to visit Uncle Bill and he said he would like to see us one day. So we thought Wednesday was a good enough day as any.

Uncle Bill

Uncle Bill had spent most of his life as a banker traveling across Canada during the 1920's and '30s. This on horseback calling in on all the outposts. He carried pay for the trappers, loggers and did banking in small townships. When he retired, he went to Jamaica and got a job as caretaker for the Forestry Commission. He was given a few acres on the hillside and started to build a house for himself. He'd build a room or two a year. He also built a little one room 'Guest House' which jutted out over the side of the hill at the back of his house. This was originally built to house his sister who came out from his homeland Scotland. She stayed for a year, as she had not seen him for many years, he had never returned home.

He was a very big man, was Uncle Bill. Always a smiling face with twinkling grey blue eyes, silver grey hair and beard, well-trimmed. To me at the tender age of nine, he seemed very old. Looking back now I suppose he would have been in his sixties. I thought then, nearly a hundred.

The unfinished room, which was then his dining room, had as its fourth wall some hessian hanging down, weighted at the bottom with a pine sapling.

The highlight of our holiday was a trek up the mountainside, for, the last four miles was only a footpath. The only way we could get up to Uncle Bills' was to walk. We left early in the morning with some fruit and water. It was about a four-mile hike. Three miles on a winding dirt road then when we reached the one shop town of Mount Pleasant, we turned off on to a narrow path leading up and over a small bridge to the path that led us to Uncle Bill's. We arrived about half past nine very tired, thirsty and hungry to be greeted by all plus two dogs, with a very hearty laugh and a cheery welcome.

"Come away in, you must be fair peckered out!"

"Hello Uncle Bill!" we all chanted together.

Arthur Scoggin, 14, dressed in his usual jeans, red and black checked shirt, was sturdily built, had dark hair compared to William two years his junior. William was slightly built and very fair. We all thought he was the better looking of the two, and he knew it. He was dressed in tight fitting pale blue shorts with a paler blue and white striped cotton shirt. Virginia, their sister was ten, and so thin we used to say one wouldn't see her if she stood sideways, except for her nose. She had shoulder length wavy, mouse coloured hair and very light blue eyes. She wore a pink checked cotton frock. Robert was the only one from the Taylor family with us. His sisters were too young to walk the distance.

My eldest brother David, nearly 11, in khaki shorts and shirt and Pat my sister who was nearly 3 years my junior. Some of us did not want her along, as we thought she wouldn't make the distance. My mother had dressed her in a pair of maroon corduroy dungarees and a pair of short gumboots. I wore my favourite green cord shorts, favourite because they had side pockets. I always liked to carry string, a penknife, matches and a large handkerchief. A green and red, small checked, shirt with pockets with button down flaps. In these I used to collect small coloured pebbles and seeds.

As we all trooped after Uncle Bill who was constantly talking. He certainly seemed very happy to see us all.

"Naicey will get us all an iced jug of lime juice and I'll open a can of some nice Canadian salmon, I caught the other day." He teased us.

"And maybe Andy (that's what I was called in those days) and David wouldn'a mind picking some tomatoes offa the bushes, William yoor a tall lad, would you mind fetching a cucumber offa the vine growing up yonder fence." He turned to see who was left, "Arth and Ginia, you two can lay the table in ma new dining room. That leaves two of you, will you go and see Naicey (that was his cook) out in the kitchen and mebe give her a hand."

So our day started as it always did with every one being made to feel quite grown up and useful. We ate the meal of salmon, tomatoes, cucumber and pickles, home baked bread with lashings of homemade butter and mayonnaise. The meal over, Uncle Bill suggested a "wee walk" So off we went up the mountainside, he with his long staff, quietly whistling to himself. His stride at least four feet to our two. In a very short time, he striding in his slow movements, was way ahead of us, we followed at a steady trot. Puffing and panting and red faced while Uncle Bill looked as cool as the day was.

Always whistling. I learned later the tunes he whistled were Scottish laments.

We were all grateful when at intervals he would stop, turn around and admire the scenery. He questioned us on birds, types of grass or just generally everything around us. We had been too busy trying to keep up with him to notice what we were passing. We learned a lot about flora, fauna and the elements around us on these stops. Then off we'd go again. The path was a narrow one. In places we had to climb onto a rock which made a very high step or jump off one depending on whether the path suddenly took a downward trend. We were following the side of the mountain as the terrain allowed.

Uncle Bill arrived at a little log cabin in the middle of a clearing, within the forest, at the top of the mountain, a while ahead of us. We arrived one behind the other Indian style. The fittest first. By the time the last arrived, usually the youngest and Virginia, he was ready to go again. But we persuaded him to stay a little longer by asking a stream of questions about things around us such as "how'd you build this cabin" and "how deep are all these pine needles on the ground?" They felt very spongy. There was a small pipe sticking out of a low bank behind the cabin, out of which, trickled deliciously cool water. Tapped from an underground spring. What a peaceful, beautiful spot it was with that damp smell of pine needles and earth. It was deliciously cool too.

I thought it would be lovely to live in a place like that. Grow your own vegetables and stuff, but of course there wasn't enough sunlight for that.

On our return to Uncle Bill's house we all had a drink of cold lime juice and a couple of biscuits out of a big square "Peak Freen Assorted" biscuit tin. Then we all trooped into Uncle Bill's workshop.

In the centre of the room was a heavy six-foot square table. On the left wall hung various-sized saws. These had neatly cut pieces of pine boards covered in petroleum jelly, tied on each side. This prevented rust in the humid atmosphere. The wall facing us had hammers, chisels and planes all neatly in their slots or narrow shelves. On the right wall there were screwdrivers, pliers, wire cutters and an assortment of other tools and rows of little drawers full of various sized nails and screws, nuts and bolts, hinges and fastening bolts. Below all the tools was a two-foot deep workbench. A wood vice attached at both end and one in the centre of the left bench. On the bench facing there was nothing but on the right bench there were a couple of metal work vices. Under these benches were various sized timbers; under the right bench were some lengths of piping. There were three doors one led in from his living come dining area, opposite a door led outside and the third went into a storeroom where he kept his timber, tins of kerosene, turpentine and paints and paint brushes.

Uncle Bill showed us how to use the different tools and again put us in pairs. We were allowed to make either a toy or something useful. On one particular occasion, Uncle Bill thought it would be nice to make something for Helen and her new baby. We decided to make Helen a box with a lid to hold all the pins, creams cotton wool etc. for bathing and changing the baby. He designated who should cut the wood to size, who should plane the wood and who to sand it, all from a plan he had drawn up. Before we knew it, it was 3:30 and time for afternoon tea before we started our long trek back to Langley. We had not finished the box so that gave us an excuse to visit again. Uncle Bill seemed as pleased as we were at the thought.

Before our long walk back to Langley we had delicious homemade brown bread with oodles of butter and jam. Some pancakes Naicey had made, again, with oodles of butter and honey or lemon juice and sugar. I liked the lemon juice and sugar. We had flapjacks and freshly baked bread with various jams. There were always at least six varieties of jams to choose from. I had never had green gage jam before so asked him what the green jam was; he teasingly said that it was made with this special fruit he grew for little girls like me. He must have had tins of food stashed away in another storeroom. It was wartime and we couldn't buy half of what he served us. After tea we bade everyone 'cheerio' until we'd meet again in a couple of days.

With our tummies nice and full and all clutching the items we had so cleverly made we said our goodbyes. Off down the winding path we went, turning at each bend to wave to Uncle Bill, until he was out of sight. The end of a perfect day. Only hope we made Uncle Bill as happy as he made us.

The journey home was much quicker as it was downhill all the way, we ran most of the way, sometimes hiding if we got far enough in front not to be seen, and then we'd jump out at the others as they went by. What a wonderful day we had, decided we'd go for a quick swim when we got back. It was still light, so we got into our bathers and ran up to the dam. Took a quick plunge and boy was it cold but so refreshing. The sun had set so we opened the gates of the dam; by the time we returned to the 'Big House' the lights were already on.

Bicycle Days

A picture in my mind of bicycles of my youth, the crazy antics my brother and I got up to. Our bikes braked by pedalling backwards or just standing on the pedal. We decided that if we removed the back fender, I think we got the idea from our gardener, there was a third form of braking. Twist around and firmly put a foot on the back wheel, against the frame. Not very good for the soles of our plimsolls, what we called our canvas and rubber soled shoes. But quite an effective way to stop. We practiced for days another method of stopping in a hurry. This was jumping off the bike backwards and catching the seat as it went from under us.

There was a very steep road running down from Red Hill which ended in a T junction. Red Hill because the earth was a red colour in comparison to the other hills around. David, Chiki (David's friend) and I rode up the hill with great difficulty and determination, the gradient was 1 in 9. In those days we did not have multiple gears, it was a very slow journey. There wasn't much traffic on this road so we started down the hill jumping off backwards, practicing stopping in this manner. Halfway down we decided to return to the top, travel longer distances as our speed would be greater. We were successful, so again halfway down we returned to the top. This time we would do the full length which was some four miles.

We started down, gaining speed rapidly. When we reached the bottom of the hill, we jumped off backwards, with great relief caught the seat and actually stayed on our feet, though the force of the speed made us run forward some distance. Fortunately, not running into the traffic on the main road below. Very exhilarating. We sat and rested deciding we'd try that again another day.

On the way home we went off the main road down an alternative route which was also hilly but not so steep. Here we competed in riding with our feet up on the handlebars steering the bike while we had enough speed to carry us forward, and not requiring pedalling. Where there was not enough incline, we would crisscross along the road to gain speed and at the same time prevent the next rider from passing. If they were too close, they would have to take evasive action, usually braking, which needed their feet.

No wonder we were never bored during school holidays, there was always something new and exciting to do.

In a small leather pouch attached to the back of the seat, we carried a puncture outfit. In this tin was a spare valve rubber, various sizes of rubber patches which had a sticky shiny side covered with a sort of material strip. A tube of adhesive, a little container of powder and on the lid was a grater with which we could rub around the puncture to clean the tube and also to get a rough surface for adhesion.

By blowing up the tube it was usually obvious where the hole was. After cleaning the area, the adhesive was spread around the hole and left to dry to a tacky feel, strip the material off and stick the patch on, first letting the tube down to nearly empty. With the rounded edge of the tin press down all around the edge of the patch, leave it for a while to seal.

Meanwhile we would probably sit around eating fruit and having a drink or we would explore the surroundings. Once I found an open-ended spanner which I bagged.

When we thought the patch was well and truly stuck, blow up the inner tube and put a lavish amount of spit around the edge of the patch. If there were no bubbles it was sealed, then we would let out the air by removing the valve, run a few fingers around the inside of the tyre to find out the cause of the puncture, sometimes ending up with a cut finger if the culprit was a tack or nail. At times of course it was a pinched inner tube or a small bit of grit that had not been cleaned out previously that caused the puncture. Sprinkle the patch with a little of the powder then replace the inner tube, pump it up a little then carefully ease the tyre into the rim of the wheel, make sure the tube was safely within the tyre, pump it up and we'd be ready to cycle again.

We had fun playing a type of Polo on our bikes, when we had enough friends around to make up two teams, sometimes only two a side. Another time we would compete to see how many tricks we could do on our bikes. Set up a long narrow plank of wood to ride along with a meter drop at the far end, not very good for the front fork. More often than not we'd fall off on landing. We'd ride along on the back wheel and see who could stay on the longest. Or ride the bike backwards standing on the pedals facing the rear of the bicycle, a fairly difficult feat as one's hands were virtually behind on the handlebars. This took a lot of coordination.

I used to ride to school in the good weather often holding on to the side of the tram so I didn't have to pedal up hill. There was a handle at the end of each seat, the seats ran the width of the tram. To prevent passengers from alighting onto the road a wooden bar was lowered the length of the tram, The conductor walked along the outside of the tram on the further side, but I still had to keep an eye on him as he would hit the hand of anyone holding on to the side. He carried a switch with him which he used if he could get close enough. These are a few of the pictures I carry in my head.

A Fortunate Childhood

My father was an accountant with Shell Oil Company. He was sent to several West Indian islands. When relocated we either went with him or followed soon after. What a fortunate childhood we had. The islands were beautiful, as were the people, all differing in many ways. This helped to make our lives very interesting and diverse.

In the early thirties, my brother David was 14 months older than me, Patricia, my sister 2 years younger. The word 'bored' never entered our vocabulary. Our life was free from morning to night. We spent most of those hours outdoors. My family was considered to be well off but we never had the abundance of toys and gadgets children of today own.

Each Christmas, we received a large toy like a scooter or tricycle or just a large car inner tube. There were no surfboards in those days. We never saw a water ski until 1946 when Errol Flynn called into Jamaica and some of the crew on his yacht skied in Kingston Harbour, just off Myrtle Bank Hotel.

Each Christmas, we also received a garment of clothing and always a book. Depending on our age the title differed. I remember David was presented with 'Moby Dick' when he was 11 and I with 'Little Women.' We had to wait for either a birthday or Christmas to receive a tennis racquet or cricket bat when we showed an interest in the game. We never received toys or anything else for that matter in between those special days.

Our pocket money started with a nickel, five cents, a week. This increased each year until we received a quarter. Of course, this amount was increased by whatever coin we found in the Christmas pudding.

We were always inventing games or making things from whatever material we could scrounge. One year, David and I had read 'Robinson Crusoe' so we decided to make a raft as at that time we lived by the sea. With some help from our gardener we put this together from some boards taken from packing crates. We were so proud of our product. We had a big launching day. After dragging the raft down the beach, put it into the water, it sank. How disappointed we were! We were so despondent; my mother took pity on us and bought a container of putty. This we preceded to fill in-between each board. On refloating the raft, the putty lifted straight out. Maybe we should have put it on the underside of the vessel. After several attempts and failures, we gave up the idea. This was probably providential as David and I were quite adventurous. Who knows, we may have ended up having to be rescued sailing out to sea on a prevailing current!

Incredible Memories

William Scoggin, Chris Bunty, Virginia & Arthur Scoggin, David and Robert Frank on top of coffee store, 'Langley' Jamaica 1944

Self, Pat, Robbie and David in the dam, 'Langley' Jamaica 1940

Chapter 3

ANECDOTES OF YOUNGER DAYS

The Tricycle

I can remember when we lived in Haiti early 1930s, when David and I owned a tricycle. There was a wheel at the front attached to a long handle with a hand steering grip. It had an elongated wooden seat that narrowed at the front and widened at the rear where we sat. It also had a backrest. The pedals were on the front wheel, there was also a footrest above the axel of the two rear wheels where one of us could stand and get a lift. We used to take it in turns and ride it around our long front veranda. David also had a red metal-bodied pedal car. This had a seat and two pedals that we pushed back and forward with our feet. The pedals were attached to the front wheels by a bent rod, which went in a circular motion. The pedals worked independently so it was quite hard work pushing them. The steering wheel was also attached to the front wheels.

While on leave in England, Aunt Enid gave Pat and I two China dolls. Pat's had blonde hair, like her and mine had dark hair like me. They had blue eyes that moved to close when we lay them down, with long eyelashes. I wasn't very interested in dolls but I really loved this one, especially because it had belonged to my aunt. It was not very long before Pat broke hers' and then proceeded to break mine. I was very upset.

When we moved to Puerto Rico, we were given a wagon. It was red with a long handle attached to the front wheels, this steered the wagon when pulled. Likewise, if we sat in it, we would put the handle backwards and would be able to use it like that. Sometimes we would be pushed or find a hill to freewheel down. It did not have any brakes so if we did the hill business we often got tossed out at the end.

Sometimes we would put Chico, our dog, in, or Pat, and haul them around.

Incredible Memories

We also had a pair of skates each, David and I became very good skaters. We could do all sorts of tricks on them.

When we had been in Jamaica for about a year, a friend of my parents, who were returning to England, gave Pat and I two tricycles. We had never seen such big tricycles before. They had a large front wheel with pedals on either side attached to the handlebars. Below the seat there was a 'y' shaped metal piece to a platform that ran between the two back wheels. This could be used as a step and we could give someone else a ride if they stood on it and held us around the waist. As we got bigger, they were handed down to our younger siblings.

I saved up and bought my first bike, for thirty shillings. That was a lot of money in those days! Pat took up horse riding. A friend gave her an ex-racehorse, called Gibraltar. We always had a menagerie of animals; chickens, ducks, rabbits, a couple of goats, a mongoose, a donkey, a pig, and two dogs.

Our dog, Solo, seemed to know when we were going to have an earthquake or tremor. He would face in the direction, his tail would go up and so would all the hairs on his back, then he would make a strange noise similar to a growl but it wasn't a growl. Just before we felt the tremor he would start barking as if there was an intruder.

Picnics

At weekends we invariably went on a picnic with friends. On one occasion we drove across the island to a most beautiful beach at Dun's River. This beach was little known in those days. We had to climb down a very narrow path from the road to the beach. There was a very wide waterfall falling down over what were like large steps. This meant there were several foaming waterfalls until the water reached the beach. Below each step there were small pools before the water flowed down to the next level. We used to climb up and sit in the pools and let the water splash on to our backs. Some of the rocks were slippery and we had to be careful.

On either side of the falls were gingerlillies, which had bright coloured flowers, and various kinds of ferns and palms, which looked very picturesque when the sun shone on them. A large tree had been blown down during a storm so we used that as a table to lay out our picnic. We used to be joined by several of our friends. They seemed to be mostly grown-ups but we children didn't mind that as we all, my siblings, played together in the shallow, clear seawater or in the falls. A few of the adults played with us.

Another weekend we crossed the Blue Mountains and went to Port Antonio to visit a friend who managed a sugar plantation and factory. This was on the north side of the island. Phil Graham had an old car with a canvas top but didn't seem to have any windowpanes. So as we drove along the wind blew in on us, free air conditioning! Phil used to drive along and then suddenly stop and we'd all topple forward, we thought it was great fun.

ANECDOTES OF YOUNGER DAYS

When we drove down the long road from his house to the beach, he would do a wobbly all over the road. As we looked out over the harbour waters at Port Antonio, we looked across to a small island, which Errol Flynn had bought. He often brought his yacht in and anchored just off it. The waters along that northern shore were incredibly clear, with white sandy beaches.

I couldn't believe how warm the water was, I'd swim underwater with my eyes open, looking at the coral and beautiful shells on the floor of the ocean. I learnt later that the Gulf Stream came around the north coast of Jamaica and that was why the waters were so pleasant to swim in.

Halfway across the mountains we stopped at a place called Castle Gardens. There were grassy slopes. David and I found a large leaf off a palm tree. At the end that joined it to the tree was like a huge scoop, this had been separated from the main branch, we sat on this and surfed down the hill. We were tossed out a couple of times ending up with a few grazes but this did not stop us from returning to the top of the hill and scooting down again.

One weekend Phil came over to have dinner with my parents, then go to some big Ball. David and I decided to play a trick on Phil as he was always teasing us. The adults were all in at dinner so decided to take the opportunity while they were all out of sight and ear shot. We pushed his car up to the end of the front veranda, David started to giggle and my father came out to see what was going on. When we told him what we planned to do he gave us a hand. We got the car up on to the veranda, Daddy went back to the table and we went back to bed. I was nearly asleep when we heard this roar of laughter, Phil took it all in good spirits and called out "I'll get you later!" While he and Daddy got it back off the veranda.

We had friends called Munn who lived on a property at Morant Bay, in St. Thomas, east of Kingston, on the south coast. We stayed there once, and I watched one day while Mr. Munn changed an old ice box to a kerosene frig. I thought he was very clever as it actually worked. Another time we visited and stayed was when their eldest daughter, Sheila, married a young man, Robbie, who worked with my father at the Shell Oil Company. We all though their affair very romantic!

The Munns had cows and they used to make butter, the only time we had real butter during the war, other than when we visited the American base. They lived in a huge rambling Colonial style house set in tropical gardens. Their property was just off the southern coast road. The land was fairly flat but appeared to be very fertile.

One weekend, I was about fifteen, a group of about twenty of us teenagers went on a trip in the back of a very noisy truck, to a beach along the south coast west of Kingston, and spent the day swimming, picnicking, shooting and generally messing about. We played cricket, volleyball, ran races and tried climbing coconut trees. Not many of us got to the top, I found it harder getting back down again. The whole day was good fun even though we got sunburnt!

Incredible Memories

Another summer holiday we stayed at a friend's property in Irish Town, in the mountains. Just above Strawberry Hill and below Newcastle, where there was an army barracks where the men went to; to get a break from the heat of the army camp down in the city. I suspect it was also a lookout during the war and radio station.

Daddy came up for weekends. Here they had coffee barbeques, as they had at Langley, these were huge concrete squares where they washed and dried the coffee beans. There was also a water wheel in a pump house, which produced the electricity for the property. A forbidden place for children, the teenagers were allowed sometimes to start up the process which only meant opening the gates to let the water flow to the wheel.

Our father had just returned to St. Andrew where we lived, when we realised Christopher was missing. Mummy ran down from the cottage we were staying in, across the barbeques, over a low wall and down some steps toward the pump house. She hit a metal bar that was sticking out from the wall, which sent her flying off the steps, nearly into the river.

I was close at her heels when I saw what happened. I scrambled down and picked Mummy up and got her onto the lowest barbeque. I don't know where I got the strength. By that time the gardener had arrived with David, Pat and Marjorie, Pat's friend who was staying with us. Pat went down to the pump house and got Chris and took him up to the cottage. The cook, the gardener and I lifted Mummy onto a door the gardener brought down and we carried her up to the roadway. Then the gardener grabbed a flashlight and started running down to Strawberry Hill, where we hoped the Da Costas had not yet left for their home in St. Andrew. I hoped the Da Costas would come and pick Mummy up and take her down the hill as she said she was in terrible pain.

It was not too long before our neighbours arrived, they said that they had phoned my father and would meet him halfway. They also brought the gardener back as he said he was afraid to walk back as it was dark and he was afraid of 'Duppies'. Our nurse, Daphne and the gardener thought my mother was going to die and didn't want to be anywhere near her if she did. Mummy wrapped in a blanket was driven away.

We children and Pat's friend Marjorie Vaz were left with Daphne, the cook and the gardener to look after us. Mummy was very badly bruised and had no broken bones or internal injuries. She just needed a good rest before returning the following weekend. Looking a little black and blue.

The Americans had a huge base on the island and we got to know some of the guys through my father's work. No one was allowed on the base unless invited by one of the men. We visited several times and were amazed at the amount of delicious food they served in the canteen which we had for lunch whenever we visited.

There always seemed to be some sort of excitement when we visited. One weekend there had been a plane crash in the ocean just off the shore of the camp and we went down onto the wharf and watched as they lifted the remains of the plane on to the pier. Another weekend as we were being driven around the camp in a small bus, David and I were sitting in the back seat, when he had a sort of fit. He seemed to stop breathing for a while and I thought he was dead. When he came around he couldn't remember anything but said he felt a bit sick. Our friend drove quickly to the hospital and a doctor came out and examined David. He said he should lie down and rest until it was time for us to go home! I never did find out why he had the fit. He never ever had another!

One of our friends was a weight-lifter and was very muscular, he was very tall too and rather good-looking. He gave David and me a go with some of the lighter weights. The next day we were very stiff and had sore arms. Sometimes we were given a box with various can foods, which were no longer in our grocery store.

We also got a chance to go to their USO canteen near Cross Roads where several film stars and crooners came out to entertain the troops. One time, Caesar Romero and Robert Taylor flew out in their own plane and we got to meet them out at the airport as my father arranged to have their plane refuelled. That was very exciting. People like Bing Crosby, Frank Sinatra, Bob Hope and several comediennes also came out.

When I was fourteen and David was fifteen my parents started to take us to concerts. Daddy knew the guy who brought the orchestras and singers or musicians out to Jamaica. This was in the last years of the war when they could be flown out. We had people like Maliza Courjuz the lead singer in 'Great Waltz', with a beautiful voice, Yehudi Menuin, he looked so young, Hiefitz Claudio Arau, a pianist from Chile. He had been a friend of my grandparents when they lived in Chile.

One day when a group of us went down to the Myrtle Bank Hotel to swim and have lunch we heard Maliza practising her singing. We went and stood by her window. She came out and said we were disturbing her but if we sat below the window and were quiet, we could stay. It was sad when we heard that she had elephantiasis, which is why she always wore long dresses. Her legs were very swollen. She was a brave lady. She died a few years later.

All these experiences taught me about life. Some incredibly memorable, happy and sad times, but that was life.

Pig Roast

One year when we were staying at Langley there was also a family called Taylor, staying in one of the cottages. Mr. Taylor and my father decided to buy a piglet one weekend, so we could have 'pig on the spit'. Several of the young men from the Shell Co. were also invited up that weekend, as nearly all were about to sail for England to join up.

Willie the headman of the property was asked to come in on the Sunday. He was to be in charge of the cooking of the pig. Naisey the cook had prepared yams, breadfruit and green bananas to be roasted on the fire under the spit.

We older children had gone off and picked trumpet leaves to use instead of tobacco, as we had none. We were caught rolling our cigarettes by my father who rashly promised to give us tobacco but only after we had eaten all the food as they had spent thirty shillings on the pig and he didn't want it wasted. The smell already coming from the pig was so good I didn't think there was any chance any of it was going to be left!

We needed no more encouragement; we went off and found some dry bamboo and cut pieces to make pipes. This kept us busy until lunch was ready. By that time the men were feeling no pain, as the saying went. Rum punch and 'Red Lable' beer had been flowing freely. As you can imagine Mummy was not well pleased at Daddy's promise.

After eating our fill of delicious pork with plenty of 'crackly' accompanied by roast vegetables, then to top it off, homemade ice cream and fruit. Then we thought it would be siesta time, but no! My father was challenged to a pillow fight up on one of the 18x18 inch beams over a double bed in one of the bedrooms. These beams would have been at least fifteen foot above the bed. I cannot remember how they got up there but all the men were cheering them on, when the wives trooped in and yelled they were being "absolutely absurd." We kids were pretty horrified by the whole thing and were promptly removed. I must say it was very frightening to see them hitting each other and trying to dislodge one another. They were both drunk, but my father, who was of a slight build, was no match for a rather large Mr Sargent. I don't remember the outcome but there was loud laughter and I think they must have called a truce and come down. Though I think they fell off onto the bed which Helen was not too pleased about.

We kids of course, badgered my father for tobacco, which we smoked during the afternoon. I can remember walking up to the cottage we were staying in that year, Nora our cook and Daphne the nurse came out when they heard us coming. Seeing us with the pipes and puffing out smoke, not too far behind our parents, Daphne tried to warn us that our parents were behind. They were very surprised when we told them my father had given us the tobacco.

Another Pig Roast

We were given a piglet as a present and we called him 'Masoomba.' When we first got him, he must have missed his Mum because he would wander around whimpering. We kept him down the back garden so Solo wouldn't get him. Masoomba soon got used to us and would follow us around and want to join in our games. It wasn't very long before he was a big pig but he was as gentle as a pet dog. One day when we were playing hide and seek, he joined into the game. He would find us and squeal with delight then shoot off and stick his head under a shrub. All we could see was a round, fat bottom with a small curly tail which was going around in excitement and expectation. We'd stand near him and say, "I wonder where Masoomba is?" He would squeal and his tail would go even faster. Then we would smack him and run off and hide.

One day while playing this game we decided to run up the stairs to the servants' quarters. Masoomba ran past grunting because he never looked up so didn't see us. He ran around the building twice and was getting very grumpy so we came down and ran off and hid behind a bush. So continued the game.

Masoomba was very naughty because when we were at school, he broke down the fence and went next door and ate all the ladies prize roses. She was not impressed and complained. Brown fixed the fence but after the third time Masoomba escaped Daddy said he had to go. So the last I remember was coming home from school to see a blue van leaving our property and we could hear poor Masoomba squealing inside it. We were very sad and really missed him.

Meeting Lady Baden-Powell

The war had nearly ended when Lady Baden-Powell announced she was to visit Jamaica. For weeks all the Guide companies prepared for a big rally in her honour. She had visited Canada and the USA and was due to fly in very shortly. Our company was to form a guard of honour at the airport. Because there was still a shortage of gasoline, we had to ride our bikes. This was quite a distance to ride. On the way we called in to join up with other girls who lived on the route.

That week the staff at the lunatic asylum had gone on strike and we had to ride past the compound. We were not looking forward to this as the gates had been left open and some of the inmates were roaming the streets. Betty and I called down a side street to pick up the Espuets and there was a guy lying in the gutter, he had his head nearly severed from his body. Well you couldn't see us for dust; we rode our bikes so fast. We rode back to the main road another way. We still had about five miles to ride out to the airport and had yet to go past the asylum. We did not know what to expect as we had already seen several people all dressed in white wandering the street. Some were laughing and dancing around and others were just wandering aimlessly.

After this unpleasant experience we finally got to the airport in time to see the plane land. We hurriedly lent our bikes against a wall and fell in on either side of a red carpet. It had been a hot ride; Sister Emmanuel gave us all a drink, straightened our ties and uniforms and put us to stand at ease until Lady Baden-Powell was to walk down the carpet. We were brought to attention and saluted at this rather slightly built, elderly lady, in uniform, she returned our salute. She was smiling all the time and occasionally stopped to talk to one of us. Then she swished off in a car and we had the long ride back, still not sure what to expect and glad to be well past that area.

At the rally Lady Baden-Powell thanked all of us for greeting her so smartly at the airport. She said she was very proud at what so many of us had achieved in our Guiding life. That we should always remember we were Guides all through our lives even if we were not in uniform. Having been a Guide has stood me in good stead all my life. I have never forgotten what I learnt when studying for all my various badges, and I try to be always prepared.

After the war there was some extreme unrest in Jamaica. The Union under Bustamante was becoming very strong. He was a tall distinguished looking man with a mop of grey hair in an Afro style. Very popular with all the working class. Men were returning from the war, many were traumatised after their unpleasant experiences during the war. Others, who had been trained in various specialized jobs, could not get work. This did not help the situation. The Island was shut down when they had a general strike.

The streets of Kingston were full of dissatisfied people. There was looting and several fights broke out. While my father was driving down to his office one morning, his car was surrounded and the people started to rock his car. He said this was very frightening. Then someone in the crowd recognised him and shouted for them to stop. "He be good man. Let 'im be." And they let him drive on, much to Daddy's relief.

We didn't go to school for days. The Governor called out the troops and peace was restored. One of our maids, the laundress, had joined the Union and when she returned became very rude and disagreeable. Her daughter was working for my mother as a seamstress, making children's clothes. She was a bit embarrassed by her mother's attitude. In the end my mother had to fire the laundress because of her going around saying' ol white peoples dem be teefs' (thieves). She had been a quiet pleasant person before she had attended the strike.

Things on the Island became very unsettled and somewhat volatile. People were being attacked. More and more houses broken into and women were being mugged when walking in the streets. My father bought my mother a small handgun, which she could put in her purse. She did not like it one bit.

We children had to promise to be home by a certain time when we went for a cycle ride. I can remember we were very conscious of the dangers and often rode our bikes down the centre of the road so we couldn't be jumped. We carried whistles with us to blow if we were attacked. Solo, our German Shepard, was a very good watchdog so we felt safe with him roaming the yard.

At the age of fourteen I realized my father was flirting and having romantic affairs. One of the girls in my class announced he was having an affair with her aunt. I was furious and told her that if she told such lies again,

I'd punch her. So she told me to get my bike and we'd ride down to her aunt's house. And there was my father's car parked outside the front. She was a spiteful girl and was always goading me. Her brother on the other hand was a quiet, very good-looking boy, who I had a crush on. He was learning to play the saxophone. We used to go for cycle rides and he'd take his sax with him. He tried to show me how to play it. It sounded terrible when I tried but he used to be able to get such beautiful notes and tunes out of it.

Visit to Willie's House

The last year we stayed at Langley, I decided one day to take Panchito and go off exploring. I got up early had breakfast then prepared some sandwiches, grabbed some bananas and a bottle of water, and told Naisey the cook I was off. I told her in which direction I was going and took off before anyone else woke up.

I walked up past the dam first stopping to close the dam gate, then on up through the coffee plantation and took a path I had never been on before. The path looked as if it had been recently used. Suddenly I came upon a cleared bit of land. Planted in neat rows were a variety of vegetables, beyond this was a small hut. A man came out and greeted me, I recognized him as one of Robbie's workers. I told him I was on 'an explore' and had hoped to find where Willie, Robbie's foreman lived. He put me in the right direction. I was walking through the thick growth, the dew was still wetting the vegetation and everything had such an earthy smell. When I arrived at Willie's house I called out. He was very surprised to see me. He introduced me to his wife and family, they were just about to have breakfast of cornmeal porridge, I joined them. Rose was such a njce quietly spoken mulatto with a beautiful smile. The four children sat quietly and ate their meal barely taking their eyes off me.

Willie was in his late thirties, he had a mop of brown curly hair. I found out that his parents had been from Scotland and had died when he was an infant. A Jamaican family brought him up in a village not far from his home. He had very little schooling and started working for old Mr Gillies then with Robbie when he took over the plantation.

I stayed about an hour in this pleasant company, then was directed to the path that would take me back to the river and the path to the bottom pool. I wandered the hills all day, stopping to give Panchito a drink. Found a lovely spot and had lunch when I was hungry, sharing my meal with faithful Panchito.

1946-1947

I had started my hard work towards the Queen's Guide Award. The highest award recently introduced by the wife of King George VI. Certain badges, the Gold Cord and Little House Emblem, all of which I had accomplished.

Incredible Memories

My parents took Pat and me from the Immaculate Conception High School and sent us to Alpha Academy. I left after the first year and started my first job. In the meantime, I met and fell in love with a young soldier our family was introduced to through Mr Paterson's brother in Scotland who was a friend of Hugh's family

Hugh and I used to go to films together and at the weekends we'd go dancing either at the Canteen or at the Glass Bucket. We would go by tram or ride bikes. He was a beautiful dancer. I remember one occasion when we were dancing down at the Glass Bucket, it was a weeknight, and we called in after a film, so one had to put money into a jukebox. We were up on the floor, one record had finished and we had noticed someone feeding the jukebox so we stayed on the floor with several other couples. The tune that came on was one we didn't know and it was like an African tune. All the other couples started to leave the floor but we decided to stay and dance to the end of the floor where our seats were. Then we found we could dance to it, so we stayed till it finished and quite enjoyed the challenge. All clapped us as we left the floor. I loved Hugh even more after that. As time went by we got even closer and went everywhere together. We were even invited to dinner to the Scotland's, a young English couple friends of my parents, Peter worked at the Shell Company with my father. They were closer to our ages and we got on very well, both were ex-army types. We considered ourselves engaged.

My parents in the meantime decided to send David to England to stay with Uncle Charles, so he could go to Art school, as by then David was showing promise in that line. He wanted to become an engineer but my father talked him out of that. It was sad to see him go, the seas were becoming safer to sail though there were a few mines floating around in the Atlantic.

I had started my first job with Mrs Gwen Brownell-Smith who ran a boutique in Harbour Street, Kingston. I disliked serving some of the stuck-up customers and certainly did not like handling the silk and satin lingerie that she was importing from Canada. Silk stockings were starting to come on the market; I had to wear them too. Yuk. We also sold some dress jewellery.

"The customer is always right" she kept drumming into me. I was expected to have a pleasant expression all the time, talk in a quiet manner and be gracious always. My fingernails were well-groomed and polished in a bright red polish. My hair and clothes to be kept neat at all times. Mrs Brownell-Smith taught me all the sales talk, she would practice with me, and she would be the customer. I found this daunting but I persevered. It was hard telling the customer how nice she looked even if I didn't think so. Some had so much makeup on I had to be careful they didn't soil any of the garments. Then there were those who didn't want me to assist them I dreaded them as was afraid they would get lipstick on our stock, then I'd get into trouble.

I developed appendicitis and was operated on at Nuttal Hospital down on South Camp Road. I had a reaction to the anaesthetic and had to be resuscitated. Things were a bit tipsy-turvey at home and I was whisked off to some family friends, the Judah's to recuperate. I was told my parents were having an auction and selling all their furniture before we went on our three months leave to England. My mother was very upset and so was I as the items, which my parents had since their marriage, went for a song. I suspect because everyone knew we were leaving for the UK in a matter of days.

Having heard of the food shortages in England I decided to take rice and red beans with us. I went out and bought myself a small white suitcase. In those days they were made of a compressed cardboard. I still have the case after all the years. I bought two pounds of rice and a pound of red beans and a bottle of my favourite" Pick-a-Pepper" sauce. To fill the rest of the case I packed a few of my favourite knickknacks.

Before I went to the Judah's, Daddy had taken me to see a Bing Crosby film. He felt sorry for an English soldier sitting by himself and asked him if he would like to join us. Big mistake. This guy thought he had a chance with me especially after Daddy asked him to come home and have a meal with us. After that he was for ever turning up and even asked me out which I refused several times. I thought I made it quite clear I was not interested but he was very persistent. When I moved to the Judah's I asked everyone not to tell him where I was. One day who should I see but this guy turning into the driveway. I rushed through and told the maid to tell him I was not there and she didn't know when I would be back. When he heard my mother was packing all her china he offered to do that for her. He said that was his job in England. He used to pack china toilets! My poor mother tried to convince him that was slightly different. He got a couple of days leave and turned up to get on with the job. We had to admit he did a jolly good job. Poor Brian he was such a bore. A twaddler of the first degree.

Chapter 4

JAMAICA '39

David was to have returned to boarding school at the beginning of September 1939. It was quite obvious that Hitler was bent on war in Europe. My father cancelled David's passage and enrolled him at Jamaica College. Thank goodness my father had the foresight to do that. The first ship to leave Jamaica with children returning to boarding school was sunk by a U-boat. There were not many survivors.

Not long after the cigar episode, we moved house to 29 Hope road, just up the road. This was more a colonial style one-story house. Two good sized bedrooms and a bathroom either side of the house. Verandahs ran down both sides with access from the bedrooms. At the front of the house a large open, square verandah, three steps up from the driveway. The verandah roof extended over the drive that ran across the front of the house then down the right side of the house to a garage.

The verandah led into a large sitting room, which opened into the dining area, beyond this the back verandah. Steps led down to a long concrete verandah off which to the left was the large pantry come food preparation room and kitchen which had a door out into a compound which housed chicken coops, rabbit hutches and enclosure to house our two goats at night. These pens were as big as the house with concrete floors to make it easy to hose down. So all the animals lived very comfortably.

Further down the verandah three bedrooms for the servants. Across from their rooms and part of the back yard were two more rooms, one a bedroom for our gardener the other a locked storeroom belonging to the landlady. These rooms were just behind the garage.

I am relating all these facts so you can get a picture of my surroundings when I write about incidents in my life for the three years, we lived at number 29.

Beyond what I have just described was a further half-acre of land. Outside the enclosure which housed the pens and coops there was a fenced

JAMAICA '39

area where our donkey lived, even further down the property one came to a quarter acre of bush land with a dry gully running through it. A wonderful place for us to play at being soldiers with our wooden guns and pith helmets an army friend had given us when he had been issued with a tin hat. Absolute heaven for us during the war years. We carried out our own warfare with our friends. Dividing into two groups our strong holds being either side of the gully. Somehow, we had to get, unseen, to the other side to capture the headquarters of our enemy. These games went on for hours ending with very grubby and thirsty children. We were always rewarded with an ice-cold limeade and cookies. Then we'd be trooped off to the bathrooms for a scrub and told if our friends wanted to stay, they had to phone their parents and ask if they could stay for lunch.

After lunch we had to play a quiet board game. Invariably it ended up being Monopoly, though if it were kite-flying time we would spend the afternoon making kites. Our mother always had a supply of coloured tissue paper. These activities we usually did in David's room or out on his verandah as my mother would be having a siesta and 'and not to be disturbed.'

Beyond the small back yard there was an area with some large trees. Our gardener and I grew vegetables there. I grew cooking tomatoes and string beans. When ready to eat I went out to all our neighbours selling my goods. My mother was mortified and said she would buy all my produce. So I started my savings toward buying my first bicycle.

During these years we were, as islands, very vulnerable to attack from U-boats, and possible landings as we were told the islands would make good stepping-stones for the Germans to attack America. So David and I decided to make an air raid shelter under the trees down the back yard. We drew up a plan with all measurements. There were to be two entrances to a large underground room. The project started during one of our school holidays. No mean feat. We borrowed tools from the gardener, a pickaxe, shovels an axe to cut through the tree roots, of which we encountered many, the deeper we went the bigger the roots. The soil was of a black clay consistency, not that easy to dig. Then we came upon a sandier soil. On reaching this we felt a bit defeated but decided to continue digging hoping we did not strike water. By this time, we had dug down about three and a half feet. The hole with steps down into it was about three-foot square and felt maybe we should start on the entrance to the room. At night we had to cover the hole with iron sheeting so no one would fall into it. Though it did cross our minds that if we left it open either a thief or a German might fall into it and we would be able to capture them.

We didn't manage to dig anymore as we were back at school. One weekend we uncovered our shelter to discover it was full of crickets and bugs. When the rainy season hit, it was full of muddy water. Then we had the bright idea to concrete the sides and make it into a pond. The powers that be

Incredible Memories

decided that was not a good idea and with the help of the gardener we had to fill in the hole. It was fun while it lasted. We then decided it was easier to construct a hideout down in the gully, this turned out to be a terrific cubbyhouse.

Our gardener, Stanley, a slightly built mulatto, was a very cheerful bloke. He spent more of his time taking an assortment of bicycles to pieces and reassembling them than gardening. My mother suspected some of the bikes could have been stolen, so our bicycle making man was given notice. Then Theophelous arrived, a very amiable, lanky six-footer who was another mulatto. We suspected he had a few marbles missing. One particular day he was down in the gully chopping wood when his ax caught on a branch above his head, fell out of his hands, the blunt end hitting him on the head and the sharp side landing and separating his right big toe from his foot.

When he gathered his not too steady wits about him, he found the toe, limped up to the house and presented it to my mother, who nearly fainted.

"Please missus you can stick it back on to me."

The cook, dear old Norrie, dropped the toe into some salty water, put Theophelous's dirty foot into a bowl of warm saline water and told him to "Wash 'im pretty good man."

By this time I arrived with the first aid kit and Norrie proceeded to re attach the toe or piece of toe, bound it up with gauze smeared with petroleum jelly and he was sent off to bed with a few aspirins and told to stay there "until an adda mornin, mitt yon foot up high."

The next morning Theophelous re appeared and said, "Be very much hungry and proceeded to boil up a big pan of brown rice mixed with chopped chili peppers. When ready he sat down and demolished the lot, it smelt revolting, to eat a pound of rice in one sitting quite an accomplishment.

"Me feel belly well now." He announced and asked if he could "go look for the ax "and "me can finish chop de wood on a one foot missus."

"Not on your life, if you chop your toe off when on two feet what will you do on one foot. You stay right here and masta David and miss Anne will go and find your ax."

The rest of the day Theophelous helped peel vegetables and cleaned cooking utensils for Norrie. Much teasing and laughter accompanied this. Unbelievably the toe healed.

"It be plenty hurt missus, meck me look like old man when he done waalk."

He did not last very long with us; he was caught fast asleep lying on a branch in one of the trees down the back yard. We no longer had to put up with the foul-smelling rice that seemed to be his staple diet. He was replaced by Stanley who returned on the understanding he spent more time on the garden and less on his private business. Stanley lasted about six months; he just could not resist the temptation of working on bicycles. The next gardener, a much younger chap who none of the other servants liked, accused him of stealing and being lazy, which he was. He lasted a very short time and was replaced by a more mature man called Brown. Some friends of my parents who were leaving the Island had recommended Brown; he was very good in every way. He was an excellent gardener and was very kind to our animals, Solo our Alsatian took to him right away. Brown was found to be reliable and trustworthy.

Brown was also interested in learning; he would ask if he could borrow our books and would sit reading them while eating his lunch. After which he would ask endless questions, he loved reading about other countries and would ask us about the places we had lived in. I remember how proud he was when my father passed on one of his suits. He was the same size as my father so the suit looked good on him. When my father had a suit made, he would always get two pairs of trousers made so Brown used one pair to work in and the other to go out in. Not that he went out very often, then we'd tease him and say he was going to visit his girlfriend. We never did find out if Brown had any family, and he never volunteered any information. I was fascinated how he could eat whole chilies, seeds and all. He would tell us not to let the chilies touch our lips and never drink water if we found it too hot. I must admit I was never brave enough to try eating them the way Brown did. His lunches smelt much more appetizing than Theophelous's, in fact at times he would give me some to taste.

Music in our Lives

We were given a Columbia portable record player. It was covered in grey-grained leatherette. We had to wind it up after each 10-inch record. The needle had to be changed frequently to prevent wear of the grooves in the record. The records scratched very easily so we had to be extra careful when placing the sound arm down or lifting it. We children saved to buy the latest records as they appeared. We'd go into Kingston on a Saturday morning, go to the music shop in King Street, sit in a small booth and listen to the record before purchasing it. We had Bing Crosby, Glen Miller, Victor Sylvester, Benny Goodman and several jazz and boogie-woogie, not my mother's favorites. Mostly dance music.

On the weekends we often went over to the Buie's to play tennis or badminton, that was David, Pat and I, we were right into sport and dancing, though David went through a stage where he wasn't that interested. There were usually the Scoggins, Cynthia Vautier, Jackie Mannion and two of the Buie girls Joan, my age and Heather, Pat's age. I think the Scoggins went to dancing lessons, they taught us all the new steps. After playing tennis we would go into the front room have cool drinks and sandwiches brought in. We'd put on the gramophone and dance. They had a stand-up record player. Each visit we'd learn new steps from Arthur and William. I recall poor Jackie always seemed to have two left feet. Poor boy, such a nice fellow but so awkward. I feel ashamed when I recall how much we all teased poor

Jackie. He finally got the hang of it but was never what one would call a smooth dancer. At a later date the Vendries brothers, Arthur and Dennis; a couple of the Mahfouds and David Squire joined us. With this group plus several other friends we would have house parties, taking it in turn going to different homes. We'd ride our bikes over; one year David Squires picked us up in the family buggy, drawn by a beautiful chestnut pony. I remember comparing the experience to the film 'Gone with the Wind' though we didn't have the regalia of that era. But I dreamt on.

For the first house party I was allowed to go to, my mother thought it was time I had a more grown up hairstyle. Reluctant as I was, she made an appointment for me to have my first perm. She left me at this hairdressers down at Cross Roads, told the hairdresser what to do, and gave me my tram fare home. When done, I hated what I looked like and hoped I would not meet anyone I knew before I got home. Once home I burst into tears and said I felt like cutting the whole thing off. When my father came home, he said he thought I looked very pretty, that made me feel a little better. Then my mother showed me some material she had managed to get to make me a party dress. It was a beautiful light green colour; I had measurements taken and several fittings before it was complete. It had a rounded neck around which my mother had embroidered very dainty white flowers and leaves. She also embroidered some larger ones around the hemline. I thought I was the kipper's knickers in it and forgot all about my perm. I must admit, though I shouldn't, I thought it was the prettiest dress at the party.

War games and plays.

During one of the long holidays David and I wrote a play based on the army. We dressed in David's cadet uniform, someone had given David a pith helmet and we had a couple of tin helmets, plus we sewed a couple of large buttons for 'pips' on David's shirt as he was to be the officer. For a swagger stick I think we had a thin piece of bamboo. Our house lent itself well to being able to separate the dining area from the sitting room with curtains. All we had to do was move the dining table out of the way, put a smaller table out of the sitting room as a desk. We came in with all the saluting and stamping of feet which always seemed to be the norm in the army films we watched, spoke very loudly with lots of 'Yes Sirs' and 'No Sirs' in put on posh English accents. My poor parents and those of our friends who were also in the play had to sit through what would have been quite amusing, but an amateurish skit.

David had a toy box in which he had some lead soldiers with little guns that would shoot out match sticks when we pulled back a small lever with a spring. There were soldiers with muskets on their shoulders, soldiers lying down with machine guns, others in running positions or squatting, there was also a bugler and a band. We'd take them into the garden and make up little hills dig small trenches and generally make up a battlefield. I'd have so many

JAMAICA '39

soldiers and David would have the same amount and we'd play with them for hours. The dead ones constantly being whisked back into action. It was amazing how accurate the guns were. Quite often one of the heads would break off if we were too rough with them, so we would break the head off a match, force it into the body part then replace the head. Often thought, wouldn't that be great if one could do that with some of our friends who were killed in the real war.

Canadian Regiments

Several Canadian regiments were sent out to Jamaica on six months tropical training. My parents with several other families were asked if they would entertain a couple of these lads once a month as they were very young and missing their families. So once a month two were picked out and they would come, very smartly dressed, and squeaky clean, to have the evening meal with us. This was usually on a Friday evening so the older children could stay up a bit longer. The soldiers would arrive around teatime they were so keen to meet people. We children just loved them. They would play all sorts of games with us and tell us about their families, or they'd teach us a game they used to play back home as kids or with their 'kid brother or sister'.

The first regiment that came out did not stay very long and we hardly got to know any of them before they were shipped out to Hong Kong when that was being threatened with being taken by the Japanese. Unfortunately, within a short time it was over run and all the Canadian boys were made prisoners for the duration of the war.

The next batch sent out, the Fusiliers, were there for a little longer and we got to know quite a few. Two lads turned up and they seemed to like our family. The following week Frank L. phoned and asked if he could bring his best friend Al G. over one afternoon, my mother said he could. A couple of days later Stan B. turned up with his best friend James H. And so our friendships with these young Canadians grew. This happened with each pair that was sent to visit us each month. In the end there were so many that my mother said that she would not have any new ones. In that regiment we had about eight that visited us regularly, sometimes a couple of them would treat David and I to a film on a Saturday afternoon. Or a couple of them would ride up on bikes and we'd take them to the club for a swim or go for a ride to visit friends. In the evenings we would play darts or they would show us a new card game. Then they left. David and I wrote to a couple of them. They were sent in with the first wave of the invasion of France. All were either killed or wounded. We found this very sad. Frank L was one of our favorites, he was wounded, and then he heard from his fiancé that she was breaking it off. As soon as he was well enough, he volunteered to go back into battle, he was killed. His friend wrote and told us. It was worse not to

Incredible Memories

hear what had happened to our friends. With some we never did know whether they survived or not.

The next regiment that came out, my parents started the same monthly visit. The usual friendships sprung up and we became very fond of a lot of them. There was Stan B. from B. C., George B. from Alberta, Arthur B. a lumberjack, he told us many a story about being a woodman. Alex K, a very quiet guy, Roy K, who I fell madly in love with at the tender age of fourteen. He came with Alex G. Roy often combed and brushed Pat's and my hair. Said he used to do his kid sister's and he missed her very much. When the regiment was being shipped out, Roy the two Alexes and George came to say good-bye, Roy asked if I would write, gave me his home address, he said he'd catch up with me after the war.

I wrote to Roy for a year, which brought us to nearly the end of the war, and then I didn't hear from him. I did not even want to contemplate that he was dead. Then in 1951 I received a letter from Roy that had been redirected from Jamaica to England on the eve of my marriage. He explained that my last letter to him had been mislaid in his father's desk and he had just found it. He had stopped writing because he had not heard from me and presumed I did not want to write any more. I caught up with Roy in Canada in 1983 when on a trip but he was married to a very nice lady. My feelings for him were still as strong. He had only recently heard from Alex G. who had mentioned my family and wondered what had happened to all of us. Unfortunately, I had already visited Alberta and was traveling east so missed out seeing him.

My memory of Alex G. was after a route march he had some terrible blisters on his feet that became infected badly. David and I visited him in the Army Hospital down in South Camp Army barracks when he was recovering from blood poison.

My Life Between 14 and 16

My life between fourteen and sixteen, like most teenage girls, was extremely full. My school, Guide and social life very active. Falling in and out of love with various boys and girls. Having my heart broken on several occasions and being thoroughly confused with life. Not being helped at all by the nuns and priests in my muddle, my parents busy with their own problems.

But I managed to sort things out. There were times when I was very unhappy but many times when I was completely happy. I had some wonderful friends, teachers and learnt a lot from our servants and the country people I was fortunate enough to know; and grew to love. When I look back on the marvellous years I spent in the West Indies, memories pour into my mind. Often wondering what ever happened once I had left those beautiful islands.

JAMAICA '39

At I.C.H.S. Constant Spring with Elsa my best friend, 1944

Daddy with Chris, self, David with Tina and Pat at 29 Hope Road, 1944

Chapter 5

EVACUEES ARRIVE IN JAMAICA

When the war broke out in 1939 no one thought it would go on for so many years. By the time Hitler's armies walked across Europe at great speed, my parents were concerned for their siblings and their families in England. They wrote inviting them to come to Jamaica. They all declined and chose instead to send their children off to boarding schools in the north of England and Scotland.

Early in 1940, some German, French and Belgian children and their grandparents began to arrive. Some were lucky enough to have their mothers with them. Many were Jews who had managed to escape. One German boy, Ivan Cohen, of 11 years who arrived with his grandparents was billeted in the Guest House next door. We tried to befriend him but found him very anti everyone, even to the point of being against his grandparents. When he did speak to us, he said," Hitler will conquer the world". This did not go down very well with us.

As less and less tourists arrived on the island the hotels were fast becoming empty. The owners decided to drop the price on their charges and offer accommodation to evacuated families.

It was very dangerous crossing the Atlantic. U-boats at times surrounded most of the Caribbean Islands. Many a ship traveling in convoy went down. We did meet a few survivors when they arrived in other ships that had managed to rescue them. A couple of lifeboats also reached our shores with some very brave people on board. We often wondered how the children survived such an ordeal.

By 1941 English evacuees arrived in greater numbers. We found a lot of them thought they were a cut above us. Real snobs. They certainly didn't know how to treat the natives. They soon found they had to work extra hard at school to keep up with the local boys and girls. Many thought coloured people didn't have any brains. They soon learnt differently. Most of the

EVACUEES ARRIVE IN JAMAICA

evacuees from the UK were mothers and children, though there were many children on their own who came out to stay with a relative.

Many of the mothers tried to rent houses and had servants which they found hard to handle, only because they didn't understand them. Some of them gave up after about six months and chose to live in hotels or Guest Houses. Those in the country were cheaper but they felt too isolated. By living in these sorts of accommodations meant they didn't have servant problems, they had company and had more time to themselves to play tennis or join the bridge group.

By this time all Germans were being interned. Some friends of ours were carted off, even though the wife was a West Indian of French descent. They had a nine-year-old boy who was interned as well. My parents used to take food to them. The wives and children were separated from the men. The conditions they lived in were appalling. They were limited to the amount of clothes they could take in with them. I remember Clause grew out of his clothes the first year there and my mother made him some shorts and shirts and passed on some of my brother's socks and shoes.

The government started to build a huge camp surrounded by high wire fencing topped by barbed wire, only two miles from where we lived. Everyone thought maybe it was for prisoners of war. It turned out that it was for ten thousand Gibraltarians who were shipped to Jamaica. The majority were children with mothers or grandparents or both. All able-bodied men remained in Gibraltar.

Food was getting very scarce for three reasons; we had some bad storms, many of the supply ships never reached us, plus the population had grown so rapidly. Gasoline was in short supply, not many were allowed cars. Horses, mules, and donkeys were in great demand. The price of bicycles doubled, if one could get one. Some by the look of them came out of the museum. The wealthier of the population had to resort to using the local trams and buses if they did not own a brightly coloured donkey cart, trap or buggy. It seemed as if everything had jumped back half a century, until a row of noisy bren gun carriers rumbled up the road to spoil everything.

Many of the Europeans must have seemed quite ridiculous, most of them acted so superior, this annoyed the Jamaicans. The class distinction caused a lot of resentment especially among the more educated Jamaican and those of us who had lived there for years. There were many cultured coloured people, and Jamaicans on the whole were charming.

Many of the Gibraltarian girls came to our school. They got on very well, as their second language was English. We tried to make them feel as welcome as possible. Some were rather unhappy, as they had left their fathers and some older brothers in Gibraltar. A Girl Guide company was started up at the camp and they used to join our school company on our annual two-week camping holiday in Montego Bay. We used the school hall as our sleeping quarters. There was great competition between the groups.

Incredible Memories

By 1942 we were beginning to wonder how much longer the war was going to last. America had a huge base on the Island. A great number of local young men joined up and were sent overseas with very little training. This left the army barracks almost empty, but not for long. Canadian troops were brought down to do their tropical training; a crash course. After their training, the first battalion was sent to Hong Kong; they arrived just before the Japs took it over. So all that lot remained prisoners of war for the duration of the war.

Many of the British evacuees were becoming restless, wanting to return to the UK. Many could not accept our way of living. To leave the island one had to get an "Exit Permit". These were not easy to obtain. The situation became even more difficult as at the beginning of 1943, two American ships were torpedoed just North of the Island. Over 800 lives were lost including some passengers. The true story was censored but we guessed the ships must have been carrying troops. Not long after, a ship arrived full of Italian and German prisoners of war, captured in North Africa. It was ironic none of their ships were ever sunk!

Food was beginning to become critically scarce. Butter was non-existent. The margarine made locally from cabbages tasted terrible. When the electricity was cut, we used coconut oil in our lamps. Bunches of bananas were being thrown over the hillside, because there were more important things to put on ships, this caused a terrible smell and encouraged fruit fly. Then someone had the bright idea that vinegar could be made from bananas; next someone opened a "banana chips" factory, someone else made banana ice cream. We were encouraged to eat green bananas, peeled and boiled as a vegetable. They were full of iron.

Meat was as scarce as hen's teeth, so many families kept chickens and rabbits. We had goats as well as ducks, so were lucky to have a variety of meats. We grew our own vegetables. We were fortunate that we had a very faithful Alsatian dog to guard against theft of our animals and vegetables.

Black outs or rather practice ones were a bit of a joke. They were usually on a moon lit night and all it meant was that we were not allowed to turn any lights on. On these nights my father had to go down to the Shell installation to see that the local troops on the anti-aircraft guns were at their posts. One night we heard some loud explosions. A couple of U-boats had surfaced and had fired at the coast. They didn't do much damage and didn't hit any important targets. On the nights of the black outs there were a lot of burglaries. Many, like my mother, who was on her own, would invite friends over and sit out on the front lawn having drinks and play card games. One of these nights I thought I heard something outside the bedroom. I got out of bed and looked through the lattice window and was confronted by the face of a man. I don't know who got the biggest fright. As he took off down the back garden, I heard a shot ring out from next door. I ran out the front and screamed "There's someone in our back garden" and at the same time someone came running from the Guest House to see if we were all right He said that he had seen some one creeping up our back garden and by the time he went and got his gun the figure was running away so he had a pot shot and missed.

The other bit of excitement we had that year was when some of the German prisoners broke out of their camp. Great fun for all the children. We grabbed our bikes and took off to find them and thought we'd capture them. We didn't get very far when someone in the home guard spotted us and told us to go home. Spoilsports! Needless to say, the prisoners did not get very far and were caught down on one of the beaches. We heard later that they were hoping to be picked up by one of the U-boats.

Through the war years I was lucky to be able to go to the Guide camps every year. We went by train. On one of these occasions on our return journey at each stop, the police would bring convicted prisoners onboard. They would handcuff them to the armrest of the bench they were sitting on. We were all a bit scared.

We were luckier than most as my father had a permit to own a car and working for the Shell Oil Co. managed to get a fair amount of gasoline. During the hottest months our family went up to a property in the hills. An American family that also went up brought a couple of French evacuees with them, that year was great fun. Food was more plentiful and life more peaceful. One could try to forget there was a war going on.

March 1944. Some of the British evacuees were being given "Exit Permits". They waited from day to day to be called at short notice, to report and be ready to sail. They were in a queue system and according to availability of ships. No one knew when a ship was due or when they were going to sail again. This was top secret. It was a very trying time for all the evacuees. A few of them had chosen to stay. They had either lost their homes in the UK, bombed by the Nazis, or they had lost their husbands while on duty in one of the forces.

I remember one poor lady had received a telegram saying, "killed in action". She decided to stay in Jamaica and had taken up a job as a teacher. Her daughter was of school age so this made life a little easier. Six months later she received another telegram saying that her husband was found to be a prisoner of war in Germany. He had been badly injured and would be one of the first to be repatriated. He was lucky and was sent to Jamaica to have treatment and convalesce. They settled in Jamaica.

Some of the Gibraltarian boys, when they turned 17, joined the Jamaican army and chose to stay when their families returned to Gibraltar at the end of that year.

That year we had the worst drought for 16 years. We had constant water cuts, for several hours per day. This extra inconvenience only exacerbated the problem with the dissatisfied evacuees. Then in June they cancelled all Exit Permits. Due to secrecy of shipping movements and the situation of the war, this left all who had expected to be leaving, rather upset. By July they decided to issue Exit Permits again. All had to reapply, on new forms which were worded slightly differently. The evacuees were full of more complaints. Many of the children were not particularly looking forward to leaving Jamaica. They had adapted to our way of life and felt at home on the island. Some were even speaking with a Jamaican accent. Those who were in their middle teens when they arrived were now courting Jamaicans and certainly didn't want to return to the UK.

The British were to be the first to be repatriated. The Allies seemed to be winning the war. 1945 brought great hope that we were actually seeing the end of the war. Ships traveling from Canada and USA seemed safer on the sea. Things like dried fruit, apples, apricots, raisins, currants and prunes appeared in the shops. We could also purchase chocolate. This pleased the evacuees that were still on the island. Probably by this time more than half had returned home. Some of the European evacuees applied to return on the ships to Canada. A few were granted permits.

After the war, a few had the courtesy to write to our local newspaper, The Gleaner, to thank all who had helped them during their stay.

The years the evacuees spent in Jamaica had certainly been a learning experience on both sides.

Lost and never found again

Eight years were possibly the happiest and unspoiled of my life. From the age of nine, I travelled through the ups and downs of a rather adventurous, exciting learning time. Mostly with the same twenty odd friends, acquaintances and mentors.

My friends Betty, Thelma, Beryl, Elsa, Helena, Marie-Therese, and three Betties, one American, one English and one Jamaican, to name a few. Betty A was my special friend in grade one and two. She was the daughter of the American Consul; we rode our bikes around the streets of St. Andrew, sometimes pretending they were horses. Stopping by her place for afternoon tea. Asparagus sticks rolled in thin sliced white bread, without the crusts, held together with toothpicks. Toasted in the oven till a golden, crisp, a yummy treat arrived on a white plate all in rows, with the toothpicks all standing up resembling a line of telegraph poles. They were served to us by one of their maids in a stiffly starched white uniform. A jug of iced lemonade, the blocks of ice tinkling into our glasses as it was poured. Then the Second World War broke out and Betty's father was recalled to America, and I lost a friend.

The friendship with Betty E was a more turbulent one. Betty had been evacuated to Jamaica to stay with her aunt, away from the bombing raids in England. Though we were good friends we seemed to argue frequently, possibly because our backgrounds were so different. She was very British and I was very West Indian in our outlook towards life, both feeling superior, to the other, in our loyalties to our countries of birth. We went through grades three four and five together. At the same time Betty J was one of my close friends too. She was a more quiet, studious type. Though we were friends for some four years of school life, I never got to know her family very well. We confided in each other about our adolescent thoughts and talked about the more serious things in life, like boyfriends, films, our dreams and what we hoped to achieve in life.

Beryl was a champion runner, as was Thelma. Unable to compete with their speed, I decided tennis was more suited to my abilities. We were all three in the school Girl Guide Company so in a way we as friends spent more time together. Going on several camping trips, competing in how many certificates and badges we could acquire and so a special bond existed between us. But unlike my other friends we never visited each other's families.

Then there were the three Teape sisters, Alda, Nora and Amy, from Columbia, South American Indians. All were in my class though their ages differed. When they came to live with an aunt, they spoke very little English. Alda and Nora attended our English and Literature classes and the rest of the time went to the Commercial Studies classroom to learn typing, shorthand and bookkeeping. Amy the youngest took part in all our studies. She and Alda were like miniature volcanoes, fiery and quick tempered, a bit suspicious of the rest of the classmates. Nora on the other hand was more the quiet carer.

Amy and I, we were the same age. At fourteen decided we were tired of school, home discipline and several other reasons in the confusion of being teenagers. We decided we were going to steal a motorboat and travel to Cuba, ninety miles north of Jamaica. The planning of the escapade took months by then we had grown a bit wiser and other interests distracted us from that venture!

The island was a beautiful one. Climatically ideal, wonderful beaches all around the coast. Rivers that cascaded around volcanic boulders and over magnificent waterfalls that flowed into very inviting swimming pools. The music was magic and constant. We all learned at an early age to move with a sway, practically dancing our way through life. All went through life with this "Easy-ozy" lay back life tyle most of the time.

The present moment was the sum of all that happened. We filled our lives with the very moment, all that we need be and not heed the things of the past or fear of the future.

I must have been about ten years old when my mother decided she should inform me of the facts of life. Little did she know that was talked about at school, especially if we mixed with older girls! Anyway, while she had her afternoon siesta she wanted me to join her. She had a Readers Digest magazine, I'll always remember it because it was a bright orange, and on the outside front cover, was a list printed in white, all the articles in that edition.

Incredible Memories

She found the page and said she would like me to read it. Maybe she thought the article would explain things better than she could. Or maybe she was embarrassed to talk about such things with me.

So I lay there reading it and when I got to something I didn't quite understand I turned to ask my mother, but she was asleep. We never ever talked about it again except when she asked me if I understood what I had read. I said I had because all I wanted to do was go outside and play. Most of it I had already heard and this from a fourteen-year-old girl who claimed she had already had sex. Most of us other girls thought she was terrible. Somehow the nuns got to hear about it and she was expelled from the school. We all had a lecture about it afterwards.

When I did eventually get my monthly periods, I thought it was terrible, the pads my mother gave me were uncomfortable and I thought everyone must be able to see I was wearing them and knew I had them.

The nuns were very adamant that we should never discuss our personal ailments and what happened with our bodies was to be kept private! We never dressed or undressed in front of anyone else. Sometimes at school a couple of us would sit in the changing cubicles talking, until one of the nuns caught us. Well we were accused of all sorts of things and got into terrible trouble. This none of us could understand because we had done nothing wrong except talk and that was not smutty. What had we been found guilty of?

Then the big reality, we had grown up too suddenly. My parents moved away from the island with all of us children, wrenched away from the familiar lifestyle and thrown into a completely new and unknown environment.

It was a tremendous loss of friends and familiar surroundings. To return after thirty-seven years, trying to reclaim some of that past proved to be impossible and a great sadness as all had changed too drastically. The island no longer the safe haven of my childhood. Lost forever in reality but not completely in golden memories.

When we moved to Constant Spring to our new school, my first teacher was Sister Adele. I quite liked her as she made it easy to understand what she was teaching. My next teacher was Sister Xavier, we were led to believe Sister Adele was her sibling; they were as different as chalk and cheese. Not many of us liked her as she was always rapping us on the knuckles with a ruler or hitting us on our heads with a book, if she thought we were not paying enough attention or if we got something wrong. She was always picking on me. One day she caught me turning around because the girls behind were pulling my hair. She made me take all my books out of my desk and told me to go sit in the hallway outside the classroom. She had a terrible temper. She would go crimson in the face before she exploded.

Sister Cordia took our next year, she was a darling. We all loved her classes and used to have such fun in all the subjects she taught. We had two

EVACUEES ARRIVE IN JAMAICA

English teachers who had been evacuated to Jamaica. Mrs. Gough taught math. She probably was a brilliant mathematician but she couldn't teach for toffee! She was a large woman with ginger hair, very pale skin, who wore dresses that showed her red neck and chest practically down to her breasts. We discovered she drank gin and sometimes slurred her words, so we used to really play up in her class. One thing some of us used to do was chew some paper then use our rulers to propel the wad to the blackboard beside her. This of course we did when she was busy writing lots of figures on the board, she wrote so quickly we could not keep up with her. Then she would come up with an answer to the problem without an understandable conclusion. I think she lasted a year. Was her disappearance due to our behaviour or had the nuns found one of her bottles of gin? Sister Anne then took us for math and that was much better.

The other English teacher was Mrs. Lithgow. She took us for English Literature. We loved her lessons, they were great fun. Every year she would have us act out one of Shakespeare's plays. We would put it on for the rest of the school. I was the chink in the wall in Midsummer Night Dream one year.

We had a lovely venue to put on plays. Out front of the building across the driveway, there were about eight wide steps down to a flat area, twentyfoot wide by about ten-foot deep, that was our stage. Then there were another eight steps that led down into a wide grassed avenue lined with rose beds. The audience sat on seats in the avenue.

The school building had been a hotel until war broke out and there were no longer tourists visiting the island. Rumour had it that one of the nuns was related to Bing Crosby and he had purchased and gifted the hotel to the nuns. It was painted pink (which looked rather shabby by the end of the war), with pale green windows and doors. All the classrooms had originally been two bedrooms but the dividing wall had been knocked out to make one large room. Our classrooms. One could enter either end through a door and there were two double doors leading out to a verandah. The walk-in robes between the entrance doors was turned into storage space and bookshelves. On the second floor where the boarders lived, the rooms became dormitories with an ensuite. The other end of the building housed the nuns.

On the ground floor was a huge reception area with steps leading down from the classrooms. We used to hold our concerts and assembly there. At the rear of that there were two passages leading off, to the left one more classroom then a large hall and to the right to the chapel. The whole of the outside of the passage were glass doors leading out to a courtyard. The opposite side of the yard was a canteen area where we could sit and eat our lunch. At the back of the school were tennis courts and sports areas. Out of the hall there was an area done in crazy paving that led down some steps to a very large swimming pool. This had a low diving board and two higher diving boards. At the shallow end there was a semicircular fountain spilling into the pool. The pool was surrounded by stonewall with seating all-round it. You could get to the pool via some stairs that led to the classrooms. More steps, down to the right, went to the male and female changing cubicles.

The school was certainly set in beautiful surroundings at the foot of the hills at Constant Springs. There was a golf course below and around the school grounds we had to walk past the clubrooms to get to the tramline.

The school swelled in numbers when 10,000 were evacuated from Gibraltar. Several of the High School aged girls were sent to our school. Some of the American families out at the American Base sent some of their girls to our school. The English girls who were sent to the convent thought they were a cut above the Jamaican girls, they got a shock when they found they couldn't get anywhere near them for a position in class. Neither could they compete with them in sport!

There were no computers or electric printing machines in those days. We had a Roneo Printer. The work was typed onto two sheets of paper, one was wax paper, and the letters went through the wax paper. Then we carefully separated the two sheets of paper and put the wax paper onto a jelly substance in a tray. Put ink on top then lay a sheet at a time of plain paper took a roller and gently rolled it all over the sheet. The print fed through and came out a purple pink colour. Each sheet then had to be dried. When the print got lighter then we added more ink. A slow and messy process but that is how we made enough copies of anything to share among the class. Later they had a drum instead of the tray and this was quicker, as we laid the paper on the drum and turned a handle and the paper fed through coming out the other side.

Chapter 6

MY SIXTEENTH YEAR

I remember my sixteenth year well. It was in Jamaica, just after the Second World War. In this year of 1946, my sixth year in the Guides, it was the first year the Queen's Guide award was introduced. A much-coveted award by all the Guide companies. Thus far our company, 21st St. Andrews' had succeeded in being the first company to have more than one Guide with the 'Gold Cords' and I had just been awarded the 'Little House Emblem' a requisite for the Queen's Guide Award. I was going to be seventeen in October and had to pass all my tests before then.

The other requirements, were, a certain number of badges and certificates in various categories, I had 22. My father used to tease me "There is no more room on your sleeves, you'll have to start sewing them on your bottom or get larger sleeves". I was very proud of all my achievements, plus being the Patrol Leader of 'Heather Patrol'. And I was determined to be the first to be awarded the 'Queen's Guide' honour. If possible, the first in the southern hemisphere.

The main thing left to do to qualify for the Queen's award was to climb an 8500 ft. mountain with a backpack. Pitch a tent and cook two meals without utensils. I had to light the fire with only two matches, all this without any assistance.

The test required that I do this trek on my own, meet the Girl Guide Commissioner, Lady Agar, at the top of the mountain. She had driven up to her house in these beautiful Blue Mountains to await my arrival.

It was decided it would be too risky my going on my own as it would be dark by the time I reached my destination. Conditions on the island had become a little unsafe. With the return of men who had served in the armed forces, the mundane life and low wages, that is if they could get a job. There was a lot of violence and unrest on the island. Beryl Williams, a Jamaican girl in my patrol, was chosen to accompany me. We got on very well, had a few scary moments on the way up.

Incredible Memories

It had been a very full year for me; I had left Immaculate Conception High School and gone to Alpha Academy but still attended Guide meetings after school on a Friday. Taking part in various sports on a Saturday, sometimes playing tennis in the mornings and baseball or badminton in the afternoons.

It was the second Sunday in September, Beryl and I met at Papina markets at the foot of the mountain in the afternoon, after the main heat of the day. We had a map, a small compass, flashlight, sleeping bags, a blanket and a small pillow, besides some clothes and washing gear each. On top of that I had a box of matches with four matches only, 2 sheets of thick brown paper, 1 sheet of grease proof paper, 2 lamb chops, 2 large potatoes, 2 large tomatoes, 2 eggs, 2 corns on the cob, a piece of yellow yam, 4 slices of bread, a couple of hands full of green beans and 4 large cabbage leaves.

We were allowed a small amount of butter and jam. I had a small ball of string, 2 oranges, some milk, cocoa, and sugar, and of course our enamel plates and mugs, a penknife, a spoon and fork each. There was water at the site.

Following the map, we found the footpath we were to take. The hike up the mountainside we did not find too hard, the path wound around in hairpin bends and as it ran up the mountainside and we did not encounter any native shacks. In places, when we stopped to rest we spotted a few houses across the valley, always singing and music of some sort, coming from them. It started to get dark about half an hour before we reached the summit. The scene was beautiful. Fireflies lit the mountainside, flicking on and off like a thousand fairy lights. We could hear water trickling down in places. The sound of frogs and toads croaking, crickets chirping. The three-quarter full moon was already high in the sky and though the trees were prolific and very tall we found in places our path well lit.

Lady Agar was waiting when we arrived. There was a flat area where I could pitch the tent; Beryl was not allowed to assist me. I scrounged around for some dry sticks and proceeded to make my fire between 4 rocks I had found. I succeeded in lighting same, with one match. While the wood was burning, I built the fire up with bigger pieces of wood so I would have a decent amount of very hot coals.

Peeling one of the bananas, which Beryl and I shared, I then put the beans into the skin. I pricked the potatoes, wet one of the pieces of brown paper and the grease proof paper and thoroughly folded the brown piece to a size just bigger than the largest cabbage leaf, on top of this I put the wet grease proof paper, then the cabbage leaf. I laid the chops on the cabbage leaves, which were on the papers, lay the banana skin on top of that wrapped the paper around the lot and tide with some string. By this time the fire was really hot and ready to receive the potatoes, yam with its skin on and the corn still with the husk on. I then wet the other piece of brown paper and wrapped it around the other paper and added the lot to the hot coals. I found a shrub and broke 2 green sticks stripped off the leaves and used them to turn the food. I filled the mugs with water and stood them on the rocks close to the fire. We had been told not to bring water, as there would be some available. So we only carried what we would drink on our journey.

By the time the green husks had nearly all burned off, the brown paper was starting to burn, and the potato and yam skins were black, our meal was ready. Lady Agar left us to enjoy our meal and said she would return in the morning and join us for breakfast. Our meal went down very well followed by a mug of hot cocoa and the other banana.

After a good night's sleep I got up and re-made the fire, softened the oranges, sliced the top off and Beryl and I squeezes all the juice into our mouths, popped an egg into each orange skin replaced the top and put them into the hot coals, put the tomatoes onto two of the rocks, and our mugs on the other two rocks. The green twigs from the night before came in handy as toasting forks. We buttered the toast and put jam on two of them and had the other two with our boiled eggs and poached tomatoes washed down with a nice hot cup of cocoa. Lady Agar had arrived with a flask of tea and some toast for her breakfast.

When we were ready to make our return journey, I had cleaned up the camping sight so no one would know anyone had camped there. The journey down the mountainside was harder as the path was covered in loose gravel, which was very slippery. By the time I got to the bottom of the mountain the soles of my shoes were flopping up and down as I walked. It took us longer to descend because the ground was so rough and we were afraid of slipping off the path and over the side of the mountain.

I was presented with the Queen's Guide award shortly after and was honored to be the first in the Southern Hemisphere. I was very proud but not as proud as my Captain, Sister Marie Emmanuel. She reminded the company every year, put a bit in the 'Gleaner' newspaper, and wrote and sent me a copy wherever I happened to be living.

A month later I celebrated my 17th birthday, left my studies and got my first job. I was chosen to represent Jamaica at the first Jamboree held in the United States but could not attend as my family left for the UK and I was required to join them. So that was the end of a very interesting and exciting part of my life as a Girl Guide.

Having to adapt to a new school, make new friends at the Sisters of Mercy, a completely different order to the Franciscan order I had been used to, was not easy to accept at first. The classes were not as big, light and airy and I had further to travel, having to get used to being down in the city minus all the open space we had around ICHS. The nun who taught religious knowledge had converted to Catholicism from Anglican; she had a different approach to the teachings of the Acts of the Apostles, which I found refreshing. I liked her lessons because she encouraged questioning. This made the lesson far livelier.

Incredible Memories

Self and Hugh Andrews, 5 Abbeydale Road, Half-Way-Tree, Jamaica 1946 & self in 1947

Ann Scotland, Hugh Andrews on wall, Peter Scotland in water, Dam Gate Far End, 1947

Book II

Leaving Jamaica

Sailed on the 'Jamaica Producer',
Tons of green bananas loaded,
Stacked in fridges below deck
To be shipped to England.
We boarded and were shown to our cabins.
I was sad to be leaving my beloved Jamaica,
All that was familiar to me.
My many friends, the Blue Mountains,
The sound and rhythm of the music,
Salt fish and ackee, rice and peas,
Yam, yampy, okra, cornmeal porridge,
Fried green banana and plantain,
Served with our weekend joint.
The clear azure waters where we swam,
Beaches lined with coconut palms.
Rivers flowing over large volcanic rocks.
These being some of my memories
Which I swap for a two-week trip,
To sail across the Atlantic.
The ship buffeted by stormy waters.
Waves way above the ship's funnels.
Skilfully the captain steers us up and over.
After the storm, calmer waters
But still, always, the threat,
An odd mine lurking.
Not all swept and exploded,
The residual of many war years.

Incredible Memories

Finally, the sighting of Land's End.
Through the night we skirt the south shores.
The White Cliffs of Dover greet us in the morning.
Our destination not far off.
Then the shock of seeing burnt out buildings
As we sail up the Thames,
The residuum quite obvious.
My idyllic island life, exchanged for 'hurry and rush',
Noise and bustle, strange scenery and people.
But all I must accept,
For there must be greener pastures ahead.
My life as an adult, in a new land.

Chapter 7

APRIL 1947 TO JULY 1968

Sailing for England

My father was overdue for leave. Because of the war we had been unable to go to England for our three yearly visits. We left Jamaica on the Jamaican Producer, a banana boat. It took two weeks to sail across the Atlantic Ocean. There were several Jamaican girls on board going to Europe to attend finishing schools. Also, there were some British soldiers returning to be demobilized, they had escorted German/Italian prisoners of war from Egypt during the war and had not seen their families for years. They were looking forward to going home.

It was fun having so many young people on board. Most of the officers were young too. I noticed two of the girls, who were cousins, being very flirtatious with some of the young men. The younger of the two was very feisty, the other very quiet. But there is a saying "Soft water always runs deep." They would leave our company early with a couple of soldiers in tow.

During the day when it was calm, we swam in the ship's pool or played deck games. We played shuttle cock or coits, which was played with a piece of rope made into a circle that we tried to throw over a peg. Sometimes they had horse racing, we had to guide a cardboard horse along a track to see who could get to the other end first. In the evenings we found a sheltered spot on deck and sat telling stories. There were two older soldiers, sergeants, we would sit and talk about the war, family and what we planned for our future. For several days we were few on deck as we went through a very rough patch.

While sitting on deck after dinner one night I watched the reflection of the ship's lights on the ocean. Swordfish were jumping out of the water, attracted by the lights. Although in the middle of the Atlantic the seas were virtually calm, far on the horizon flashes of lightning played in the black sky. Halfway through the night, I was rudely awoken by being tossed out of my

Incredible Memories

bunk onto the deck. The bulkhead seemed to be at a forty-five-degree angle from the position in which I had been thrown.

The tannoy blurted out, "Unfortunately we have hit the eye of a severe storm. Would all passengers put on their life jackets which are housed in the lower part of the cupboard beside your bunkbed. Then proceed to the upper lounge as quickly as possible". With great difficulty we all followed instructions.

The ship pitched up and down. Sailed up massive waves then ended up in the belly of the ocean. Or so it seemed. There were times when I thought we were done for and would never see the sky again. The ship was bobbing around like a cork; the seamanship was incredible as the crew kept the ship upright. At times we could hear the propellers screaming as they were lifted out of the water. The noise was horrific, deafening and also quite terrifying. The sound of the waves buffeting the ship, the creakiness coming from the interior of the vessel, it sounded as though the whole ship was being torn asunder.

The breakfast gong sounded, but there were not many who had the stomach to eat.

We were not allowed out on deck so those of us who were not seasick, played card games. Often my father joined us. We were also entertained by a strange little man who had learnt to control all his muscles individually. Some of the things he did with his stomach and back muscles I found quite repulsive. He hoped to make a living in a side show when he reached England. He taught a couple of us how to control our face muscles and how to wiggle our ears one at a time. He also showed us how to move our fingers apart and to bend each joint of every finger separately.

The first land we spotted was Lizard Point. During the evening we could see lights in the distance as we sailed slowly along. The next morning as we steamed through the English Channel the White Cliffs of Dover stood majestically to our left. The rising sun shone on them, what a sight!

We passed several strange looking fortifications along the coast. They appeared to be sitting in the water. We were told they had been used as anti-aircraft positions during the war. Finally, we turned into the mouth of the Thames River. On either side we could see terrible destruction of buildings. The charred remains stood roofless, three walled, windowless houses and sheds with mounds of rubble heaped alongside. I had seen this sort of thing on the news reels but to see it in reality was a shock.

The ship was stopped and a launch pulled up alongside, the customs and pilot came aboard. The customs to check all passports and papers and to look for contraband, the pilot to guide the ship up the Thames safely. We were neatly put along the side one of the piers at Tilbury Docks, tied up and the gangplank put in place down the side of the ship. It was time to farewell our new friends.

I was about to enter the next stage in my life. My childhood left behind, only memories. So many happy recollections of my first seventeen years spent growing up in the West Indies.

Settling in England

After docking at Tilbury Docks, East London, we were ready to disembark. We had gone through customs while we sailed up the Thames. Our luggage all accounted for, we were taken by taxi to a London Hotel where we stayed for three days. On our journey we passed many ruins, large craters where once stood a building or buildings, the East end of London having been targeted by many a German plane. As we drove along the destruction was unbelievable.

We arrived at the Hotel; my first impressions were that it smelt musty. All furnishings and carpets looked a bit the worst for wear. My bedroom which I shared with my sister Pat, had dark wardrobes and beds, very tall windows with grey net curtains. They looked as though they may have been white when new. I soon learnt that because the air was so full of smog, all white garments became this shade of grey. The beds were high, topped by dull looking eiderdowns. A distinct chill in the air.

When I looked out of the window I was confronted by a large Plain tree, below which lay a very busy street. There was a constant flow of black London taxis. People walking on the sidewalk were well rugged up and all carried umbrellas. They seemed in a great hurry to be getting somewhere. I remember thinking that maybe by moving quickly it helped to keep them warm. The way I felt then was that "I would never be warm again!"

There were radiators in the rooms which were only turned on at a certain time. To take the chill off the room. Can't say I noticed, but I knew they were on because they made strange noises and felt slightly warm to touch.

The hotel only served breakfast and dinner at night so we had to go out for lunch. We found a small restaurant fairly close. There were two things on the menu, sausages, mash and peas or stew, which tasted fishy, so I suspected it was whale meat. The peas, I had never tasted the like. I found out later that they were dehydrated peas which were then soaked in water before being cooked. Of course, they did not taste like peas! The mashed potatoes were made from a powder that was questionable, as it certainly didn't taste of potato and it was a grey colour. Dessert was a steamed pudding, called 'Spotted Dick'. It was a steamed pudding with currants in it, a sweet white sauce poured over it. I only ever had it once, which was more than enough.

David, my eldest brother, who had been in England for a year, came down from Birmingham to be with us. My parents had business to attend to, so David took my sisters, Pat and Teresa, and myself for a trip to London

Incredible Memories

Zoo. He walked us for what seemed miles through streets full of craters and charred buildings. He knew where we could catch a bus to the zoo.

The bus arrived, David hopped on, the rest of us sauntered along in our slow Jamaican way - "One foot down and the other foot soon follow" as they say in Jamaica. The bus took off and left us standing on the sidewalk. David got off at the next stop and ran back to us.

"Cha man what happen there?" we asked. He told us we had to get on the bus 'real quick' which caused us all to double up laughing. What kind of country was this where we had to rush, rush for everything!

We spent a lovely day trying to get used to things. This strange new life. When the east wind blew, it brought very cold air straight from the Artic. It went straight into our bones. Boy, were we cold. I didn't think I was going to like living here.

My mother's eldest brother had offered the top floor of his very large three-story house to our family. The house was in a suburb of Birmingham called Edgbaston, where there is a famous cricket ground.

We all piled into a couple of taxis which took us to a very noisy, large, rather grubby train station. The platforms seemed endless. The trains, with many carriages, varied in colour and on the doors in gold lettering there was painted 1st for 1st class ticket holders and others had 2nd which is what we were looking for. A couple of porters in uniform, took our luggage and tickets and led us to the right carriage, as we had booked seats.

There was constant blowing of whistles. Some trains moving out, others arriving, all at a slow pace. I must say the seats, which were of a dark green leather or similar material, were decidedly more comfortable than those I had experienced in Jamaica. We had a compartment to ourselves. On the wall above the seats, which were long and faced each other, there were framed photos of beach resorts. In the centre a mirror. Above these were racks to put hand luggage. These consisted of a saggy net on a shiny rail with brass fittings to hold them to the wall. Opposite the door we had entered, there was another sliding door leading to a corridor. At the end of the corridor were some toilets.

Talking of toilets, we discovered that to use any public toilets, one needed a penny to put into a slot, before we could open the door. Hard luck if you didn't have a penny!

With whistles being blown, doors being slammed shut, smoke belching out of the engine's funnel and a loud tooting, we moved slowly out of the station. As we travelled out of London the train gained speed. The scenery we saw while passing through the London suburbs was very dreary. Everything around a shade of grey to a charcoal colour. A depressing sight.

The countryside beyond was greener. The English landscape sped past us at a rapid rate. The windows were very dirty so I decided to open one and admire the scenery. *Not a good idea.* I ended up with a bit of soot in my eye. I got a terrible fright when an express flew past us, going the other way. What a racket it made a swooshing, clickety clack noise. When we went through a tunnel the sooty, smoky, coal smell was not very pleasant. Some of the tunnels were very long.

On the whole I found the trip quite exciting. The scenery so vastly different to the West Indies. It was late spring so the countryside was very colourful. There were fields with freshly tilled soil, some with horses, feeding on lush looking grass, others with cows, some lying down chewing their cud. In other fields a red brick farm cottage with chickens scratching around. A little boy sitting on a fence waved to us. We flew over bridges, through boom gates, with traffic banked up on both sides of the rail tracks. Our train was an express so we did not stop at any other station, though we did slow down sometimes while going through larger stations. We passed many towns and villages. Some of them had suffered through the war and the ruined buildings were very apparent.

The green of the fields, trees and hedgerows was a different green to that which I had been used to. The hedges were not yet in full leaf, along the edges of the fields and roadside the flowers of the wild turnips and dandelions were colourful. There was a pink flower among them, I did not recognize.

We finally arrived at Birmingham. As we moved slowly down the platform people were running along-side the train. We came to a halt; my parents recognized my aunt and with her was my handsome cousin Paul. Once on the platform we were fondly greeted, porters collected our luggage and carried our bags out to waiting taxis. The two youngest children and my mother went to my aunt's car. We were whisked off to our uncle's home.

Chapter 8

EDGBASTON

Uncle Charles's house was a very big three-story house set in a sprawling garden. We had been offered the top floor. At the rear of the house was an enclosed, cobbled courtyard with a row of stables; above which there were servant and grooms' quarters. Some of the stables had been removed to make room for a couple of garages. The spaces above these had been hay storage lofts but were now used as storage for things like ladders and building materials. Behind these buildings a long glasshouse ran down the side of the vegetable garden, all this was hidden from the house by a high hedge. A huge expanse of well-kept lawn ran the length of the house and around one end. This continued down a slope to the outer fence and a railway line. To the left, close to the railway line was the shell of a building; it had obviously scored a random bomb. This building, though probably not very safe was a great attraction to myself and older cousins, as a cubby-house.

One could climb up to the second floor via a tree which grew alongside. It never crossed our minds that the outer walls could crumble and fall. If a train rumbled past the building would shake, this sensation was not unlike an earth tremor which I was quite used to as we had several while living in Jamaica.

Our family had to enter the house by the back door, through the kitchen dining area, to reach our living quarters via the back staircase. My mother did most of the cooking and preparing of meals, supervised by my aunt. My aunt made me feel as though she would rather we were not there and treated us as inferiors. The 'Wild West Indian' cousins! Food rationing was in full force, it took some getting used to the small portions of everything we were allowed.

Twice a week my father took Pat and me to a hall where food was being served to subsidize the rations. We were able to buy a meal of sausages, mashed potatoes, carrots and peas, with gravy, followed by a steamed pudding of sorts, covered in custard. All of this for one shilling and six pence. This being washed down by a very strong brew of tea or a ghastly cup of coffee made with some liquid stuff out of a bottle called 'Camp Coffee'. This certainly wasn't coffee as we knew it. Someone told us it was made from acorns!

How I missed my favourite Jamaican dishes, yellow yam, plantain, salt fish and ackee (a fruit), or rice and peas, where the red beans were cooked in a stew with pork, carrots and scallion, served with white rice.

Our aunt would not allow us to put our jam or marmalade on the side of our plate, as we had been taught. We had to put the butter straight on to our bread or toast, the same applied to jams. Having so many ration books between both families did allow us to buy a joint of meat when available. It was so difficult to get used to being allowed two bananas a week and a small bar of chocolate a month. My aunt pooled all our rations and stretched them out in very small portions.

Before leaving Jamaica, I had bought a small white suitcase. It was made of compressed cardboard lined with a checked brown and white, stiff paper. I still use the case after sixty-four years. The case measured 24 inches x 18 inches x 5 inches. On each corner a hard, plastic material shaped to fit and held on by studs. It has a metal handle and two metal fasteners which I could lock.

I was determined to not go without my rice and peas, ration or no ration. So into my little suitcase I stashed two pounds of rice and a pound of red kidney beans; I also bought a bottle of my favourite "Pick-a-Pepper" sauce. It was a brown coloured chili sauce. Needless to say, I had to share these things with all in the household. It was a question of "what's yours is mine and what's mine is my own" where my aunt was concerned. My mother made a big pan of rice with stewed beans. I enjoyed it while it lasted. My cousins didn't take to our Jamaican dish, so we West Indians enjoyed a couple of meals of rice and peas.

In my little case I had also packed several of my favourite belongings. The case was full. My mother had some large trunks to take my clothes and a few books I wanted to keep, plus my gun, a 22 rifle, which a friend had given me several years before. I dismantled it so it would fit in with our luggage.

My parents had decided to separate which was quite a shock to all of us. After three months my father returned to Jamaica, I wanted to return with him but was not allowed. After his departure I felt that my mother was being treated more like a servant, which I resented. I and my older siblings had duties, like laying and clearing the table, and doing the washing up, we were always being picked on. My cousins seemed to always have something else to do. At one mealtime, I didn't like the way my aunt spoke to my mother, I had enough and lost my temper and told my aunt I was fed up with the way we were all being treated, especially my mother.

Incredible Memories

I was soundly reprimanded by my mother and told I should be grateful that my uncle and aunt had offered us a home. I still could not see that was a reason to be treated as we were.

My two youngest cousins, who were the same ages as Christopher and Christine, were having their tonsils out. My uncle who was a doctor, suggested it would be a good idea for my brother and sister to have theirs removed at the same time! Just something else to add to the trauma of our huge move. He also prescribed some pills for me to take, as he told my mother he thought I had an overactive thyroid and they, the pills, would quieten me down. I promptly poured them down the sink!

Cousins Paul, Peter, Marianne, Mark and Aunt Adelaide, Edgbaston

My uncle Robin, my father's youngest brother came to visit for a couple of days. He was still recuperating from being in a Japanese prisoner of war camp. He had been on the Burma railway line and had suffered considerably. He was very good looking; in appearance he was similar to an Anglo-Indian. Quiet in manner and in speech, with a very dry sense of humour, not much older than me. On the Saturday night we went into Birmingham to a dance hall but did not stay long as he said he was not feeling very well. The next day it turned out that he had the mumps! Needless to say, my aunt was not over pleased to hear this. He left for London the next day, which was the last time I saw him. I never got the mumps and neither did anyone else. When Robin got over the mumps, he left for South Africa to work in the office at a mine site. He did correspond with my father until he died in the early seventies, when he very generously left some money to his many nephews and nieces.

After my uncle Robin left, my aunt divided the garden in half with a rope, the Johns on one side and the Burns on the other. This was just in case we had caught the mumps. Needless to say, the young ones found a way of getting together to play!

To get away from the house and have some sort of independence I decided to get some gardening jobs. I didn't fancy an indoor job. There were several gardens around that area that had been left to the weeds during the war. It was great being out on my own cleaning up these gardens, some were very overgrown. I could imagine what they would be like if they were well kept. I discovered overgrown rose gardens, gravel and brick pathways, and raised beds, some full of bulbs. Hidden hydrangeas, rhododendrons, blackberries, redcurrants, raspberries and many more forgotten plants, struggling to survive. This was exciting and I was enjoying myself and getting paid for it! The best part was I had my own money. Then my aunt suggested I pay board also, but my mother said I was included in what she was paying for the family to stay there. Soon I had more jobs than I could cope with, as by word of mouth more and more people were asking for me.

Pat and I used to go to a movie or just into Birmingham to have a good look around. We both missed Jamaica and our life out there. Away from 'the house full of rules' we could laugh and feel free. David was studying at the Birmingham Art Centre and during the summer holidays we both went off to a harvest camp where we joined many other young and older people who worked on farms helping with the harvesting. The Land Army had been disbanded and a lot of the farm hands were still in the forces or didn't want to return to the land.

We were billeted in Nissan huts, men and women separated, and we were given our meals in a dining hall near the kitchen. German prisoners of war did the cooking and cleaning. We travelled to the farms on the back of a truck and were dropped off at various farms in the county of Rutland. I did mainly spud bashing, which was potato picking. We walked down rows of dug up potatoes, collecting them in baskets and then dumping them in large bins that were dotted around the field.

The farmer's wife brought us very strong tea and cakes and we ate our sandwiches that the camp had provided. We had another break before we were picked up and returned to the camp, exhausted. At the weekend I went, with a group of ladies out of my hut into town, to a dance hall, which cost us one shilling and six pence to get in. This also covered a cup of tea and biscuits at the interval. Army and air-force personal went to these dances so we never lacked for a partner. On one occasion I met up with a couple of Jamaican guys and got right into Jive dancing. One night I walked back to the camp with a very handsome Polish airman. When we got back, he was in the middle of telling me about his family, so we decided to go into a field

Incredible Memories

just opposite the gate to the camp. He took off his coat and laid it on the ground and we sat there talking for another hour. I heard all about his escaping to England to join the free Polish air-force. He didn't know if he would ever see his family again whom he had left in Poland. He had not heard from them for over a year. We said we'd see each other again the next Saturday but he never showed.

David had to go back to study, so I stayed on for another week. While there I got friendly with one of the older prisoners, though we were not really supposed too. During the war we were so patriotic, our feelings toward Germans, Italians and Japanese literally boiled down to hatred. With all the propaganda and news reels we were shown, of the atrocities these nations were inflicting on our allies, it was hard not to hate. Man's inhumanity to man. However, this fraternizing rule seemed a bit of a tall order when some of the men looked so unhappy.

Fritz was a quietly spoken man in his late thirties, he had been a submariner and had been rescued somewhere in the Atlantic. He carried with him a rather soggy looking photo of his wife and two children, whom he had not seen for over three years. At eighteen he decided the navy was to be his life. He was not enamored with the way things were going in Germany. When he left school, it was near impossible to get a job. The world was in a depression, so he joined the merchant navy; this enabled him to support his parents and younger siblings, a brother and two sisters.

His life was good and Fritz was free. So much was changing in Germany, by the time he was 25 years old Hitler had taken over the running of the Fatherland. Fritz feared for his parents, being good Christian people, he knew they would not agree with some of the drastic changes. His fears were realized when his mother wrote and told him his father was in prison awaiting trial for treason. He never saw his father again.

In 1938 Fritz received calling up papers, he was to join the German navy, to be trained as a submariner. Life in a U-boat was very dangerous but he had no choice. He hated Hitler and all he stood for. There was no way he could show his feelings and had to obey orders, he still had his family to support.

On one of the occasions when we sat talking, I realized, here was a very sad man and I had hated him. It was a great relief to him when he became a prisoner of war. Fritz was not very popular with the younger Germans at the camp, for they had been staunch Nazis. I remember one young fellow, around my age, one of the handsomest young men I had ever known, except for his cold blue eyes. Nothing would convince him the war was over, he truly believed Germany would rise again and conquer the world. His arrogance and hatred bristled out of him. Because of Fritz I learnt not to hate a nation.

When we were at the camp I used to run around with bare feet, everyone thought this was strange but I was just so used to doing it and feeling my feet were free. I remember an elderly lady telling me that I would get a tapeworm or if I cut my foot, I'd get blood poisoning. She couldn't understand how I could walk on gravel paths without feeling it.

Myself 17 and a half years old

Chapter 9

MOVING ON

At about the age of 17, I returned to Edgbaston after six weeks and my mother said that my aunt Alice, who lived in a village called Well, in Yorkshire, would like me to go and stay to help her with her two youngest. Tom was four years old and Alison was two and my aunt was expecting another. Her three eldest were away at boarding school, my uncle was working away from home and as she was getting close to the delivery time, she was finding it hard to cope on her own.

They lived in a big rambling house on a hill overlooking the village. The house was surrounded by a large garden, vegetables growing in all sorts of places. There was a chicken pen some distance from the house, up near the front gate, sheltered on one side by the garage. Aunt Alice liked working in the garden but there were quite a lot of things she couldn't do, as she was so large with child! She didn't much like looking after the chickens, so I used to do that and any jobs she couldn't manage. I got on very well with my aunt. I also enjoyed looking after my cousins. Alison used to call me 'lovely Anne', as she followed me around all the time.

Aunt Alice used to prepare some wonderful meals but I have never seen such a cluttered kitchen, she seemed to use umpteen pots and pans and when she was finished with them she would discard them on the kitchen floor. The result was a massive washing up after the meal. I never knew where to start.

To get down to the village we had to go down a path that started at the back of the garden and led to the lower road. In the house at the end of the lane there lived a man who was a bit simple and he used to dribble, the Milroy's, Alice's family, called him "Dribbly Binks". Alison was a bit scared of him and would have to be carried till we had passed him. He couldn't talk properly, he just mumbled and then he would laugh. He always seemed glad to see us.

MOVING ON

Maimo and Heather, Ian, Tom and Alison, Well, Yorkshire

Well was a pretty little village. I loved listening to the church bells ringing on a Sunday morning and evening. Everyone was very friendly, though a bit curious as to whom I was. The day came when my aunt went into hospital and produced Antony. Uncle Bill came down, from a small town in Durham, northeast England, to see his new son. I was on my own for a few nights with my two cousins and was managing quite well. One night I was awoken by a terrible scream. I discovered it was a rabbit that had been caught in a trap. As you can imagine I was a bit worried until I knew what it was. When my uncle was down, he said he would feel happier if I, Alison and Tom went back with him.

We were going to a place, if my memory serves me right, called Barlow. Bill boarded with a mining family. They had brought up a large family in this three-bedroom house. The house seemed very small after the house in Well, it had no bathroom and the toilet was outside in a small courtyard. Bill and the Scottish guy who he worked with, who also lived there, shared a room, the parents in another room and their eighteen-year-old daughter, the only one living at home, shared the third room with Alison, Tom and me!

They were very warm and friendly people but I had never known that there were people living in these conditions. Downstairs there was a parlor (they called it) to entertain special visitors, like the vicar and his wife. I never saw it used while I was there. The rest of downstairs was one large room; this is where life was lived. There was a sink at one end under the only window in the room, next to that was a door leading out to the courtyard.

Incredible Memories

There were two comfy chairs either side of the open fireplace. A very large kitchen table and chairs in the centre of the room.

When the men came in from work they would strip off to the waist and have a good wash in the sink, the said sink was used to wash the vegetables, after being peeled, I had also bathed Tom and Alison in it, and after the meal the dishes were washed in it.

After their ablutions the men sat at the family sized table for their evening meal, which they called tea. The meal had been cooked on the coal fire. Swinging hooks hung on one side of the hearth for cooking pots and on the other side was a type of oven. There was also a ring on an arm which swung in over the fire; this is where the kettle sat all day. Always ready to make a pot of the proverbial cup of tea, should anyone pop in. But it was quite natural to drink several cups during the day.

I had to look after my cousins and all their needs as well as peel the pounds of potatoes and do some of the housework. The daughter went out to work. The old boy joined his cronies at the pub until lunchtime, after which he spent many hours reading the daily paper, smoking his pipe or just snoozing. I remember his face looked as though it was covered in blackheads. It was a build-up of coal dust in his pores from working down a coal mine all his life. He said he started at the tender age of thirteen!

In the centre of the courtyard, which was only about ten foot by twelve, there was a well, the toilet at the far end, and a small room with a copper over a fire hole for doing the washing or to heat water for the weekly bath. There was a huge metal bathtub hanging on the wall. No way was I going to sit out in the courtyard having a bath, so I went to the public baths and paid my one bob for a towel, soap and a hot bath.

The daughter asked if I would like to go to the Saturday night dance with her. Uncle Bill said he would keep an eye on the two bairns. We could go in by bus but the dance ended too late to catch the last bus, so we had to walk back, the two miles. I went and quite enjoyed myself but found it difficult to understand some of the lads and girls. Their accent was broad Geordie; I think they made it even stronger for my benefit, so they had a good laugh at my expense. Some of them accompanied us part of the way home, stopping off at various points where they lived. We lived the furthest away. I took my shoes off long before we got back, my feet were so sore.

We stayed with the family for two weeks then went back to Well to help Aunt Alice. The two weeks were certainly an experience I shall never forget. Once back, there were many chores to help with. When Antony was to be baptized the three eldest children came home from boarding school. Godparents arrived and the house seemed crowded. After the baptism we had a big spread before all were leaving to return home and to boarding schools. My cousin Ian, who would have been about eleven years old, was very upset. My aunt tried to cheer him up by saying she had packed a tin of golden syrup in his bag. His favourite. This didn't help very much. We later heard the tin had opened and gone all over everything in his suitcase, poor Ian!

After a few weeks I left for Edgbaston and returned to my gardening jobs. One weekend my mother and the two youngest, my aunt and her two youngest, went to a school run by an old family friend of the Burns', the Arbuthnots. My cousin Mark was at school there, hence the reason we were there, for their sports day. We met up with the Floods, also old family friends. Mrs. Flood was a sister to the headmaster, and they also had a son at school there. They had an adorable si- month old baby, John, with them, who took to me right away; much to his mother's delight. She was looking for a Nanny; it was arranged between them and my mother that it would be a good idea if I went and worked for them. One way of getting me away from Edgbaston and embarrassing my mother any further.

Within a week I was on my way down to Wimbledon. The Floods lived in a large apartment. I had my own room. My sole job was to look after John and help with meals. I ate all my meals with his parents when they were home. Gradually the jobs grew. I was asked to get breakfast ready. Doctor Flood had to leave early as he worked up in London, his wife often stayed in bed.

Not long after this, they bought a huge three-story house in the posh part of Wimbledon and we moved in. Again, I had my own room which was larger than the previous one. While there I decided I wanted to do a correspondence course in Electrical Engineering. After only two weeks into the course the four older children in the family came home for school holidays. They ranged in age, eight to fifteen years old, and I was then expected to look after them as well. The older ones resented this as I was not much older than them; they started to give me a hard time especially the eldest boy.

The next thing on the list was, "Would you mind lighting the boiler down in the basement first thing in the morning?" This was so there would be hot water when everyone got up. The hot water went through the radiators, which heated the house. It was a bit spooky going down there while it was still dark, especially as the door exiting to the garden did not lock properly.

I felt all these extra tasks was asking a bit much of me, for thirty shillings a week, so I asked for more. There were some evenings when it was my time off, and then Molly would phone to say she was staying in London and would not be back till 8 o'clock. I was supposed to finish at six on my weekdays but would stay back to look after John as a favour. One night I was supposed to be meeting my sister Pat, to go to a film, Molly did the same thing again, phoned and said she would be late. I was very annoyed as I had no way of letting Pat know, so I told her I could not stay, Molly was not very happy.

Incredible Memories

My mother had bought a house in lower Wimbledon. At night after work I would walk two miles down to the house to start renovating and painting. My mother was to move down from Edgbaston shortly with the rest of the family. I also got the electricity and gas put on. It was very creepy walking back up the hill in the dark.

Anyway, the culmination of having asked for a rise was that 'I was very ungrateful for having been given a job and they couldn't pay me anymore'. In those days everyone had to have a job or join the forces, so I decided to join the Navy. Molly phoned a friend she knew quite high up in the Woman's Royal Naval Service (WRENS) and got all the information on how to join up. So that is what I did. Later I heard they had got an au pair girl from Switzerland and were paying her three pounds ten shillings a week! I bet she didn't have to do all the jobs I had done. That taught me never to get a job with friends or relatives; they always take advantage of you!

Girls I joined up with, 1948

Chapter 10

I JOIN THE NAVY

It wasn't long before I received my call up papers. I was instructed to go for a medical to a place I cannot remember; the whole episode was such a nightmare I preferred to forget it. They sent me a ticket to wherever it was. I took several trains and then had to walk a fair distance, following a map they had sent. Finally, I came to a large, very ugly brick building, I was directed to the second floor. I gave my name and was handed a small jug and told to go into a cubical, strip and put a white garment on. There were women stripping off all over the place and they didn't seem to mind who saw them in all their glory. I, on the other hand, had never undressed in front of anyone else I didn't know and was very embarrassed. I had been given a form to fill in; I grabbed my clothes and joined a long queue. When my turn came, I was told to 'go wee in the jug,' normally I had no problem but this day, nothing, so I was told to go and drink several glasses of water. By this time, I was freezing as the white garment was very skimpy. A doctor checked my breathing, heart, reflexes, feet, eyes, 'open your mouth wide and stick out your tongue', then they pressed my tongue down and peered down my throat at which point I nearly threw up. After this I was finally able to present them with a jug of wee. I was told to get dressed. By this time nearly everyone had left. "We will be in touch" I was told.

Off I went accompanied by a lady who announced she was Romany, which meant nothing to me. She told me she could show me a quicker way to get back to Wimbledon. We ended up at a place called Elephant and Castle; I remember thinking, what a funny name. This is where my new friend got out and so did I, as by then I was bursting for the toilet, after drinking so much water, so made a dash for the ladies. Had to produce the proverbial penny and by that time I was nearly wetting myself. Then my new friend told me what trains to catch and where to change. Well the journey took forever. Each stop I made a dash and was beginning to run out of pennies. I finally got back to Wimbledon. I think I had been all the way around London.

Two weeks later I received notice that I had been accepted into the Women's Royal English Navy or WRENs, as we called it. I would commence training immediately. There was a train ticket and instructions on how to get to my destination, and what I was allowed to take with me. My little white suitcase, which I had brought from Jamaica would be just the right size for the few things I was permitted to take. I had to have a warm skirt, two blouses, and a cardigan, change of underwear, toiletries and a pair of sturdy shoes. Fortunately, I had all of these items because otherwise, if I had to purchase them, all of these things were rationed. I was permitted to bring no more than ten shillings. I was to report at Reading Station by 11:30am on the 27th January 1948.

Needless to say, I was very nervous and wondered if I was doing the right thing but in my heart I knew that it was what I wanted to do. At Reading a group of young ladies and I were met by, what I learnt later, was a Petty Officer, about twenty of us climbed into the back of a Naval truck for the trip to H.M.S. President at Burghfield, in Berkshire. My stomach was churning; we all sat in silence except for two noisy women who never stopped talking and laughing. Some of the things they were saying were quite funny and we all started to loosen up and joined in the laughter. All through the days in the Navy I found those who thought of life as one big joke. We seemed to be driven for miles but finally arrived at the gates. The driver checked in and we were allowed to drive on. The barracks were referred to as a 'Stone Frigate.' Arriving at a parade ground the truck stopped and belched out twenty-seven new recruits. A pleasant young lady in uniform met us and announced she was the Petty Officer in charge of our group.

We were told to fall into two lines and follow her. Once in what looked like a classroom, she asked us to find a seat. I was now a Pro Wren and was in a group of twenty-seven other women under Petty Officer Chalmers and Third Officer Collin-James. We were told we would be put into double cabins, luckily a nice quiet lady asked if she could share with me. Before we were taken to our cabins, Petty Officer introduced us to a few rules: address an officer as Mam, when we met them outside, when in uniform we saluted them but if we were not in full uniform we gave them a smart 'eyes right'. I presumed this meant I always walked on the left side of the path. Time was announced in a twenty-four-hour day. One pm became thirteen hundred hours; midnight was twenty-four hours and so forth. Every order was announced over a Tannoy. Our meals were at a certain time, for which we had to line-up and walk past a counter where the food was more or less chucked onto our plates. At the end of the meal we had to return our plates to a pile at the end of the counter but keep our cutlery which we had to wash ourselves and keep them handy for the next meal.

I JOIN THE NAVY

We would wear our civilian clothes for the first week, at the end of which we were given the choice to leave or stay. Those who stayed would be issued with uniforms. During that week we were training on the parade ground. Forming ranks with commands being shouted at us like 'right dress' where we would do an eyes right to get the line straight. We'd do right turning, quick marching, form fours, about turn, mark time etc. I was amazed how many girls couldn't coordinate arm and leg movements. They looked so funny marching with their left arm moving with their left leg and vice versa. While we marched in formation, we had to keep our lines straight. While marching we had to do eyes right, to see the line was straight and at the same time not walk up the back of the girl in front. All this came easy to me as I had done a lot of marching when I was a Girl Guide. Quite often half were out of step and had to do a little skip to get back into step. We drilled in the morning and went to class in the afternoon.

In training

We also did exercises, but most of the first week we spent in the classroom. We were taught all the ranks in the navy, how to recognize the different types of ships, also all the different categories there were and generally how the navy worked.

Our cabins were just big enough to hold double bunks, a small chest of draws each and there was a very small hanging cupboard set in the wall, to hang our uniforms in. There were two sheets, two blankets, a pillow and two pillowcases neatly folded on the end of each bunk. Beside these was a blue and white, single bed cover with a crown and anchor at the head, also neatly folded.

Each day started with the tannoy blaring "Wakey wakey, rise and shine!" I'd fall out of bed make for the ablutions, down the hall, in my PJs.

Incredible Memories

We had fifteen minutes for this and to get dressed before falling in on the parade ground. We had to then march down to the dining hall to join about 900 other Wrens, grab our breakfast, which was always very substantial, eat it and return to our cabins to make our bunks, neatly for inspection. The sheets had to be tucked in hospital style, as were the blankets. The coverlet was to be over the pillow but pulled back a bit so it could be tucked under the front of the pillow. The crown had to be central on the pillow and the anchor just below, about six inches down. If it was not satisfactory on inspection, we had to start all over again!

I found meals very traumatic as I was shy sitting among 900 rather noisy women. This put me off my food. All around me ate so quickly and I was a slow eater. Our meals at home were never hurried. Invariably forks were aimed in my direction and part of the food on my plate would disappear. I never had time to eat my puddings so that would vanish too. I survived on biscuits from the canteen.

During this period several of the girls were curious to learn more about my life in the West Indies. I was amazed at how little they knew about where I came from. Most thought I came from the western part of India. They wondered how I was so white! Our cabin would be full of visitors until 'lights out', I know it was probably terrible of me, but I couldn't resist spinning a yarn, or as they said in the Navy 'swinging the lead.' What sort of house did you live in and did you have shops and schools and the list went on and on. I told them we lived in a tree so the wild animals and snakes couldn't get us, that I wore a grass skirt, ran around in bare feet, this being the only truth. I hated wearing shoes, still do. At the end of our ten-week training we were given a weekend pass, so I brought my photo album back with me. Well they nearly killed me when they saw I had been leading them on.

After our first week at Burghfield three of the girls decided navy life was not for them. The rest of us were trooped off to the storeroom and dished up with our uniform which we carried back to our cabins. I was now Pro Wren Trainee Anne John 71222. One thing I always remember PO Chalmers teaching us was that one should be able to laugh at oneself. It was not easy living constantly with people you have never known, so a good sense of humour helped. Our messmates were from all walks of life.

When we were dressed in our uniforms we had to go to the classroom, there we were asked which category we wanted to be in. I said I would like to do something mechanical or to do with signalling, only to be told there were no vacancies. I had the choice of ships or officer's cook, ships or officer's steward. I plumped for cook(s), with a choice of changing my category at a later date if a vacancy came up.

So off to the storeroom again to be issued with blue and white striped overalls and clog shoes. The shoes were heavy leather, steel capped, in case we dropped anything heavy on our feet. We were also given a couple of pairs of thick black stockings, a webbed belt plus two chef's hats. The overalls were

I JOIN THE NAVY

very ill fitting; mine was down to my ankles, so we all had to do some adjustments before reporting for duty at the galley. With our gear we were issued with a cloth roll with needles, thread and a pair of small scissors plus spare buttons and a thimble. We were also given a shoe-shining set of brushes and a tin of black polish. We had to do a fair bit of spit and polish. This is when I learnt that spit does help to put a lasting shine on one's shoes and I was getting quite good with my aim when I spat. So unladylike!

Those of us who chose to be cooks were marched off to the galley to be introduced to the Chief Petty Officer, Petty Officer and Leading Wren in charge of our watch. We were divided into three watches, each doing eight hours duty. The watches sort of over lapped. Sometimes we did a bit more than eight hours!

Then the fun began! We were cooking for 900 Wrens so there were a lot of potatoes to peel, luckily there was a peeler, something like a large cement mixer. It sort of knocked the skin off as they tumbled inside. We tipped them out into a huge bin and removed the eyes manually before tossing them into another bin full of cold water. If chips were on the menu, we had to put them through a chipper before dropping them into the cold water. They sat there until it was cooking time which was usually the job of the next watch.

The early morning watch prepared breakfast, so we started at 0500, we would also prepare the vegetables for lunch, for the next watch who came on at 0800. After serving out the breakfast we would scrub out the galley, clean all the gear we had used, by then it was time to knock off. We'd have our breakfast and return to our cabins and change into our uniforms.

There were huge ovens and steam chests, the like I had never seen before. Plus large fryers, like there are in fish and chips shops. We even fried the eggs in them. Thirty at a time. By the time you had cracked the last egg the first was ready to come out, so it was a constant pop them in and take them out. I got splashed with hot fat quite frequently so my arms were covered in small red blotches. Just had to get used to it.

One day when we were making Toad in the Hole, which was sausages laid in batter and put in a hot oven, the oven caught fire. So we were given a lesson in fire extinguishing. First, we had to remove the cooking trays then chuck heaps of salt on the fire. As all the ovens were electric, we had to switch them off. Once the fire was out we had the terrible mess to clean up. So after that we made sure we never let the oven get too hot.

During my training in the galley we had a visit from the Queen, King George the VI's wife. I was very busy making mayonnaise when she approached me; needless to say, I became nearly speechless when Her Highness asked me what I was doing. "I am making mayonnaise, Mam," "Well I never, such a large quantity! But I suppose you need that amount for the number you are catering for." "Yes Mam." "Thank you, my dear, good luck." And she moved on.

Incredible Memories

During my training I met up with the Gypsy I had met when I went for my medical. When we were off duty at the same time, we would borrow a bicycle and go for a ride around the countryside. We both relaxed being out in the country enjoying the scenery. During these rides we learnt a lot about our families and life before joining up.

A lady, who lived about a mile down the road from the camp, opened her house to the trainee Wrens. In the evenings we would walk down to enjoy an evening of music and yummy home cooked scones, cakes and pies for a very reasonable price. We also got to meet some of the local lads. As we had to be back in camp by 2000 we had to make sure we kept an eye on the time. When it was time to leave, I noticed most of the girls I had walked down with disappeared with some of the lads. There were no streetlights on the way back so the walk was a very dark one. Luckily one of the older guys offered to walk me back and he treated me with great respect, he didn't try to take me off for a 'snooky' as the girls called it. Most of our evenings were spent having a sing-a-long; the lady also provided board games for those who preferred. It was certainly an enjoyable break away from training.

At the end of ten weeks we were put through an oral, written and practical test. I was presented with a menu which absolutely floored me. Fortunately, we were allowed to use recipes. But with a seven-course meal I couldn't see that I would pass. It looked as hard as trigonometry. My menu consisted of a consommé soup, the garnish of which was strips of carrot the size of match sticks. A fish dish, main course was roast beef with Yorkshire pudding, something I had never heard of before coming to England. Roast potatoes and three vegetables, and a steamed pudding made with Golden Syrup. This thank goodness turned out very light, more like a sponge. The pudding was served with custard sauce. I also had to make a fruit cake. All of the meal preceded by hors d'oeuvres.

After the meal came the pudding, cheese and biscuits, which I had to make and finally, there was coffee and fruit cake.

Well I didn't know where to start, so I was doing a bit of cake mixing, a bit of the pudding and then thought maybe I should start the consommé, but then didn't the hors d'oeuvres come first? The PO kept on coming over and suggesting things to me. My head was spinning, I was nearly in tears. I couldn't see how I was going to get everything done in time, but I managed somehow. I got 60% for my marks so I couldn't have done a bad job! That was on April 20th. After all this we were all given a long weekend to go home. We were now considered to be Wrens. When I returned from the break, I was told I was to be drafted to H.M.S. Mercury.

Chapter 11

H.M.S. MERCURY

H.M.S. Mercury, another Stone Frigate, a training ship for 'Sparkies' at a place called Leydene near Petersfield in the county of Hampshire. All my new made friends were sent to other postings in the UK. I packed my kit bag, was given a ticket and was on my way to being a ship's cook after only a few weeks training.

I was as nervous as a mouse in a cattery. Here I was, at the tender age of eighteen, joining a ship with 1000 ratings aboard. A real Sprog and quite frankly, with a little trepidation. When I arrived at Petersfield, a Wren driver and a naval truck called a Liberty Boat, met me, I jumped aboard and was then driven for miles through some beautiful countryside. I was accompanied by matelotes and Wrens returning from shore leave. A couple of the Wrens spoke to me but I still felt like a Sprog, my bag and uniform looking so brand new and I probably looked a bit lost. All this being new to me, after just getting used to life at Burghfield.

We finally arrived on the Quarter Deck, where the truck came to a stop. I jumped off the truck, grabbed my kit bag, saluted the Quarter Deck and entered the office of the duty Wrens Officer of the day. Nearly forgot to salute her, she soon put me at 'easy', read out a few rules and regulations, welcomed me aboard and gave me directions to my quarters. After saluting her I slung my kit bag onto my shoulder and started off towards a row of Nissan huts. Lordy, Lordy how does one salute an Officer when you've got your bag on your right shoulder? Oops one big mistake, always carry it on your left shoulder.

In the confusion of trying to get it changed to my other shoulder I knocked my hat off, sort of remembered something about "You do an eyes right when without head gear." Next thought "could I be put on a charge for being without it?" Did a smart eyes right, replaced my cap and continue on my journey. Arrived at a flight of steps and noticed the hut with my number on it was the one right at the top. I arrived slightly out of breath, knocked at

Incredible Memories

the door and opened it. Inside I was greeted by a very buxom lady who introduced herself as Doris.

"Hi there, you must be our new cook eh? welcome to your new abode. You will be on my watch; we are on duty at 0800 tomorrow, in the meantime make yourself at home. Your bunk is the last on the left. "Nelly, can you show Anne John the ropes and where everything is? See you a bit later 'Johnny'."

I guessed that was to be my new name while in the Navy!

I walked the length of the hut with my eyes down, only to raise them when I was quietly greeted by one of the girls I shared with. There were a few snoring their heads off as they had been on early morning watch.

Fortunately, I had a bottom bunk. A face appeared from the top bunk. Her hair was not quite a ginger colour and she greeted me with an Irish accent.

"My name is Mary, the chest of drawers on the left is yours, and you can hang your great coat and uniform in the wardrobe at the end of the bunks."

"Thank you," I replied.

I unpacked and stowed my kit bag on top of the wardrobe and went back down the row of bunks. There were twenty of us billeted in the mess. Nelly showed me where the ablutions were, at the far end of the hut, just past the door I had come in. Opposite the door was another door and a separate cabin which two Leading Wrens occupied. Nearly in the centre of the hut was a large pot-bellied stove which I was informed "we all take turns to keep clean, polished and always to replenish wood and coke, both in huge bins outside the hut."

Nelly was a very quiet lady, slight of build, who seemed to spend her entire day wrapped in a rather grubby dressing gown. While awake she very seldom was without a 'Woodbine' cigarette in her mouth or between her fingers, which were an orangey brown colour. Though some of the other girls ribbed her about her appearance it made no difference. She was very good-natured and the remarks just slid off her back. I often wondered what experiences she had during the war, she had served with Doris the latter part of the war, somewhere on the east coast.

After my tour it was time for tea. The dining hall was on the same level as our hut, also a Nissan hut, but wider than ours. Mary and I walked over together. Though I was hungry I was still shy and found it difficult to enjoy a meal with a crowd of noisy women. But at least here, Mary announced, we could scrounge slices of bread, some butter and she would get some cheese and jam from one of the stewards.

After tea I sat on my bunk writing to my mother to let her know I had arrived safely, when the whole mess erupted into loud laughter. Peggy, the other Leading Wren, and Doris appeared; she called out in a booming voice. "Come on mates, let's make Johnny feel at home."

H.M.S. MERCURY

Doris wore a white shirt with a pink 'bra' on the outside, huge black silk bloomers with a pair of suspenders on the outside hitching up a pair of bright red and white striped stockings. I wondered where she would have got all this gear during ration times. For shoes she and Peggy wore galley clogs, with steel tips on the toes and heels, these made good tap-dancing shoes, though a tad heavy. Her hair was done in very small, short plaits tied with various colored bits of rag. She had big dangly earrings.

Peggy was in similar garments but she had a green 'bra' and green striped stockings. She was blonde and had a pigtail, surely false, down to her waist; she had a comb covered in a piece of tissue paper and two dessert spoons which she used to clap together on her thighs or on her head.

Doris for her musical rendition had a mouth organ attached to her head somehow, and a small saucepan with a wooden spoon.

We grabbed chairs and joined others already sitting around the pot belly stove.

Peggy had made up a poem in which I featured and they sang it to the tune of "I know a Lassie". Doris disappeared and returned wearing a sort of long net skirt over her bloomers and carrying a stick with a star on the end. They started singing "Walk Right In" and most joined in. They pranced around. They looked a right pair. They continued with "A-Tisket a Tasket Top Hat White Tie and Tails" then they put on their caps, back to front and great coats. They did a bit of a tap dance in their clogs, then removed their coats and started "Ain't Misbehaving" to which they attempted to do a tango, clowning around in between.

We all sang things like "Dinah, Somebody Stole My Gal, Is You Is or Is You Ain't My Baby". Doris was a regular clown with various facial expressions, every now and then dropping her four front teeth, which were on a plate. Looking cross eyed, when she sang "Sweet Georgia Brown". By this time the very large kettle on the stove had boiled and we all made a cup of hot chocolate before lights out.

All this, to make me feel welcome. I must say I did feel more at home but did not quite know what to expect next.

Incredible Memories

Officers' quarters in the background, HMS Mercury

Looking down on camp from sick bay HMS Mercury

Chapter 12

FIRST TASTE OF A REAL GALLEY

After our usual routine of the day which was ablutions, put work clothes on, make up bunk, breakfast and then report to the main galley by 0800, I was greeted by the early watch scrubbing out the galley. The floor was red tiled and showed up all the marks made by Wrens walking around spreading black streaks off their clogs, having crunched bits of coal. I couldn't believe it; the ovens and stoves were coal fired. A row of stoves ran down one side of the galley, opposite the fire box was a hole in the wall which was spilling out coal. Next to each, a huge shovel to feed the fires. Against the opposite wall a row of steam chests. At one end of the galley was the dining hall, divided from the galley by long serveries below which were heated shelves to keep the food hot.

At the other end there was an area where the potato peeler was and where we prepared the vegetables. A door from this lead out into a yard and another smaller room where the potatoes and vegetables were stored. The potatoes were in one-ton bags, built up one on top of another to the ceiling, I had to climb up and haul the highest down and carry it through to the peeler. No mean feat, but one learnt how to lift them with the least hardship.

Beyond this prep area was the Chief Petty Officers and Petty Officers dining area, then a door leading outside to where the pig bins and garbage were stored. Opposite the dining room was another small room where their stewards ate and did the washing up. The male stewards who looked after the CPOs and the POs would collect the food from the galley and serve it out. They kept the place clean and made sure everything was ship shape. They were a good set of young lads. Always cheerful and sometimes would make us a cup of tea with a piece of bread and jam, if they saw we were too busy to make it ourselves. We often played tricks on each other.

I remember one young matelote joined the group and he was a bit scruffy, after several warnings to get himself cleaned up the other stewards

Incredible Memories

got hold of him and put the hose on him and scrubbed him with one of the galley brooms. He soon got the idea about cleanliness.

It didn't take me long to settle into the routine. Two jobs I did not enjoy were stoking the fires and preparing the Brussel sprouts. If you can imagine how many bags it took to feed 1000 men. We had to tail and remove any yellow leaves, slice the stem and chuck them into a huge bin of cold water. Being a winter vegetable, I felt as if my hands were frost bitten by the end of the exercise. After getting the potatoes to the peeler, I and another Wren would empty half the bag into the machine. While they were being peeled, we had to get on with another job and try to remember to go and empty the potatoes into a bin of water before they ended up half their size.

The enamel dishes we cooked our puddings in were two foot by one and a half inches in size. We also roasted the joints of meat in similar dishes which were very heavy to handle when there were three joints weighing about six pounds in each. The days we had roast on the menu we also had roast potatoes and Yorkshire pudding in these huge dishes and all to be cooked in the ovens. The ovens were deep enough and wide enough to take three dishes or trays as we called them, one behind the other and another row next to that. We'd haul the back trays out with a long hook. Of course, we would have to see the ovens were kept at a steady heat. When the meat was cooked, we had to let it stand for a while before slicing it up and laid in yet other trays for serving, we did not have electric knives in those days. We would be told off if we cut the meat too thick. The gravy was made in the trays we had taken the meat out of. There was enough fat and juices to add flour to, once that was absorbed and cooking, we'd add water and stir until we had the right consistency.

The menu varied and the food was very good and wholesome. It took a little time to get used to the sizes of the utensils, the speed with which we had to prepare a meal ready to be served at a specific time. If we were at all late the men would start to beat their plates and chant "Oh why are we waiting."

During the first months I was at HMS Mercury there was a flu epidemic and there were only three of us cooks left standing with the Chief Petty Officer, so we had to do extra hours. After a week the authorities sent up some cooks from Portsmouth to help us out. I ended up in sick bay after three exhausting weeks, very sick. I lost my voice but because I could speak like Donald Duck I rested my throat. When I was discharged from the sick bay, which was on the top floor of the mansion the officers were billeted in, I bumped into the 1st Officer Wren as I walked out of the building. I saluted her and she asked how I was and I answered her like Donald Duck, I had got so used to talking like that. "You still don't sound too good." says she, well I wished the ground could have swallowed me up. Found my real voice and replied "Yes Mam." Then took off to my quarters.

FIRST TASTE OF A REAL GALLEY

Officers' quarters and sick bay, HMS Mercury

For my first leave I got a pass to Scotland and went to stay with Hugh's mother. Though Hugh and I had kept in touch with each other and I had only seen him once since he left Jamaica, it was obvious our relationship was about to end. Though we got on well with each other we had grown apart and I found him very changed. I had too. While staying with his mother, I realized how anti Catholic his family and friends were. He took me dancing and we went rabbit shooting and a couple of times I went with him if he had a job out of Kilmarnock, so I saw a bit of the countryside. That was the last time I saw Hugh and I discontinued writing. Because his father had died from a massive heart attack the doctor told him it was hereditary and Hugh said he would never get married.

I loved the grounds of Leydene, the property we were stationed on. I used to go for walks through the woods with my friends and listen to the birds; there were some woodpeckers and lots of wood pigeons. The rabbits would scamper away and one day I saw a small snake lying on the path and stepped over it, one of my friends yelled "That was an adder."

There were sweeping lawns down to the woods and halfway there was a shooting range. I got quite friendly with the VADs (Voluntary Aid Detachment) when I was in sick bay, one of them wanted to join the shooting team so I joined too. We had to shoot 303s which gave quite a kick, but I got very good at it and used to get high scores. The Chief said I was good enough to shoot at Bisley but I was drafted before I had the opportunity.

Incredible Memories

Self on shooting range with Chief PO

I was fortunate that girls I was friendly with enjoyed going for walks. One of the guys told me there was a small village with a pub about two miles down the road, so I and a friend went for a stroll one day. The road was very narrow and winding, it had high banks with hedges perched on top on either side. There weren't many houses but the quaint little pub stood out to the left of us. Outside there was a notice which said the first game of cricket was played on the village green. I never investigated the fact! We had a shandy each and started the walk back; we picked some wildflowers on the way back to brighten up the mess.

The only other buildings on the camp were the classrooms for the Sparkies to learn their trade, a huge workshop where vehicles were maintained and a large storeroom. The side wall of this was where couples used to end up after a movie or our monthly dance. Attached to the storeroom was a room with a bar which served cider and coffee or tea as well as soft drinks. There was a dart board and a few tables and chairs. This was the Wrens canteen. We could buy biscuits, potato chips, cigarettes and matches, as well as toiletries. Beyond this was the men's canteen. They had a bar where they served beer. There were a couple of billiard tables and a snooker table. Wrens were allowed in on a Friday night. Not popular with some of the older ratings. One night I went down with one of the male stewards to have a game of billiards. We put our florin on the side of the table and waited our turn to use the table. I won the first game. A little Irish guy put his money on the table and said he'd take me on. The loser always had to buy a pint for the winner. Three pints later he decided to give it away. By this time quite a crowd had gathered and they started to rib Spud. I had enough beer to last the night.

Halfway down to the front gate there was a long building which was used as a cinema and was also where we had our monthly dances. The floor was slanting down to a stage and the film screen. This was great for sitting and being able to see a movie but was hard work while dancing uphill! One year they put on a Christmas ball before we went on leave. For this I drew some caricatures of some of the officers and they were stuck up around the walls. They all had large heads and small slim bodies, recognized by the pips on their shoulders. They came out very well and I hoped to get them back after the dance but they all disappeared before I got the chance. Never did find out who removed them.

One day we saw one of the ratings being taken off in hand cuffs, escorted to a police car. Some days later we were told he had been stripping down motorcycles and taking them ashore over the back fence then re-assembling them at his mother's house and selling them on the 'black market.'

When we went on leave the chief store man used to give us cooks a half pound of butter, a pound of sugar, a packet of tea and if we wanted, a jar of tomato sauce and a bottle of brown pickle sauce. These he saved up with what accumulated because all the stores weren't always used up before he ordered more for the monthly allowance according to the amount of ratings. The navy allowed one shilling and a farthing per rating per day but of course there was not always a full quota of men aboard for meals. As all the items we were given were on short rations ashore and we were not allowed any ration cards while on leave it helped out wherever we were staying. But if caught we were put on a charge and we had to promise we would not divulge where the stuff had come from.

Chapter 13

PROMOTION

After I had been in the Navy for six months. I was put forward to do a Leading Wrens course. As I was a Portsmouth rating, I was sent to Victoria Barracks to be billeted while I did the course at the Dockyards. It was quite a walk there and back each day, never mind the weather. The course was very intense and after a day of lectures and practical we had to leave the galley in top shape. And I mean top shape. The saucepans had to be scoured and cleaned so the Chief could see his face in the bottom of each pan. The Chief was a very good teacher and I passed with flying colours.

While I was down there, I caught up with the Leading Wren that had taught me while in training. I had kept up with her by letter so she took leave as she lived near Portsmouth and we used to go to a film or on a nice day we went to the beach. What a shock it was for me the first time I went to the beach. Well it was two shocks, the first was that there was no sand and the second was when I dived into the water, it practically took my breath away, it was like diving through a thin sheet of ice. I tingled from head to foot, my teeth were chattering and I thought I would never be warm again. As luck would have it the sun was still warm as it was not long after lunch. I never was brave enough to do that again. Sitting on a towel laid out on stones is not exactly the most comfortable past time either. Elsie Bullock and I went to the beach a couple of times if the weather was good. It was strange listening to the waves breaking on the beach and turning the stones over as it rolled back into the ocean, On a bright day the beach was covered with very white bodies lying around soaking up the sun, very few ventured into the water!

In the evenings if I missed the evening meal I would go to the Canteen in town and get a cheap meal. I had met a Canadian and an English lady who enjoyed playing Bridge so I would sometimes join them if they were there. The English lady had been in the Navy all through the war, I never did find out what category she was and why she was still in the Navy. The Canadian had been an interpreter during the Nuremburg Trials and after the war could not settle in civilian life so joined the Navy and worked in administration. I think her name was Elizabeth; she was good fun and had a terrific sense of humour, so I got on very well with her. On some nights they had ballroom dancing which I really enjoyed. We girls never lacked for partners. The music was the popular records of the day, Victor Sylvester and Glen Miller being the most popular. The dance floor was always packed.

Off duty

One weekend I met Elizabeth and she said she had met up with some American Service men who had hired a car for the day and had asked her if she would like to join them. She said she didn't want to go on her own and thought I would like to come along. I did. We had a great time traveling around the countryside. The guys treated us to a meal and they were very good company. There were five of us altogether so a bit of a squash in the back seat. But we hardly stopped laughing all the way. It was the first time I had ever tasted Bourbon, it was a special American brand and very smooth to drink. The boys dropped us off at the canteen just in time to have a light meal before returning to the barracks and getting an early night before facing my exams the next day.

While in Portsmouth I met up with several Wrens and ratings I had known before, which was nice. In the days when I was in the Navy it was possible to have a platonic friendship. I met some real nice guys. I went out with a guy for a while, a bit older than myself, who had a very traumatic time during the war and then came home to find his wife with another man. I hope I managed to help him to cope with it by being a good listener. He got drafted and I never heard from him again.

Incredible Memories

There was a constant Fair down at Southsea, so on a warm evening me and whoever I was with used to walk down to it. Here I was introduced to mussels and winkles, quite an experience! Also cockles, by a Londoner, apparently a favourite with Eastenders. He was a 'Barra –boy' in 'civvy street'. He would park his barrow, with fruit, at a specific spot, usually near a Post Office and yell his wares. I met up with him one day, when on leave selling his goods near Wimbledon PO. He had a real Cockney accent, very clipped words and certain sayings in rhyme. Fascinating to listen to.

I passed my L/Wren exam and returned to HMS Mercury until August 10th 1949. Before I left to go to my next posting there was a new P/O in the Wren's galley. She had been in the Wrens all through the war and had been trained in the latest type of torpedoes. It was a little-known fact that some Wrens went to sea. She had been put on submarines with other Wrens. They plied the seas from UK to South Africa, up and down the West coast of Africa and the Atlantic Ocean chasing German and Italian ships. After the war she wanted to make the Navy her career, she became a Ship's cook. What a come down, but she was happy she could remain in the Navy.

The Chief Petty Officer in charge of stores had been going out with her, unbeknownst to any of us, until he proposed. She just announced one day that she was to be demobbed, so we had a tea night in the P.O's mess to wish her well. They all asked me to read their teacups, most of this I just did as a joke but some of the things used to come true! I read Dot's cup and said she was going to get married; one of the last things any of us thought would happen as she was getting on in years. She was over forty. She blushed madly and asked me how I knew. "I saw it in your cup," says I. It was then she told us that she was in fact going to get married, and to whom. We all nearly fell off our chairs. How could she have kept it such a secret for so long? One thing she did tell us was that when she was in Civvy Street she was going to have a fish and chips shop.

We also learnt that she and her betrothed had been taking quite a lot of stock ashore, like drums of oil and several bottles of sauces plus bottles of vinegar. All this to start her off on her new project, we never found out how they managed to get so much ashore without being caught! Both left the Navy and set up somewhere in Portsmouth.

I was quite friendly with the Chief PO in charge of the main galley. We both enjoyed doing crossword puzzles and used to do them together when we had a bit of a slack time, which wasn't often. My father had taught me how to do the crosswords so I was pleased when I found someone who was also interested in doing them. Some evenings I would go across to the PO's mess and do the puzzles as Chief always bought a daily paper. She was a very nice lady and had also been in the Navy all through the war, she never spoke of the war years. Chief was very popular with all the Wrens, always very fair and had a lovely sense of humour.

PROMOTION

Though my L/Wren was nice and I got on alright with her she tended to be a bit sarcastic. I recall one occasion when I asked her if she knew where the colander was, she lifted her arm and said, "well it ain't hanging on a curl under here."

Self, Chris and Dorothy, HMS Mercury

Self with two stewards, HMS Mercury

HMS Mercury Self with ship's cook, Dot Woodcock and stoker

Incredible Memories

PO Stewards outside main galley

Self, Chris and Elsie

Daniel and self

Self, Elsie and Dorothy

Chapter 14

H.M.S. GAMECOCK, BRAMCOTE

Not long after I passed my exam I was promoted to L/Wren and was told I was the youngest L/Wren in the Navy. There were enough L/Wrens at H.M.S. Mercury so I was drafted to H.M.S. Gamecock, at Bramcote, near Nuneaton. This was a Naval Air Station. I was sent on leave and then had to proceed to my new ship. It was sad leaving all my new friends but that was the way in the Navy. I arrived there in August 1949.

HMS Gamecock Naval Air Station, Bramcote Nr Nuneaton

I was met at the train station by a Liberty Boat, as they were called, but this time it was a bus. We arrived at the gates and had to get off and salute the Quarter deck, to the left of the Quarter deck was a building with the Officer of the watch and Quarter Master, I was told to go across the road to

Incredible Memories

the Administrative block to report to the Officer in charge of Wrens. After reporting I was driven up past the Parade ground on the left, on the right was a large building which was the main galley and men's mess. This galley catered for 1,000 Naval Airmen and ratings. Beyond this was a smaller building, the NAAFI, behind that a small building which was the Wrens' galley and mess deck which fed 108 Wrens and PO's.

The Quarters were quite different; the camp had been an Air Force Base before the Navy took it over. I was driven further up the road between some double-storey red brick buildings which housed the men. The last one on the right was the Wrens' Quarters. The Officers' Quarters were behind this. Some of the higher ranks had married quarters. If you continued around the corner was the Chief Petty Officers' and Petty Officers' Quarters, mess and galley. The Wrens non-commissioned Officers had cabins in the Wrens' block. Around another corner was another row of ratings' blocks.

Quarter deck and Admin block

As one entered the Wrens' Quarters there was a passage facing the door. To the left there was a large room with windows down both sides looking out onto well-kept lawns. There were comfortable armchairs with occasional coffee tables where the Wrens could relax and entertain friends, at certain times of the evening. We were only allowed to entertain guests in this room. On the ground floor, off the corridor, at each end were the Wrens' sleeping mess with double bunks for ratings and single bunks for L/Hands. There were 20 to each mess, and there was a mixture of categories in each mess. In between the messes was the ablution blocks, a small room with a bath at each end, in the middle wash basins and mirrors, on the other side of the corridor were the toilets. The stewards were on this floor. The 1st floor was

H.M.S. GAMECOCK, BRAMCOTE

a replica of the ground floor but where our lounge was situated was a laundry and cupboards with all the cleaning gear.

This accommodation was luxury compared to H.M.S. Mercury. The whole building was heated by radiators which the stokers kept going during the wintry months. The only disadvantage was the dining area was a fair walk as it was next to the Wrens' galley.

I was assigned to the main galley and was L/Wren of one of the watches. I didn't enjoy working an early morning watch during the cold weather as I had to walk quite a distance to the galley. Fortunately, we didn't have to light and stoke the fires; this was done by stokers and a couple of civilians. Quite often one of the stokers had a nice hot cup of tea waiting for us as well as a piece of toast.

The main galley, like my previous galley had a red tiled floor but coal was stored down some steps behind the very long ovens we worked with. There weren't steam chests but steam pipes which we lowered into large bins to cook whatever! So I had to learn how to use them. We even made custard using the steam pipes, but I soon got the hang of it. The galley was very bright with high ceilings which had sky light windows so we could open them in the summer if the galley got too hot. Off the galley was a large pantry where we could prepare the vegetables, store the trays of prepared food and also do the washing up. Next to this was a caboose which also acted as an office where the chief and leading wrens could make up the menus and orders for food. There was also a large clock on the far wall and a telephone. We all stowed our hats, gasmasks and coats in there too. There was a man, Chief Petty Officer in charge of the main galley, then we three L/Wrens. There were four ratings on each watch, wrens and men, and a Petty Officer in charge of the Wrens.

On my watch I had a little Welsh woman who was a kleptomaniac. Her gas mask was never in her case, she would fill the empty case with sugar, tea, tinned fruit or anything else she could lay her hands on. Though the door to the caboose was mainly kept closed and there was always someone around she still managed to stow these things without being noticed. So I had to check Taffy's bag before we knocked off, but somehow she always managed to get off with something.

The last watch of the day would open large cans of fruit and put them in trays and stack them on a bench in the caboose, if that was dessert for the next day. This is when we had to keep an eye on Taffy. We had to keep the door locked all the time unless there was someone working in there. The law finally caught up with Taffy. One leave she was caught with two train tickets, so she was given a dishonourable discharge. Three months later she was brought back, somehow she had managed to get a book of passes and was caught using one when the conductor on the train asked to see her pay book.

One day when roast lamb was on the menu, a Wren and I were taking the trays into the pantry. Each tray held four legs of mutton, each oven held twenty trays, so it was very heavy work. The girl in front of me slopped some fat out of one of the trays which I stepped on and slipped and fell. I went arse up spilling all the contents of my tray over myself.

The hot fat burnt the whole of my left hand, I fell sideways onto the handle of one of the huge containers, we soaked the veggies in, twisted my back and got the handle between two of my ribs. So I ended up in sick bay. It was fortunate the Sister in charge had nursed badly burnt airmen during the war. She wrapped my hand in Vaseline gauze and bandaged it up and left it for nine to ten days. When she took the bandage off, my hand smelt terrible but the hardened fat came off on the bandage and the new skin had grown under the bandage. It was still very tender and red and I was surprised the skin was not tight. She re-bandaged it with more Vaseline gauze. Then I had a dry bandage for a week to protect the hand from being damaged.

In the meantime, I was having infrared treatment on my back and rib area. My ribs had not been broken and I had torn muscles on the left side of my back. Both still very painful and I had difficulty sleeping at night. I had spent most days in the sick bay. The Doctor was an alcoholic and I found him a joke. If it had not been for the Sister, he would have sent me back on duty.

The end result was the MO (Medical Officer) sent me down to the Naval Hospital on Hayling Island. And was that an experience. I was examined by a doctor who asked me why I wanted to get out of the Navy. I told him I didn't want to, his reply to this was that he could find nothing wrong with my back and sent me to a psychologist. I felt completely helpless and wrote to my mother and told her what was going on. In the meantime, I was taken on a tour of the psychiatric ward and shown men in padded cells and others very heavily sedated and was asked if that was what I wanted to happen to me. This scared the hell out of me. Luckily my mother wrote to the MO and I was allowed home on leave. My mother took me to a clinic where my Godmother worked. They found I had a slipped disc beside the torn muscles. They manipulated my back and I didn't have any more of the severe pain.

The same MO at Gamecock sent another Wren to hospital. She came to me in tears and said the doctor, who had first examined me, had given her an internal examination suggesting she was pregnant and wanted out of the Navy. Poor girl didn't have any family to turn too, so I suggested she return to Gamecock and tell the 1st Officer Wren what had happened. The drunken MO was moved on. I returned to a month of light duties.

During my time at Gamecock on my days off I used to go into Nuneaton, the nearest town to us, with a couple of friends. We usually went in pay week as we got paid fortnightly. We'd have a meal before going to a film and then we'd go for a drink at a pub, close to where we had to catch the last Liberty Boat back to camp. On the Liberty Boat there were usually quite a few drunken guys, they'd get rotten drunk on pay day. One weekend,

H.M.S. GAMECOCK, BRAMCOTE

my uncle Anthony invited me and a friend to a play, Macbeth, that he was putting on in Nuneaton. I went with Fizz, a girl I worked with as she had said she enjoyed plays. My Uncle met us at the door and gave us our free tickets. After the play we went and had something to eat and a couple of drinks before returning to camp.

One weekend a friend and I decided to hitch hike to London, both of us were broke and it was blank week. We started off in the direction of the London road and were lucky enough to get a lift to the main road. After that no one stopped for us. We walked and walked and finally gave up when we got to a phone box and it was getting dark. We spent the night in the phone box, both propping each other up, and spent a very sleepless and uncomfortable night. At about 5am a cop car pulled up and asked us what the story was, when we told them they said they would give us a lift back to the Bramcote Road. So that was our weekend in London gone for a Burton!

Church parade, Ratings Quarters in the background

One afternoon when Fizz and I decided to go for a country walk we were walking along next to a field where they were harvesting some hay when this young bloke called out to us and asked if we'd like to make a few bob. We jumped at the offer, he showed me how to drive the tractor and Fizz helped stook the hay. It was great fun and we arranged to do it again the next time we were on middle watch. At least it meant we had extra cash for the blank weekend so we could go somewhere.

One week end we went with our friend Chris to stay with her mother in Birmingham. Her mother had one huge room, part of a very big house that had been split up and let out as flats. Everyone on each floor shared a bathroom and toilet. In the corner of the room was a cabinet with an electric cooker and a toaster, beside that was a basin, with hot and cold water. There were five single beds, three in a row and two others against a wall, which were used to sit on during the day while we ate or played cards. So many people lived like this in the cities as there was such a shortage of houses after the war. It was a fun weekend as we were made so welcome. We managed to take some rations over with us to help out.

At one stage I went out with one of the pilots, a ginger headed guy, he just lived for flying. Then one day for some reason his plane took a nosedive straight into the runway, it left a huge crater, and Jim never had a chance.

One of the girls in my mess was a telephone operator, sometimes I would go down with her when she was on night duty. She would be on her own as it was not very busy at night so we used to play a board game or cards or just talk. She taught me how to operate the board so I used to answer the calls and put people through to whatever number they wanted. Some evenings I used to baby sit for one of the officers. I would go over for dinner and then they would go into town to a show or to visit friends, for this I was given five shillings for every two times I baby sat.

H.M.S. GAMECOCK, BRAMCOTE

Dot and Fizz on motorbike

Fizz and self

Self, HMS Gamecock

Chapter 15

JOCK, TOM IN MY LIFE

Another day when I was wandering around the galley, checking on the various jobs that had to be done on my watch, I looked across the galley and saw a handsome young man standing in the doorway of the caboose. He looked across and smiled at me. It was like an electric shock went through me. I asked Fizz if she knew who he was, she said he was called Jock.

That evening there was a film being shown on board. Fizz and I went and just before the film started a voice said, "May I sit with you girls." To my utter surprise it was Jock. He plonked himself down beside Fizz and seemed interested in her. After the film he offered to walk us back to the Wren's block. He walked between the two of us. We said our goodnights but I couldn't get him out of my mind. I had noticed what lovely blue, grey eyes he had, always with an amused look in them. The next day he came into the galley again, one of his jobs was to go around synchronizing all the clocks on board. He came over to see what I was doing, then asked if I was going to the dance on Friday night.

We danced together nearly all night, and he walked me back to the Wrens' quarters. Jock and I went ashore a couple of times and we got to know each other a bit better. Because he was a Boson, one of his jobs was to wake the cooks on early morning watch. He appeared one morning much to my surprise, with a cup of tea. Another time when I was on early morning watch, Tom came in, woke me up and gave me my cup of tea but also gave me a kiss. Unfortunately, Fizz saw this and I got ribbed about it.

We had been going out for a couple of months when he got drafted to a frigate up in Scotland. We wrote to each other and then arranged to meet in Carlisle when we could have a long weekend together. I got in touch with the Council and was sent names of Bed & Breakfast accommodation. I booked two rooms at one of them. We met there and had a great weekend together. Jock, whose real name was Tom, even came to Church with me on the Sunday, though he was not a Catholic. I had to explain the Mass to him, but I really appreciated that he had accompanied me.

Tom (centre) outside WREN's galley, HMS Gamecock

During the weekend he asked if I would like to visit his family on our next leave. It was then he told me that he had spoken to his mother and said, "the girl I bring home is the one I want to marry." He also said I was from the West Indies; his mother thought Tom was bringing a black lady home. I was very embarrassed when I heard that, and as Tom had never mentioned marriage that was also a new one on me. I had thought nothing about visiting his family as several of my men friends had come home to my mother's and I had visited their families but there was no mention of a lasting relationship. I must say I was very fond of Tom and wondered if our relationship would go further.

After that leave we both decided we wanted to go steady, a bit difficult when we were so far apart. We kept up writing to each other, he wrote every day.

Just before Tom was drafted, I was transferred to the Wrens' galley, I was put in charge. As we were only cooking for 108 ratings there were only two on each watch. I was very fortunate to have some really nice girls working with me; we used to have great fun. I had to do all the menus and ordering of food. I was allowed one shilling and a farthing per day to feed each man or Wren. As the ratings were not always eating on board, I found

Incredible Memories

certain things accumulated in the storeroom and so I would order less the following month. After a few months the Commander sent for me and asked if I was starving everyone, so I explained. He decided it was time I applied for my Petty Officer's Rating.

When going through the haricot beans one day I found a sunflower seed and planted it on some soil at the back door of the galley, it grew. Before long it was taller than me and produced a huge flower, I was very proud of it.

Sunflower I grew outside Wren's Galley

While I was stationed at H.M.S. Gamecock. I visited my Uncle Anthony and Aunt Mary at their home in Kenilworth. Their home was just below a castle, I used to love going over there for a weekend. The only ones of the family home at the time were the two youngest, the others were all at boarding school. There were no spare beds when they were all home. My Uncle and Aunt were a lovely couple and I got on very well with them, especially Aunt Mary. She told me how she and Uncle Anthony met during the war and how hard it was to be separated but they both agreed that they were free to go out with others during their separation. They both trusted the other to stay true to one another and were certainly very fond of each other. I could see they were still very much in love. At that time, they had five children; I think they ended up having eight.

While I was in charge of the Wrens' galley, I caught one of the stewards taking food, tea and sugar out of the storeroom. I taxed her about it and she became very violent and threatened me with an egg slice. Her language was not the best either, so I put her on a charge. It was a very unpleasant week after she was told she had special duties and was not allowed ashore for a couple of weeks. I had all sorts of threats from her and her boyfriend, so I took her into the storeroom and had a good talk with her. We became quite good friends after that.

This same woman and another steward, Mary a Scottish girl, went ashore a few times. Though Ellen was several years older than me she would come and ask my advice about certain things. She had met a Dutch man and was going out with him. He asked her to marry him and go and live in Holland, so she wanted to know what I thought of it. My answer was that she would have to decide for herself. She ended up in Holland and I never heard from her again.

Tom, self and Tom's mother

Chapter 16

I MEET TOM'S FAMILY

On my next leave I met Tom in Glasgow and we travelled up to Inverness together. I was not sure what my reception would be, Tom assured me all would be well. Mrs. Aitken was a large lady; she was very reserved for the first few days I was there. Gradually she relaxed, and so did I. We experienced beautiful summer weather. Often Mrs. Aitken and I would sit on a bench in the back garden getting to know each other.

I shared a room with Tom's two youngest sisters, Sal and Rose. I wasn't quite sure where Tom slept. His mother had a room next to the girls' room, next to that was a smaller room, so he may have slept there. I think it was his brother Ted's room. Ted was away up North working as a carpenter, as was his older brother Andrew. Andrew's bedroom was downstairs just to the right of the front door. Both came home for the weekend during my visit, both carrying heavy wooden boxes with their carpentry tools.

Andrew was tall, he had piercing blue eyes, was a terrible tease, so I didn't quite know when to believe him. Ted was shorter, more Tom's height, about five foot eight. He could have passed for Tom's twin, though he was fair and Tom had dark wavy hair. His mother said Tom was the spit of his father who also had wavy hair and was dark.

Sal was about eighteen, she worked at the swimming baths in town. Rose was turning seventeen; I don't recall where she worked. She would come home from work, eat her tea, usually eating her sweets first. I thought this strange but she said she liked it best when the custard was still warm. Then she would have a wash, change and go out, so I hardly got to know her. Sal was a cheerful, fun sort of person. At the time she was going out with a young fellow in a wheelchair. He had been crippled with Polio around the age of thirteen. The two of them were childhood sweethearts. Sandy was a lovely young fellow; Sal had been pushing him around since they were at school together. She and Sandy eventually married and had two handsome little boys. While I was visiting, I met another older sister, Babs, her husband

I MEET TOM'S FAMILY

Arthur and their four young children. They lived down in the cul-de-sac beyond the Aitken household. Babs was expecting her fifth child at that time.

Tom with Sal and Rose, David, Paul, Derrick and John

Tom took me around all his old haunts. I must have walked miles that leave. One day we took a bus out to a town named Beauly, where he introduced me to some great friends of his, the Cormacks. It seemed everyone we visited would produce a great spread, we usually were there for their evening meal, which they called 'High tea.'

In the Aitken household the lads ate first, in the kitchen dining area. The lassies ate in the sitting room. The bathroom was used to have a wash but to bathe, all would go into town to the Public Baths. I would arrange with Sal to go during a time when she was working. She always had a nice warm bath ready when I got there. Next to the baths, in the same building, was a very large swimming pool, always fully occupied. I remember it being steamy and smelt strongly of chemicals.

I had been made very welcome by all and I felt very at home so I decided to meet Tom the next leave and go North. This time I only stayed a week as my father was coming over from the West Indies. That was a memorable leave as Tom managed to slam the train door on my thumb. I spent a very painful journey down to London. Though I managed to sleep I must have been moaning and a very kind gentleman had wet his handkerchief with cold water and wrapped it around my thumb. It was very swollen when I arrived in Wimbledon.

Incredible Memories

Tom's sisters, Sal and Rose with Ma   *Andrew, Tom's eldest brother*

Babs, another of Tom's sisters

Chapter 17

FURTHER PROMOTION

Tom and I wrote regularly to each other. He was on a course in Boom Defense. In between leaves I was sent down to Portsmouth to do a Petty Officer's course. I was stationed at a base a few miles outside of Portsmouth and would travel to and fro by bus. We were issued with a special bus pass which allowed the other Wrens and myself who were on the course, to travel from the Naval Dockyards to Eastney. I was amazed at the amount of bicycles that used to come out of the dockyards and surrounding factories while on the way to the barracks. Simply hundreds of men and women in their work clothes all in a hurry to get home. The bus would have to stop while they all poured across the road. Some days we were lucky to reach that point in the journey before the whistle blew for the end of the day.

The course was being held in a galley in one of the big, red brick buildings in the Dockyard. There were twenty of us from various ships, and the course was of a very high standard, equal to London City and Guild. The Chief Petty Officer who ran the course was very strict, though fair. We did practical in the morning, preparing a meal for lunch. Then had lectures in the afternoon.

The dishes were very fancy. For instance, creamed potatoes were served in silver, oval platters with piping around the edges done with the creamed potato squeezed through a piping bag, in little dollops, then brushed with a little melted butter and popped into the oven to keep hot.

One day the Officers were entertaining some dignitary and we had to prepare the meal. We started off with Hor d'oeuvres, Consommé, a fish dish followed by the main meat and veggies. All this was followed by individual trifles served in glass dishes. As if this wasn't enough, they had a cheese platter and coffee. The last prepared by the Officer's stewards.

We had to leave the galley and all the utensils we used, absolutely spotless, as we did when I went on the L/Wrens course. I must say we ate very well as we ate whatever we prepared. One of the questions in the test at the end was, "What would you require to set up an emergency kitchen to cook for one hundred ratings?" This out in a field as presumably the galley had been destroyed during enemy attack. At the end of a month I passed with flying colours and was sent on leave before returning to HMS Gamecock.

On my return I was sent to work in the Chief and Petty Officers' galley. The building was just around the corner from the Wren's quarters, so I didn't have so far to go. The galley was about the same size as the Wren's galley but better equipped and we had our own sitting room with comfortable arm \chairs where we could relax and eat or just read when we got a break.

The PO in charge was having an affair with the Chief PO from the main galley. She would disappear for an hour in the afternoon watch. It was a quiet time in the building as all the CPOs and POs were all doing their various duties in other parts of the ship.

In those days I smoked and found it difficult to afford the habit, so I found a non-smoking rating and asked him to draw his ration of tobacco. They paid seven and six pence for a tin of cigarette or pipe tobacco which was a month's supply. So all I had to buy were the cigarette papers and I bought a special gadget to make the rollies, as we called them. One month I got the guy to draw some pipe tobacco, as a few of us smoked pipes when we were in our quarters. That was a lot cheaper. The pipe tobacco lasted more than a month, whereas the other only lasted a month.

One occasion I recall while at Gamecock and working in the main galley, was a Christmas I spent on board, and we made a Christmas cake in one of the huge metal containers. We put all the ingredients in and stirred it with a couple of scrubbed oars. The Captain, his wife and the Commander came to pour in a large quantity of rum and each had a stir. We were all given a tot of rum to celebrate the occasion, it was a very good drop, nothing but the best for the Navy and its long-standing tradition.

We then put the mixture into trays and cooked the cake to perfection, one of the nicest Christmas cakes I've tasted. On Christmas day the mess was decorated. We cooked turkey, ham, brussel sprouts and baked potatoes with brown gravy, Christmas pudding which we had made a month previously, with brandy sauce. After that, a slice of Christmas cake. The single junior officers joined in the fun. Those of us who stayed on board for Christmas had leave in the New Year.

FURTHER PROMOTION

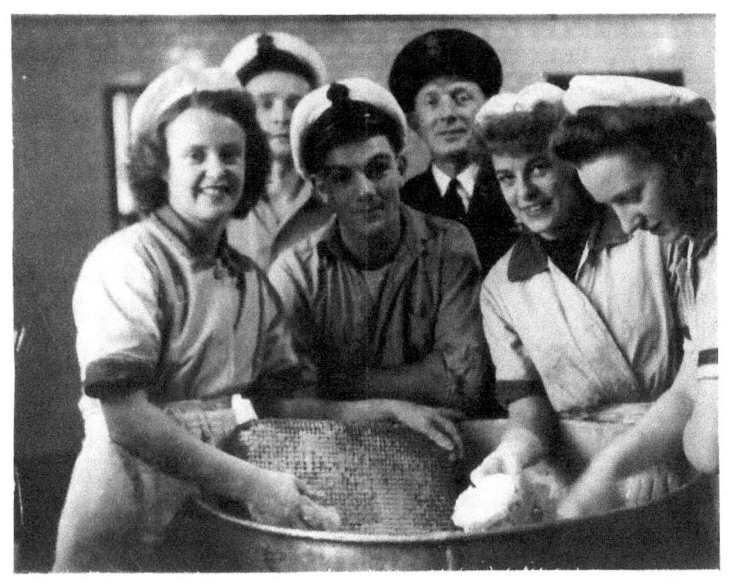

Grating suet into Christmas pudding

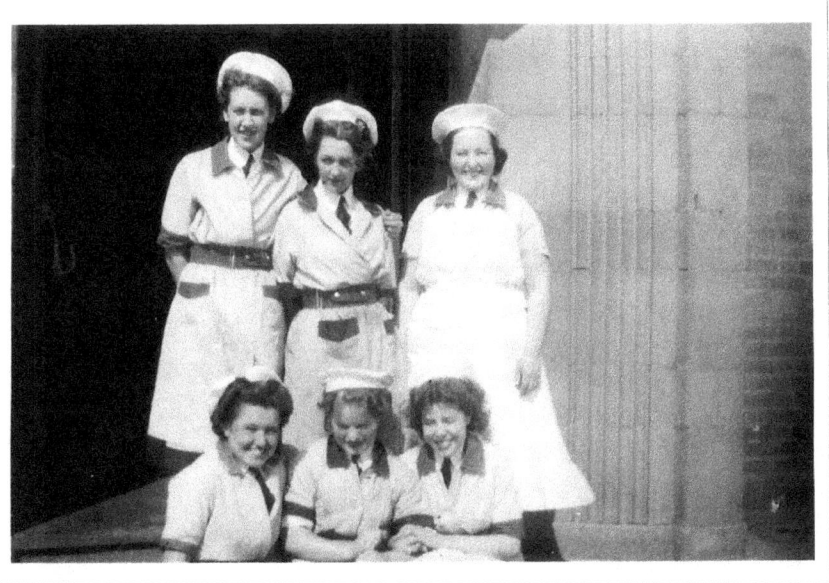

Our watch, Main Galley, HMS Gamecock

Incredible Memories

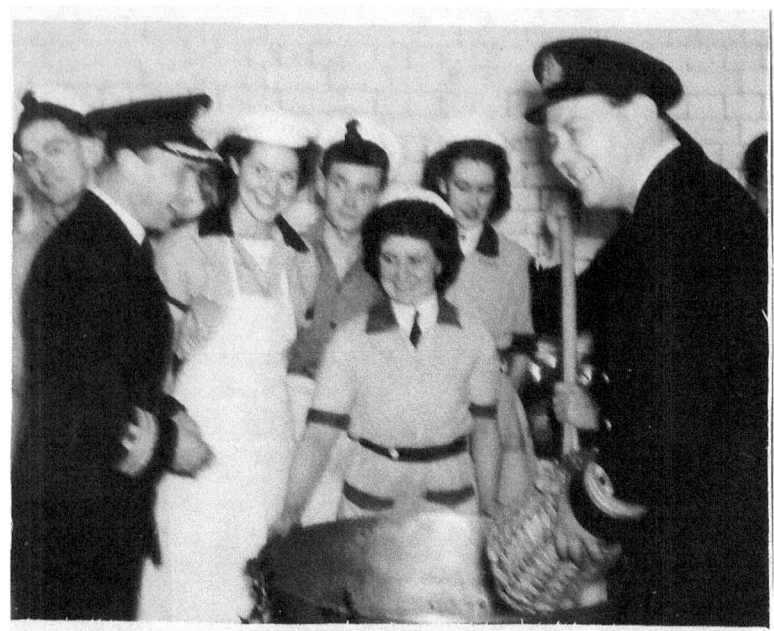

Pouring rum into Christmas pudding

Crew from WRENs galley, HMS Gamecock

Chapter 18

TOM AND I BECOME ENGAGED

Tom and I had leave at the same time. He came down to Bramcote, HMS Gamecock and we travelled to Wimbledon together. It was his turn to meet my mother and family.

For some reason my mother took an instant dislike to Tom and let it be shown in no uncertain manner. I was both ashamed and embarrassed. Tom felt very uncomfortable. We were to become engaged that leave. Tom wanted to break it off. But I said he was marrying me, not my mother. We spent most of the time away from the house. One day we went up to London to buy the ring. I spotted a sweet ring with two small sapphires with small diamonds on either side in a band of gold. It was in a Pawn shop, so was quite a bit cheaper than a brand new one. Of all the rings I had seen, I liked this one the best.

I took Tom to meet a couple of friends of the family, the Millens, they liked Tom and made him feel more welcome. I asked their opinion about our relationship; they gave us their blessing and offered us their lasting friendship. While on this leave, we visited places like Hampton Court Palace, the Tower of London, and Buckingham Palace. On the visit to the Tower there was a man outside the gates singing 'Pennies from Heaven', those were the only words he sang while the crowd that gathered tossed pennies into the air which landed all around him. Some young men were making fun of him. He ignored them and scrambled around picking up the pennies. He made a mint in the short space of time we spent watching him. A very easy way of making a living if one had the courage to do what he was doing.

At Hampton court we fed the deer and wandered the very green grounds. We also visited the part of the Palace that was supposed to be haunted, the indoor tennis court and saw the hundred-year old grape vine. We took several walks up on Wimbledon Common. One night we went to a very nice pub in upper Wimbledon to have a quiet drink, when a couple asked us to join them in a game of darts. We joined them several nights later, they were a very friendly couple, quite a bit older than us but very good company.

It was a sad leave but we also had some happy experiences. Then it was time to part again and return to our respective ships.

Tom in Civvies 1951

Chapter 19

COURSES BEFORE DEMOB

Before I was demobbed, I was offered one of several courses. I chose Auto Mechanics. The course was to last a month, but I completed it in three weeks, so was offered another. I chose Domestic Electricity.

During the mechanics course I had to strip down the engine of a Vauxhall, then put it all back together, making sure it worked. The Chief Petty Officer who took the course was very thorough. He had been semi-retired as he had been badly wounded during the war.

As I took the engine apart, I had to draw detailed diagrams of the engine parts and describe their function and how they worked in conjunction with other parts of the car. I had to change a tyre, mend a puncture, and return the wheels to the vehicle. I also had to replace brake discs, bleed the system and check all leads.

The other part was drawing a diagram of the electrical system. In those days the indicator consisted of a lit up, small arm, lifting out between the front and back doors. It had an orange light and there was one on each side of the car, to indicate which way one was turning. The wiring was not as complicated as today.

Chief took the group out in a small truck to teach us how to drive. He first drove us out east of Portsmouth, up a hill, turned it around and said," OK Johnnie you're first to drive," I got into the driver's seat and had a small panic attack when I saw how steep the hill was. Going there I had been sitting in the back of the enclosed truck so hadn't been able to see much of the scenery!

Luckily the drop off the road was on the right side and being a left-hand drive, I was hugging the side of the hill.

The advice I remember the most was Chief saying, "Don't speed, it is better to be five minutes late and arrive alive."

I passed the course with flying colours.

Incredible Memories

The next course being Domestic Electricity was taken by another semi-retired Chief, he was blinded in one eye. I had to wire an entire two-storey house from the meter box. In the lounge was a three-way lighting system. On the stairs there was a switch that turned the light on at the bottom and an off switch when you got to the top. It also worked vicki verky. We were also taught how to renew elements in electric irons, kettles and anything that had an element. For instance, toasters, electric fires and electric cooking pots also had elements.

When I had re-wired the whole house and passed the element's part, I had to wire a caravan, to be run from a generator but so it could also revert to mains electricity. All the work had to be drawn in detail using all the electrical names and points, and why certain plugs or connections were used. I got 95% out of a 100% at the end of both courses.

I found both courses very useful when in civvy street as I was able to do repair jobs which saved dollars in expenses, or pounds depending on where I was living at the time.

Prior to my demob, January 1951

Chapter 20

WE MOVE ON

I was to be demobbed in February. In those days we were not allowed to remain in the forces if one got married. Tom had completed his 'Boom Defense' course and was to be stationed in Portsmouth. As I was a Portsmouth rating, I had to go down to Portsmouth to be demobbed. We looked around for a flat and found one in Southsea. We were lucky it was the winter months, as in the summer landladies would put tenants out of the flats so they could ask a higher rent from tourists. Portsmouth and Southsea were summer resorts.

The nouveau riche in the UK bought large houses and turned them into flats. Some of them were let out at reasonable rents, others were determined to become wealthier. The one we chose was owned by a rather weird, elderly couple. We had two large rooms, one on the ground floor which was our living and kitchen area and the bedroom on the first floor. They provided Tom with a single bed in the living area until we got married. We shared a bathroom, also on the first floor. The hot water was an instant gas heater over the back of the bath, it was very old and blew up the first time Tom lit it. It ended up in the bath. Luckily, they were insured and a new one replaced the ancient one.

The rooms were fully furnished, though mostly old stuff. There was an open fire in the living room and the landlord supplied the coal. The hallway was very dingy and unlit. Nearly every time one of us went to get fuel the landlady was creeping around. She had a sinister grin on her face and struck me she was 'two bob short of a quid.' Her husband was out all day, so we presumed he was working, though he seemed pretty old. There was an eighteen-year old daughter, who also seemed a bit short of a quid, who tried to befriend us. Whenever we opened our door she would have a quick sneak look inside. We guessed she and her mother spent their time eaves dropping.

Incredible Memories

As neither door locked, we did not leave anything of value lying around and we would set little traps to see if they were going into our rooms when we were out. Not the most pleasant way to live.

In the meantime, Tom was having religious instruction with the Naval Chaplain, as I was Catholic and Tom a Protestant. In those days a mixed marriage was frowned upon and one had to get a dispensation. Incidentally the Chaplain announced he had a letter from my mother asking him to prevent the marriage. He said he could find no reason to do this. I later learnt my mother had sent a very hurtful letter to Mrs. Aitken, which, thank goodness, she ignored but kept and I saw it many years later.

I went to see the priest at St. Swithans, at the Catholic church in Waverly Road, and arranged a marriage ceremony. Tom met the priest who tested him on what Instructions he had been given by the Naval Chaplain. The date of our marriage was to be the 28th of March 1951.

I had kept in touch with several of my Naval friends who were now married and living in and out of Portsmouth. Before I left HMS Gamecock I had baked a huge very rich fruit cake for our wedding. It was still in the specially made tin I had baked it in and it had a tight lid, so was still very edible a year later.

When I was demobbed I had to hand in my uniform, I was paid a fortnight's pay, given civilian cloths coupons, a train ticket and was shown the gate.

Our wedding day, March 28th, 1951

With our two witnesses

Chapter 21

THE START OF MARRIED LIFE

None of Tom's or my relatives attended our wedding. We had two friends as witnesses, then we went back to their place for a cup of tea and a piece of cake, which another friend had made. She was an ex Wren and her husband, a rating we both knew, were the only others present. After that Tom and I walked down to the lake at the end of Herbert Street, where we lived. We hired a rowing boat and bought two ice-creams with our last half crown. We rowed around for an hour and that was our 'Honeymoon.'

We had to wait for Tom's next pay-day but I had enough food to see us through. Tom had most of his meals on board. In those days, food was still rationed. I was allowed two chops a week, I could not get rations for Tom. He sometimes managed to get his rations ashore, plus a bit extra, which helped. He said he didn't like meat anyway as the Navy didn't cook it like his Mum, so I didn't have to share my small portions. That is until he tasted some meat I cooked and he couldn't resist a taste because it smelt so good!

About a month after we were married, I had a miscarriage and was very upset as I desperately wanted a baby. It wasn't long before I was pregnant again. I used to write to my mother regularly but she never answered. Occasionally I had a card or letter from my sister Teresa. She came down and spent a weekend with us and we took her over to The Isle of White for a day. It was a beautiful day, warm enough to go for a swim and to sun bake. The beach was sandy, not pebbles like at Southsea, and the water was not as cold. We enjoyed Teresa's visit and managed to catch up on family news. After her return home, when she told my mother that I was pregnant, I started to receive mail from my mother. This baby was to be my mother's first Grandchild.

The Boom Defense which Tom had been trained in, was an anti-submarine device stretched across the entrance to the Solent, at the Spithead. The Solent being the gateway to Southampton and Portsmouth Harbour. In

THE START OF MARRIED LIFE

those days there was still the uncertainty that we may have a war with the USSR. They and the Allies were competing with nuclear arms and power. The days of the Iron Curtain, as it was called, and the Berlin Wall. Both sides busy spying on each other. There was a lot of fear, Britain had gone through a lot of suffering and loss. It had barely rebuilt towns and cities devastated by the ruthless bombing of the Germans.

We settled as best as we could in our small flat. I got a job at a Guest House at the end of Herbert Street. The lady who ran it had bought two houses next to each other. As they were identical, she had each floor in both houses opened up so one could walk through from one to the other. All the bedrooms were on the first floor. By knocking down walls, she had converted a large dining area opposite a lounge. The dining room was set up with tables to seat six, four or two people. The lounge was comfortable with armchairs, coffee tables and a couple of tables where one could play cards, dominoes or board games. This room was well used in the evenings. The guests could make themselves a cuppa before retiring to bed. The daily paper was there to be read with a variety of magazines.

My duties were to help with breakfast. I would walk along as far as the church with Tom when he was going on duty, go to early Mass, have a quick breakfast and report to the Guest house. Breakfast was served from eight to nine each morning. I'd clear the tables and then go upstairs to make beds, empty 'potties' and clean the rooms and bathrooms. The worst job was emptying the china potties which were under each bed. This saved the clients from having to go down the passage to the bathroom during the night.

The worst experience was finding a used 'French Letter' under a pillow, when making a bed. I was nearly sick, I told my boss and she printed up a notice which I put on the back of each door, asking the guests be more considerate of staff.

I had to help in the kitchen and serve at the tables. Having been a cook in the Navy stood me in good stead. While there I learnt how to make individual Yorkshire puddings, the lady used beer in her mixture, which made very light and tasty puddings.

That winter I was troubled by chilblains on my toes. I first experienced them when I was working in the Wren's galley, it was from standing on the cold concrete floor. My circulation from the constant standing meant my feet would get very cold, then I'd warm them up in front of the fire, get into a hot bath when off duty, or stick them up against a radiator. They are a very unpleasant ailment to experience. Your toes itch like hell at times but if you rub them, they are very painful, red, swollen and sometimes the skin breaks, that's when you're in trouble.

Tom and I were invited up to Wimbledon for Christmas. Tom managed to get leave over Christmas so we went up for a week. The wounds were healed, my mother never really apologized, but she was quite surprised how handy Tom was about the house. He was always very considerate and she could see how much in love we were. He accompanied me to church, it was the first time he had ever been to midnight Mass, this pleased my family no end. My mother was worried that Tom would get drafted abroad before the baby arrived but he told her that they had been told that the job in Portsmouth was to be no less than two years.

By this time I was quite heavy with child, being due the end of March. I worked at the Guest House until the end of February. I had saved a few pounds for a rainy day which I had put in an account for when the baby arrived. I had been told how expensive it was to raise an infant. As fortune would have it, my Spanish aunt had recently had a baby and handed on several items like a baby bath and cover, and a pram which her boy had grown out of. She also gave me a carry cot, which was exactly that. It was a blue plastic cot with handles on both sides, a thin mattress and small pillow, several small sheets to go with it. I knitted matinee jackets, booties, and hand sewed little nighties, as I did not possess a sewing machine. I embroidered several place mats, so I kept myself quite busy and the time before the baby arrived went very quickly.

While stationed at HMS Gamecock, one of my friends, Chris, had taught me how to knit and I had knitted Tom a sleeveless pullover, it was maroon, done in a cable stitch pattern. I found it very challenging but as all my mess mates seemed to know how to knit, I was always helped out if I made a mistake. I was glad I had learned as I could see I was going to be doing a lot of knitting. Babies soon grow out of their garments. Plus it was much cheaper to make Tom or myself jumpers or cardigans and one could nearly always buy wool. At times I bought a knitted garment from a second-hand shop, washed it and took it to pieces and re-knitted it into whatever.

I met a very nice French lady, four doors down from where we were living. She invited me to visit her and we became quite friendly. She was a beautiful seamstress and did a lot of church work. It was the first time I had ever seen anyone work with silver and gold threads. So she did a lot of mending for the priest, in the way of worn out alter clothes and all the gear they wore for different ceremonies. She also served at Mass early in the morning.

I confided in her and told her I was not very happy with our living arrangements. One day she told me that the lady next door to her had a couple of rooms to let. Though the rooms were up at the top of the house, at least both rooms were on the same level. The whole house was a lot cleaner and our rooms would be much lighter. In the living room there was a huge bay window, the bedroom looked out onto the back garden. They were fairly large attic rooms converted. We still had to share the bathroom, which was on the floor below. The one she and her husband lived on.

The landlady and her husband were probably in their forties. A very quiet couple, she was thrilled to know there was a baby on the way. Her very strange mother lived on the ground floor and looked to be Anglo-Indian.

THE START OF MARRIED LIFE

We had three flights of stairs to reach our abode. Our bedroom consisted of a comfortable double bed, a large chest of drawers, a basin with hot and cold water, and a curtained off alcove the depth of our landing, where we could hang clothes and store things. Our living room had two large armchairs around a gas fire, which we had to feed shillings into a meter box, to get gas. Against one wall there was a roller-top desk which smelt very strongly of sandalwood. There was a small table and two chairs and in one corner a sink, a stove, and a food cupboard, the top of which I could use as a workbench. Certainly more comfortable than the other flat.

I kept up with a couple of Wren friends who were also married. On my days off we would meet up for a cuppa and a bit of a chin wag, in one or other's flats. Pat Smith already had a baby, a gorgeous little boy with red hair. Pat and the wife of a First Officer, who I also got to know, passed on some baby clothes. They also gave me some information and recommended the Nursing Home down the road, near the paddling pool and park.

Chapter 22

OUR FIRST CHILD

When I gave up work, I had more time to visit my friends I heard regularly from my family, my mother had made me some lovely maternity smocks and skirts. She also sent me down two dozen terry towelling nappies and a dozen muslin ones. Teresa, my sister, sent me a bed jacket to wear in the nursing home.

I had a wonderful pregnancy. No morning sickness and was able and fit enough to work. In the evenings I wrote letters did some embroidery, knitted for the expected and also made two marquetry pictures.

There were nights when Tom was on duty but he was mainly at home. On a Friday or a Saturday night, depending whether Tom was on duty we went down to the local pub and met up with a few locals. Had a couple of drinks, I mainly had lemonade but occasionally a glass of stout if the evening was cool. Sometimes one of Tom's mates would join us for our quiet evening of chit chat.

All good company and we always had a good laugh. My new landlady Mrs Roe was very kind, she never intruded. At times she would call up to me but by the time I got to the door she was gone and there was a cooked dish of some sort on the steps. Sometimes it was a pasta cheese dish another time it would be an apple pie or a fruit crumble with a bowl of custard. Quite frequently a cut flower lay beside the dish she thoroughly spoilt us.

During her young married life while living in India she lost her only child while riding on the back of her husband's motorbike. They had an accident and she miscarried. She never became pregnant again though she loved children.

They were a very quiet and considerate couple, probably in their forties. Her mother lived on the ground floor and professed to be a fortune teller. One night she held a séance in her daughter's lounge. The sounds that rose to our flat were very eerie and sounded rather strange. Fortunately, this did not happen too often.

OUR FIRST CHILD

The Christmas of 1951 my mother invited us up to Wimbledon, where she lived to celebrate the festive season with the family. It was a custom in the family from when I was a child that we would always invite a friend who was on their own.

This year she invited a rather eccentric man friend of my brother David. He used to write strange poetry and announced in the middle of lunch he found that he wrote the best poetry while sitting on the toilet. My mother looked a bit put out as there were certain subjects, we learnt, that were never broached at the table during a meal.

We had all been to midnight mass on Christmas Eve so did not feel like getting up early. My mother had made the Christmas pudding a month prior. The turkey which was not easy to buy had been dressed, stuffed and in the larder ready to pop into the oven. Potatoes had been peeled and put into water over night. Beans had been rinsed from the salt they had been preserved in. So all was virtually ready to go. Tom had managed to get a small bottle of brandy for the brandy sauce, to accompany the pudding. There were silver thripennys (three pence) and sixpenny bits boiled in the pudding. Always a cause for excitement from the younger members of the family when they discovered one or other in their slice of the pudding. Some not really interested in the actual pudding but expectant in finding a hidden coin.

Tom and I returned to Portsmouth on Boxing Day to miss the mad rush of returning travellers. It was a relief to find that Tom was more welcome on this visit.

I was fairly large with child who preferred to be very active at night. She still is nocturnal. The last couple of months she became extremely active. Our armchairs had arms that were low and one night the whole of my stomach literally moved over to the right and practically landed on the arm of the chair. I prodded and cajoled but there was no way it was going to return to the normal position. I presumed the baby was in the process of turning itself but chose to do it in slow motion. A rather uncomfortable position but all of a sudden with a lurch I was back to normal.

The 25th of March arrived and I started labour about 5am. Tom had to go on duty so we both got up and dressed. I already had my famous little white suitcase ready packed with things I had to take to the nursing home. It was nearly opposite the guest house I had worked in so we walked up the road and rang the doorbell and I was admitted after kissing Tom goodbye. He went off to his ship and I was formally admitted, examined and put into a labour ward. I had read Doctor Ried's book "Natural Childbirth" so knew what my body was doing and reacted as suggested.

I practiced my relaxation exercises and slept in between contractions. About 9am a lady came in with a bucket of water and a scrubbing brush, got down on her knees and started to clean the floor. There was a clock opposite where I lay so I was to monitor the times between contractions.

Incredible Memories

At about 9.15am I said to the cleaning lady that I think that she should call the Matron as I was about to have the baby. Her reply was "Is this your first deary? Well you probably won't have it until about 4pm at least."

I pleaded with her to ring the bell. When the Matron took a look, the cleaning lady had to take herself and her cleaning gear out of the room and a nurse was called.

Anne Bernadette arrived at 10.20am. She was given to me to hold while the cord was cut and necessary things done before being whisked away to be cleaned up. She was returned to me and lay on my stomach while we were wheeled into a ward with three other beds. Two were occupied and had already had their babies. Anne was put into a cot at the end of my bed and I fell asleep. But it didn't seem very long before I was woken for lunch which I devoured as I was very hungry

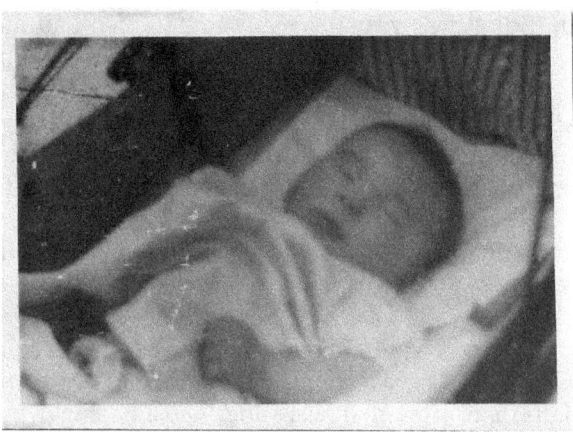

Anne Bernadette 16 weeks old, Wimbledon

By this time the occupant of the fourth bed was in labour and let all the neighbourhood know about it. I was glad I hadn't had to listen to that performance before I went into labour. This was her fourth child, but her labour was much longer than mine. I presumed it was because she didn't know how to relax.

I was given Anne to put to my breast to bring the milk in. What suction for one so small, her gums felt as if she had a mouth full of teeth. She had weighed in at 7 and ¾ pounds and looked like a beautiful little china doll. She slept well through the day but come 7.30 in the evening she thought it was play time. At night she was taken with all the other babies to a nursery where she was fed by bottle with some of my expressed milk. This gave me a good night's sleep.

Tom had been phoned to tell him he had a bouncy baby daughter. He arrived about 4pm much the worse for wear as all his mates had toasted him with a share of their grog.

OUR FIRST CHILD

The Matron and nurse thought this quite funny while he joked with them. I was not very impressed as he hardly noticed Anne or me. I remained in the nursing home for nine days while I was shown how to fold nappies and put them on correctly, I was shown how to bath a baby but because I had younger siblings all my experiences returned.

Tom called a taxi for my return home. My landlady was in tears of joy on our arrival. She had cooked our evening meal and had a wee present for Anne. A beautiful embroidered sheet and small pillow slip and a bottle of 4711 eau de cologne for me plus some red roses, so sweet of her.

Then started the process of changing nappies, feeding every four hours. One forgets how many pooey nappies an infant can fill. At times having to change vest and night dress as well. I then found if I wrapped a muslin nappy around Anne over the towelling nappy it saved a bit of mess.

I was only home a couple of days when Tom announced he was to be sent abroad. That was quite a shock as we had banked on him being in Portsmouth another year. But being married to a service man one just had to expect the unexpected. He didn't know when it would be so we arranged to have Anne christened so he could be present. We asked Jim Millen a family friend to be Godfather and my sister Pat as Godmother. Ted, Tom's brother was doing National Service in the RAF and he came and visited us one weekend and my mother and sister Christine came down as well.

Tom was with us for nine weeks so he had time to bond with Anne. I found him very good at changing nappies. Anne was a good baby but was still nocturnal and used to demand attention between 7 and 9 pm every evening.

By the time Tom left for the Mediterranean, Anne at nine weeks was sleeping from her 10pm feed until 5am which was good as it meant we got a good night's sleep. I used to go for a walk in the mornings with Anne in a pram given to me by my Aunt Mabel. I would do a bit of shopping and sometimes visited the French lady. People were all so friendly always wanting to have a glimpse at my baby.

Not many weeks after Tom left my landlady's mother objected to my leaving the pram in the front hallway. So I used to haul it up the three flights of stairs. I found it too much of a strain so my landlady said I could leave it in the coal shed. This was awkward too as sometimes the back gate was bolted which meant I had to go up and through her kitchen and down the back stairs to unbolt the gate. Her mother made it quite clear we were not welcome. This went on for some weeks. When I mentioned it to my mother she came down and suggested I go and stay in Wimbledon and see if I could find a place to live there. I packed up our belongings and my mother helped me on the trip to London.

It was virtually impossible to find a place to stay. There were dozens of couples on the housing list and I was told it could be years before I found a place. Things were a bit cramped at 5 Delamere Rd. Anne and I had the downstairs back room which had been David's room and workshop. Things were getting a bit awkward living with my mother. She was always complaining about "so many nappies and baby's things in the airing cupboard". It was rather difficult not to have nappies with a young baby.

During the year I lived at Delamere Rd I did a night course in pottery at Wimbledon Art School. It was convenient as I would settle Anne for the night, she always slept right through to the morning.

While I was living with family in Delamere Rd, we had visits from Aunt Clarita and Uncle Tim. Clarita was one of my mother's sisters, Uncle Tim was holding Anne on his lap when she lurched off his lap. He very deftly grabbed her by one foot and hauled her back onto his lap. He calmly said, "that was a near miss".

We also had my Godmother, Aunt Betty, no relation, to lunch on several occasions. Also my Aunt Enid, the very amusing sister of my father's. For some unknown reason my mother didn't get on very well with her but felt it a sort of duty to invite her to lunch every so often.

We were all instructed to dress properly for the meal when she visited. She arrived one day with her fox slung around her neck. Immaculately groomed. David had been asked to wear a tie, something he rarely did. When he was called for lunch, he entered triumphantly adorned with three ties at the front and three at the back. My mother was mortified, Aunt Enid thought it hilarious. David stood in the doorway giggling. All except my mother thought it very funny. My mother never asked us to dress "proper" again.

Aunt Enid had a wonderful memory of all our visits when on leave from the West Indies. She would recall incidents and funny sayings we children had said that made her laugh.

Another visitor was Uncle Eric my father's eldest brother. He was a chauffeur to some wealthy man so when in the area he had some time to himself, he would pop in. He was another one my mother didn't seem to like. I used to feel quite embarrassed at my mother's rudeness. Never did find out what the problem was. We children always enjoyed his visits, short as they were.

David and Marianne were getting married, my mother said "I am going to visit your father with the younger members of the family and I have told David and Marianne they can have the house while I am away so you will have to make other arrangements".

Fortunately, our friends the Millen's said I could move in with them. They lived only a street away, had two small children and Mary was expecting her third. They were so warm and easy to get on with and I was able to help Mary with the children who adored Anne.

OUR FIRST CHILD

We decided to call Anne by her second name, Bernadette, as it was difficult with two Annes in the house. While there Bernadette developed German measles. It was a bit of a worry with Mary being pregnant.

Self with Tom and Anne

Ted, Tom's brother with Anne

Chapter 23

RETURN TO DELAMERE RD

When my mother returned from the West Indies, David and Marianne bought a house on Bucklebury Common and I moved back into Delamere Rd. At this time my father was still in Jamaica. He paid his regular three yearly visits which we all looked forward to. My mother was very civil on his visits. I suspect she still loved him. They certainly seemed to get on better together than when they were living together. They never got divorced only separated.

My mother had to go out to work as my father was not supporting her constantly. I visited David and Marianne at their cottage with Bernadette several times. In fact I stayed with them for some time and was able to help when Marianne had Clare, one year younger than Bernadette and Helen newly born. I used to enjoy my visits as it was away in the country and I would get into the garden and dig furiously. David had a workshop some distance away which he cycled to daily and we never saw him again until the evening, in fact when Marianne was in labour with Helen, David got on his bike and went to the workshop and Marianne delivered Helen on the bathroom floor. Helen was a beautiful baby and I remember one occasion when she was sitting on my lap she was staring into my eyes and looked as if she wanted to climb into them.

Tom and I wrote regularly to each other but I could tell from his letters that things were not the best. He had been sent from Malta to Greece and various parts around the Mediterranean. He wrote and asked me to join him. I had saved a bit from my allowance so booked a flight for Malta.

Chapter 24

FLY TO MALTA

Bernadette was fourteen months old when we flew to Malta. She was a little chatter box, out of nappies and running around. I remember little of the flight. It was strange being together again. Tom found it hard getting used to Bernadette. He had found an apartment to rent but there was no privacy. We had a couple of rooms upstairs in a very large house. We were given the front door key which led into a large marbled area, wide stairs led upstairs to several rooms around a balcony, two of them being ours.

The landlady was always hovering around downstairs and was not exactly friendly. So we looked for another apartment. The second apartment was smaller but at least the top floor and the flat roof above was ours. Both were in a town called Paula. There was a small covered balcony from the bedroom where we could sit in the evenings and watch the world go by.

I had only been there just over a week and Tom was shipped off to the Persian Gulf. And there he stayed for ten months. There were wives of two other sailors who sailed with Tom, they lived in apartments just across the road. We often went out together to a movie or into Valetta to the canteen for a meal. One of them found it a bit of a tie having Bernadette along all the time so after that I didn't go out with them very often.

One day while in the canteen I ran into a Wren, Celia, who I had been stationed with at HMS Mercury. She was married to a sailor who I also remembered. Celia and her husband had Bernadette and I around a couple of times for meal. While her husband was on duty, we went on bus trips to visit places of interest around Malta. They had no children and enjoyed having Bernadette around. Celia, Bernadette and I visited several towns, exploring each and finding out the history. At one town they had discovered the remains of a Roman villa and were in the midst of restoring the beautiful mosaic floor of the courtyard. We also visited catacombs.

Incredible Memories

Bernadette aged 2, Malta   *Tom in the waters of Drepano, Greece, 1952*

During World War II the people would take shelter down in the caves and catacombs whenever they had air raids. A lot of Malta was terribly destroyed in these raids. After the war the island was presented with the George Cross for bravery shown by all the citizens.

The landlady and her husband were very old and could not speak much English but were very kind. Every now and then they would share a meal with us. The milkman called around before the sun rose yelling "Halip" which means milk. My landlady would get my jug filled when she got hers filled. The cooking facilities were rather primitive. There was a homemade cooker which burnt kerosene. The whole place smelt of kerosene. There were two burners and a small oven, which I never quite got the hang of the whole ten months I was there.

Then I got news that Tom's ship's company were being flown back to Malta. Tom seemed glad to see me but was acting a bit funny with Bernadette. She slept in a large cot at the end of our bed and Tom seemed to resent her being in our room. Because of mosquitoes and other flying insects, we had to sleep under a mosquito net. It was like a tent which hung from the ceiling. One night a cat came into our room. We slept with all our windows open plus the doors leading onto the porch and our small kitchen area. The cat went around to Tom's side of the bed and clawed at the net and gave a yowling sound. He leapt onto my side of the bed. He hated and was a bit afraid of cats and they seemed to know that. Another night, one of the few when Tom was home, he sat reading with his legs over the arms of the armchair when a massive flying cockroach flew in and landed on his leg. Tom jumped up and flew into a rage, he ranted on about how he hated Malta and couldn't wait to be at sea again. He came home drunk the next few nights. He came home drunk one night and started to accuse me of having an affair while he was away. Talk among the men was very catching, some of the men came back to find their wives had been unfaithful. Tom became quite violent which rather frightened me plus embarrassed me as the landlord and lady would have heard the commotion. Their daughter came around the next day to find out if I was alright. I spoke to the priest next time I went to confession and he suggested I get in touch with the Naval Chaplain.

The landlady's daughter invited us to her daughter's First Communion meal. We arrived at Rosita's house about 2pm to find the house overflowing with friends and relatives and hordes of excited children. Bernadette clung to me, many of the children came over and tried to get her to join them. Luckily most spoke good English and we were made very welcome. The dining room table was laden with all sorts of delicious food and in the centre a very large green and white cake which when cut was a light sponge with swirls of green going through it. Each guest left with a little muslin bag full of almond bon bons.

Then we heard we were to be flown back to the UK within a week! I didn't bother to get in touch with the Chaplain. So I had to start packing again. In a way I was sad to say goodbye to all the Maltese neighbours I had got to know. But in another way I was glad to be going back to England as I thought Tom would give up drinking.

We were moved to an army barracks where we stayed for several days. Not the most ideal place to be with small children and there were many of them. One poor lady had three under the age of five so I gave her a hand to look after them. I often wondered how they would get on as they had nowhere to go when they got back to the UK. Neither had family to help. At the barracks we were only allowed to go certain places. We could go to the canteen between 10am and noon to buy things like milk, biscuits and bread plus toiletries.

We all had to share bathrooms and toilets. I dreaded going to the toilets as they were not very clean and extremely smelly. I used a potty for Bernadette and I was constantly washing her hands. Our meals were served at the canteen. We never knew from day to day when we were to fly out. In the end we had 12 hours' notice. Bad luck if we had done a load of washing. The lady with the three children had done some washing and it wasn't dry so she folded it up and tied it down in her pram when we got to Gatwick airport the customs had her take everything out of the pram. The poor woman, with bawling kids and damp clothes strewn all over the counter.

The plane we were put on was not very big, not the most comfortable flight I have been on. We had a stopover in Nice, south of France for a two hour refuel. We were served sandwiches and some of the most delicious peaches I have ever tasted. The waiter who served us slipped me another peach "for cherie Bernadette." That was the only thing she would eat. Then I remembered that I craved peaches when I was pregnant with her! The trip seemed endless, I can't remember how many hours we flew from Malta to Gatwick. It certainly took all day. All the Naval personnel were bussed to Victoria Station in London then we found our own way to our destination. We had been given train passes to Wimbledon where we were to stay with my mother. I had sent a telegram to let her know the day of arrival. Tom had been given two weeks leave so we decided to go to Inverness to visit his mother and family as he had not seen them for several years.

When we arrived in Inverness after an overnight train journey. We were warmly greeted by Ted, Kath and Sal then went by taxi to 39 Kessock Avenue where we were met by Ma, Tom's mother. She was quite overwhelmed and had tears in her eyes. It was the first time she had met Bernadette and thought her a *bonny wee lass*.

Not long after we arrived Babs, Tom's eldest sister came over with her three youngest, the others were at school. Bernadette was very shy but soon went out to play with her cousins. During the afternoon Babs' three eldest Arth, Christine and Andrew came in. They were in the habit of calling in on their way home. Their grandmother had a jar full of sweets, they were given a couple each, asked about school and then went home. It wasn't long before Arth returned and he took Bernadette out into the garden. He was very good with younger children. He was twelve years old and the eldest of Babs' children. One evening Ma said she would keep an eye on Bernadette so Tom and I could go out for the evening. Ted and Arthur, Babs' husband came over and we all went out to the dance hall and had a great evening.

On the Friday nights we went to the catholic church hall, they always had a dance on. The week we were there Tom caught up with a few of his old friends. We went out to Beauly by bus to catch up with the Mackie family who were great friends of Tom's. We were very warmly welcomed and had to stay for tea so we could catch up with Davie when he got home from work.

The week was a very busy one and soon came to an end. We returned to Wimbledon and Tom had to report to Portsmouth barracks. I and Bernadette stayed at Delamere Rd for the next two years and Tom was stationed at Portsmouth. He came up every weekend he had off which was once a fortnight. While there I became pregnant with my second baby. On one of Tom's leaves we went back up to Scotland to visit his family. Bernadette turned four years in March that year 1956 and Marie-Therese was born in May.

My pregnancy was very uneventful; I craved dark chocolate and loved the smell of Life Buoy soap. I was booked into St Theresa's Maternity Hospital. It was run by the order of St Anne, an Irish order. Because I was so large they gave me an x-ray, they thought I was expecting twins! I was 61 inches around my non-existent waist. Again, I had a very easy delivery. In fact, the young doctor who sat next to my bed taking notes was most surprised when I said I thought the baby was about to arrive. *But I haven't noticed any contractions.* So I told him it was because I was practicing relaxation and having a *natural childbirth.*

After I had Marie-Therese he came and visited me in the ward and said he hoped all his deliveries would be as quiet and uneventful in the future.

Marie-Therese was born sucking her thumb. The nun said she had probably been doing that for some time while I carried her. After about the fourth day I had to go in the lift to the nursery to pick Marie-Therese up for feed time. I noticed that she held her breath while the lift was moving and I wondered if that had anything to do with the fall I had when crossing the road in Edgehill after mass. The road was very steep and I sort of rolled down until Tom caught up with me and helped me up. We called into Laura Sydnham's to sit for a while as it happened just outside her house. Laura was a family friend. She gave me a cup of tea and I felt alright so I continued on our walk back to Delamere Rd.

There was another mother in the ward who had had twins and was unable to feed them. So I had milk extracted, a rather uncomfortable procedure, as I had so much milk. I fed both twins as well as Marie-Therese.

In those days, children were not allowed in the hospital so I did not see Bernadette for nine very long days. I was very upset when she and Tom met me at the door the day I was to go home. Bernadette would have nothing to do with me. She looked at me as if I was a complete stranger. It took a couple of days for her to come around. I used to get her to help me bath Marie-Therese and I would let her hold her so she finally accepted the fact that she had a sister.

Tom had been demobbed just before I had Marie-Therese. He got a job with an ice cream company selling ice cream from a cold box attached to a bicycle. He was over in Roehampton by the common. My mother took Bernadette over to see him one day. He was kept extremely busy as the weather was very warm. A van would come around about every hour and replenish what he had sold. Because the evenings were so light, he would get home about 9 pm at night very exhausted. We had made plans to go up to Inverness as he thought it would be easier to get a job and a state house.

One day I went through to our room to tell Tom lunch was ready. I'll never forget the look on his face as I entered. He was as white as a sheet and handed me the mail he had just received. It was an envelope with his navy papers and his birth certificate which they were returning to him. His birth certificate read that he could use Fraser or Simpson as his surname but he had always known himself as Aitken. It was a terrible shock to him. *So I am a bastard I suppose you'll leave me now. What would I want to do that for you are still the same person I married.* That information doesn't make the slightest difference. But you will have to sort it out with your Mum.

Incredible Memories

His father had left them when Tom was seven years old and he had always presumed his father was Mr Aitken. He never knew his father and his mother had never been married.

Tom stewed over this for weeks and made me promise I would not mention it to my family. He was so ashamed. I couldn't understand why it made so much difference to him. As far as I knew his family had always been very close and Mrs Aitken had worked very hard all their young lives to keep her and eight children fed and clothed and schooled. His attitude to his mother changed completely and here we were about to go up to Scotland and live with her until we found a place.

We decided we were going to drive up. Tom had done a mechanics course before leaving the Navy and he had a driver's license. We saw an Armstrong Sydney advertised selling for 36 pounds. It had been up on blocks since her husband had been killed during the war. It was a 1936 model with preselect gears in excellent condition. Tom checked it over and could find nothing wrong with it so we bought it.

When Marie-Therese was four months old we took off. The car was loaded to the hilt with all our belongings. Marie-Therese in a carry cot on top of boxes on the back seat, her cot tied on the top of the car. Bernadette shared the passenger seat with me. We stopped about every four hours to feed Marie-Therese and get Bernadette and ourselves something to eat and drink. Our first night stop was in Glasgow where we stayed with the Graham's, family friends of ours from Jamaica. Then we cut across to Edinburgh and stopped in a B&B. Then onto Aviemore where we spent the night in a lovely hotel. We had homemade pork sausages for breakfast with lovely rolls which tasted so different to any I had tasted. The scenery on the drive from Perth up through the mountainous country was so beautiful. So little traffic and housing in comparison to the first part of our journey. The hillside purple with the covering of heather. The slopes on either side of the road rose to quite a height. As we neared Inverness the land was not so mountainous. Still great distances between villages. The journey was a bit of a trek but we were looking forward, full of hope, to a new life. As we neared Inverness Tom's mood started to change. I tried to talk him into not blaming his mother and just find a quiet moment to broach the subject of who his real father was.

As we drove up to 39 Kessock Avenue, a welcoming party rushed out to greet us. Tom was like a thunder cloud and nearly bit his mother's head off. I tried to smooth things over and said we had travelled a long way and Tom had done all the driving and was dog tired.

Bernadette was looking rather pale and said she felt sick, little did we know there was a hole in the exhaust pipe and we had all been breathing in carbon monoxide. She was affected the most as she had been sitting over the hole. Thank god it never affected Marie-Therese. How I will never know. Ma showed us where we were to sleep and we unloaded the car. Ma and Sal,

FLY TO MALTA

Tom's sister, looked after Marie-Therese and Bernadette while we got settled. Thank goodness it was good weather and both the children could get fresh air into their lungs. We had tea and got an early night. The next day we discussed the possibility of a job and state housing. Housing had a list as long as the one down in London. Tom's brother Ted worked at the post office so he and Tom went up to see if Tom could start as a mechanic. He started as a *B* mechanic as that is what he had got a certificate for. Tom's hopes of working in the hydroelectric scheme were dashed as the work had been completed and we were well behind the times.

Tom was a bit moody still but at least he had a job so was out of the house most of the time. I did my best to fit in with our new life, to fit in with Ma's routine. At the time Sal and Rose, another sister, lived at home. Ma said she would cook the main meal for all the adults and for Bernadette if she liked the food. Bernadette was a good little eater and ate whatever was put in front of her. I was still breastfeeding Marie-Therese and had started her on solids which I prepared for her. Bernadette got on very well with everyone and loved her cousins.

Babs, Tom's eldest sister lived at the end of the cul-de-sac. Ma had her rituals, always went over to Babs' for morning tea and a wee blether (chat).

I usually took Bernadette and Marie-Therese for a walk. Both Rose and Sal came home for lunch, but at different times. Rose never stayed very long before she was off with her friends. I never did find out where she worked. Sal worked as an attendant at the public baths. I arranged to go to the baths twice a week with Bernadette, Sal would have the bath ready and would look after Marie-Therese. Sal and I got on very well together and often when she was home she would join us on our walks. She took us to places that had been Tom's boyhood haunts. Ma went to the flicks twice a week. She would walk up to Kessock Rd to the bus and catch the late afternoon show and would have tea out. Don't know if she met anyone up in town. She was a very private person. Sometimes she would talk about a film she had seen.

Ted and Andrew were still living at home but worked away during the week so were only home at weekends. When they were home they always got fed first in the kitchen and Ma said I had to keep out when they were eating. Sometimes it was awkward if Bernadette decided she was hungry or thirsty. So I kept some biscuits in our room and would get a drink of water from the bathroom.

After the men ate, they would have a wash and a shave at the kitchen sink and then get dressed to go out. Both were courting at the time. They all made me feel very welcome. There was always a bit of an undercurrent when Tom was around. He worked shift work so sometimes he left very early in the morning other times he was home in the morning and went to work in the afternoon.

My father sent me 365 pounds which would have been a very good deposit on a house if not the full price. So when Tom was home we traipsed around looking for possibilities. We saw some really good places but Tom always shied away. The best place was a three-storey house just below the hospital. Two old ladies were selling and we had enough money to pay nearly the whole amount. I suggested we could turn the top floor into a flat and let it to a nurse as they were always looking for accommodation. But he said no way. He admitted before he died that he didn't want to buy it because he didn't want his family to think he was going to live up with the *toffs*. *(The rich people)*.

On a Sunday Bernadette and I would walk up to go to mass in town. Sal looked after Marie-Therese and then she would walk up to meet us to walk home. Tom had met up with some of his old mates and started drinking so he would be sleeping in. One night he got really drunk and stared to abuse me, luckily he didn't wake the children but I ended up going down to ask Andrew to get him out of the room.

One day Bernadette and her cousins were out front playing on Bernadette's scooter and one of them fell and ended up having a green fracture in her right leg. After that I was ostracized and Bernadette was not allowed to play with her cousins. So things were very awkward. Sal was the only one who never changed. I told Tom I couldn't go on living like that. By that time, I was pregnant with George. We went looking for somewhere to rent.

Someone had opened up a yard and put old single decker buses and they were little huts which were virtually one room bedsitters. All very run down and very unhealthy to live in. All in a very muddy yard. We were shown a blue bus, a wood stove faced the door. The whole interior was a dirty grey from the smoke that had billowed from an inefficient chimney. With the door shut at night and on inclement weather we would all be breathing noxious smoke. So the only alternative was to get a job with a house. Tom was very much against it but living with his mother had become impossible. Eventually Tom agreed to get a job with the forestry commission. While in Inverness we had seen a little stone cottage, it was a little bit out of town, it was on about half an acre of land. I fell in love with it. It was small but had possibilities Tom said it would need too much done to it so we gave it a miss. When we announced we were moving out and going to live in Glen Urquhart, Ma got friendly with me again. One day she took me into her bedroom and started to talk about her eldest daughter Edith. She had gone off with Tom's father when Tom was about seven years old, she had been gone for a few years when she tried to get in touch with Ma. She sent her a letter and enclosed a photo of a little boy about three years old and a baby about six months old which was sitting on Edith's lap. Ma had the letter in a shoe box behind her bed. She said she did not reply to the letter and she never heard from Edith again. I don't know why she confided in me, I told Tom but he didn't want to hear about it. He never ever did talk to his mother about his father.

FLY TO MALTA

I and the two children were once more allowed to grace the lounge. Babs' never changed her attitude towards me and Bernadette was still not allowed to play with her cousins. Young Arth still came for walks with us if he saw us going up the road.

First thing in the morning while Marie-Therese was still asleep I would go up to the kessock with Bernadette when the herring boats came in and get a bucketful for a shilling. These I shared with Ma, I would clean them and she cooked them. What a delicious taste, freshly caught fish. So fresh and tasty with a "buttery", these were fresh rolls sold door to door early in the morning. Inverness was the only place I have ever tasted such fresh rolls. They were still warm and only a shilling for six. All pleasant memories I carry with me through my life.

It was during the last week or so that we were still at 39 Kessock Avenue that Ma showed me the letter my mother had written to her before Tom and I got married. I was so embarrassed and angry that my mother could have written such a hurtful letter. I apologized for my mother. Ma said she could see Tom and I were making a go of it and hoped Tom would keep off the grog, as she knew what it was like to be with a bloke who drank. She said Tom was so like his father in mannerisms and with his wavy hair. In the end I think she was sort of sorry that we were leaving and going so far from Inverness. She told me which grocery store to go to so I could order food to start us off and said they would deliver it to Glen Urquhart. Of course, when I told them the address I did not say URQUHART as Scots would so they had a good laugh at that. Ma said it was pronounced ARKART.

Chapter 25

MOVE TO SHENVAL

We moved out to Shenval in Glen Urquhart some thirty miles out of Inverness. We had no furniture except for a single bed for Bernadette which my father had bought for her, and a cot for Marie-Therese. For the first week or so Tom and I slept on the floor on corrugated cardboard. Not the most comfortable while pregnant. So we went in to Inverness and bought a lounge that opened out into a double bed.

The house was quite big there was a very large room which had a wood stove and oven which I could cook on and which kept the room warm. There was a bedroom downstairs and two upstairs with a bathroom upstairs also. There was a small laundry and toilet downstairs which led out the backdoor. I did all the washing by hand in the sink in the laundry.

The floors were concrete with some sort of screading in a dark brown which stained anything wet. And it was very cold. When Marie-Therese started crawling I had to put her in warm trousers. Her little hands would be nearly purple with the cold.

Marie-Therese was crawling around the room and discovered an electric point on the skirting board. She lay on her stomach and looked from the point to the plug on the end of a lead to an electric heater. She did this for a while and then picked up the plug and fitted it into the point. I went over and picked her up and said she must not do that again. Then removed the plug. Luckily, I didn't give her a chance to work out how to switch it on. She never did it again. I watched her work several things out so I knew she was very clever but she was not an early talker.

My mother made some nice warm clothes for the children. When I told her what I was cooking on she sent up an electric hot plate which was a lot cleaner to cook on, though expensive to run.

There were ten houses altogether, most of the people were nice and friendly and had moved as we had because they couldn't get a house. I became friends with the forester's wife who lived in the first house in our row

MOVE TO SHENVAL

of eight houses. They had a daughter Bernadette's age. On the way in to Shenval there were two cottages, the MacDonald's and their teenaged son lived in the first and the second was on a small farmlet where the Lee's lived with two young sons and a daughter. Everyone called Mrs Lee, *Mamma Lee*, she was Austrian and we became great friends. Mr Lee, her husband was Scottish. Both small quiet people some years older than Tom and me. When I had George at home Mamma Lee would collect Marie-Therese and any washing and look after anything for the day. Then she would bring Marie-Therese back about four o'clock, all the washing done, dry and folded and sometimes she would bring a rabbit stew or some vegies from their garden. At the weekend Bernadette and Marie-Therese would go down to play. The Lee's had a pet deer which was a great attraction. Bernadette started school at a small one room school a couple of miles down the road. All the forestry children would meet up and walk there and back every day, and in all weathers. In those days one didn't have to worry about traffic as very few vehicles passed that way. The worry was when any of the children decided to take a detour through the woods.

The post office was in walking distance, in the opposite direction and could be seen on the hill across the valley. The midwife also lived on that hill side. She would ride her bike over when she came visiting me and other families at Shenval. The midwife in her forties was always very cheery when she arrived in all weathers. It was probably two miles by road, not that far as the crow flies. The post mistress was a very comfortable friendly body. We had no shops close by. One grocery shop at Drumnadrochit fourteen miles away on the way to Inverness overlooking Loch Ness. It was called *Leslies*. The other shop was in the other direction at Glen Cannich. Leslie's sent a van around the Glen once a week. We would take it in turns to go out and buy groceries from him. Sometimes he would bring a parcel from the post office. Our next-door neighbour would spend ages in the van while she flirted with the driver. Sometimes he would save the jelly out of the ham tins for me which I used as stock for soups.

There was no mail delivery so we would walk over to collect mail and to use the phone if we had to call anyone. While our car was running, we used to drive over to Cannich on a Sunday to mass. Once a month the priest came to the school hall to say mass and weather permitting, we would walk over.

I loved the Christmas of the highlands. The pine trees dotted with rowan trees with mottled gray and white trunks. Along the road the pine trees varied in size depending on how old they were. Every now and then we would get a glimpse of a deer or young doe. The fir trees in winter were very beautiful as the snow ladened their bows. The outlook in front of our house was a field going down to the river. The ground rose on the other side of the river and main road which ran parallel to the road in front of our house. To the right there was a farmhouse some distance away. Tom sometimes got work on the farm and made a bit of extra money. One entered the farm through a gate at the end of our road. To the left the road led down past first the Lee's wee croft to our right then to the MacDonald's which was the first house one came to once one left the bridge that crossed the river. The road rose up and curved around the MacDonald's. There were huge pine trees on the right all the way from the bridge. The forest ran along the back fences of all the forestry houses.

Our back door opened to face the next door's back door. An Irish couple with five very young children lived there. There was always a strong smell of dirty nappies. I told the midwife and she visited them and found they were living in squalor. She told the lady she had to keep the place clean and to look after the children and keep them clean. I felt very sorry for them. In all weather the children would run around in skimpy clothes, no socks just gum boots. The boys in shorts, their arms and legs crimson with cold. The little girl in a summer dress also crimson. Their noses constantly running, five blonde blue-eyed children always hanging around our fence. None of them spoke very well so I don't know what part of Ireland they came from. They came over because there was no work in Ireland. All the children's clothes were stained with the brown stuff they had painted our floors with. I think the mother just soaked the clothes in water and then hung them out. I tried talking to her but she would hurry inside.

The nurse said they had a couple of chairs and a table and all slept on the floor. She scrounged around and found some warm clothes and a few sticks of furniture for them. The father went mad and said they didn't want charity. But they were told if they didn't change their ways the children would be taken away. That would have been a shame as they were a very loving family. Not once did I hear them raise their voices. Tom said the man never mixed, he kept to himself and went off away from the other men to eat his piece. The children were always hanging on the gate waiting for him to come home. He would pick up the two youngest and the others clung to his jacket with beaming little red runny nosed faces. That would be the last we would see of the children. But about an hour later the father would go out back and start to chop wood. Sometimes the two eldest probably aged 9 and 10 would come out and carry the chopped wood inside. The three eldest went to school and I believe had a hard time from the other children. So very often they did not go to school. Beyond them lived an English family with four very skinny children, the parents were slight too. I visited a couple of times as the mother was very friendly. The children were always very clean and well-dressed but I realised they seemed to subsist on potato soup. The children were served a bowl of this as soon as they got in from school. They must have gone to bed very early as there was never a light on. The Irish family never had their lights on, they used candles I could smell that smell one gets when candles are extinguished. Two doors down from us on our right as you face the house was a young Glaswegian family with a family of five boys. I got on well with the mother and Tom seemed to like the father. They were very strict with their boys and one quite often heard them getting a hiding. Never-the-less they all seemed a happy bunch and she kept the house and the boys spotless.

By the time I was to have George we had acquired a single folding metal bed which we put up on boxes to heighten it. On August 14^{th}1957 about 5am I felt contractions. Tom got on his bike and rode down to the midwife. He then took Bernadette and Marie-Therese down to Mamma Lee's. I had a very quick labour and very easy birth. George only weighed 7 and ¾ pounds. He had flaxen hair and bushy eyebrows and very long eyelashes. He was a very hungry baby, luckily I was able to satisfy him, but when he was about 3 months old he developed colic, so cried a lot. The doctor prescribed some medicine which helped him but he was still very restless. About that time while Tom was chopping wood out the back of the house, he put the axe into his leg. That laid him low for a few days. I had to go out into the woods at night to collect wood. I had to go at night as we were not allowed to take wood out of the forest, but that was the only way we could keep the fires going. It was about that time that George got the colic and I wondered if it was the extra stress that caused this.

The forestry commission would sell us a load of wood for two pounds and ten shillings. That was about half of Tom's weekly wage. The load comprised of huge tree trunks which we had to cut with a cross saw and then chop into smaller pieces.

At that time our Armstrong Sydney decided to play up. Tom couldn't find out what was wrong and refused to pay a mechanic to fix it, he sold it to the farmer down the road for 25 pounds so that meant we were without a car. No buses came out our way so we had to rely on either the MacDonald's or the forester to give us a lift. Tom heard they were looking for men to work in the engineering department to work on road and bridge building for the forestry commission. He got a job with them which meant we had to move to Glen Cannich.

Incredible Memories

Marie-Therese, 1 year old, Shenval, Scotland

The Armstrong Siddeley we owned

Looking down at houses in Shenval

Chapter 26

MOVE TO CANNICH

Mr Baird the forester let us borrow a truck one weekend and we moved down to a two-bedroom cottage in Cannich. Life was quite different there, it was a village, with a grocery shop, post office, catholic school and church. There were several state houses, the forestry houses were separate and across a wee moor from the village. The cottage was so much smaller than the house in Glen Urquhart. One came through the front door into a small hall, two bedrooms to the right, the bathroom straight ahead and the lounge to the left. The lounge was the size of the two bedrooms. This we used as dining area as well. The kitchen backed onto the bathroom so it was the width of the bathroom and the length of the living room. The backdoor went out to the back garden from the kitchen. Beside the door were double sinks under a big window. There was a decent sized gas cooker, a work bench with cupboards below. An open fire in the living room to heat the house. The whole cottage was clad in Canadian Cedar slats. A very neat looking building. A small enclosed garden out front, a path from the gate to the front door continued to the right to the back door. Outside the back door was a coal bunker. A clothesline ran from the house to a high pole. We had a wooden horse on which we used to cut up wood for the fire. I had a small vegetable garden and to the right of this a lawn for the children to play on. The whole garden was fenced so it was quite safe for the children. Our house was semi-detached and the last in the Cul-de-sac.

Our next-door neighbours were from Aberdeen. Their accent so strong I could hardly understand them, they had two small children.

There were ten forestry houses similar to ours, except two were three bedrooms. Just beyond the houses was a large single men's quarters which also let rooms to backpackers who were passing through. Across the road from the forestry houses nestled among large fir trees, was the Catholic church and schools. This meant Bernadette didn't have to walk so far to school. Her teacher was Miss Chisholm, a single lady just ready for retirement. Father Kerr was a very down to earth man, his house was attached to the school. Bernadette made her first Holy Communion there and seemed to settle quite well to her new school.

Tom quite often worked away for a whole week and only came home at weekends. One weekend we went down to the river to picnic. The next thing I knew George was in the river. I had to go in after him large and pregnant and wearing elastic stockings. I always took a couple of towels with me.

The first year we were there, Tom worked on a road and bridge several miles away from Cannich. He used to leave early in the morning being taken by truck to the site. He'd work a 12-hour day so used to come back exhausted. I would have to make sandwiches for him to take and also a flask of tea. We made friends with an English couple, when Tom and the husband were away, she would come over and we would play Scrabble.

We acquired a small car while we were there; a two door Vauxhall. This meant we could go to Beauly ten miles away to visit friends. Tom took Bernadette to Inverness to Andrew, his eldest brother's, and Christina's wedding. I was pregnant at the time so stayed home with Marie-Therese and George.

The midwife was a bit of an alcoholic and when I got Braxton Hicks, she called an ambulance and sent me into Inverness. I kicked my heels there for four days. My mother was visiting at the time and looked after Bernadette, Marie-Therese and George as well as Tom. Then I saw a doctor and he wanted to know what I was doing there. I told him I thought the midwife had panicked a bit and sent me in.

I phoned Bill Duncan at the grocery store and he sent a message to Tom to pick me up. It was another month before I went into labour but I left it for the last minute to send for the midwife. Bernadette ran across the moor to fetch her. Tom was home at the time. My mother had gone back to London. Not long after the midwife arrived, I had Margaret. Much to my disgust she would not give Margaret to me and dumped her in a carry cot and said she had to attend to me first. I told her if she didn't give my baby to me, I would get off the bed and fetch her myself. Margaret was screaming her head off and I was determined to hold her and quieten her down. I was glad to see the back of the midwife so I could nurse Margaret. Tom had got me some lunch, I was ravenous. Then the other children came in to see their new sister. About two days after I had Margaret I must have dozed off. When I awoke the house was so quiet, I wondered where Marie-Therese and George were, I knew Bernadette was at school. I got up and went through to find Marie-Therese was up on a chair at the sink and George was on another chair next to her. They were doing the washing up. Marie-Therese only 3 years old and George 2. There they were whispering to each other so they wouldn't disturb me. I burst into tears, mainly out of relief that they were alright, but also to seeing these two wee mites doing the washing up. I just hugged them both. They were a bit disturbed at seeing me crying but I explained it was because I was so happy. I doubt they understood the contradiction of emotion. Four days after Margaret was born, she started choking. The midwife had not cleared her throat so I had to clear it and resuscitate her.

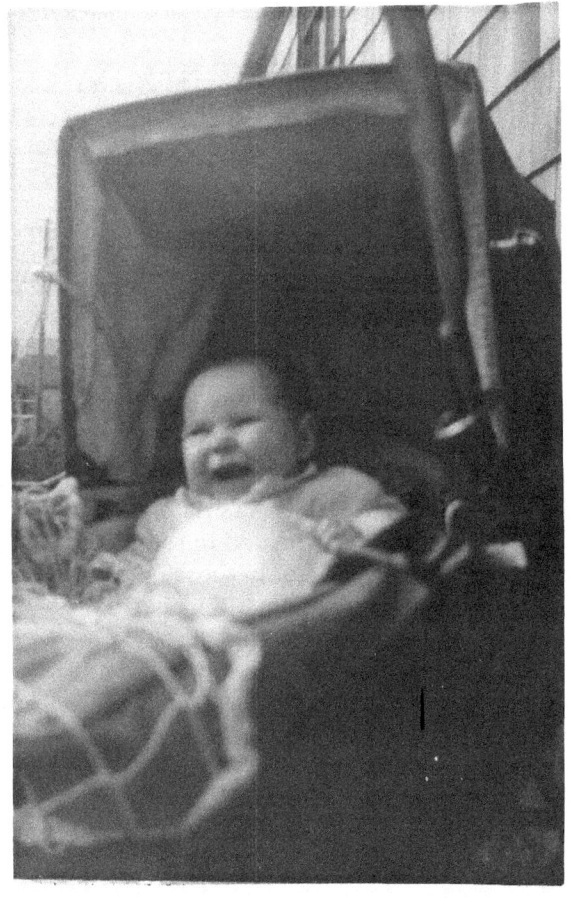

Margaret 4 and a half months old, Glen Cannich

Chapter 27

AN EVENTFUL YEAR

When I was seven months pregnant with Margaret, our little car started to give electrical problems so we sent to London for a complete set of wiring for that particular model. When it arrived, I lay it all out on our lounge room floor and tagged all the wires leading to various points of the car. There were wires which came out of one central clump all taped together. It was very confronting

Tom asked the Camp electrician to give him a hand. But for some reason he found domestic electricity was different to mechanical electricity! So large as life, hardly able to fit behind the steering wheel, I went out and gave them a hand to work it all out. In those days, on either side of the car, half-way up, between front and back door there was a little flicker which indicated which way one wanted to turn. I remember two yellow wires led to them. I must say it was a mighty job, not one I would want to repeat. And no, I did not have a miscarriage but I was a bit stiff in certain parts of my body the next day. The job was successful.

Another was, one weekend, when Tom was coming home from a job, the car conked out about three miles north of the village. So the next morning I made a picnic lunch and we all trooped out to the car, to find out what the matter was.

I had taken a sheet to hang between branches of a tree for some shade for the children and our food. It was a hot sunny day and there were a lot of little flying insects. The sheet being white attracted them. On looking up Marie-Therese spotted them silhouetted against the sunlight and refused to stay under cover. Anyway. we found that by placing a match stick in a certain position in the cut out, the engine kept running

We used the matchstick trick for several journeys. But it was constantly dropping out so eventually we bought a new part.

It was a horrific winter. So cold the main water pipe running under the bridge, on the Cannich to Beauly road, froze. The whole village was without

AN EVENTFUL YEAR

water. Quite a nightmare with three young children and a new baby. To wash the nappies, if they were not soiled, I rubbed them in the snow and then hung them on the clothes-line. Within a minute they were as stiff as a board, very difficult to unpeg them, but when thawed in front of the fire were as soft and sweet smelling as one could want. My mind is a blank about what I did with the soiled ones, and these were many. I know I had several very stained ones as one does with an infant!

We used to have to cut up large branches and tree trunks with a crosscut saw. It was a large saw with a handle each end and required two people to use it. One pushed and the other pulled, then reversed the proses. Halfway through the trunk we had to turn it on the wooden horse, then cut through the other half. When we cut through the first half, I went to lift out the saw and my hand stuck to the saw blade, it was so cold. That was when we had a snap freeze in the middle of winter.

We had icicles hanging down in front of our front door. They were so big we had to go in and out of the back door. It snowed so heavily overnight, covering the roof and filling the gutters. When the sun was at its hottest for the day it would melt the snow which dripped on to the already formed icicle from the previous day, froze, and built up to a single mass of ice.

The children loved playing in the snow but it used to get down into their gum boots, melt, and then as their feet got colder it froze between their socks and boots. Of course, when they came in I'd remove their boots with great difficulty, and their frozen, purple feet started to thaw it was very painful. I had to rub their feet until the circulation returned and try to stop them from getting too close to the fire, to prevent them from getting chilblains. The result was, I had wet clothes, socks and gloves hanging all over the place, trying to dry them out before the next episode. It was only fun while they first went out to play.

The only place near the village which had running water, was a spring coming out of the side of the hill, just over the bridge on the Glen Urquhart road. I'd take an empty bucket fill it up and as the top froze very quickly, I did not lose much on the walk back. I had to do this a couple times a day so we had drinking and cooking water. I found it took many buckets of melted snow to get a small amount of water in the bottom of a saucepan.

The sky had looked strange all day. As I looked out of the front window, I saw flashing lights in the sky and then it was like we were enveloped in a brightly coloured tent. It was quite frightening as I didn't know what it was. Frightening though exciting, a spectacle I had never seen before. Gentle but bright colours spread over the sky. Frightening because it were as though sounds were muted. Flashing lights but no thunder. The blue sky had disappeared as were the few clouds I had witnessed earlier in the day. Exciting in that the whole picture was so colourful and because it was so quiet. The enclosed imaging of the various lights and colours did not appear to be threatening. I had no idea what I was witnessing, never having lived in such a northerly Hemisphere. I was rooted to the spot, I tried to memorize the scene. Brilliant green wispy clouds mixed with pinks and reds, swirling in the sky. Illuminating the northern horizon as a greenish glow and sometimes a faint red as if the sun were rising in the north. The aurora appearing as a diffused glow, as curtains that extended across the heavens. A mixture of green and red, behind a pink then all of a sudden there were shades of blue. I was later told I had experienced an "Aurora Borealis" The Northern lights.

On another occasion I heard a swishing noise and at intervals a honking sound. When I went out and looked skywards there were several V formations of Canadian geese migrating over the north of Scotland flying south to warmer climates. It was a thrilling sight to see hundreds of these large birds flying overhead, knowing they had flown all the way from Canada.

One day when I was through in the bedroom feeding Margaret, George got on his tricycle and rode it through to the living room. The next thing I knew he had fallen into the fire knocking the fire guard, which was airing nappies, sideways. Luckily it was not a blazing fire and was just hot coals. He burnt the side of his face and his ear. I remembered when I got burnt while in the Navy, the nurse put Penicillin gauze on the burns and bandaged it. I had some gauze in my first aid kit so I put strips on George's face and ear and bandaged it for a couple of days. When I removed the bandage all the ash and blackness came off. All looked quite clean so I just put more gauze on and bandaged it and left it for several days. The result was he wasn't scarred.

When Margaret was about eleven weeks old, came the big thaw, and we had some really nice sunny half days. So one weekend Tom suggested we drive out of the village into the forest where he was working to see the progress on a bridge they were building. We arrived and all got out of the car to walk up to the area where the bridge was nearly finished. It was a beautiful spot. The whole area had been cleared to make a sort of turning point for the trucks to turn around in. Tom said to get into the car and we'd find a nice spot to picnic, before it started to get cold. I said I'd wait with the children till he turned the car around. Luckily Tom was in the habit of leaving the driver's door open as he backed. Suddenly, the road gave way and he just had time to jump clear before the little car plunged down some twenty feet down the side of the hill. It landed on its side at the bottom. We were several miles from the nearest croft, Tom scrambled down and recovered our food, then we all started the long trek.

On the way we came to some huge concrete pipes, lying on the side of the road so I suggested I and the children shelter in one of them while he went for help. It would be quicker for him to go on his own. I with three children and a baby huddled up in the pipe away from a cold wind which had sprung up. We had our picnic in the pipe and I fed Margaret. By then the sun had started to sink in the west and it was getting colder and the village was ten miles away.

When Tom got to the farm there was only a ten-year-old boy there but he said there was an old Army jeep which Tom could borrow if he could get it started. Tom arrived turned the jeep around and then it was "How was I going to get the children safely into it". It was open all around and had very hard seats and no restrainers for the children. Finally, we were all settled and made for the main road. Halfway back to Cannich we met the owners going home, we all stopped and the farmer offered to drive us home, His wife drove the jeep back to the croft.

After lighting the fire and getting everyone warm once more with a hot bowl of soup, all were ready for bed. It had been a very traumatic event for the children. One they would not forget in a hurry.

The next day the car was hauled up onto the road. The battery fluid had leaked out acid all over the passenger seat and door and burnt big holes where it had dripped. What a trauma. One of the experiences in our lives.

To order meat from the butchers in Beauly, I would walk up to the old post office and put a note on the window. The local bus driver would pick it up on his way back to Beauly and the next day the butcher would send my order up on the morning run, to be left on the windowsill for me to collect. One summer's day I didn't get up until the afternoon and my packet of liver was fly-blown. The blood had seeped out of the butcher's paper and the flies had got in. I took it home and buried it. After that I made sure I was there when the bus arrived. Quite often it was a long wait as the bus was not very punctual. It depended on how many deliveries the driver had on the way to the village and whether he stopped to have a blether (chat). We paid for the meat the next time we went to Beauly.

Often while I waited, villagers walked past and greeted me. They were all very friendly but none ever called me anything other than 'Mrs Aitken'. I only really became friends with a few people, a couple, he worked for the Forestry Commission and another couple, she was Scottish and he was Irish, their children went to school with Bernadette. Then there was Mrs MacDonald, who lived just behind us, she was always very kind but we never got on Christian name terms. And the other was Bernadette's teacher, who was nice but very 'proper' an old school type. Both of the last two were much older than me but I appreciated their friendship. The Parish Priest Fr Kerr was well liked by all the congregation as he was with many of the non-Catholic villagers.

Incredible Memories

Marie-Therese 2 years old, Glen Cannich, Scotland

George, 3 years old

George 14 months old, Glen Cannich, Scotland

Chapter 28

VISITORS WE HAD WHILE IN CANNICH

While we lived in Glen Cannich we had several visitors. The first was a surprise visit from Basil Cousins. a family friend from Wimbledon. He was in the Navy doing National Service and was up near Edinburgh studying Russian. With him were three other hefty young men, classmates of Basil. They hired a car and drove up to see something of the Highlands, for the weekend! Luckily Tom was able to get accommodation for them over at the Hostel. It was a bed and breakfast at a reasonable price and they could have an evening meal if they ordered it in time.

All very likable blokes. We took them up to show them the Hydro Electric Scheme. I made a picnic lunch which we stopped and enjoyed at the next village up the valley. Thank goodness the weather was very kind to us so we were able to get out and about as our cottage was rather cramped when all four were visiting. The kids loved having them as they played games with them and took them for walks. All together it was a very pleasant visit which we all enjoyed.

My youngest sister, Christine, came up for a week with an exchange student from Belgium, called Huegette. Tom and I slept in the living room on the pull-out lounge. Bernadette, Marie-Therese and George slept in one bedroom and Christine and Huegette slept in the second bedroom. The weather again was very kind to us and we were able to go for walks and picnics. There were some lovely spots just outside the village. Down by the river was beautiful and peaceful. I was quite pregnant by this time but still very fit and able to walk a fair distance. We had to watch George all the time as he had a habit of invariably ending up in the river then would have to be rescued. That summer and spring were so enjoyable. Very sunny days with a spot of rain over night or a very heavy dew.

Incredible Memories

Our next visitor was my mother, a month before I had Margaret. She stayed for three weeks and more or less took over the running of the house, and children. She was amazed at what brisk walkers the children were and what a distance they could walk. Even George at two and a half, she would take the pushchair but George preferred to run and walk with the girls. The weather was not quite so kind as it rained quite often. I was in hospital in Inverness the first four days of my mother's visit. A false alarm and a panicky midwife. So my mother had gone back to London by the time Margaret was born.

When Margaret Mary was about two years old, we had a visit from my eldest brother David and his wife Marianne. They slept in the living room as Tom was working away at the time.

David had a long chat with Bill Duncan the owner of the village shop and between them they decided it would be a good idea if Tom went down to the midlands in England to a place called Corby, to see if he could get a job there. Corby was a big industrial town, producing steel. After David and Marianne left Bill had a long chat to Tom and persuaded him to accept a loan to take a trip south.

Tom being Tom and not liking to be beholden to anyone, hitch-hiked down, got a job and hitched back again. He gave Bill back his money and we started packing to move south. Tom received severance pay so we had enough money for train fares and the move south. Tom's brother Ted and his wife Kath asked us to spend a couple of days with them so we could say our farewells to the family. They only had a small place but made us very welcome. Tom was in a terrible mood all the time we spent there. Margaret was being very difficult as she had to share the bed with Tom and me. Tom lost his rag and threw Margaret down to the end of the bed and then stormed out of the house. I was very embarrassed and said it would probably better if we cut our visit short. We said our good-byes to Tom's family and took the night train down to London. It was a long and not too easy journey with four young children. A journey I do not remember too much about.

VISITORS WE HAD WHILE IN CANNICH

Marie-Therese, George, Bernadette, baby Margaret, Glen Cannich, 1960

Chapter 29

OUR STAY AT WOODLEY

We were met in London by my mother and brother David who went with us by train to Reading. At the time David and his family lived out of Reading at a place called Woodley. I was exhausted and do not remember how we went on to Woodley. I remember being welcomed by Marianne who announced that three of their children were up in bed with the mumps.

The house at Woodley, on the main London Road, was a large three storey one, which both families shared for the next eleven months. There were nine children under ten years old, between us. Quite a handful as soon after we arrived David went down with the mumps and was very ill. Not long after that Marianne went down with rheumatic fever and remained in bed for a spell.

There was five days difference between our two youngest, who were both two years old. Sarah, David and Marianne's youngest, a very placid child, and not too fussed about learning. Our Margaret, five days younger, was very active and decided she was going to get Sarah up on her feet. She succeeded. David talked me into sending George to school so there would be less in the house during the day. I was very reluctant as George was not yet five years old. Poor wee chap he was very unhappy but luckily the nuns allowed him to stay with Marie-Therese the first term.

The school was not very far away but the children had to cross the very busy main road. David and I took it in turns to walk up and meet them. As you can imagine my life was very busy. The neighbours thought I was running a kindergarten when they saw me trooping along the road with nine young children in tow.

It was a very difficult eleven months as David didn't believe in saying 'no' to his children whereas mine were quite used to me saying no to unreasonable requests. So we ended up having a few words over that. I appreciated being able to stay there but I had to stand my ground. It took Marianne a long time to recuperate.

David had a studio attached to the back of the house, where he spent many hours sculpting. Luckily. they had a Mrs Skeats come in a couple of days a week, she cleaned, washed and ironed.

The house was situated in a large garden with fruit trees a vegetable garden and a green house, which was at the bottom of the garden. There were high hedges down both sides of the garden which ended at a point just behind the hot house. The front garden was wider with hedges across the front but there were no gates.

One day, Margaret decided she would take Sarah for a walk. They were brought back some time later by a kind lady, who found them wandering down London Road, which they had managed to cross. The angels sure looked after those two. At that age one only had to be distracted for a few minutes and they were off like a shot. They had been playing in the playroom when they moved off far too quickly and silently.

There was fruit to be picked and stored up in the attic, the plums were ready to pick and jam to be made. Seville oranges from Spain arrived in February, so marmalade to be made. Some of the fruit to be stewed, meals to get ready, tea break morning and afternoon made life pushed to full speed. Then there was shopping to be done as well. When Marianne was better, we took it in turns shopping and cooking.

Tom was working at Corby and came home at weekends if he didn't have to work overtime. The pay was good but Tom had to pay board so we had to watch the pennies.

One weekend Tom and I took the five eldest down to Sonning River. It was a beautiful warm summer's day and all were in bathing suits. The spot we chose had a nice little beach, the children were only supposed to paddle in the shallow. Next thing we knew Simon, aged six was out of his depth and Tom had to dive in and rescue him. That caused a bit of excitement.

Before we left Woodley, Tom and David took the five eldest down to the New Forest camping. I had presumed all had enjoyed themselves, I later heard how Bernadette had not enjoyed any of it, especially the boring food they had prepared. Baked beans on toast and fried onions. I don't think that was all they ate. Fortunately, all the children got on very well. All being so close in age they sort of paired off. It was a marvelous garden for children, big enough for them to ride their bicycles around and great for playing hide and seek or chasey. On inclement days they were occupied in the playroom, the older ones improvising plays and skits. There were dressing up costumes, board games and plenty of paper and crayons or watercolor paints to occupy them. The older ones were very helpful in organizing the younger ones.

After ten months, a friend of Tom's in Corby, who were going on holiday, offered their house for a week so we could look around for a house to purchase in the area. David lent us two hundred pounds for a deposit.

Incredible Memories

When we arrived at the house it was filthy so I had to set to and clean. There was food on the walls in the dining room, all the furniture was sticky, the stove, sink and bathroom needed to be scrubbed before I let the children use anything. I had to change the sheets on all the beds and wash everything. Tom took the children for a walk and got them something to eat. They brought back some groceries and some fish and chips, I was starving.

I felt everything was a bit cleaner. None of the cutlery, cups and plates had been cleaned properly either. I couldn't believe people would live like that. Tom said "But they have four children" I replied "so have we."

We didn't want to live in Corby, so we looked around a town called Kettering not too far away for Tom to get to work. After looking at several places we found a double story, semi-detached on London Road. It was near a lovely park called Wickstead Park and overlooked the playing fields of a boys' college.

We paid a deposit and got a solicitor to see to the paperwork. Our offer was accepted so we went back to Woodley to gather our things together.

Chapter 30

KETTERING OUR NEW HOME

The house cost us 1,400 pounds. It was on the top of a hill along the main road to London. Just beyond our house about four houses and a shop above our house there was a road going off to the right, to a village called Pytchly, not far along we were in the country with fields both sides of the road. It was a good road to go for walks and picnics.

Our house was the central one of three. At the front left was our front door of 306 London Road. The door to 308 was right next to ours. On the right was a big bay window, this was our living room. Facing as we entered, a long hall, to the right, just past the living room door were stairs going to the upstairs. Further along a door into a big room, this became the playroom, where we put the open out lounge in case we had anyone to stay. The hall ended in our dining area with a door to the right leading out into the back garden and down a path to the toilet which was attached to the end of the house. Beyond the dining area was the kitchen, not very big but serviceable. There was a gas stove and a stone sink under a small window, with one tap, to the left of that was a pump handle for me to pump water up form a well below the house. Every now and then I had to prime it. There was a leather washer that had the habit of drying out during the summer months. There had been some modern plumbing done in the house, the only hot water being up in the bathroom using an instant gas hot water system.

There was just enough room to put a washing machine between the stove and the sink. This we were able to afford after a year. This had an overhead manual wringer. The first washing machine I had ever owned, quite a luxury. From the kitchen one went down two steps into a small larder which had a window looking out to the back garden. This faced the south so never caught the sun and was always cool. There was a marble slab below the window. We didn't possess a fridge or ice box but our meat, cheeses and anything else we wanted to be kept cold, that's where it went.

Incredible Memories

It did not take long to settle. Both neighbours introduced themselves over the back fence. The Walkers lived to our right, a couple in their late forties. Mr Walker was a bus driver, Mrs a housewife! Their son John, late teens, lived with them. They had a married daughter. The Drages lived to our left both in their middle sixties, they had two sons still living with them. All the men were farm workers and worked on local farms. I hardly ever saw Mrs Drage. She was always inside housekeeping and cooking for three hungry men. Sometimes when I looked out of the larder window, I would see a hare hung over our back fence, noses and tails peppered to prevent being fly blown. Mr Drage said we had to hang the hare in our small shed at the bottom of the garden for a couple of days. He showed us how to skin them and dress them for cooking in a stew. Hares being much bigger than a rabbit, one hare would give us three meals. We had a door leading out into a lane, the wall of the shed was our back boundary. The lane went past and up the side of the Walkers to London Rd.

Our back garden was covered in crazy paving, good for the children to ride their tricycles. We dug up part of it and made a sand pit. To the right at the bottom of the garden there was a small triangle of earth in which I grew some flowers. Mr Drage told me that I could get what they called 'an allotment' just down the road from our house, This cost us ten shillings a year from the Council. It consisted of a quarter acre bit of land with a small shed at the far end, with a door one could lock.

It wasn't long before I had vegetable garden growing. With Mr Drage's help, I turned the soil and he started me off with seedlings of all the greens, like cabbage, broccoli and Brussel sprouts. He got some seed potatoes from the farm and also gave me hints on how to successfully grow everything.

For my birthday present I asked for a load of manure. Everyone thought I was a bit strange but thought this a very practical present. I didn't plant carrots, turnips, or swedes as Mr Drage always supplied me with sufficient for our needs.

Bernadette went to the Kettering high school in town, Marie-Therese went to St Hilda's, which was a bit further away. She was a year too young for the high school. George went to Hawthorn primary in Hawthorn Rd. All walked to school.

The town was walking distance, there was a market day on Friday and Saturday. If I went in late on Saturday, I could get fruit and vegetables much cheaper. There was a grocer shop at the bottom of the hill run by a very nice couple, Mr and Mrs Hairsine. He would give me credit until Tom got paid which was very handy at times. We had been living there a year when Tom got fed up traveling daily back and forth to Corby.

He got a job with a firm that was laying pipes to new estates. He ended up driving the bus as well to carry the men back and forth to the job. Extra money was always welcome.

KETTERING OUR NEW HOME

By August 1962 I was very heavily pregnant and could not go very far after 11 am as I had a very bad prolapse. I had a nice midwife who brought along a Nigerian nurse who was in her final year of studying midwifery. She was such a nice person, very homesick, as she missed her husband, who was a lawyer, and her three children. They had stayed in Nigeria. She made a big fuss of my children and one Saturday she was going to Leicester and asked if she could take Bernadette.

They got back about 5.30pm after having a wonderful day shopping and window shopping. It had been a beautiful Indian summer day, which had added to the enjoyment.

At the church fete, Kettering

Chapter 31

ALISON'S ARRIVAL

I started labour at about 4.45am but I didn't tell Tom, as he was starting a new job. He had to leave the other job as the strong toxic glue they used to join the pipes was beginning to affect him.

I got his lunch ready and said goodbye, then started to get things sorted out for the delivery. I sent Bernadette next door to tell Mrs Walker I had started labour, so she came over to see that all was alright. I got George and the girls ready for school with Bernadette's help and then Mrs Walker went down to the post office to phone for the midwife. The Nigerian nurse turned up as the English midwife was delivering another baby. Mrs Walker took Margaret over to her house.

I delivered a nine and a quarter pound baby girl, Alison, just after 10am. Everything was going alright but the nurse started to look a bit worried when my waters broke. She told me later, because the water was black, she thought something was wrong with the baby. Apparently, the reason was that I had had the chickenpox when I was 7 months pregnant.

Alison was a beautiful, healthy baby but looked more like a three-month old baby. Just after I had her the other midwife appeared and was well pleased how the Nigerian nurse had handled it all. Later in the day Dr Bill Drake-Lee came in to see everything was alright. I was allowed to have someone to help for the first month after having a home birth.

This very round, jovial lady arrived. She was a short lady, very large who bounced around performing all the household duties, with such speed and efficiency. I was terrified she was going to have a heart attack she was so out of breath when she climbed the stairs. She was a very capable lady in her late forties. All the children took to Mrs Bartlet. The first week she came early and saw the children off to school then got on with all the chores, with Margaret trailing after her. She would give Margaret little jobs to do. The second week she did not arrive so early and would stay until she got the

ALISON'S ARRIVAL

children's tea ready. I was up and about by then but still not able to cope with everything.

That winter was a very cold one and Tom was off work for eleven weeks. A bit of a worry as we didn't get any financial help and were worried how we were going to get the children Christmas presents. I put all their names in a hat and said that who's ever name they picked out they would have to make a card and some sort of present for them, out of whatever they could find around the house or outside of it. This project kept them busy for hours. They made some beautiful cards for each other, for Tom and me, and for their Grandmothers.

What we were going to have for Christmas dinner was another thing. One day when I was down at the grocer's store, I bought a shilling raffle ticket for a Christmas hamper, which I won. So that solved the problem of dinner. There were tins of ham, corned beef, peas, a packet of dehydrated potato and tins of fruit, a Christmas pudding and a cake. Two days before Christmas I went into the larder and saw something white hanging on our back fence. When I went out, I found a large dead goose plus carrots, turnips and a couple of onions.

So sweet of the Drages and they got so embarrassed when I went to thank them with a card from the children. On top of that, I ended up with a packet of tea and a bowl of custard for the children.

We lived at 306 London Road for just over seven years. So much happened in our lives in that time. I will not record every detail as this book would go on for too long. I expect a lot of the things were no different to what happens in a lot of families. Amazing things like having such caring friends and neighbours. That Christmas was one of the happiest we had.

After signing up with Dr Drake-Lee I found out that, though younger than my father, he went to Stoneyhurst College run by Jesuits. He was at school with one of my Uncles. His wife Angela again younger than my mother went to the same Ursuline Convent. In their young days my Grandparents on both sides would have house parties during school holidays so that was how they all got to know each other. Our children loved going over for afternoon tea at the Drake-Lee's because they had a large garden with an underground air raid shelter, put there during World War II. Always an exciting place to play and it was close to where Angela and I were having tea and a chat. They had also made the top floor, the attic, into a playroom. There was a big rocking horse, a huge doll's house, a collection of lead soldiers, a miniature train set and umpteen toys. The children were allowed to play up there as long as they didn't take anything out of the room and put everything back as they had found it.

Angela always had a delicious spread. It was lovely to sit and chat in such beautiful and peaceful grounds. In the spring all around the air raid shelter mound, were dozens of tulips, daffodils, crocuses and jonquils. Quite a picture. My dentist was just down the road from the Drake-Lee's so Angela used to baby-sit Alison when I had an appointment. Though she knew Angela, Alison cried all the time I was away, it didn't matter how Angela tried to console her. Fortunately, I didn't have to go very often.

Tom had taken to bouts of drinking heavily. Bill Drake-Lee came over and had a good talk to Tom and he went off the grog for three months which was great. I could never make out how he could get so drunk but still hand me his pay packet in-tact. I never broached the subject. He was not a pleasant person to have around when he was drunk, so unlike his sober self. Tom didn't like the children around while he ate his evening meal, so I would have to feed them before Tom got home.

Tom became very suspicious and jealous of me. He even accused me of having an affair. I don't know when I would have had the time or opportunity. I remember one night there was a meeting called down at the church hall, we had just got a new priest, a convert from the Anglican Church. It was also about the time the Catholic Church decided to have all the ceremonies said in English instead of Latin. Many of the older parishioners were dead against it. The meeting was to try and make them see why the church had chosen to do so. After the meeting a dear old lady, who lived beyond us, at Burton Latimer, offered me a lift home. She was in such a terrible state over the whole thing, when we arrived at our house, I tried to persuade her to come in and have a cup of tea to calm her down. She refused. We sat talking in her little car for ages, finally she seemed a little calmer so I bade her 'good night' and asked her to drive carefully.

When I got in Tom was still awake and was as white as a sheet with rage and jealousy accusing me of carrying on with some bloke out front in the car. He swore he had seen it all and would not believe me when I told him what had happened. From then on, he wanted to know all I had done during the day and who I had seen. The only times I went out in the evenings was P and C meetings or something at the church, I was learning to be a Catechist up at the convent, so I would get him to drop me up there and then pick me up. In those days we owned a small station wagon.

This was very handy for the size of our family. At weekends we tried to always take the children out to a village near Kettering. We'd visit the little old churches and wander around the graveyard, finding the oldest gravestone. There would be more recent ones which were covered with colourful wreaths and bunches of flowers. All the head stones with loving messages on them. We would try to imagine what sort of a person the deceased was. Sometimes we found a whole family had died in the same year. Some illness of great proportions or by fire, nothing on the stones to enlighten us.

I would pack a picnic lunch and we'd find a suitable place where we could enjoy this. Quite often a villager with some knowledge of the village, would spend some time making us aware of certain historic events in that district. They were so happy we were interested in their village and that we

ALISON'S ARRIVAL

had brought our children there to share their history. Those weekends were some of our happiest times as a family. Some of the churches certainly felt as if there was some sort of spiritual presence. One week the local paper had a photograph of what appeared to be a monk kneeling at the foot of the alter. A young man had been out to the village to take photos as he said he had definitely felt a very strong presence.

Of course, there was a stream of letters to the paper with various opinions regarding the snap. The photo was sent away for tests to see if the figure had been super imposed or was it truly fact. That was one of the churches we had felt a presence, so we did not need to be convinced. On weekends that I had to get on with something, Tom would take the children over to the park to vent their energies, ending up with a Wickstead Park specialty, an ice cream made from goat's milk. Sometimes if I had finished what I was doing I would go over and join them.

We were so fortunate with the weather. Often it would rain at night and we would have a beautiful day, a bit wet under foot if we went into a field. Sometimes making it a little difficult to find a dry spot to enjoy our picnic.

Alison, 4 months old, Kettering

Chapter 32

VISITORS

Several relatives visited us while at London Road. One year we had a visit from my Uncle George. He was a Jesuit priest who had just returned from South America. He asked if he could stay a month as he was writing a book. Amazing that he chose us, with five children, I would have thought he would have picked somewhere with peace and quiet, but I think he wanted to stay with a family. I didn't have to keep the children quiet or change any of our habits and George really enjoyed the children.

I let him have the front room. He had a comfortable chair to sit on, a small table and a single bed. There was a large bay window with plenty of light and the room was far enough from the rest of the rooms that were full of active children. In those days, priests wore black suits and a 'Roman collar,' this he wore all the time. He was a smoker and invariably had cigarette ash down the front of his suit.

Uncle George was a big man with a loud voice to go with it so the children were a bit afraid of him. He was a terrible tease and often played tricks on them. They really loved him. I was in the habit of making homemade wines which I kept in the cupboard under the stairs. They shared this space with all the jam jars and preserves I bottled.

One evening I asked George if he would like a glass of wine, he chose parsley wine and thought it was quite delicious and 'could he have another glass?'. I told him it was very smooth but extremely potent, his retort to this was that he was used to drinking wine. Though the glasses were small he felt no pain after the second glass. He came down our long hallway singing a hymn in his very loud, though harmonious voice. I just burst out laughing as this huge dark figure walked towards the dining room. The children were terrified, he must have seemed so much bigger to them.

He would have us screaming with laughter at some of the tales he told us about all the years he had travelled around South America. The last place being Chile, the land of his birth. I wish I had asked him more about our

VISITORS

relatives in Chile, where my mother was also born and my maternal Grandmother hailed from.

I found him very easy to get on with, so down to earth and with such a great sense of humour and understanding of humanity. After a month we were sorry to see him leave. He went to Stoneyhurst the Jesuit College in Lancashire. Quite a change for him from his many years as a missionary in South America.

We had regular visits from my mother. She would come up from Wimbledon by train and bus on a Friday, arriving in the evening. The children looked forward to her arrival as soon after, one of us would go down to the fish and chips shop at the bottom of the hill. The children were all bathed and ready for bed when my mother arrived, so after the fish and chips treat, they were off to bed.

My mother would always take over and she would have the children up to their rooms after breakfast, to make their beds and tidy up. During the day they would all troop off to Wickstead Park while I got on with the mundane chores. On a Saturday evening we would go into the markets, weather permitting, this being the cheap time before the vendors packed up for the weekend.

On one of my mother's visits she had gone into town on her own. While coming across a small park, with crazy paving paths, she tripped and fell and broke her collar bone. She arrived back in great pain so I went to the post office to get Margaret, the Campbell's eldest daughter, they were the owners of the PO. She came up and babysat while I took my mother by taxi to the hospital. I was shocked to see how roughly they handled my mother though she was in such pain. Her arm was put in a sling and I persuaded her to stay a few more days. The following weekend I travelled down to Wimbledon with her.

We had several visits from cousins of mine. One week my cousin Ian came. I was very worried by his state of mind and called my Aunt who came down to take him home with her. He had just had an unhappy romantic break-up plus he was finding his studies at University very taxing. He had joined the Navy and they were paying to put him through University but at the same time he had to return to his ship and carry out certain duties. He found this a great strain, was burnt out and needed a good rest.

My cousins Heather (Boo we called her) and her sister Alison also visited on a couple of occasions. Alison was living in Cambridge at the time while studying, so the trip to Kettering was not too great. Heather was working in London. It was always nice to catch up with them, they were very helpful with the children who enjoyed their company.

My cousin Peter also visited and stayed a few days. He had entered the Dominican Order of monks but did not fit in with their monastic life. He still felt he had a calling to the priesthood and then entered the Benedictine Order

Incredible Memories

at Ampleforth. He settled better there. My cousin, Dominic had joined the same order some years earlier.

My cousin Tom, who was studying at Cambridge, also visited a couple of times. One weekend we went by car over to Cambridge to visit him and to catch up with his sister, Marian and her Husband Edward. They were sharing a house with a Chilean family. We had a wonderful visit, it was sunny all weekend so the children were able to be outside. We sat around on deck chairs, having all the meals outside.

While in Kettering we also had a visit from Tom's youngest sister, Rose, who was staying with friends in Leicester. His brother Ted also visited us for a weekend. I was horrified to see how fascinated the younger children were in his chewing his fingernails. Two of them ended up with the habit. It was still lovely to have him stay and see how close he was to Tom.

It was so nice to have all staying as they were all very easy to get on with, and the children always enjoyed having visitors. Our house was big enough to accommodate them too and have such lovely countryside around, plus the park made life so much easier. In the evenings when the children were in bed the adults were able to catch up with each other. I was so lucky to have such close cousins. Then we all went our separate ways, Maimo to New Zealand, Boo to Italy, Alison to France and Tom's family to Scotland. As I did with my sisters, Pat in the West Indies, then the States, Teresa in Brazil, then Italy, Christine in Canada. In those days we kept up by writing to each other, quite a time-consuming occupation but very rewarding when we received mail by return. We all looked forward to hearing from each other. I also wrote to my mother, a couple of aunts and also to a couple of friends in Jamaica. I remember one Christmas I sent 76 Christmas cards and received about the same in return.

My Girl Guide Captain, Sister Marie Emmanuel wrote to me every Christmas and sent all the latest news including newspaper cuttings. That was a real connection to friends of my youth. I also wrote to my father who had returned to the West Indies, it was nice to occasionally get a letter from him.

When I think back on all the things I used to do, I am amazed I had the time, I made jams, bottled fruit, preserved string beans in salt in large jars, plus I used to make a sort of cheese by putting sour milk in muslin, hang it and letting all the water drip out, then tighten the muslin around what was left, to shape it. Very nice with jam on crackers. I also made about two hundred jars of marmalade during the Seville orange season, half I would sell to the shop up the road and that helped to pay for the sugar and oranges.

Chapter 33

MORE ABOUT LIFE IN KETTERING

While in Kettering I grew all our own vegetables up in our allotment. I shared some with a family who lived near us. There were five children, their father was a bit of a con man, he spent time in and out of jail. When he was home, I noticed the children with bruises and suspected he was abusing them. His wife was very loyal to him and would not hear anything against him. I used to have the children up during the day at times.

Our house was always full of children. A couple that lived nearby, whose two eldest went to school with ours, well they had a late arrival, who turned out to have Downs Syndrome. The mother who suffered Post Natal depression did not want to look after the baby. The father would drop the infant off on his way to work. I would look after her during the day and she would be picked up at the end of the day. Her brother and sister just adored her, she was also loved by my children and she reacted to their loving attention. She started to put on weight and as the days past I found it easier to feed her. When she was a few months old, her mother decided she would look after her.

There was a family down the road from us, they had twins six months older than Alison. When they were about 14 months old, I took on the job of having them during the day, until they started school at five. Both parents worked. Maxi proved to be a bit of a handful but over time realized if he was too much out of control, he ended up sitting at the dining table for a 'time out' spell. This he did not enjoy. When their mother arrived to pick them up, both boys would get right out of control. After they crayoned on the hallway wall, I asked the mother 'just pick them up at the front door and leave'. All the boys wanted was their mother's undivided attention after being with me all day. It was different when their father picked them up. He had a more calming response from the boys.

Incredible Memories

Though having the boys was a bit of a tie to the house until they were about four years old, the thirty shillings a week was a great help. Then they were five and all started school and I only had the boys for a spell during the school holidays.

I dreaded the day I was to take Alison as she always proved to be a bit of a mummy's girl. So contradictory to my expectations, when we arrived at the gates of Hawthorn Road Primary School, she said goodbye and trotted in with the others. Not a tear from her but a couple from me!

One day there were panic stations, Margaret did not arrive home. Mrs Matthews called in to say Margaret was not waiting for her, as she used to bring Margaret home when she picked up her boy. So a search party was organised. When I passed friend's houses, I popped in to find out if they had seen Margaret. They hadn't. So they joined in the search. As I walked up one road, I heard Margaret's voice and laughter in a backyard so I called out to her. She very happily came out the back gate as if nothing was wrong. She had gone home with a friend who had no siblings but had a key to let herself in, Margaret thought she would keep her company. What a relief, I didn't know whether to hug her or reprimand her. I tried to explain that she must always tell me first before going to anyone else's home.

Another rather traumatic occasion was when George chased Marie-Therese into Bernadette's bedroom, she shut the door and when he reached it, he tried to push it open but instead put his arm through the glass in the top half of the door. Next thing I heard the most terrible screaming from Marie-Therese, George came down the stairs with blood spurting out of his arm. I made him sit on the steps and remembered there was a pressure point on his arm which I pressed to stop the bleeding. I then asked Bernadette to stop someone in the street and tell them I needed help then to go to the Post office and get Mr Campbell to phone for an ambulance. A very nice young man came in and said he was a Scout and could he help. I asked him to go upstairs to see if Marie-Therese was alright, she was. Then Margaret Campbell came in just as the ambulance arrived. The medic told me to keep putting pressure and I would have to go in the ambulance. When we got to the hospital we were rushed to the operating theatre and I had to sign some papers and was told to go home as they would keep George in overnight. After three days I got a message to pick George up as he wasn't eating and would be better at home. When I got home, which was just after lunch George sat at the dining table and said he was hungry and wanted baked beans on toast. He managed to get a whole large can of beans and several pieces of toast down before the other children came home from school.

George ended up with several stitches and was very lucky he did not cut any tendons and did not lose the use of his arm, but he ended up with a big scar. I had to take him back to the hospital to have the stitches taken out, I had to go in with him as he refused to go without me. It was then that I had a reaction and nearly fainted when I looked in the mirror which enlarged the site and made the stitches look so much bigger.

Margaret, 3 years old, Kettering   *Alison, 3 years old, Kettering*

Marie-Therese, Grannie, Bernadette, George, Alison and Margaret, Kettering, Feb 1966

Incredible Memories

All five children in the yard at Kettering

Margaret, George, Marie-Therese, Alison and Bernadette, Kettering, December 1966

Chapter 34

PLANS TO EMIGRATE

Tom and I talked about emigrating, either to Canada or Australia as we thought we would have a better future for the family. We proceeded to get all the information. A family we were friends with up at the allotments had already applied for papers to go to Australia. They gave us a lot of information about the procedure. We started to get newspapers from Australia giving us information about houses and jobs.

When we weighed it all up, we decided Australia would be the place to go. If we went to Canada, we had to repay the air fare. The climate was another consideration as their winters were so cold, we would have to spend a lot on clothing for five children and ourselves. Whereas to go to Australia would only cost ten pounds each for Tom and me, and if we stayed for two years, we didn't have to repay the fare. Also, the climate seemed more inviting. Most cities seemed to be near the ocean and beautiful beaches. There was also a possibility of a job for Tom with a building firm and they would help us to own our own house,

There was endless correspondence and at great expense, visits to London, to Australia House. We would have to take the train, with five children, spend the day having interviews. I would take a packed lunch with plenty to eat and drink for the children and a supply of reading matter for them while Tom and I were interviewed. The man who we saw went through all our history. Took photographs of all of us. They gave us a choice of flying or taking a boat. Asked us which State we would prefer. We chose Queensland or Western Australia. Luckily, they said we would be going to Western Australia as the possibility of jobs and housing was better. We were also told that if we had two thousand dollars in the bank, we would have no problem getting a mortgage.

In those days I used to run a little haberdashery and stationary store from home. I made sure we all had at least half a dozen pairs of undies, socks and other garments each. John, who interviewed us, said it could get very

Incredible Memories

cold and wet in the winter months, so I made sure we were all prepared. Not much different to what we were already experiencing.

We put the house on the market. I made inquiries about crating our belongings, which included folding beds and mattresses for the children, toys books, cooking utensils, various household tools and many personal items such as photo albums. If there was any space while I packed, I'd slip a few more things in. The whole thing was to cost two hundred pounds, delivered to the wharf in Fremantle and would take three months to get there.

I tried packing the things as carefully as possible into two large crates we were sent. I had to itemize all in boxes and crates. Label them and address them to Fremantle Port to be collected.

It did not take long to sell the house and we got the price we wanted. Settled our mortgage and with what we had left we had our two thousand dollars. My brother David and his wife Marianne invited us to stay with them until our flight date. I was a bit concerned about the weight we were allowed to take on the plane, so there was constant weighing of bags. We were sent our flight number and identity papers with all our photos, the children were all on my paper and Tom had a separate one of his own.

The week before we were to go down to David's, I got a telegram to say they wanted to interview me again. I promptly went down to the Post Office and phoned them to ask why, and a very officious voice said,

"You were born in Haiti."

"Yes, so what? We have had lots of interviews and already have our flight number, so what is the problem?"

"Well I would like to interview you."

"Why? Do you think I am black?" (Australia at that time had an all-white immigration policy). "Have a look at our photos. We have been accepted and I am not traipsing down with five children in tow at this point. You look through all the information you have." And I put the receiver down. I was furious and thought that wasn't a very good start.

After settling the house and having the crates collected, we all drove down to Woodley. I was rather exhausted to say the least.

The winter before we left had been a bit trying. Tom had got a job as a truck driver, carting coal from the midlands down to London. Tom found the driving through London very taxing and would come home exhausted and covered in coal dust. It was a difficult time for both of us. Tom suddenly decided that emigrating was probably not a good idea. I managed to talk him around to seeing all the good reasons to go.

The spring before we were to leave, we hired a van and drove up to Scotland to visit all of Tom's relatives, to say goodbye. We called into Kelso to stay with Aunt Alice and Uncle Bill. Heather and Angielo, her husband were over from Italy so we saw them too.

PLANS TO EMIGRATE

We had lovely weather and a very happy, though sad visit with all. Saying farewells is not always nice. Then we drove down to visit friends in Bristol and across to the New Forest, where we camped a couple of nights.

When we went to stay with David and Marianne it was a bit of a crush as the children were so much bigger than our previous visit and there were two more children. We took some 8mm film of both families around the garden as a souvenir to remember our visit. I also did an audio of the children eating in the playroom. My mother came down for a weekend to see us before we launched out on our new venture.

My mind a bit muddled as to what went on while staying in Woodley. There was so much coming and going, invitations to meals or just a cuppa with friends we had made during our previous long stay at No 1. My brother Christopher and his wife Basia came down one Sunday for the day to wish us well.

Marianne, sometimes David and I played Scrabble in the evening, when the children were in bed. Marianne was a walking dictionary and invariably won the game. I enjoyed playing, it stimulated my brain and I found it took my mind off all the mundane things and also what we were about to launch into. When David played, he used to make up words and when challenged would have a little giggle.

I do remember I went for long walks in the park with the younger children.

Would I miss the greens of England, the colourful gardens? Surely there were comparably beautiful things of nature to enjoy in Australia. Certainly, I would not miss the long damp coldness of winter.

The day arrived for our flight. We were well overweight so we all wore about three layers of clothing and carried on coats. Of these we were very grateful as the airplane was very cold when we were at a high altitude. We were boiling hot when we landed in several very hot countries to refuel. After thirty-six very long hours we finally arrived in Perth, Western Australia.

But that is another story.

BOOK III

Chapter 35

THE START OF A NEW LIFE

Certain events in my life have been related in the previous two books. Those incidents made up half of my time on this wonderful earth of ours. The second half of my existence I am finding harder to set up in one book. The fifty odd years I have lived in Australia could possibly fill several books. So how do I begin to write all the exciting and adventurous episodes that have taken me on this long romantic venture?

When Bernadette, my eldest, was sixteen and Alison my youngest was five we migrated to Australia to start a new life in Western Australia. and were accepted on the 'Ten Pound' scheme. I thought the move and making a new life would make a difference to Tom's drinking habit. I was soon to learn that heavy drinking was a norm in Australia. Tom soon found mates who he could drink with who also had weird ideas about respect for women. At times Tom became very abusive and violent when under the influence, he also became very suspicious and accused me on several occasions of having affairs. He even accused me of being a prostitute. I prefer not to write in detail about that part of our life as when Tom was not drunk, he was a very good man. We got divorced not many years after our arrival.

It was a thirty-six-hour flight from London to Perth with three stopovers. The longest was a couple of hours in Singapore. When we arrived there, we were still suffering from our touch down in Bahrain, where the plane had refuelled. At this stop we had to walk across a sweltering stretch of tarmac. The temperature was 45° C and we were all muchly over clothed. We had been limited to the allowed weight so anything over that, we wore! Our stopover in both Singapore and India gave us a taste of very uncomfortable humidity. Mind you, we were glad of all the extra clothing while flying at high altitudes. The planes in 1968 were not as luxurious as the modern Qantas flights.

THE START OF A NEW LIFE

My entire time was spent in looking after the younger ones. Frequent toilet trips, 'want a drink!', 'can you read to me?' or various games to distract from the lengthy journey - 'are we nearly there?' umpteen times. As we flew into Perth the sight below was straight lines of streetlights crisscrossing the city we were about to make home. My initial feelings were of relief, we had landed safely and were about to launch into a new and exciting life.

By the time we had passed through customs it was well past 3am and I was beginning to feel quite sick. I was so tired. We were put into two taxis and drove off into darkness, as in those days the streetlights were turned off at midnight! The three youngest were in my taxi. Aged five, eight and eleven, they were nearly asleep. After twenty minutes of driving I started to feel quite concerned, where were we being taken? The driver said we were going to a place called Bicton. Finally, we arrived. From the taxi lights all I could see were a row of Nissan huts, Surely he had it wrong, in the glossy literature we were to be housed in a neat looking house with green lawns. A short solid man with a round face, under a multi-coloured beanie approached us carrying a torch. Finally, the other taxi arrived and the family was reunited. Our luggage was unloaded and the taxis departed we were told to leave our bags and followed the wee manny down to the canteen where we were offered very strong tea which had probably been brewed hours ago. I asked for milk for the children and then a bed "if you please". We followed the torch, picked up our belongings and walked past several darkened huts. Jim unlocked a door and left us to make seven bunk beds but we were far too tired to make them properly. The two rooms we had been given had no other furniture and no heating. We all turned in fully dressed and fell into a deep sleep until the middle of the next afternoon.

This was July 1968, my first impressions on opening the door was: had Tom and I made a terrible mistake in choosing to bring our five children to start a new life in this far off country? I was faced by some strange trees and the sound of an unusual bird call, this turned out to be a kookaburra. There was also another cry that of the local magpie, this was also strange to me. Beyond this there were the green lawns of a golf course, so at least we were close to civilization. The glossy pamphlets and promises we had been made on our several interviews were not true.

We all staggered down to the ablutions and certainly must have looked a sorry lot. Next thing was to go to the canteen to see if we could get some food. We were greeted by a very kind Irish lady who said the next meal was at five but she could give us a packet of biscuits. We were then told that the nearest shops were a mile and a half down the road but it was half day closing so this meant we would have to spend another cold night in the hostel.

In my younger days I was taught one should consider the consequences of one's actions. Most of my magical experiences came as a result of ignoring that rule and acting out of wild abandon as I will try to tell in my writings of various episodes and incidents in the next 40 odd years of my life in Australia.

I chatted to the lady next door and was filled in with the times for meals, certain families we should avoid, and was shown where the office was. This was already closed so we took a walk down to the beach. The children brightened up when they saw how close we were to the Swan River and somewhere they could swim. This venue turned out to be our salvation and helped to keep me sane while we lived under the conditions to which we had been delivered.

The second night we were there my eldest daughter, Bernadette, left her watch in the shower block. When she went to retrieve it, one of the other children had smashed it so badly it could not be repaired. This was very upsetting as it had been a gift from my father. A few of the children that had arrived before us turned out to be very rough and bullied the newcomers. This meant an adult had to accompany a child every time they went to the ablution block.

The day after we arrived we went down to the office to meet the Administrator, a very friendly and helpful fellow, only to be told that Tom did not have a job waiting for him with any building firm and that it was very difficult to rent a place with so many children. Not the sort of news one wanted to be given on arriving in a new country. The alternative was to find a property to purchase!

One of the men who lived in a caravan with his family, offered Tom a job as a brickie's labourer, at least this would tide us over. Families appeared and disappeared. A ship came in the week after our arrival. The new migrants were brought in on buses. I happened to be passing and noticed a guy who had tried to befriend us when we arrived. The newcomers were greeted by this fellow, who was completely negative about everything to do with life in Australia. Not an ideal greeting when one has travelled so far to make a new life. Life was bad enough as it was to find things were not as we had been led to believe. But what choice had we, we just had to make the best of it and get on with life.

Tom went off to work very early and the Administrator drove me around the suburbs and up into the hills looking at properties we could afford. There was a one room school where the four younger children went, Bernadette our eldest took a bus to Curtin High School which left me free to get around house hunting. I looked at a five-acre property with a three-bedroom home set among fruit trees on what appeared to be very good soil. This was situated just outside a town called Armadale. I could see possibilities but there was no transport, Perth was some distance away and job options nil. A car was a necessity to get around to find a house, on weekends we would drive to several destinations from New Norcia to Geraldton. We were told there would soon be a University built in Geraldton but none of us warmed to the town. Another weekend we drove down south

THE START OF A NEW LIFE

to Albany, we quite liked the town but again too far from Perth if the children wanted to continue their education. Finally, we found a place in Palmyra and put an offer in only to be knocked back by the bank. Before leaving the UK we had been told we had ample deposit for a house of that price. The owners of the house were even prepared to carry us but again the bank knocked us back.

By this time Tom was beginning to drink heavily and was being thoroughly put off our move to Australia. This did not help the situation. After eight weeks we were moved to a two-bedroom duplex in Beaconsfield. Our beds and belongings had not yet arrived from the UK the Saint Vincent Society lent us cutlery and cooking utensils until ours arrived. They also gave us a couple of wardrobes, a dining table and chairs and a lounge. The store man at Point Walter lent us a couple of bunk beds and three single army cots and mattresses, also some sheets and pillows with cases. We purchased a second-hand washing machine and a couple of lounge chairs and then made do with what we had.

Duplex in Beaconsfield, December 1968

Again, nothing of our surroundings resembled anything remotely like the glossy pictures we had been shown. I was shocked to find there were four children under 10 living in the other half of our duplex. Their mother had taken her life and their father was in jail. I will never understand how the children were not taken into care. Trying to befriend them without worrying about my own children was very difficult. I could never go out and leave washing on the line as when I returned half had disappeared. Then to my horror one neighbour said not to let the girls go to the local shops as a convicted rapist was hiding under one of the houses on the way there. Another headache, having to see children safely to buses and school. The three youngest were at Beaconsfield Primary school, a fair hike to it. Bernadette and Marie-Therese were at John Curtin High School, bus trips away.

Two Scottish families had been living in these conditions for twenty years. They made us feel quite welcome. The family got their first experience of an earthquake on October 14th1968, no damage done in this area.

I got my driving license and drove around daily trying to find a home. This proved very difficult as the bank was not prepared to give us a mortgage. People grumble these days about the interest they have to pay on their loans. To finally be able to purchase a house, a kind agent managed to get me two loans! One was a fixed loan at 9% the other was a reducible at 9% both were from wealthy farmers. This after trailing around for eleven months and unsuccessfully being able to raise a loan. Apparently, Poms, as they called us, were not reliable enough to repay loans, especially with a large family.

During our stay at the hostel a very kind lady called Nelly, called to see us. She had come out here with three sons from Kettering, the town we had come from and had heard about us from another family from Kettering who we had kept in touch with. They told Nelly we were having a hard time. Through her we joined a group of migrants from various towns and villages around Kettering. It was nice to have contacts and Nelly very kindly used to ask us up to visit her home in Subiaco, a suburb of Perth. We also went down to visit our friends, the Brights, who lived in a place called Collie. We found the town very friendly but again too far from Perth. The group used to hold a soiree once a month which Tom and I attended until Tom started to drink too much and it spoilt the evening, so we stopped going.

The house was in South Fremantle, we were close to the Indian Ocean, with beautiful beaches, and the children could remain at the same schools.

The weekend after we moved into our new home, I awoke to find our outside toilet had overflowed into the backyard. What a shock! Were our troubles never going to end! I found a plumber, recommended by our very kind neighbour, he announced there was a very serious blockage. The grapevine in one of the houses out the back had sent roots into our ancient sewerage pipes. They and the whole system had to be dug up and replaced. Not the sort of news one really wanted to hear but the good news was that there was a park across the road which had public toilets!

THE START OF A NEW LIFE

Our first home and car in South Fremantle, Commercial Road April 1969

We discovered drive-ins; these were open air cinemas. One drove our car in passed a pay kiosk, found a suitable parking bay next to a stand which had a loudspeaker which we hung on the front door. Facing us was a huge screen on which the film was shown. Behind us was a shop which sold ice creams, lollies as they called sweets, hamburgers, something new to us, and packets of crisps which they called chips. Inside the packet of crisps was a little blue packet of salt. They also sold sausages and chips. In fact, one could buy tea. We took sandwiches to save money but the children could go up in the interval and buy an ice cream. This was our entertainment for the week.

We used to go down to South Beach to swim. Our first Christmas promised to be hot so we made a picnic and went to South Beach, found a nice shady spot under a large Norfolk fir tree surrounded by green lawn. The temperature reached 114° F. Strange to have such a hot Christmas with no snow or icy east winds, no holly or the things we were used to connect with the festive season. When we felt too hot, we had a dip in the Indian Ocean. Unbelievable.

Incredible Memories

Port Beach, Fremantle 1969

Being new Australians was not made easy for any of us. When the children grew up, they related some horrific stories of what they had put up with at school, this from pupils and from some of the teachers. A couple of months after we moved in, I became ill. I knew from my doctor in England that I needed a hysterectomy operation. I went to see a doctor, and the week after I saw the doctor, I was put into hospital. I was operated on and only just made it.

I had the most extraordinary experience while on the operating table. Most will find it unbelievable. Why was I floating up on the ceiling? As I looked down, I could see Me lying on the operating table. All around me, nurses and doctors were trying to resuscitate my body. Their voices were hardly audible. They seemed agitated. There was blood everywhere. I was haemorrhaging. A mask was put on my face, an injection into my arm.

All of a sudden, the scene changed. I was in a long tunnel. My body didn't seem to feel like my body. I was as light as air. Where was I traveling to? I didn't care very much, if at all. It was a wonderful feeling this weightlessness. My surroundings were not at all clear. It was as if I was in a comfort zone. It was very peaceful, extremely quiet and trouble free. A very bright light appeared, it lit the tunnel I was in. My thoughts suddenly turned to my children, for I was able to think. I needed their love and support. They needed mine. Without any sort of announcement, my whole being stopped advancing. I was being dragged backwards. There was a terrible jolt. A voice said, "I think we've got her."

My whole body felt very limp and completely drained. All I wanted to do was sleep but this distant voice kept repeating.

THE START OF A NEW LIFE

"Can you hear me, wake up Mrs. Aitken. Anne can you hear me?"

My mind seemed to be working in slow motion. I didn't recognize the voice. Why didn't they just leave me alone, to drift into sleep? Then someone started to slap my hand.

"Can you hear me? Do you know where you are? What is your name?"

There they go again. How was I supposed to answer, I had a mask on my face? Why don't they just let me sleep?

I felt them roll me onto a softer surface. I opened my eyes slightly and saw four nurses around me. One was sticking something into the back of my hand. Another was putting white socks onto my feet. The other two were turning handles. My legs were being raised. I couldn't imagine what they were doing all this for.

I just wanted to sleep and didn't much care what was going on around me. My whole body felt very cold.

My outlook towards life had changed. Everything I had and was later to gain in life, my thoughts only "that I was fortunate." I had some Guardian Angels that were around constantly to guide me on my path, the lengthy journey of life.

I was very weak when I got home and it took a good 4 months before I was back to normal. Some very kind friends would call around during the day and make me a cuppa or heat up some soup for me. Bernadette had been given a few weeks compassionate leave from Teachers College and looked after everything for the family while I was in hospital and the first couple of weeks, I was home, which was a great help. Trips down to the beach with friends was a great healing. Tom was being very understanding and caring but he could not give up work.

My maroon dart blazer, I captained the Fremantle team in the inter districts competitions, winning all! 1970 - 1976

Incredible Memories

Family in South Fremantle 1971

Christmas 1978

Chapter 36

MY DREAM - THE AUSTRALIAN TRIP

From an early age I dreamt of visiting and traveling Australia. I finally succeeded in becoming a resident and citizen in the 1970s.

The Islands in the West Indies were so vastly different to the wide-open spaces here in Australia, yet so alike in many ways. The easy-going lifestyle being one, the climate another.

What a country, somehow I felt I had been here before, I felt so at home. I loved it from the minute we stepped off the plane. The first few years were hard, getting the family settled, holding down a job and bringing up the family.

It was not too long before Tom was back on the drink again and financially we were struggling, so I went and got a job down at the drycleaners at the bottom of our road, as a van driver, collecting and delivering dry cleaning. It was very heavy work. I ended up with a prolapsed uterus. I tried to do less of the very heavy work.

We made several short trips down South when the children had school holidays. We'd go down the coast one time to Australind, Bunbury, and Busselton (all coastal towns). The distances seemed vast, the roads wide and fairly good to travel on. Then another time inland and down the South Western Highway to Albany, returning the coastal route. We stopped at several places on the way to camp, like the delightful little township of Denmark, with its sleepy river lined with huge shade trees. Then at Pemberton, in the heart of the Karri forests.

One summer, I think it was our fifth, we decided to go on a longer camping holiday. George, my son, two of his friends, Margaret, my daughter and her friend, Alison and I went. Leaving the big city was not exactly their cup of tea but after two weeks enjoying the beauty and tranquillity of the countryside, they decided it was a better type of life. All but George's two friends, who after a couple of days, decided to hitch back to Fremantle.

Incredible Memories

This time we had driven down the Brookton Highway through the wheat belt towns of Narrogin, Wagin, Katanning and joined the Albany Highway at Cranbrook. It was a fairly dry and dusty drive until we neared the Porongurups where the scenery changed to the blue-green of the hilly country side. At Albany we found some nice swimming beaches, there was a lot to explore in the old Whale-fishing port city. As the children got older they would take off with their friends on their own camping trips. I told them that when they were grown up I would go around Australia.

While I worked for Gibney's Drycleaners, I found out the pay was well below what I should be earning. I was not very popular when I asked for a rise. I heard about a job with TNT auto transport which I applied for and got. This meant I had to drive a variety of vehicles during the day. Mainly delivering new cars to sales yards all over the metro area. Or drive truck cabs and chassis to yards where bodies were built on to them. Other jobs were to go to private houses to pick up a car to be delivered to a train terminal to be transported across the country. For three days work I was earning more than I got in a whole week. One day I was told I was no longer required. A friend who knew the owner of another dry-cleaning company, called Richardson's told me to phone the owner as he had put in a good word for me. This I did and was told to start the next Monday.

When I arrived, I was given a brand new 'Combie Van' and told to go out and find some new customers. By the end of the day I had 14 new customers and the boss was quite surprised. Over a year I had my full quota for the size of the van and the boss took on another driver to take over some of my work. After several years I was made manager of the firm. I still did jobs on the floor and also did deliveries when there was a lot of work on hand. I kept a check on all our agents and also got more agents and the business doubled. Then over a stupid incident the boss accused me of not paying $1 dollar for petrol I had got several weeks before at one of our depots, I had paid the lad who served me and he must have put it in his pocket. I was furious and told the boss I was quitting, I would stay until after Christmas so I didn't let down the customers. The boss gave me an excellent reference, I think he regretted the whole episode and would have liked me to stay on.

I decided it would be better for me to try and get into teachers' college as the pay and conditions would be so much better. I took the exam and passed, much to my surprise. In the interim I needed to be earning some money, a friend offered me a job at a games room up in Perth. The place was in Hay Street, there full-sized pool and billiard tables on the lower floor and on the ground floor there were Pinball machines. The boss wanted a mature woman in the job to try and talk the street kids to go back to school or for them to have someone they could go to if they had a problem. It was a real eye opener to see how many young children had left home or been kicked

MY DREAM -THE AUSTRALIAN TRIP

out of home. Some used to sleep under the bushes down at the Supreme Court Gardens or in railway carriages out at East Perth.

During the day it was fairly quiet, though I used to get truants coming in and I would have to ask them to leave suggesting they go back to school before getting in trouble with the law. At weekends there were crowds coming into the Pinball machines. Downstairs only two to each table and two were waiting to play. Of course, there were always those who tried me. Next to the fire escape door at the rear of the lower floor was my office. This was kept locked when I was not in it. There was a one-way window where I could view the whole of the floor and also the stairs leading down into that area. I had a phone with direct access to the office at the game's rooms in Murray St. In those days we did not have mobile phones.

Upstairs, on the ground floor were a row of Pinball machines, a couple of machines with grab arms which one fed 20 cent pieces and hoped to hook up one of the small prizes. Very seldom was anyone successful, so this was a good money spinner. At the bottom of the stairs into the lower section there was a video screen which showed the whole of the ground floor. I could keep an eye on what was going on in the upper floor while keeping an eye on the game's tables.

Only two were allowed to play on each table at the one time. Anyone who wanted the table for the next game placed a 20-cent piece on the side of the table and they then played the winner of that game if he chose to accept a challenge, or he played a game with his mate. Those waiting their turn to play had to sit on chairs provided. One had to be very strict with the rules otherwise there would be too many people down in that area.

If I had to open the centre, I'd go up to Perth by train as I would be finished by 4 o'clock. I had two young men working with me, one was Polish and the other was an Aboriginal. During the week there was only ever one of us working but on Friday and Saturday evenings there were two of us. I always had to work those two nights so I would drive up and try to park my car as close to the venue as possible. In those days it was free parking after 5pm.

When I closed up, I would get everyone out and shut one of the front doors, padlock it and then shut and lock the other one on the inside. Then I would make sure no one was inside and go into the office and sort out the petty cash. Sometimes the Aboriginal guy would stay back as I would give him a lift home which was on my way.

When it was the school holidays there was always full house. If anyone misbehaved, they were banned from coming in, if they did not leave when I asked them to I would phone through to the office and they would send a bouncer around. I learnt to play quite good pool as there was always someone who came in on their own and if it was quiet I would give them a game.

Incredible Memories

The weekends were not too good for me as I had to work late shift, but I always had a guy working with me so we could keep an eye on both floors. On the whole everyone behaved well until the 'Bikies' started coming over from the Eastern States. I found I could usually handle them. With a little bluffing, and somehow it got around that I was a black belt in martial arts. In the meantime, I had an interview at the college and the head decided it would be too much for me to study, have a job and run a household. So I stayed at The Blue Pumpernickel. The venue was situated in Hay Street between the Mall and Pier Street.

When I first started there some of the young fellows used to try me. I had one young Aboriginal guy pointed out to me who had been banned for a month, he had two weeks to go. As soon as my boss left this kid tried to walk in.

"Sorry you're not allowed."

"Not me."

"Yes you, don't think just because you've changed your shirt I wouldn't recognize you." He and all those with him started to laugh, but they left. Two days later he tried again. This time he had his hair cut short and thought I wouldn't know him, He didn't try that again.

They were banned for all sorts of things, damage to machines, swearing, fighting or abusing another patron. No one was allowed in with bare feet. They were not allowed to carry weapons. They were not allowed in more than 4 in a group and they were not allowed to crowd the place. One day a guy came in and started to kick and thump one of the machines. I walked over to him and asked him what he thought he was doing.

"This bloody machine isn't working right."

"Well kicking it ain't going to help, so I'm asking you to leave."

"You going to make me."

"Yes!" I said.

"You and who else?"

"Me and no one else."

And he started to thump the machine again. By this time the place had cleared.

"Right that's it!" I doubled my fist, as I'd been shown when I learnt self-defense, and whacked him in the ribs, at the same time said, "Now leave before I throw you out on the pavement for all those guys out there to laugh at you!"

Then I removed my sandals and started to hit my hand on the side of one of the machines like I was hardening it up. He just put his hands up and said, "Ok." And left. By that time my knees felt like jelly. Slowly people started coming back in.

Soon after my boss came over from Murray Street, with a bouncer, someone had run down the alley and told him there was trouble at the 'Blue Pump'. All he saw was everyone playing the games as good as gold. Well

MY DREAM -THE AUSTRALIAN TRIP

after that word spread that I was a black belt and you don't want to mess with Mum, as all the regulars used to call me. There were several other incidents which I managed to bluff my way out of.

One Saturday night there was a crowd gathered out on the pavement and the guy in the café next door called the police. When I went to the front to see what was going on a drunk came over and started to abuse me saying he was going to punch me for calling the police. A couple of Aboriginal guys, who I knew, grabbed him and told him I would never do that and to settle down. He came and apologized later that evening but I told him to come back when he was sober. I got to know Chris quite well.

One New Year's Eve when driving up Pier Street to get to Wellington Street, I could hardly move the car. There were guys jumping onto the bonnet and boot of my car and thumping on the roof when I suddenly spotted Chris, the drunk, I yelled to him and waved. Before I could say 'Happy New Year' he was over like a shot dragging guys off my car and yelling at them. Next thing I knew I had blokes making a path for me to drive through. Boy I was glad to get going! It was a most unpleasant experience. This happened back in 1970s. How things have changed.

When the Bikies started coming over from the Eastern States it was the beginning of trouble. After six months and being followed late at night to my car, I decided it was too dangerous to be up in Perth at night by myself.

In the meanwhile, my mother had decided to come out to visit us. She was supposed to stay six months. By that time my girlfriend Vera and her youngest daughter had moved up from Bunbury. Her daughter had moved up earlier as she wanted to go to High School in Perth so she boarded with me. Vera and I moved into the unit out in the back yard so there was more room in the house. With my mother's arrival we decided to fix the unit to accommodate my mother so it would be quieter for her and she would have all her meals with us and was free to come and go but she also had a private place and she could entertain the children there if she wished.

Unfortunately, my mother wasn't happy with the arrangement until I explained the reason we had that arrangement. I was still working up at the Blue Pumpernickel so had odd hours but tried to spend a lot of time with my mother, one day she came up to Perth and visited me at work, She was a bit horrified at the conditions when she saw some of the types that frequented the joint. By that time, I had decided to throw it in and I got a job in Real Estate which were very long hours.

One day when I got in from work, I found the kitchen and dining area had been completely changed, both Vera and Mum had decided to remove kitchen cupboards and the fridge and put things the way they thought they should be. Needless to say I was not too pleased and voiced my opinion. There were other times when either Vera or Mum took things into their own hands which caused a bit of friction as all was done without consulting me. Mum decided to cut short her stay and Vera and her daughter moved into a unit in Fremantle and life was a bit more peaceful. That year I did quite well at selling properties and arranging rentals. About six months later Vera and her daughter asked if they could move back so after agreeing on certain arrangements, they were back living with us.

Soon after I lost my job and was told I was entitled to go on a pension, so I did as I was tired of working hard for someone else and working hard building up their business and then getting laid off. Vera managed to get work and by then we decided to buy a home on wheels and planned on taking a trip around Australia when the last of our children was able to cope on their own.

When talking one day to Vera, I found she also had the same idea. We decided we would work towards the day we would achieve this together. We bought a home on wheels together. It was a custom-built home on a three and a half ton Bedford truck chassis. When we could, for we were both working, we'd take it on longish trips to see how it handled steep hills and gravel roads. Testing mileage per gallon, and several other things.

I did odd gardening jobs and Vera and I cleaned a block of offices at night. Vera left her job at an hotel and got a job cleaning daily at an Indian family's house, she also got me a job there ironing. As they had three children there was quite a lot of ironing, the father was a businessman so there were lots of shirts to be washed and ironed. He complimented me one day by saying he had not had his shirts ironed so well since he left India.

Sometimes we went away to various places testing out the van as we wanted to be certain it was road worthy to take on such a long trip. It proved to be very comfortable and drove well and when we found anything needed to be done we had it fixed.

Finally, when Alison was at technical college and 16 years old and Nola had got married and left home, I sold the house in South Fremantle and the three of us moved into the unit I had bought in East Fremantle and paid off all the mortgages. Alison had less responsibilities living in a unit. I made her responsible for paying gas and electricity and looking after my affairs while I was away. Then we decided on a date having made sure our van was all set up with spare parts

Making lists and more lists. What does one need? We had never done anything like this before. To start with spare parts. Everyone told us, "You must take as many spare parts as possible, most essential with *your* vehicle!" Very cheering they were! Fan belt an absolute must. No one told us that our fan belt pulley was to sheer clean in half 135 km from the nearest town. But that is another story. Water hoses, spark plugs, points, spanners, inner tubes, on and on went the list. I might add all this information from men who thought we were absolutely crazy to even contemplate such a trip on our own.

We tried the jack, that worked OK, greased it well, stowed it away and hoped we never had to use it. Got a short length of pipe to use as a lever

MY DREAM -THE AUSTRALIAN TRIP

while undoing or tightening the nuts on the wheels. Garages have a habit of replacing the nuts so tightly with their little guns, daring us to remove them with our puny hands. Condenser, light bulbs, nuts bolts, more tools, then on to the food list, camping gear and clothes.

Clothes, now that was a very difficult subject. This being a working holiday we had to be prepared for everything. We had made up our minds we would take on any job that was available so we needed a variety of clothing, we also needed some formal dress when we visited friends and stayed in town! So we also required shoes for these occasions, boots for hiking and climbing. Then we ran out of storage space. Out came everything, reorganize, eliminate. Would we ever get going?

We had our mobile home for a year. After our trial runs, we felt we had chosen the right vehicle, we had all the comforts one could wish for. A good-sized fridge, a gas stove with an oven and two burners, a sink with running hot and cold water, a shower and chemical toilet, Comfortable bed and plenty of storage space. We carried two 20lb. gas bottles for stove, fridge and hot water, a 12-volt heavy duty battery for lighting if we couldn't plug into mains. The fridge could also be run off mains electricity.

We found the fridge a good friend especially in the out-back, always a nice cold 'white one' as the Northern Territory people called their cans of beer. Our plan was to use it for all the fish we were going to catch, as it turned out we didn't catch as many as we had hoped. We did use it however for fresh vegetables which meant we didn't have to rely on dried or canned varieties. How soft and reliant we had become living in a city. Half the things on our list we never used and were not essential, especially on a trip like ours.

We had one door on our van, which when locked on the inside could not be opened from the outside. Or so we were led to believe until someone proved different, but not until our return! Having one door was an asset, a safety measure, the colour of our van was a matt gun-metal, a good camouflage when parked in the bush. The roof was white and therefore easily sighted from the air. On one side I had painted a large map of Australia, on this I drew a road showing all the towns and cities we visited, entering them as we travelled. From reports in the media and listening to people's tales we really didn't know what the wide-open spaces held for us.

Packing our van turned out to be the least of our worries. The comments from people we told of our impending trip were many and varied.

"Two ladies traveling on their own, quite crazy!"

"What if you get a blow out or break down?"

"Well we'd change the thing, if we had a break down we'd check it out and if we could do something about it, at least to get us to the next town, we'd do it."

"There's some terrible things happen to people when they're traveling."

"You should take a CB radio with you just in case you need help."

I wonder how many people have hiked, biked and driven across without a CB.

"Oh, but you're two ladies on your own."

"I bet there's been a few of them too." Wondered if they were trying to put us off ever going on our trip. Another popular one was.

"What if you get hassled?"

"We'll cross that bridge when we get to it. They might even end up with a bit of buck-shot whizzing over their heads."

"Oh, you're taking a gun then are you? That's good. Yes, oh well you'll be right. Do you know how to use a gun?"

"No, we'll send for you. Ask a silly question, what do you expect mate!"

"Oh well you'll be right."

"Yes we'll be right for a couple of rabbits, maybe. Got to live you know."

"What, do you mean you'd skin them and all?"

"We don't exactly fancy eating them skin and all." A horrible silence as they check us out, this insane couple.

"See ya. Have a nice time and take care."

Then there's the big Aussie male. "Got room for us to come along and keep you girls company? Well I mean you might need help if you get a flat tyre or something. Or might meet a bunch of black fellas."

"Maybe they'd be better than a bunch of you. Well we'll take the chance." Can see the disbelief and hurt ego creeping in, but back they come for more.

"How are you two ladies going to travel so long without the company of a male?"

"Quite well thank you."

Actually this turned out to be one of our hassles while traveling. These characters, married or not, thought that two ladies on their own must be looking for a mate. All through our trip we never failed to get amazed looks when we told of incidents we had experienced, and we had managed without the help of a man.

Date Set

We set the date for departure, June 10th1980. Within three weeks of telling the families of our intended plans two of Vera's daughters announced they were pregnant. Nola her youngest, due in September and Diane her eldest, in November. Then one of my daughters, my second, Marie-Therese due in January. Phew what timing!

But we had made our plans, all agreed we should not put off our trip. With eight children between us we might never get away if we were to stay home for every grandchild. We must go while we were still young and strong enough to work our way around.

MY DREAM - THE AUSTRALIAN TRIP

For days before we left the phone ran hot, friends wishing us well. Some asking if we'd like to squeeze them in. The morning of departure, just about every member of the family came over for breakfast. The ones who couldn't make it phoned.

Time was slipping by and we realized it was going to be difficult to do any more organizing, so we grabbed the last-minute things, threw them into the van and tore ourselves away. At last we were on our way and a dream was coming true.

We travelled slowly out of Perth collecting some more spare parts on the way out, water hoses (later we found out we had been sold the wrong ones, but luckily we found out when we were in a town). We also picked up some extensions for the valves on the inner wheels, there were dual wheels on the back. The extensions made it easier for testing tyre pressure, also when getting air.

After only traveling a couple of hours, it was already 4 o'clock, we decided it was time to find a nice quiet spot to park for the night. Off to the left we found a strip of disused road running parallel to the Highway. Parked behind some bushes, sheltered from view by mounds of blue metal, very handily left there by the road board. This was between the town ships of Moora and Carnamah, half a mile south of Watheroo.

This first part of the journey had been pleasant, nice scenery, good road and excellent weather, but, maybe because everything was so new and we were possibly a wee bit anxious, nothing we passed at this stage of our travels seemed to make much of an impression…From memory, we were both excited at finally starting our trip but a little sad at leaving our families and familiar surroundings.

Took stock of everything, poured ourselves a sherry and commenced reading farewell cards and messages. We also played a tape which Nola and her husband, Gavin had given us with strict instructions we were not to play it until we were on the move. Both of us dissolved into tears and felt very homesick and alone, wow and that was only our first day away. It was a very touching and rather emotional message.

After a second sherry and a good meal we felt a little better but rather tired so decided on early bed as we planned to travel at sun rise.

So ended the first day of our 'Dream Trip.'

Chapter 37

ON THE MOVE

In the middle of the night we were rudely woken by a train thundering past. We both sat up wondering where we were and what the hell was going on. Could it be an UFO? We had not noticed a railway line running only a hundred yards beyond our camping spot. A goods train hurtling by at night sounds so much louder.

The birds had started with their morning songs just before the sun had actually shown itself. Always a good start to the day. We watched the sun rise as we battened down, put things away, then we were off again, up the Northern Highway. It was a beautiful day and we were truly on our way.

We stopped in at Mingenew hotel to visit some friends then slowly moved on to Dongara and Port Denison, on the coast, a delightful little fishing harbour where we wandered around and stretched our legs. Dongara is a picturesque town, with a population of just over 1,000, sheep and wheat farming other than cray-fishing and oil drilling are the main industries. But it is also a very popular tourist resort.

On to Geraldton via the by-passed hamlet of Greenough. This is a town well worth seeing as several of the oldest buildings dating back to the pioneer days have been very cleverly restored, and here is true Australian history. Quaint twisted 'lie down' trees dot the countryside. These trees have been pushed over by strong, salty Westerlies that blow in across the plains from the Indian ocean. Overland the settlers toiled to clear and plant some of the first crops ever to be grown in Western Australia.

Only completed 179 miles, other travellers we'd seen seemed to be in such a hurry to get to their destinations. We had been traveling at a steady 45 mph, saving our vehicle, also seeing more by doing so.

As we'd driven along the highway a flock of pink and grey cockatoos (galah) flew up from the side of the road, what a wonderful sight as they glided in unison. When they changed direction, the sun caught the silver of their wings, in the next second they turned again and they were all a reddy-pink. There must have been a few hundred of them. We had also seen a fox and several kangaroos, but they had been hit by fast moving night traffic.

After arriving in Geraldton, we decided to drive out to Bluff Point and park for the night. We found a quiet spot down by the sea. It was such a restful sound listening to the small waves slowly falling on to the beach then even more slowly sliding back into the ocean turning the sand and the pebbles as it went. The sunset was breathtaking, first a golden sky then a rich red dotted with grey-blue clouds barely lying on the horizon.

Our bus, parked by the beach, Geraldton 1980

So careful we thought we had been in our packing! How difficult it is to open a can with a penknife, but it gave us one of the many occasions when we laughed at ourselves. At this point our water pump packed up. A blessing in disguise as showers would mean so much more water being used. We were soon to learn how to stretch out the water ration, a precious commodity in the outback. We, at this stage, felt we needed the use of the pump and spent the next day trying to find parts to fix it. We drove around to several places that had been recommended to us to no avail. But at least we had pretty well covered all of Geraldton and had met many people who tried to be helpful. We phoned Perth to get a part sent up to us.

We waited around for six days during which time we found out that the stove needed a service, we also needed to have an adjustment to the timing in the engine. We had the van completely serviced before leaving Fremantle, another thing that had not been done properly.

Incredible Memories

The seaport of Geraldton is the principle town north of Perth. Its hinterland covers millions of acres of good arable land and is one of the greatest wheat producing areas in Australia, one of the biggest grain terminals dominates the harbour. Another major industry is cray-fishing and the main source of supply are the Abrolhos Islands. A group of islands about 50 miles off the coast, in the Indian ocean. In the close vicinity of the farming area, tomato growing has become a profitable industry, supplying early markets in the south and in the Eastern states. We found most of the farmlets were owned by Asians.

During our six day stay, we explored the town on foot visiting several places of interest including the Cathedral. While wandering around we met a few other travellers, one such person was Wal Birk from Sydney. As we were walking up one of the backstreets, we saw a mobile home with dozens of place stickers and thought we'd check it out. A rather distinguished looking gentleman stepped out. Tall bearded but minus the moustache, softly spoken and with a twinkle in his eye. We exchanged notes and found he and his wife, Ol, had travelled thousands of miles and were over in Western Australia visiting one of their sons.

We were to find out that while traveling one tends to bump into the same people again even if it's a year later and several hundreds of miles away. At this stage of our journey we were a bit shy and reluctant to make it known we were two ladies traveling on our own. It was amazing how many presumed we had husbands with us.

On the sixth night we changed our parking spot. We went to a beach south west of Geraldton, just for a change of scenery. About 7:15 the next morning we had a knock on our door, to our surprise a middle-aged couple stood there claiming to be the designers and first owners of our van! We got a bit of a run-down on the history of our home on wheels. They were pleased to see nothing had been changed but a bit concerned that the guy who sold us the van had been less than honest about the mileage done. It was certainly a shock to learn the engine had done more miles than the speedo reading. We now knew to expect a certain amount of break downs if we didn't treat the vehicle with great respect, and possibly even then. But not to worry, onwards we must go, our adventurous spirit still with us.

Geraldton the town from which the great explorers left, John Forrest, 1874, and Ernest Giles, 1876, to journey east over land to Peake Station, South Australia. Now we were starting North on our exploration!

We waited another night, the part for our pump was to be delivered to us by courier out front of Kentucky Fried. Again, no luck and in the meantime a carload of young people parked their car across the front of the van. When asked if they would move, they just laughed at us. So I just got in the van and started the engine blew the horn and advanced very slowly, they sat there laughing, all except the girls who were screaming for them to get out of the way, which they did. We took off and drove North to another car park near a beach and bedded down.

After collecting mail the next morning, we decided to forget the water pump. We drove on towards Northampton, the rains keeping us company all the way. We drove straight through, what could one see with it teaming down by the bucketful. At times the rain was so heavy we wondered whether it would be safer to stop, visibility was almost nil.

We drove on, paid a visit to Horach's Beach. A holiday resort where we saw an assortment of sandstone rocks, wind-blown into weird shapes. Then on to Hut River Province, which was not very well sign posted. Interesting but not quite what we expected, actually we didn't know what to expect. I think we thought we'd see more houses, looking back on that visit all I can remember which made an impression on me, was the little chapel. Did the usual things tourists tend to do, we bought souvenirs, sent postcards to the family and took posed photographs. It was a hot dusty place devoid of atmosphere. We met the self-proclaimed ruler, dressed in working gear, we would have missed him if the lady in the little shop had not pointed him out to us.

As we continued our journey, we were to find we could enjoy and see far more in looking at what nature had provided for us and that was free.

It was very windy, the road going North was never far from the coast. From the appearance of the trees it looked as if the wind had never ceased as all of them had a decided lean to the East. Some actually lying on the ground. The paddocks were quite wind swept and barren, to the left there seemed to be for as far as the eye could see, nothing but huge sand dunes, white patches, then yellowish stretches. In some places the vegetation had reclaimed the dunes. To the right it was more of a scrub country, with spare stunted mulga in reddish earth.

As we left Northampton the highway took a path further inland, still scrub country. Not long after passing the rabbit proof fence, we turned off the highway into Kalbarri, what a beautiful drive that was. The road no longer a dirt road, as we both remembered on our last visit, it had been widened and sealed.

Some forty miles from the highway, laid out below, around the mouth of the Murchison River, was the coast and the township of Kalbarri. It is a very popular fishing and holiday resort. We were both surprised to see how much it had grown. On the way in there are some meandering gorges, the Murchison River has carved a winding course, it has eroded fifty miles of gorges hundreds of feet in depth through sandstone, creating a multi-coloured horizontally banded white, red and yellow wall. At the bottom of these gorges the river water is nearly always clear. One can see wild goats and kangaroos coming down to drink.

We had witnessed a magnificent sunset as we drove down into Kalbarri. The weather was beginning to improve and the evening was warmer. There

Incredible Memories

was a sheltered spot down by the river where we camped for the night, kept company by some mosquitoes that managed to find their way into the van.

It was our eighth day on the road, we had been getting up early every morning, raring to go, to see new things, meet new people. We went for a wander along the beach shell hunting, not many to be found so tried our hand at fishing. After two hours and not even a nibble, plus a biting cold wind which had sprung up we gave that away and returned to the van.

A young couple from Perth parked their Kombi van near us, they were on their return trip. They had spent their honeymoon traveling around Australia. After tea they joined us for a few games of cards, told us a tale or two about their trip. We were able to glean a fair amount of information from them re good camping spots, swimming and fishing holes. They also told us how friendly everyone had been across the top of WA. Maps had been spread out and little Xes marked the spots. At that stage we omitted to make a note on the side of the map explaining what each X was there for. But we learned as we travelled, if not from our mistakes, from other more experienced troopers who still made mistakes!

Always make a note, even found it interesting to put down the name of the person who gave us the information and where they hailed from.

After having a bright day, it turned to rain early the next day so we refuelled and headed out. The further we drove the worse the weather got, it rained all the way to Carnarvon. Very heavy at times, impossible to see the countryside. We called into the Overlanders for lunch and a break. We heard stories of how wet it was further north. Never seen so much water, it was just everywhere. The last time through these parts we had seen emus running across the road and wil flowers along the road side, now there were lakes on either side of the road. Not one parking bay was safe to drive into.

It had been difficult driving under such conditions and we were pretty tired on arrival in Carnarvon. All we wanted to do was find a nice quiet place. We drove around for what seemed like ages trying to find a decent spot, finally parked in the town car park. It was well lit and had half passable toilets and the ground was level. Our first night in Carnarvon and we intended having a good night's sleep. Little did we know at that stage we were to stay many more nights in this northern township.

Chapter 38

THE FLOODS CAME

Carnarvon, some 600 miles north of Perth, is the centre of the Gascoyne sheep raising district. Thousands of acres have been irrigated along the Gascoyne River turning the area into a big fruit growing district. The climate being well suited to tropical fruit and vegetables. There is a large prawning and fishing industry. The Carnarvon Space Tracking Station played an important part in America landing the first man on the Moon. The establishment of the Tracking Station supported facilities for NASA's scientific satellite program, the tracking stations are a part of worldwide networks. Carnarvon is also a base for the Royal Flying Doctor Service. The population is growing at a steady pace and is a tourist attraction- the "Tropics" of Western Australia.

At the mouth of the Gascoyne River lies this interesting town. The terrain not many feet above sea level and fairly flat, has virtually one main road, a wide one. This street runs from the mouth of the river, East to the junction of the North West Coastal Highway and is about three miles long. It runs parallel to the river and is lined with coconut palms. A pleasant walk is along the coastal front of the town and over a foot bridge to the other side of the river.

It was humid, hot enough to get into shorts. We called at the post office and found there was no mail- very disappointing. As we walked out, we noticed two girls we had seen down in Geraldton, sitting on the steps. Made ourselves known to them. They were sisters- Demaris and Beate, from south west Germany, hitchhiking north, hopefully to Darwin.

Our tenth day on the road- we decided to stay over the week to await mail, visit friends, and catch up on letter writing. We wandered around the river front to a pub and had a couple of games of pool. While there we met a few friends of Vera's up on holiday from Bunbury (a town south of Perth). We played a couple of rotten games: both needed to practice before being challenged by anyone else.

Incredible Memories

The weather forecast was not too promising. While we walked back via the river we could see that the river had risen quite noticeably. Not to worry, this was the dry season so it wouldn't last too long or so we'd been told! When back at the car park we decided to back the van down behind the loos as it was a more sheltered spot for the night.

We enjoyed some fresh mullet for tea which had been locally caught, not by us I may add. Neither of us had tasted mullet for years. What a way to live, fresh fish, not the frozen variety, lots of fresh fruit and vegetables.

The news was that it was raining very heavily inland, that all the rivers and creeks were flooding and several roads were being closed. This was so hard to believe as it had been a warm sunny day in Carnarvon, with hardly a cloud in the sky.

Next day after breakfast, we went for a long walk around the river and the town. The Gascoyne was still rising, the bridge on the road north had been closed. Only people traveling south could leave town. This was very disappointing news for us. We drove around looking for higher ground, ended up parking in Rushton Street, under some shady trees, next to the Jubilee Hall, across the road from the Catholic church. We spent most of the day down by the river. It was still very warm and sunny. The river was turning a muddy red colour, with bits of debris coming down. The water line was still about ten feet below the top of the banks. There seemed no immediate danger of the town flooding, so we moved back down to the car park for the night.

Next morning, we noticed a young couple with two children, parked near us. They were in a station wagon and towing a covered trailer. Larry and Gloria, with Timmy, two, and Roxanne six months old, of Port Headland. They were on their way home from holidaying in Perth. In cramped space with two young children and no cooking facilities, we told them where we planned to park and that they were welcome to join us if it would make their situation a little more comfortable.

While walking along the banks of the river we met the Catholic priest. This was out near the suburb of Morgan Town. He showed us photos of the 1961 floods. We only hoped there wasn't a repetition. The Gascoyne was flowing much faster and rapidly rising. We moved back to Rushton St. and parked, leaving space behind the van in case Larry and Gloria should join us.

We walked into town, down to the river, several times during the day to check the level of the water. It was certainly rising at an alarming rate. The news was that it was still raining very heavily in and beyond the Kennedy Range, the source of the Gascoyne River.

We were parked as I said, next to the Jubilee Hall. This had been taken over as an emergency radio station so we were in a great position to be able to get first hand news. Bulldozers and large machinery had been busy all day building levy banks along the south bank of the river. All the roadside drains

THE FLOODS CAME

had been topped with sandbags to stop the back wash flooding the streets. We heard later that day that all the market gardens and plantations were flooded and that several people had been rescued. Others were stranded awaiting rescue. The river had risen four feet above the Ten Mile bridge. The railings had been removed to try and save the bridge. The Ampol service station at the junction had been flooded. We wandered down to see how the levy building was going. The banks were eight foot or so higher with one of the levy banks already breached. A bit of a worry. No one could leave Carnarvon except by air.

Gloria and Larry joined us for a cup of tea, Timmy thought our van was great and made himself quite at home. He sat in the driver's seat pretending he was driving a boat.

Two of the caravan parks had been evacuated, everyone was moved just up the road to the football oval, though it looked pretty wet from where we were. There was a great feeling of comradeship with nowhere for anyone to go. Several people strolling around the streets stopped and talked to us. Had there not been the flood we would never have met these folk. A situation like the threat of a flood and the thought of being cut off from any provisions coming into the town caused people to panic. The supermarket shelves were soon emptied.

At the time the State bowling championships were being held in the town. Several of the competitors had travelled up in their own accommodation. As some of them had to return to work, the authorities started flying them out.

On Monday, June the 23rd, the Gascoyne was still running very high. Roads along the river front were flooded. The river was full of foam, branches, trees, sheep, and cattle carcasses and debris all floating out to sea. It was still raining inland and the forecast, 'more rain.' We were to be there a few more days. The sea, seventeen miles out, was red and muddy. The fishing boats were forced to pull their nets because of the debris, so returned to port.

We went down to the only caravan park still open, had ourselves a shower and did a bit of washing just in case Carnarvon got some of the rain which was so doggedly hanging around. Later in the day we walked around to the Carnarvon hotel and played a few games of pool; a good way to meet some of the locals as well as those stranded by the floods.

We ended up with a group of younger local guys who gave us a few good hints on how to sink the balls in the right pockets. My first game was a very short one. I sank the black ball on my second shot- very embarrassing. When we walked back along the river front, we noticed that sand bags had been piled up in driveways and entrances to all the houses.

The following day it rained and we didn't get out much. It was still hot but squally. The football oval was under about a foot of water and had to be

Incredible Memories

evacuated. The foot bridge and Babbage Island road were closed. *Everything was very wet.*

Gloria met an old school friend at the shops who offered to put them up, which was great news. Vera and I spent most of the day in the van reading. We were beginning to get a wee bit impatient about getting on the road again. On Wednesday the level of the river dropped considerably. Everyone was starting to get itchy feet. None of us could complain, we had been made to feel quite at home. The hospitality and friendship was amazing.

At the bakers we met the German girls again. They had been evacuated from their caravan park and put on a hill, the other side of the Highway. Their daily provisions were taken over to them by boat. That day they were able to wade across and walk into town to do some shopping and collect mail.

Being parked in the same spot for a week, with no set itinerant time means nothing. It's very hard to remember what day of the week it is. We spent several hours in the library, and the librarian said we could borrow a couple of books. Carnarvon was still completely surrounded by water. It was difficult to get to the airport as the creek that runs between it and the town was in full flow.

Amazing how dramatically the level of the river had dropped. It hadn't rained for 24 hours inland. We checked with the Road Board to see whether we would be able to move on. The roads going north were still closed and we overheard at the radio station that a semi-trailer had tried to come south and had got himself bogged to the axles. There was a pretty hefty fine for anyone traveling on any roads that had been officially closed.

It had been rather cloudy and turned cold first thing in the morning but would fine up into a beautiful day. The river was down some more but the water still a dirty muddy colour. We heard on the news that the Murchison was in full flood and that it was a bit risky to attempt to travel to Geraldton. More people were being flown out, a few were contemplating traveling inland via Gascoyne Junction to Meekatharra and the Great Northern Highway and so continue their journey. There was more rain forecast and they were advised against such a move. On the Friday things looked a bit more promising. Larry came around and told us that there was a possibility cars and light vehicles would be allowed to move out the next day if they travelled with caution. That was real good news for them.

The day had started off very cold and then changed into a very warm and sunny one- everywhere was drying out a treat. Gloria and Larry came around to say good-bye and extended an invitation to stay with them when we arrived in Port Headland. We had a farewell cuppa with them and exchanged addresses. They planned to leave at daybreak next day.

The radio people at Jubilee Hall were getting ready to move so things were looking up. They had done a tremendous job.

THE FLOODS CAME

On Saturday morning the weather was fine, we went for a drive out to the junction. We drove out as far as Plantation Caravan Park and were we shocked to see how deep the water still was there. Cars were having to travel at about five miles an hour or stall. When we got back into town, we made inquiries about traveling and were told to come back on Monday. The authorities did not want anymore heavy vehicles getting bogged or breaking up what was left of the roads.

That night we decided to treat ourselves and went out to a Chinese meal at the Pearl Dragon. We had a very enjoyable evening. We were included in the fun at all the tables around us and had an excellent meal into the bargain.

Traffic over Babbage Island had started again. For several days the island had been cut off and anyone coming across had to wade over or come by boat. The bridge was under about eighteen inches of water. Many homes had been flooded and had suffered hundreds of dollars' worth of damage. Several had to be evacuated since the river level dropped, the ground started to dry out. The massive job of cleaning up got under way.

Sunday turned out to be a beautiful sunny clear day. We lazed around reading and writing. All we could think of was getting on the road again. At this point it seemed we'd never get to the other States. On Monday the Road Board told us we could proceed to Exmouth with great caution. They told us the Lynden River was still flooding over the Exmouth road, so as long as we checked out the situation again further up the road, we would be OK.

We called at the bakers and met the German girls again. They had got a job at the Junction cleaning up the garage so would not be leaving yet.

As we drove out of Carnarvon the road had been so badly washed out, we had to drive on a detour through a plantation. The water we'd driven through was deep and as we joined the highway, I suddenly realized we had no brakes. This was a frightening experience as we approached the sharp turn onto the road. Luckily, we didn't have to stop and managed to get the van safely around the corner with just the slightest bit of a skid.

We had heard the force of the water had moved the bridge four inches so didn't look forward to the crossing. When we got to the river the water was running about five feet below the bridge. We drove over very slowly as the railings were still missing. On checking the rear-view mirror, to my horror I saw two trucks also on the bridge. We just prayed the bridge would stay together until we got to the other side.

When we reached the north side, we found the roads very badly damaged. At times we had to drive on the wrong side of the road as that was the only part left. The Road Board had really been on the ball and had marked the bad patches with red flags where it was dangerous.

At least the weather was good. All around was evidence of the flood waters. The scrub was coated with a red-brown layer of silt and the odd tree showed how high the water had reached leaving its dull water mark. There were places where the water still lay in large puddles. When we arrived at

Incredible Memories

Minilya we inquired about the road into Exmouth and were told the Lyndon River was still flowing over the road but there was traffic coming out of and going into the town.

We drove on and turned off the Highway. About nine miles west we came to the crossing and started down the hill to the causeway. We drove over in first gear. The water flowing over had a very strong current and we could feel the van being pushed - not a pleasant experience. The main thing was to keep the van moving very slowly and in the centre of the road. When we arrived on dry land again, we were without brakes so drove along pumping the brakes until they dried out.

The road was very straight with barely a tree in sight, a bit of scrub and lots of sandy coloured ant hills dotted around. Halfway to Exmouth we decided to pull over to the side of the road and park for the night. Someone else had previously had the same idea as there was a campfire already set up. We scouted around for a bit of firewood. It was nearly as scarce as hen's teeth. This was the first time we had cooked out in the open since we'd started our trip.

What an eerie night we spent. The last vehicle passed us at 6:20 that evening and then not a single sound all night. It was a beautiful moonlight night, neither of us slept well. When we looked out of the window all we could see were rather ghostly looking ant hills. The absolute stillness kept us awake. There wasn't even the bird song one expects at sun rise.

The first car passed at eight o'clock. In the early morning light, the countryside reminded me of the Scottish moors, except for the ant hills. The warm sun rose but there was an ice-cold wind. The road was very straight and the ground rose slightly away on either side. Between the ant hills was some spinifex and a shrub with a delicate pink, bell shaped flower. The leaves were an olive green. The highest turreted ant hill was a mass of yellow-grey, and at least five and a half feet high.

I decided to go for a walk to see if there was any sign of life other than the ants which we could neither see nor hear. I saw signs of rabbits and roos a quarter of a mile from our camping spot. I had gone up over a small hill and when I turned around the van was out of sight. There were so many paths, possibly sheep tracks, though there were no sign of animals other than droppings. Some of the ant hills were at least six foot high. There were literally hundreds of them and all the surrounding hill side looked the same. It looked like a hillside covered in sand coloured wigwams. When I got to what I thought was the top of the hill, it turned out to be another ridge. No sign of the road. Now I could see how easy it would be to get lost.

The sun was behind me when I left the van so as long as I kept walking towards the sun I would soon see the road. The spinifex looks nice at a distance. A soft green, like a nice long grassed lawn. Very unpleasant to walk through without boots, as it is terribly spikey. The secret to not being pricked is to walk one foot in front of the other. As I walked along I kept bearing to the right. After ten minutes I saw the road directly in front of me, but no sign of the van. I was well off course, a hundred yards and around a slight bend and there it was. It was a relief and boy was I ready for breakfast!

Chapter 39

FREAK WET SEASON

Since starting our journey we had seen so much rain, flooding and water. Had we picked the wrong year to go on our trip?

Not to worry, on we went. Nearing Red Hill crossing, about thirty-four miles north of Nanutarra, we had to pull over as there was a car and caravan jack-knifed in the middle of the road. An elderly couple had been told that the creek up ahead was five-foot high and they were attempting to turn around and return to higher ground. We got out and gave them a hand, turned around ourselves and joined them. When we got to the high ground, we pulled over behind them and parked as level as we could.

It was a sunny day so we sat on the side of the road eating our lunch. The couple from the caravan joined us. They decided that they were returning south. We sat there talking for an hour or so and when a car came toward us from the north, we hailed it down. They had successfully crossed the creek but had got a car full of muddy water and were in a hurry to get to the next roadhouse to dry out. We bid our new friends farewell and turned north once more. After traveling a few miles, we stopped behind seventeen other vehicles all parked on the side of the road. As we were walking up front to investigate the hold-up, who should we see running toward us but Beate and Demaris. They greeted us like long lost relations, said they had a lift to Karratha Junction and should they still be there when we arrived would we pick them up. We said we would.

They told us what they had been up to since we last saw them and were quite interested in what we had been doing. We hung around for an hour or so, walked down to the creek and a few of the vehicles were braving it and starting to go across. We were waiting our turn when we realized some in front of us were not going to attempt it even in a 4-wheel drive. Some of the 4-wheel drives didn't look as if they had ever had a bit of mud on them and they "certainly weren't going to start now thank you very much."

FREAK WET SEASON

As we approached the creek the car in front of us took off at such a speed, got himself good and thoroughly drenched and stalled right in the middle, in our path. Then as if he thought we were as silly as him, beckoned us forward. That is something one never does- go on a floodway two abreast. The water invariably washes the lower side of the road right out and it could be several feet deep. So we just had to sit and wait until the car was towed out the other side by a truck. Everyone was quite good about the whole thing. A couple of guys waded in and tied a rope to the front of the car and away they went. Everything in the car was saturated. I bet they wished they'd never come.

We were taking it in turn. Half a dozen cars from the north would go through then six from the south. We got through to the other side and dried out our brakes. The rain was pouring down and we wondered what awaited us further north. We had already been disappointed that the road into Onslow had been closed. This was to be closed for a month. How lucky we were that we had not gone in and been stranded there for that length of time.

On we went. The Robe River was in full flow, then further on the Fortescue River was also flowing very fast. The rain abated for a while. On we drove.

We reached Karratha Junction and there they were, Beate and Demaris, thumbs out. They seemed very pleased to see us. We picked them and their gear up and turned into Karratha to the shopping centre, bought some fresh bread and told the girls we were going out to Dampier to see some friends. They said they would go with us, if that was all right with us. So off we went and as we did, looked for likely places to park for the night.

Dampier was a neat little place right on the coast. We called at the hotel and met a friend of Vera's. We had a drink and they caught up on family news. Then we and the girls drove back toward Karratha and turned off on a track we had noticed on the way out. We drove into the bush a few hundred yards, well out of sight of the main road. It was still raining off and on. There was a high bank on either side of the track so we thought it would be quite dry for the girls to set up their tent. While they put up their tent Vera and I got some tea ready and the girls joined us. We were all a bit tired after all our ordeals that day and decided to have an early night, we'd get to know each other better the next day.

It rained incessantly all night. We were all eaten alive by midges during the night. When we got up in the morning the girls were lying on a waterbed and we were parked in a lake. Normally when we parked anywhere, we would always park facing the way we would be going out. This night of course we didn't.

For two hours we cut branches and tried to find things to fill the track in. There were some fairly deep potholes. We couldn't believe that we couldn't find one single rock or some stones to help with the filling. After getting absolutely drenched, covered with mud and succeeding in getting the

Incredible Memories

road filled in, we decided to have breakfast. Then came the job of getting the van out.

First the van had to be turned around. To do this I had to drive it up off the track. As luck would have it there was a fairly level bit of ground, not too far from where we were parked. So off I went and managed to get up on to the bank. With the help of clumps of rather coarse grass that was growing there, the wheels were able to grip and I turned it around. Vera and Beate had their cameras out, at the ready to get it all on film. Demaris was going to guide me out. I drove back down onto the track where we had carefully laid the branches and started the nightmarish drive out. I knew I had to keep the van moving otherwise we'd really and truly get bogged. I put my foot down in first gear, then I felt the back of the van start to slip into the bank. So I hurriedly drove up on the bank again. Luckily there were no trees there. I drove along the bank for a stretch and then there was a tree facing me, I had to take off down on to the track. Slipping and sliding, feeling the wheels start to get bogged, then up onto the bank again, down on the track, then thank goodness onto 'terra firma'. All the while Vera and Beate would get the van in their sights and I'd take off in another direction and they'd be there with a look of disbelief on their faces. So they never ended up getting a photo.

Everything was so wet. The van was in such a mess but we were all thankful we had got out and were on our way again. Surely to dry weather and better road conditions. What a laugh we had about the whole episode. The road to Wickam, Port Samson, and Cossack were closed to all traffic except residents. We had hoped to go in and see Wittenoom Gorges, but all the roads off the Highway were closed. We stopped at Roebourne and made ourselves a cuppa, then drove on. Not exactly the weather for sightseeing.

A couple of miles out of Roebourne we heard a terrible noise that sounded like a machine gun under the van. We pulled over, had a look around the van and could see nothing so, we all climbed in again and drove about a hundred yards up the road. The same sound again. So out we all piled and noticed only half of our inner dual wheel tyre was left.

Right away the two girls asked where the gear was to start changing the tyre. They got stuck straight into changing it and we were soon on our way. The rain had left us at that stage, in fact we had a nice sunny spell as we travelled up through Whim Creek. The Yule and the Turner Rivers had a fair amount of water in them and as we got closer to Port Hedland the sky was very black. We took the girls to a caravan park and arranged to see them the next day, then went around to Gloria and Larry's. They lived a mile or so away from the caravan park. We were very warmly greeted by them and were asked to tea.

After tea we sat around and talked and watched TV. Gloria and Larry made us feel so welcome. It was as if we'd known them all our lives. We got the extension out and Larry plugged us into electricity. The rains were still with us, though it was only a drizzle.

FREAK WET SEASON

The next day we rose early, did some washing, then drove around. picked up the girls and headed for the main town. Gloria and Larry lived in South Hedland. At last we had quite a collection of mail. We drove down to a car park the other side of town and sat reading our letters. There were some belated birthday cards for Vera, letters from various members of the family and a couple of friends. The girls went off to shop, we wandered around looking at caravans and mobile homes. We met a couple from New South Wales and another from Victoria. They told us about places they thought we would be interested in calling at as well as road conditions and places they thought we shouldn't attempt with our van. Actually, we were to prove several people wrong as to where we could take our van safely. Being rather low in the body and long based from the back wheels to the back of the van, but driving very carefully, checking out the distance between dips in the road, we managed quite well to get into a lot of the out of the way places.

Port Hedland lies on the coast, about 1,200 miles north of Perth. It is the main northern port, inland from there is one of, if not the biggest reserves of iron ore. It is a tidal port with a well-protected harbour. A very red township. Everything is covered with a red dust. We were amused to see even the town's road sweeper was the same colour from head to foot. Standing leaning on his broom, I thought at first he was a statue. He was apparently quite a notorious character.

The area where Gloria and Larry live is a newer suburb, built away from all the ore dust. The iron ore berths at Port Nelson, in the inner harbour, are over 2,000 feet long. There are some very deep channels dredged to allow huge ships to dock there.

After lunch we went out to Finucane Island with the girls to look up a friend of theirs. We found Maureen working at the club there. Vera and I played a few games of darts while the girls chatted to Maureen. We then drove around the industrial area, got the gas bottles refilled and had our tyres checked. Larry managed to get us a tyre to replace the one that blew.

It was depressing still getting so much rain. The next day it was still very wet. We had our tyre changed but found the garage didn't have a jack strong enough to lift our van. So we had to get our own out and took the wheel off. They changed the tyre for us and the inner tube as that had been chewed up. We put it back on the van ourselves, much to the surprise of the girl working there.

We spent a considerable time looking around the shell museum down at the waterfront. There are certainly some beautiful shells up in that area. The tide was out, so we drove out to Cooke Point and looked for shells. That is the best time to go out to that point, when the tide is out. The sand left in ridges with grey and black patterns with many shells left high and dry. Sticking out of the sand was also the wooden remains of a jetty.

Saw a beaut sunset. It is more tropical here in temperature and flora and fauna. That night after tea, which we cooked, we were taught how to play

500. Had a late night playing cards and enjoying the company of the Howsers. Larry cooked us a very tasty pancake breakfast the next morning. Later, while he was fixing the exhaust pipe on the van we wrote several letters.

We dug up the shell; it didn't smell much better. Washed it out and filled it with bleach. We then walked over to the caravan park to see if the girls had decided if they were still traveling with us. Found they had made friends with some other young campers and were sitting around playing a guitar and singing, so we joined them. They agreed to continue with us. We went back to a BBQ that Larry and Gloria had organized for our last night with them. Gloria's brother from Darwin arrived and joined us. We had a very happy evening with them but as usual no one really wanted to say goodbye.

The next morning, we got up with the sun, early enough to see Larry before he went to work. Then we went over to the industrial area and got our reserve petrol tank filled. As we drove out of the driveway and made a sharp right turn, a drop of eight inches or so and at the same time the front wheels rising to the centre of the road, BANG, we knocked the corner and tap out of our drainage water tank. Thank God it wasn't our petrol or water tank.

We went around to the caravan park, met the girls, had a quick shower and were on our way into the town to pick up a fibre glass kit to do a repair job on the tank, at the first suitable stop.

It was about 11 o'clock when we left Port Hedland, too late to be starting as it was already getting hot. The road took us in a north easterly direction. Brown and red ridges extended on either side of the road with blue hills in the distance. The roads even as far north as this had been affected by the unusual wet weather. The road into Marble Bar was closed, so we travelled on. The bridge over the De Grey River was very low, more like a causeway, but luckily there was not all that much water flowing and we were able to cross with no trouble. We heard later that we had been very lucky to have crossed when we did as a few hours later the road and bridge were impassable and all the traffic had to cross over the railway bridge. Rather a bumpy way to travel!

I remember thinking what a scenic crossing ours had been. The gum trees along a sandy bank and the water flowing slowly. The crested bellbird or panpanpalala, as the Aboriginals name it, after its song, which is two slow and then three quicker notes; the red capped robin, a restless, fluttery little bird and lots of tree martins were in these parts. Of course, the pink and grey Galahs appeared now and again to show off their beauty, the small Corellas were roosting by the hundreds in the trees in the mid-day heat. On a hot day it would be nice to have a dip in the river and then sit under these smooth barked, pinky coloured, shady trees. But we had to keep going.

FREAK WET SEASON

Once past the turn off to Goldsworthy, the sealed road was at an end till about forty miles south of the turn off to Broome. On we went driving along a dirt road. Every now and again we would come to parts of a brand-new highway and we would have to go on a detour as the highway was not opened to traffic yet. The countryside around us was getting more and more like desert- not a house or even a road or track leading off. The girls were getting very quiet and looking rather worried. They asked if we were going the right way, and how long before the next town and where were all the stations? It must have been so different for them from traveling in Europe where there would be villages or towns every so many miles. Here we travelled at least a hundred miles and had seen nothing except an odd car traveling in the opposite direction.

Arid and semi-arid terrain stretched on either side of us. Everything was so dusty and it was fairly hot traveling. At long last it was not raining. We drove on as far as Sandfire Flats and stopped at the Roadhouse. Everyone had a couple of shandies and chatted to the owner who told us we were welcome to have a swim in the water hole. He also told us it was not safe to swim in the ocean, so we were quite glad we had missed the turn off to Eighty Mile beach. We had turned in a track but found it too sandy to attempt to drive any further. He told us the road into the beach was only for 4-wheel drive. Later we met a few people who had gone into the beach and found the going not too bad. Maybe the guy at Sandfire was having us on.

About seventeen miles beyond the Roadhouse we spotted a nice gravel pit off to our right and decided to call it a day. We turned off the road and drove in a few hundred yards and set up camp. The girls found a suitable bit of ground to pitch their tent. We all wandered around checking the place out and picking up firewood as we went. As everything around was so dry and there was a bit of a breeze, we thought it safer it dig a hole and set up the fire down in it. While we waited for the fire to turn to hot coals we relaxed with a cold flagon of Moselle, a packet of nuts, recalling incidents during the day and watching the sky turning pink, a sign of another good day to come.

For tea that evening we had a large flat-head, done in foil in the hot coals, carrots and peas. Beate and Demaris contributed spaghetti in tomato sauce with plenty of garlic. We enjoyed a real feast out there in the outback. After eating we felt very satisfied and sat around the dying embers chatting until ten. This is a very late hour to be retiring while traveling, but it was such a warm and pleasant night and we were enjoying each other's company.

We had witnessed a very colourful sunset, listening to the last of the birdsong. Everything was at peace except the rustle of a couple of small mouse-like creatures in the undergrowth and the distant sound of a road train or car rushing over a cattle grid. It sounded loud and close, carrying in the silence of the night!

Incredible Memories

The next morning, we were up with the sun. When checking the van before departure, we discovered a flat tyre. Why when there are dual wheels, it is always the inside tyre that goes flat? We finally got on the road at 9:30. The road was long and rough. We were still traveling on several detour tracks.

We called into 'Grisly' camp to visit a couple of guys who's names we'd been given by a friend in Perth. Well what a surprise! We were shown into an air-conditioned dining hall, and there in the kitchen stood a chef in tall hat, checked trousers, and spotlessly white apron. There were white tablecloths on all the tables. A menu that would compare quite favorably with a top restaurant in any city. And here hundreds of miles from nowhere!

We introduced ourselves and were told we were a bit late for a meal but were welcomed to a cup of tea or coffee and biscuits. I think they were as surprised about four ladies bowling into their camp unannounced, as we were to find all the good living so far out in the "out back."

After a couple of cups of good coffee, we decided to make a move. When we got outside our van had attracted quite a lot of attention.

Fifty miles or so of very hot and dusty traveling up this un-made road, we found a spot to stop and cool the engine and tyres. Half an hour later we continued our journey. Some few miles south of the turn off to Broome we hit bitumen. This was around a place called Roebuck Plains. Just before turning into the coast we stopped and talked to some hitch hikers, they said they had been waiting there for three days for a lift south. We were glad it wasn't us, it was so hot, dry and isolated.

Very hot, dusty, and thirsty we arrived in Broome. The first hotel we came to we found a shady tree to park under and all piled out to have a nice long cold shandy.

Our 1st flat tyre North WA July 1980

Chapter 40

A VISIT TO EXMOUTH GULF

The scenery as we drove Westward, was very uninteresting, dry grasslands dominated by spinifex. The ground between was bare with a few low trees and shrubs, spaced far apart but as we neared Learmouth we started getting glimpses of the Gulf. Close to the coast the scene changed yet again to sand dunes and grey coloured limestone. The blue of the water very pale and in some places quite clearly a green.

It was nearly noon when we turned into the little fishing settlement of Learmouth. We called in to visit friends, Rosalind and Neil and little Natasha. There was a nice shady tree to park our home under. After being warmly welcomed we exchanged the latest family news then Vera and I drove into Exmouth. On the map it looked like we would drive straight through the town, we saw some buildings off to our right and kept driving. We stopped and asked a chap on a bike, directions, no wonder he gave us a strange look, we'd missed it two miles back. As we had driven out this far, we decided to continue to Point Murat, North West Cape, where we were told, on a notice board, was the furthermost point west in Australia's mainland. We had passed the US Communication Station on the way.

The Indian Ocean looked very inviting, such a clear blue. Only tropical waters seem to have that hue. It was a glorious, warm sunny day and we were glad we had arrived at such a beautiful place.

Exmouth is quite a neat little township, we called in for mail, didn't miss it on the way back. The residents were mainly United States servicemen and their families, reminded me of Puerto Rico. There were also Australians employed at the station, plus their families. Of the many engineering projects this station played a vital role in communication. The giant station with thirteen masts taller than the Eiffel Tower, dominating the skyline of this lonely headland. Spread over four square miles in a complex tangle of lofty antennas. The VLF Transmitter is the most powerful ever built. As I write this many years later, I presume these facts are history.

Incredible Memories

While in town we bought a few groceries and some fresh bread. We both have a weakness for bakeries and the other goodies they sell.

After a very tasty fish dinner Ros and Neil took us over to the club. We met several of the other inhabitants of Kailis Village, very impressed with the friendly and welcoming atmosphere.

The club room was a large lounge, a bar at one end, tables and chairs on either side, two pool tables and a couple of dart boards. There were sliding glass doors down both sides of the lounge. Outside on the South side there was a grassed enclosure where the children could play quite safely. The complex included an enclosed swimming pool, which the older children made good use of.

We had a few games of darts, a few drinks and met a lot of the locals, then returned to the Macs' for a nightcap. Neil's father was up from Perth on holiday. It was quite nice relaxing inside a house again.

This little fishing village consisted of about a dozen homes, single quarters for male and females, with a canteen where they had their meals. There was a fairly large processing factory, a shop where one could buy just about anything required. Huge freezer rooms and workshops where they could repair machinery or fishing gear.

Some of the workers chose to live in their own caravans situated in a small park just off the main road. Down at the beach were a boat ramp and a jetty. It was a sandy beach, a popular fishing spot for tourists, there was always bait available and it seemed fish to be caught. Even we were in luck here. During our entire stay there we had a variety of fish dishes.

A daily routine, that the ladies called on each other for morning coffee, or was it a "stubby" They certainly enjoyed their beer. We'd see them wandering over to visit each other, with their stubby or can in their individual holders. Having done their daily chores, they would relax out on a lawn looking out on the gulf. Then at lunchtime the club rooms seemed to have a magnetic draw, over they'd all troop, children in tow. There they would have a game of darts or pool or just sit talking. It was terrific to see what a generally happy atmosphere there was. Living in such close proximity to be able to get on so well with each other, they needed to have a sense of humour, theirs was unique to that spot. We certainly had a great time and found it a place we could have quite easily stayed. It was very pleasantly warm during the day but a bit chilly at night.

We used to get up very early and while the tide was out we'd go beach combing. In among the rough rocks that were half buried, just off the shore we scored several fishhooks and sinkers, sometimes a whole line full of gear. There were also some small pools where tiny fish and crabs were trapped, left behind by the outgoing tide. As our shadows fell across these pools the fish would dart for cover under the rocks. We found a variety of shells on our walks.

A VISIT TO EXMOUTH GULF

I enjoyed watching the crabs scurrying around in their side-ways walk, also the sea snails. As I sat there watching there would suddenly be a bubbling up through the sand, spitting the small grains of sand up into the water, slightly clouding it, but no sea creature followed, I never did discover what caused this to happen. The water was so clear, the sand very fine, a grey colour not a yellow, left in ridges by the receding water.

On the morning of the fifth of July Neil asked if we would like to go out in his boat for the night as they were only going out on a one-night trip. We agreed it would be a terrific experience. At 4 p.m., we joined Neil and Tor, one of the crew or deck hands, down at the water's edge. We had to go out to the trawler, the Kayama, by dinghy, as it was anchored a couple of hundred yards offshore. When all the gear was on board, we set sail out into the Gulf. Vera and I sat in the bow and watched a magnificent sunset out at the mouth of the Gulf. They put down the first nets at 7:30pm. The nets were held by ropes along long arms jutting out either side of the boat and in this manner were dragged around the gulf.

We climbed into a couple of bunks, below deck, for a bit of shuteye, before the first pull or "shop" as it was termed. The nets were down for about two hours then we heard the engine slow to near stop, the skipper called down "wakey wakey" and we all got up, pulled our coats and boots on and made for the deck, pulling our beanies on to keep our ears warm.

We watched the first 'shop' come up over the side and aloft, the nets were emptied onto the sorting top. What an amazing assortment. There were three varieties of large prawns, Tiger, king and banana; these were what we were there for. Sorting them into their individual crates, everything else was swept down a chute straight back into the gulf waters, to the waiting dolphins and hundreds of sea gulls that had joined us as soon as they heard the engines slowed.

A dozen trawlers watching out for each other on radar screens as they trawled up and down the gulf, doing figure eights. Dropping their nets and pulling them every two hours. After each shop we would go down to the mess, have a cup of tea or hot chocolate and something to eat and a short sleep before the next call. There were four shops altogether. The dolphins and seagulls must spend the whole night traveling from one trawler to the other every time one slows down. As soon as the floodlights went on, there they were waiting to be fed. In every catch there was such a variety of fish. Little tiny thin long ones, small flat ones, some very brightly coloured, octopus, gardie, bream, crabs, squid, and sometimes even sea snakes. While helping to sort we had to be careful our hands didn't touch a rockfish or a cobbler as they could give a very nasty sting and a painful wound.

On the last I looked up to see if there were any snakes and there was a huge shell. It must have been all of eighteen inches long. I was told I could keep it if none of the crew wanted it. They didn't. What a wonderful souvenir. After the sort was finished and the nets were made secure, we

Incredible Memories

made for shore. Loading the catch into the dinghy, we got into a very wobbly boat, as the water was a bit choppy. We got ashore about 9:30am, good and ready for breakfast.

That day there was a show out at the American base and we were asked to join the McCulucks. It was a scorcher of a day but they put on a beaut show. There were sideshows; games for the kids, there were stunts by planes and helicopters. In the evening a barbecue with tons to eat and drink as well as an iced cake at least five feet square. Then they put on a dance at night with a couple of excellent bands. During the day it had been so hot I had a terrible thirst, so tried a beer, as they seemed to be the coldest of the drinks. I acquired quite a taste for it.

We all had a really enjoyable day and went home pretty tired but happy in more ways than one. It was so good to see everyone mixing and being friendly, drinking together, no one becoming intoxicated. The men on the base being perfect hosts.

The next day we went for a drive into Exmouth and took Natasha with us for the drive, she had become quite attached to us. No mail. We checked out the Buldara road with the police as we thought it would be shorter going that way and possibly more picturesque. A semi-trailer had got itself bogged and the road had been closed. We got both our petrol tanks filled and our gas bottles and made ready to move on.

That night we were invited to a dart match at the Truscote Club, we called by the Kailis club to say goodbye to a few friends we had made.

The Kailis team won their game against the Kooranwara team, so of course we had to celebrate. We had a hilarious evening, what a good bunch of jokers they all were. Real good fun to be with. When they heard we intended leaving the next day, they tried to find all the excuses in the world for us to stay a bit longer.

Ros took us for a run out to see the Canyons the next morning. Got a wonderful view of the Gulf. The fleet and Kailis village lay down below us; it was a beautiful day and a very pleasant picture to take away in our memory.

When we returned, I took my shell out of the freezer and left it in the sun to thaw before hosing it out to try to remove the animal inside. After about two and a half hours I managed to get most of it out but not without quite a struggle. After lunch we said our farewells and were on our way once more. The Lynden was easier to cross, we drove to thirteen miles south of Barradale and turned off the road to a windmill we had spotted two hundred yards off the road.

We set up camp, did a bit of washing then went for a scout around. It was refreshing being out in the quietness of the bush again. To cook on an open fire once more. This is without a doubt the best way to cook most things, but fish is delicious done over an open fire.

A VISIT TO EXMOUTH GULF

It had rained overnight but we had no difficulty getting back on the road. Headed north, soon after we crossed the bridge at Nanutarra, we saw one of Adventure Tours vehicles coming down the road towards us. We had worked out that our friend Hazel, from Perth could very well be one of the group traveling with them, so we did an about turn and followed them into the roadhouse. Sure enough there she was. It is so nice to see a familiar face so far from home. We went and had a cup of coffee, all talking so quickly to tell each other what we'd been doing since we'd last seen each other. Time was too short. Hazel's party was moving off again. Had we had the space I think she would have joined us.

Hazel warned us that a few of the creeks were fairly deep. With this in mind we drove on but not very far before we noticed deep water on either side of the road. The first creek we came to was a wide one and the water deep enough to run in under the door, which was eighteen inches off the ground. We drove through very slowly, dried out our brakes and kept going wondering if we were doing the right thing.

The scrub on either side of the road was coated with a thin layer of red silt. In places the ground had been washed away leaving roots bare. The scrub in this area is an acacia. Mulga is the most widespread form but there is also Gidgee, umbrella mulga, witchetty bush and lancewood, the bushes can grow to a height of eighteen foot. The countryside was just completely unreal. The dirt is red and since the floods most trees and plants were painted this colour to the height the water had risen.

Chapter 41

TROPICS AT LAST

Broome dates back to the 1880's. When it was found, the local waters were rich in pearl shells. In its heyday over 400 luggers used Broome as a base. They were mostly manned by Asians. The beef industry has become the area's major industry. The Gantheaume Point dinosaur's footprints can be seen, fossilized. About 126 km north, the famous Beagle Bay Church can be seen, with it's pearl shell doorways and windows. The road out was not too good. There is a wildlife sanctuary between Waterbank and Beagle Bay Aboriginal Reserve. There are a large variety of birds in the area, blue-winged kookaburras, a relative of the laughing kookaburra, and spotted nightjar, seen by car headlights with its bright ruby red eyes. Also, there's the noisy little grey, white and yellow faced cockatiel, their call can usually be heard before they can be seen. These are a few that can be found in this area.

We found an hotel and jumped on to the verandah, stepped over a few bodies and ordered drinks. The place was packed. We hadn't been standing too long at the bar, when a young guy came over and invited us to join his party. He introduced us all around. It was such a good feeling, this friendly and warm welcome. Later we were told that it was supposed to be the roughest pub in town! When we returned to the van a couple of hours later, we were confronted by several very drunk bodies leaning against and lying around in the shade of the van. We greeted them and politely asked them to remove themselves, as we would like to continue our journey. They were full of apologies, that was, those that were capable of speaking. The older Aboriginals in this area we found hard to understand as they hadn't a vast knowledge of English. We found them on the whole very friendly. It is a sad sight to see all these basically good and spiritual people, in this drunken state.

Our first impression of the town was of colonial style wooden and fibro bungalows, sitting on large blocks. Shops, mainly general stores were scattered through the town. The streets were wide and lined with shady trees, not all the roads were sealed.

We drove out to Cable Beach and parked in a large parking area on the beach front. The girls booked into the caravan park next to the car park. Near to where we parked there was a shower and toilet block. What a sensation to have a nice cold shower and wash one's hair. We had an early tea and just fell into bed. It had been a rather tiring day.

Early next morning we were woken by a high-pitched twittering and this was before dawn. It turned out to be the Fairy Martin. As soon as the first starts the twitter another joins, and yet another, and the sound increases until they depart their nests at daybreak. They are recognised by their rust coloured head, white rump and square tail. They have a rapid, swallow like flight and feed on flying insects. During such flights they often hesitate and dip their bills in the water to drink or catch insects.

I got up and climbed down to the beach. The tide was out and the pools and rocks left high and dry were full of little shells, crabs and some small fish. I also found a large, perfect starfish; red on one side and yellow on the other.

After breakfast we talked to a couple from the Eastern States who had parked near us over night. They were traveling with a caravan and were on their way to a job at Tenant Creek. As usual we exchanged traveling stories and they told us of several places we should call on in our travels. Beate and Demaris came over and we were all going into town together but we couldn't get the van started. The girls decided to hitch a ride into the shops. We cleaned the battery terminals, checked the acid content, tried again and the engine started like a song.

When in town we bought a new inner tube and had the tyre, which had gone flat earlier, checked. We changed the PCV valve- it was a warm job. After filling our second petrol tank we went and parked under a cool tree for a couple of hours. When we were rested, we called to see if there was any mail. None. Mail from home is very important and a real highlight of the day.

We drove around the town then out to the jetty where we met an elderly couple from NSW. They had been parked down by the jetty for a few days fishing and had been lucky enough to catch their tea each day.

Back to Cable Beach to witness yet another exquisite sunset. A sun setting over the horizon of a becalmed ocean is really something. Beate and Demaris came over after tea to visit us and we all decided to stay another day in Broome. The girls told us that while they were wandering the town, some Aborigines had come up to them and asked if they were looking for their van with their friends. They described us and told them where the van was parked and how to get to it- which just goes to show we wouldn't be able to get away with very much in a town like this! It turned out to be quite

Incredible Memories

a warm evening and night. They were very good company and we always had a great time together, and a good laugh.

I got up at sun rise and went down to the beach to collect more shells. While I was down there, the owner of the caravan park went over to the van and told Vera we were not allowed to park there another night. Vera got under the van and tried to clean and clear the corner of the tank we damaged, but it was too windy and dusty to mend it. After breakfast we put more drinking water into the water tank and moved the van over near the park under a shady tree. We caught up on some writing and then went into the park and lay under a tree, talking to Demaris. Beate had gone into town. As we had been asked to move, we decided to move on after seeing China Town. The girls got their things together and we all went to the tourist bureau which was in an old DC3 aircraft parked near the Great Northern Highway, on the approach to the town.

We left Broome about 4:30. It was a little cooler traveling at that time of the day but the trip to Fitzroy River seemed endless. This was one of the spots we had been told was a good camping area. We travelled on in the dark which was one of the things we swore we would never do again.

Our instructions had been to turn off just before the river. The next thing we knew we were at Willare Bridge, the bridge which spans the Fitzroy. We then had to retrace our steps. We turned around and went back over the bridge. It was so dark we couldn't see the turn off. Beate and I got out and looked around with a torch. We found it and then had to guide Vera down by torch light. She drove down into a picnic area and parked near a suitable place for the girls to pitch their tent. Not far from there was a BBQ fireplace with seats and a table, all under cover.

While the girls put their tent up, Vera and I rustled up tea, curried vegies and rice. After a satisfying meal we all turned in early. The girls weren't too happy about sleeping in the bush, there wasn't a clearing except the track we had come in on. I think they were afraid there may be snakes in the undergrowth.

It was much better traveling later in the afternoon, cooler, but not nice setting up camp when one can't see the surroundings. During the night there were several disturbing sounds. Animals crashing through the bush, and they sounded quite large. The moon rose and showed the trees around us were quite tall and beneath them thick undergrowth.

As the dawn broke and the sun rose, we realized why the traffic had sounded so close. The track had doubled back and we were very close to the bridge. We got up and walked back towards the way we had driven in and found another track running north. The scrub became less dense. We proceeded very quietly taking yet another track to our left. The land rose slightly and there on the brow of the hill were three kangaroos, with a couple of 'joeys'. We froze, they must have picked up our scent because, as one, they bounded off.

TROPICS AT LAST

The track we had taken was taking us away from the river so we retraced our steps and took a right hand arm of the 'Y' tracks which when we took a further right turn brought us to a beautiful clearing and so close to the river. We hurried back and met the girls and told them what we had found. By this time the billycan was boiling.

We all moved after breakfast. The girls found a wonderfully secluded clearing to put their tent, only a hundred yards into the bush behind our van. We all decided it would be a good idea to stay a few days and relax in this ideal surrounding.

It was now the 18th of July. We had been on the road just over a month and had travelled 1446 miles and this spot was truly the best we had stopped at since we left Perth. We were far enough away from the road to make us feel isolated. We were in good company, doing our own thing and yet according to the map we were walking distance from Willare Bridge Road House.

Demaris arrived, book in hand, and said she was going to walk to the Road House. She felt like being on her own with a cup of coffee. We could not persuade her that the hotel was closed and there was probably no where she would find a coffee strip until Darwin. Off she went. When she returned, a wee bit disappointed, we made her a strong cup of instant and she went off to a quiet spot to read her book in solitude.

By this time, I and my shell were very unpopular. Vera had been rather embarrassed while getting petrol at Broome. The lady serving had apologized for a bad smell. Vera had tried to steer her as far away from the front of the van where the offending shell was tied up in a sack, fastened to the roo bar! I had been told "either the shell goes or you both go" So I got a bucket, some bleach, a scrubbing brush, and the shell and wandered off a few hundred feet down the river. During the two hours it took me to clean the shell, the direction of the wind changed. There were loud shouts of protest and I was asked to go even further away. By this time I had got used to the smell and thought all was well and so started back to join the others, much to their disgust. I was allowed to remain as long as the shell was filled with bleach and placed some distance from the van.

The girls had been sitting down by the river reading for several hours, all the while checking out if there were any signs of crocodiles. Referring to the map, the mouth of the river didn't look too far away and we weren't sure how far up the river they would swim. There was quite a lot of water in the river but we didn't want to take any chances. By mid-day it was getting hot, so we decided to risk it. We all plunged in for a skinny dip. The girls had a blow-up mattress which they chucked in and Demaris fetched her book. What a way to go! We had a very lazy day enjoying our surroundings.

Beate had brought her violin and it had got broken during her travels. We went through our toolbox and found some picture wire some strong glue, and she went off to the tent to mend it. I practiced my accordion for about an hour. I had bought it before we left as thought it a good opportunity to teach myself a tune or two while traveling. Vera had seen more kangaroos and also a rabbit when she went for a walk.

The girls said they had chased a cow during the night. As there were signs of cattle activity, rather large round cowpats, some very recent, in the vicinity of their tent, we decided to make them safe for the night. We built a barricade across any paths that led to their clearing and gave them a Girl Guide whistle to blow if they heard any cows investigating them. We had an early tea and sat around the campfire singing. Beate played us a few German tunes and Demaris played and sang to her guitar. Had a very happy evening. As the embers died, the moon rose, and we sat there, all of us quite glad to be such good company in this beautiful spot. We heard the nocturnal birds and beasts venturing forth to see who had so rudely entered their terrain.

The weather was fine though humid. Vera and I thought it would be nice to go and get ourselves a 'roo', to give the girls a taste. They did not think that was a very good idea and made us promise we would not kill any animals while they were with us.

I had risen very early and gone for a long walk and saw lots of 'roos' There was an amazing amount of birds all happily singing their morning songs, they didn't seem timid. Quite an assortment of colourful tropical birds. A few budgerigars, who would later shelter in trees and shrubs from the heat of the day, flew past. There was the blue-winged kookaburra, the little brush cuckoo, grey and yellow cockatiels and the crested pigeons. There had been a couple of coots in the shallow waters. There always seemed to be a carrion hawk or two or whistling eagle gliding up in the sky. Some of the smaller birds were hard to recognise as they darted around.

The bank down to the river was fairly steep. It was lined with bright green Pandanus palms- these are typical of wet tropical regions. The huge Fitzroy River cuts its long winding way through gorges and mulga scrub plains from the Durack Range to Mowanjum, West of Derby. We were fortunate it was so deep where we were, the water a rather murky colour but very refreshing to swim in. There were parts where the sun shone through, making that part of the water look a little clearer. A few hundred yards down the river it became quite shallow and flowed over a cluster of rocks and on either side there was a sandy beach. On a dead branch over hanging the river was a sacred kingfisher with its rich ochre-buff breast, its turquoise-green head and dusky turquoise-green shoulders, grading to bright turquoise-blue on the lower back and tail. It sat there completely still, then swooped down to the river showing off the beautiful colours.

The trees all around were beautiful too, the werekaranda paper barks, ghost gums and apple gum, some with vines growing up and around them. We all went for a swim again and Demaris threw her air bed in and climbed aboard and lay there in all her glory, reading.

I dug a deep hole and set a fire in it, then prepared some bread and put it in a big thick saucepan to bake underground. It came out a bit heavy but tasted OK. Vera and I were told to go for a long walk, say for an hour or so. Beate and Demaris were going to give us a surprise for tea.

We wandered off towards the road as we had heard voices in the distance, so thought we'd investigate. There was a car and caravan parked where we had been the first night but the occupants didn't seem very interested in exchanging notes. Not far off was a motorized home, so we tried our luck there and found a friendly couple from South Australia; Roy and Margaret from just out of Adelaide. We sat talking with them for a long time, in fact the girls came looking for us to tell us tea was ready. While we had been talking to Roy and Margaret, two more vehicles drove in. Quite a well-known and popular spot.

After a delicious tea we sat around the fire and sang while Beate played her violin. Then the girls told us about their family and life back in their hometown, Ettenheim, in southern West Germany, and how they came to be in Australia. While we were sitting singing the McLeods arrived in their van and parked 50 yards down the track, backing their van in under a ghost gum. They then joined us around the fire and sang along with us. We exchanged addresses and promised to look them up when we got down to South Australia. We retired early as we'd planned to move on the next day.

We would miss this camping spot. It was so refreshing being so close to water and being surrounded by beautiful paperbarks, gum trees and some tropical palms. During the days it had been warm and humid. At night it had also been warm but comfortable. There was always signs of wildlife, day or night, though so close to the highway.

We were all up early only stopping to have a cup of tea before breaking camp and making for Derby. Our first stop was at the Boab prison tree. This is a huge hollow tree with a door like opening which we climbed into and all fitted quite comfortably. The branches stuck out untidily at the top and there were no leaves on at this time of the year. At the top of the trunk there was an opening, above us was the clear blue sky, as only a tropical sky can be. The tree is reputed to be 1,000 years old and held as many as sixteen Aboriginal prisoners on their way to be tried. What cruelty!

Walking a distance from this was Myall's bore, the longest cattle trough in the Southern hemisphere. This was used in days past, to water the cattle being brought on foot to the slaughter.

We called in to market garden to buy some fresh vegetables, on the way into Derby. We had breakfast on the roadside then paid a visit to the tourist bureau.

The tidal port of Derby lies at the southern end of King Sound. The town has a population of around 3,000. It is the most rapidly developing town in the Kimberly and is the centre of the cattle raising industry. Derby has an all steel jetty with a concrete top. It is 1,834 feet long and is curved to give complete turnabout of vehicles and trains. At the ships berths there is twenty-six feet of water at high tide, which is sufficient for existing coastal ships. At low tide the ships are left sitting on the bottom alongside the jetty. Low tides leave a quarter mile stretch of muddy sand between the jetty and the sea.

As it had been fairly warm, we stocked up on beer from the Spinifex hotel. We cleaned the van out while the girls went shopping. Then we met at the Boab Tree Inn and had a refreshing cold shandy. We returned to the Spinifex and all had showers and washed our hairs as we knew we wouldn't be staying anywhere except the bush for the next few days.

We drove out of Derby to the junction and turned east. We travelled about seventy km, turned south down a track for two Ks, we found a nice spot under a couple of very large Boab trees. The girls pitched their tent between the trees. A few feet beyond was a windmill and water hole.

Just after settling for the night, the loud screeching sound we had heard earlier was getting closer and a bit louder. We then realized it was the bellow of a bull. As he got closer we found out that he was accompanied by a large herd of females. There was also another bull approaching from the opposite direction, with his lady friends. It was a bright moonlit night. When we looked out of the window, there was this very big beast, a hundred yards or so behind the boab trees, with his head down pawing the ground and roaring his throat out. The next thing, the tent was unzipped, Beate appeared in only her knickers. She picked up a stick and started beating it against the tree and yelling something in German. There was complete silence. We couldn't believe our ears, or our eyes for that matter. I don't think the bull could either. Our next fear was that perhaps he would charge when he got over the initial shock of this abuse in some foreign language. So we suggested the girls grab their gear and sleep in the van, then we'd all get some sleep

We'd all just got settled when we heard another noise in the distance. It was a dingo howling. Well the cattle milled around for quite a noisy while, until they'd had a good drink. Then I suppose I must have fallen asleep because the next thing I woke to the sun rising and it was time to get up and think about moving again. We made our way to Tunnel Creek.

Chapter 42

MAJOR BREAK-DOWN

After a substantial breakfast around the campfire recalling the events of the previous night, we moved out to the main road again and were on our way to the next camping ground. We were about 135 km from Derby, driving along having a good laugh about the bull episode when the engine sounded as if it was going to fall apart. I turned the engine off and stopped by the side of the road. Looking under the bonnet we discovered the fan belt pulley had sheered in half. We couldn't start the engine so with great difficulty we pushed all three tons off the road, down a slight incline to a level bit of ground.

The girls were terrific. They didn't mind getting their hands dirty and knew as much about engines as we did, if not a bit more. A Bedford being a short-nosed effort, getting the radiator out was quite a feat. Some bright spark had soldered the radiator to the frame, so we had to take the whole thing out. When we finally got it loosened it took all four of us, and a jiggling job, to remove it. Vera and I balanced on the roo-bar above and Beate and Demaris on their backs under the van. We stopped a road train to ask the driver if he knew anything about this model and how to get the fan off. He didn't and said he was behind schedule so wouldn't be able to stop but would radio our plight to other trains coming through. We discovered we didn't have the right spanner to remove the nut that held the fan on.

Not long after an elderly couple in a Kombi pulled up and asked if they could help. As luck would have it, they had the right sort of spanner. By that time some friends of theirs pulled up. I think they were quite amazed that we were game to do the job ourselves. While doing this a small flat-topped truck pulled over with a station owner or manager and an Aboriginal station hand and asked what the problem was. He said he was in a bit of a hurry but if we were still there in the morning he was going into Derby and back and would give us a lift. After removing both parts of the pulley, the second Kombi driver offered a lift to the Derby junction as they were going to

Incredible Memories

Broome. We decided that it would be better if Vera went as she was an Aussie. My having a bit of an American accent, we reckoned, people on the trip used to overcharge us, especially when they looked at the size of the van and thought that we must be wealthy. Beate won the toss to join her. They grabbed a bag with fruit and some food plus a large bottle of water. We waved them goodbye and good luck. After being dropped off they soon got another lift straight to Derby.

Replacing the radiator 135 kms from Derby, WA

They took the offending parts into an engineering shop and were promptly told by the lady there that they would have to wait at least two days for a part to be sent up from Perth. Vera and Beate told her they were sure something could be done right away and asked to see the manager. As soon as he saw it, he agreed that it could be bronzed together. Within half an hour Vera and Beate were on their way south again.

They had found it extremely easy to get into Derby but the trip out was to prove a bit longer. Before leaving Beate said she wanted to buy a 'billy'. So armed with a billy, a cool drink and an ice cream they started out of town. They recalled that at least fifty cars passed them. No one seemed happy to pick them up. Then a carload of Aborigines came along and offered them a lift. They said they were only going twelve miles down the road and then turning off to a station. In they squashed for a very speedy journey, but at least they were a bit closer to the van. They bid their new friends goodbye and started to walk down the road. As so many cars passed them, they were trying to find every excuse why people were not stopping to pick them up. Beate said "Maybe she was too ugly so she would hide in the bush until somebody stopped."

MAJOR BREAK-DOWN

They walked for ages and then another car of Aborigines picked them up, apologizing that they were not going very far. A few more miles closer to the van, but still cars were passing them by. Vera and Beate were still taking it in turns to put their thumbs out. They were nearly to the junction by then and Beate was thinking they would be camping on the side of the road for the night. As they walked along Beate spotted some large ant hills and decided to investigate. As she took off through the long grass Vera reminded her that there were probably some snakes hidden in the grass. Well her feet hardly hit the ground as she returned to the roadside. She found herself a stout stick and returned stamping her feet and hitting the ground with the stick as she went. By this time Vera was doubled up laughing.

Several more cars had passed by the time Beate came out of the bush and announced she had a billy and Vera had a light, so how about they find a nice spot to camp the night. There wasn't a drop of water to be had except a small amount in the bottle they had taken with them. The sun was very low in the west and things were beginning to look a bit grim. By this time, they had reached the junction and were walking East along the road towards the van but still about a hundred Ks away. Next thing they knew, the small truck that had stopped in the morning flew passed them. It got a couple hundred yards up the road, screeched to a stop, did a U turn and went back to pick them up. The Aboriginal guy had recognized them and told the boss. Vera and Beate climbed up on the back of the truck and made themselves as comfortable as they could among bags of feed and a couple of large gas bottles. Off they hurtled at top speed, both hanging on for dear life. As they travelled east, they witnessed a most beautiful sunset in the west at the end of the straight stretch of road they were hurtling along. It wasn't the most comfortable way to travel but at least they were getting a lift right to where they wanted to go.

Vera and Beate had left for Derby about 9:20. During their absence Demaris had found a level spot off the road shaded by a couple of small trees and set up the tent. I generally messed around in the van. We had ourselves a morning coffee and lay on a rug by the side of the road talking and reading. We gathered some wood and took it across the road to a cleared area to make a fire for the return of the others. Very little traffic past all day.

After lunch we were sitting on a shady bank. Out in front of us to the south, was a very large area of semi-arid land; it stretched for as far as we could see. In the distance there were dark blue to purple hills and some sand dunes. A hot barren land, except for a bit of scrub by the roadside; an unusual landscape. Behind us the land rose very slightly into red sand dunes with a few rock crops and a bit more scrub and a few trees running in from the road a couple of hundred yards east of us. During the heat of the day, it was 40° C. There wasn't a sound or sign of life except the constant marching up and down of bull ants, which we avoided as they give a nasty bite.

Incredible Memories

All of a sudden, the trees to our left started swaying madly and making a frightening noise. The noise was coming towards us. A swirling of leaves torn off the trees came rushing up the road. We dived for the van. Just before it reached us the swirling leaves turned across the road and travelled south, then were sucked into the sky in a cylindrical shape to as high as we could see them. Then another spiral, but of sand, was sucked up into the air a bit further away. All together we experienced four of these unusual sights; a small tornado, known as a 'Willie Willie'.

It was quite a frightening experience, especially as we didn't know where the next one was going to be. They were getting further away but we decided to move the tent in case any of the branches should fall after the shaking they had been given. What a bit of luck the tent hadn't been blown to bits.

By late afternoon Demaris was getting a bit concerned that the others would not return. I said that I felt they would return by evening. At sundown we had ourselves a drink and decided to get the fire going and a meal on the way for the return of the others. It was nearly eight o'clock by the time they were dropped off by the station owner and his stockman.

While sitting around the campfire two road-trains pulled up to ask if we were all right. The other driver had radioed in the morning that we had broken down and they thought they would be able to help us. We were not so isolated after all. They offered to park their trucks with the lights shining in such a way that we could see to mend our van. As it was so late, we told them we would start first thing in the morning. They said they would give us a hand if we would like. We thanked them for stopping and asked if they would like a beer. They wouldn't be in it but left us a couple of cold ones. They said they'd be on their way if they couldn't be of assistance. I think they were quite surprised that we were able to manage and had already got the part fixed.

After a good tea we turned in. Vera and Beate were very tired after their exciting day. None of us felt like a musical evening. There was also the thought of an early morning. Being right on the road could prove to be rather noisy with passing traffic.

Next morning, we were up with the sun and got straight into the job of replacing the pulley. It was easier doing the job this way around. A quick breakfast and we were on our way by nine. We turned in to see Tunnel Creek. It was 76 Ks of pretty rough road and several creeks to cross. At some we had to walk through with a stick to see how firm the ground was below the water. One crossing was very wide and the bottom very muddy so we marked the path we were to take with sticks stuck in the ground. Further on we stopped by a creek full of boulders and had lunch in the shade of some grotesquely shaped red gums. They had white and grey smooth barks and lined the banks of the creek. It had turned pretty hot, so we had a rest and cooled the engine, before our next stop.

Chapter 43

FINAL DAYS WITH THE GIRLS

We arrived at Tunnel Creek about four o'clock. As one drives in you are confronted by a wall of rock. When you look up it, there are young trees clinging on by exposed roots. It is amazing that they survive growing as it were out of the surface of the rock. The top of the wall is fringed with grass and trees. We found a spot where the girls could pitch their tent near the van. There were several vans and a few tents already there. Once we were organized, we went off to find the entrance.

We climbed over some large rocks and under a fallen tree, we found an opening to a cave. As we proceeded it got very dark but we were all right as we had a torch. We met a couple who told us that if we followed the tunnel to the end, we'd come to a nice pool which was deep enough to swim in. So we returned and got our towels and some soap. They were right, it was a beaut swimming hole.

Halfway through the tunnel there was an opening to the right. We followed this and climbed right out of the top of the rock face and looked out for miles on any side. It was a glorious view.

There is an underground stream running through with tiny white fish swimming around. In parts we shone the torch upwards, way above our heads where there were some unusual stalactites. Some were shining with the water on them, others were sparkling like crusted jewels, and yet others had traces of pale green on their cream colour. There were also some bats hanging around up there. There were a few nests that looked like rat's nests.

When we got through to the end, we all stripped off and plunged into the cool water. What a change to the heat we had experienced all day. We couldn't dally as the sun was sinking fast. We had a fair hike back to the van. We were quite amazed at the size and splendour of the tunnel.

The story goes that there was an Aboriginal police tracker, Jandamarah, nicknamed Pigeon, who went bad and was being chased for months. No one seemed to be able to catch up with him. Someone would send a message to say he had been seen several miles west of the rock and within a matter of hours he was sighted several miles east of it. Then within an hour or so he'd be sighted on top of the rock. People were beginning to think he was the fastest runner in the west. Pigeon could appear and disappear so quickly. Would he ever be caught? He was finally caught when the entrance to the tunnel was discovered.

When we had found our way through the tunnel back to the van, we had tea and the girls retired. Vera and I went over to talk to a couple from City Beach, a suburb west of Perth. As usual we exchanged travel tales. Tunnel Creek is a real nice place and we felt it was worth the rough ride in.

We woke early, had a quick breakfast and hit the road. It was a very hot day. We stopped along the way to cool off as we had always to consider our engine and tyres overheating. Then we continued to Fitzroy Crossing. The township is sort of scattered; the first thing one comes to is a roadhouse, more or less right on the highway. We turned left and down a street. There was a sign to the left which said to the police station and to the hospital, to the right there was one to the Post Office and the hotel. It was nearly eleven o'clock so we decided to call in to the hotel and have a cool drink. None of us had ever seen so many 'tinnies. There were simply piles of them everywhere, especially under the trees. The pub was not open until eleven. There were dozens of people standing around, mostly Aboriginals. They were nearly outnumbered by mangy dogs. There was a shop on the right end of the hotel and on the left was an open bar. You walked up three or four steps, the area was enclosed by a wooden balustrade. There was a U-shaped bar, no gate at the entrance but a sign saying, "No Dogs Allowed." At the far end of the bar, was the public bar I am describing. It was open and one stepped out into a courtyard. We thought this was hilarious. There was no way the dogs would stay out of this area!

Beyond the public bar and to the right there was a small saloon bar which we went into. We ordered a large shandy each and sat at a small table in the far corner to take in our surroundings. On the walls there were a set of old reins, halters, stirrups, and an assortment of old farm implements. The atmosphere was very warm and friendly. We asked what the road into Geikie Gorge was like and were told we would find it difficult to get in with our van.

When we left the hotel, we drove around to the post office which was a couple kilometres to the east. It was a pale green fibro building set back off the road with a nice flower garden and green lawn. Quite refreshing after all the dry and dusty land we had passed. The post office was closed for their siesta, so we drove on towards The Gorge. It was a very hot and dusty drive out. We came to one creek which we thought we would not be able to cross. Someone had already tried to cross it without caution and up turned their trailer. It lay upside down in the creek. A challenge!

FINAL DAYS WITH THE GIRLS

We drove into the creek at an angle, then turning slightly to the opposite direction we drove out of the creek without becoming suspended halfway across. We had several deep potholes to contend with before we reached the Gorge. In parts the road was very sandy and we feared we may become bogged.

What a welcome sight when we saw the beautiful river water in the Gorge. The camping site was under shady trees. We chose a nice secluded corner. The National Park had provided BBQs and there was one close to where we parked. After a bit of a rest we wandered off for a swim. The boat that takes sightseers down the Gorge was completely booked by a couple of busloads of tourists, so we had to stay overnight if we wanted to see the Gorge.

The water was nice and clear where we were swimming. We were told there were Johnson Crocs there but that although they weren't man eaters, they weren't sure if they liked ladies! Anyway, we didn't see any. When we got back to our camping spot, we lit the fire and while tea was cooking Beate played her violin and Demaris her guitar and we had a bit of a sing song. It was funny being with so many people around, after being so long in the bush.

The next morning Vera and I got up very early and walked down the banks of the Gorge for about a kilometre, to look for crocs. We watched the sun rise above the Gorge and saw signs of rabbits and got a glimpse of some roos going off into the bush to find a cool place to sleep the day away.

Geikie Gorge, in tropical Western Australia, has the Fitzroy River running through. This has cut a long winding trail through limestone. It lies ten miles in from Fitzroy Crossing at the junction of the Oscar and Geikie Ranges in the Kimberley. The river pools remain through the dry season. Besides the freshwater crocodiles there are fish including the delicious eating Barramundi. The rock face is rather beautiful, scraggy, grey-green at the top with splashes of pink here and there. Down some few feet from the water line, the rock is white, marking the water line when the river is in spate during the wet season

The lower banks are lined with paperbarks and gum trees. The foliage a refreshing bright green. There are lush ferns in the shadows of the overhanging cliffs. It was a very interesting trip in the boat and we did see some crocs. On our return we hit the road again and had an uneventful drive out. But we were saddened when the girls told us they would be heading back to Perth. We had got so used to having them with us and would certainly miss them and their good company.

We had a last shandy together then unloaded their gear on the side of the road, wished them a speedy return for Beate to catch her return flight to Germany and promised to keep in touch. We hung around for a short time and then felt we should get going.

Chapter 44

FITZROY CROSSING TO KATHERINE

We were already missing driving along with the girls. We drove along the Northern Highway to Hall's Creek where we were met by the statue of the big Russian who pushed his sick mate for miles in a wheelbarrow to find medical help. It didn't seem to be a very big town. At the post office, we were told that not far out of town was the ruins of the old town. We decided to go on an explore and drove down Duncan Highway not far along. Over a creek and to our left, on a rise, were the remains of some old, what looked like mud brick buildings. Or rather what was left of the town. We pulled up and had a bit of a wander when we noticed a caravan parked not too far down the road so decided to pay a visit.

There was a middle-aged gentleman on his own up from the South doing a bit of prospecting for gold in the creek. He hadn't found much but was having fun. He told us a bit about how to prospect and also a bit about the old town. We decided to return to a small lake we had seen on the way in to have a dip but when we got there we found a religious group in a baptismal and were asked to join if we wished but we decided just to sit on a far bank until they had finished. We had our dip then returned down Duncan to find somewhere to camp for the night.

In the morning, we returned to the Great Northern, passed through Turkey Creek and on up to Wyndham. Not far along the road it looked like we were headed for a bush fire. When we got close to it, we decided it was worth risking it and drove straight on. It was not very windy and it was a slow burn. About a mile down the road we noticed a creek just off the road, we parked the van and clambered down with towels, and lay on some huge flat rocks. I heard a rustling sound to my right when I noticed a huge snake come crawling out. I said to Vera maybe we'll be okay if we just lay still, and it continued on its way. Phew, that was close! So we returned to the van and continued to Wyndham.

FITZROY CROSSING TO KATHERINE

When we arrived, all was closed so we found a nice shady tree to park under. We had something to eat and had a bit of a siesta. When the town came to life again, we went to the PO to see if we had any mail. While wandering around we spoke to a couple of locals then proceeded to the abattoir, talked to a couple of the workers who enlightened us about all the procedures. We were told we could have a couple of horns and told how to soften them when we wanted to clean them. When we returned to the town centre, an Aboriginal Pastor introduced himself and offered to pick us up in a ute and drive us around to see some of the sights. One was a drive up a very steep rocky road to a lookout where we could see for miles. Vera and I climbed onto the back and held on for dear life as he drove, not too gently, to the top. Our legs felt like jelly when we alighted, but before us lay an extraordinary view. He told us five rivers met and flowed into Cambridge Gulf then into the Timor Sea. On the trip down, the ute slipped and slid around on the road, quite a frightening journey.

On driving out of Wyndham to the Victoria Highway not far to the left there was a parking area where we decided to spend the night. Not long after we got ourselves settled a station wagon and motorbike turned in and parked behind us. They were a German guy and a Swiss guy both named Martin. They introduced themselves and said they had a sick girl in the back of their ute and did we have any medications to bring down a fever, we gave them a couple of aspirins. The next day before we moved out, they said she was better.

Our next stop was to be Kununurra where we were to catch up with some friends of a lady I played darts with. We hoped to get work there and stay for a few days parking at their place. We were warmly greeted and joined them for a BBQ that evening. Jim, (not his real name) offered us a few days sorting fruit and vegetables to be shipped to Perth markets, then believe it or not they were then returned to the supermarket there! It was a good job and beside being payed we could help ourselves to any rejects. By the end of the week we decided to move on. We drove around the area and discovered a small hill encrusted with seashells left there from the days when that part was under the sea. While driving around we took a road which led us to a weir which we did not cross with the van, to the left there was a nice wooded area which we thought would be a good spot to park and possibly spend a couple of days. We were well hidden from the road or so we thought because the second day we were there, who should turn up but the station wagon and motorbike! They said they spotted the roof of our van as they drove down the hill to the weir. Vera and I made a hasty retreat as we had been sitting in only a pair of shorts cleaning a couple of horns. Swiss Martin knocked on our door and asked if we would mind if they joined us, we suggested they put their tent up in a clearing some distance behind us. During the night we heard someone wandering around outside the van, I called out and a voice said, "Please sorry to destroy you but I bite by spider which I have to show." When I opened the door, Swiss Martin showed me a red back spider which was in his pyjama pants. After making sure he wasn't feeling sick or had a headache, we sat him down and told him to drink plenty of water and that he was a strong young man and would probably be all right after a good night's sleep! We teased him about his poor English and often laughed about that!

In the morning they decided to move on, thanked us and said they hoped to see us again. We were on our own again, stayed another day before making for Lake Argyle, from the turn off it was a 14-mile drive in through very pretty country side, a dingo crossed the road in front of us and we wondered if that was a good omen! We were not disappointed when we arrived at such a beautiful spot. While walking around we met a local who showed us a shiny stone he carried around, rubbing it with his fingers, it was a polished emerald which he told us were lying around on the ground just waiting to be picked up. So we started looking and were rewarded with a few small ones. We also came across a bower bird's nest, very exciting.

While there we visited the homestead which had been moved before the dam was filled and met the couple who were living there. We decided to move on as we didn't want to stay and pay at the village and soon found a pleasant spot to spend the night. Rising early, we were soon back on the highway. Just past Timber Creek and before Victoria River we spotted a track going off to our left and decided to check it out, found a nice flat mound to set up camp then walked down to where we could hear water running and found a middle aged couple with an in-law camped near a Combi van. We made ourselves known to them then walked back to have our evening meal, with a glass of sherry while we waited for it to cook. I told Vera I felt like stopping a couple of days to do a bit of painting as we had seen such lovely scenery and would like to try and get it on canvas.

Vera found it very hard to understand that a painting took so long and was itching to get on the move again. So after three days we were on our way to our next stop, Katherine. It was quite a trek but the scenery was a change as it was lush and various shades of greens in the shrubbery as well as the types of trees. A few unfamiliar to us, we promised to look them up but there are so many distractions and I was very tired at night so that never happened. As we drove along, we came across a small lake, this was very inviting, so we pulled up and decided to take a dip, never entered our head there may be crocodiles in the area! As it turned out they had not yet travelled that far inland. The rest of the drive has slipped my memory but it was getting late by the time we reached Katherine, too late to look for mail, so we bought some bread and milk and drove eastward passed the hospital to a track down on our left which led us to a river. We found a beautiful spot to park and went for a bit of an explore only to find out we were at a river crossing mentioned in the book we had been reading on our travels, "We of the Never Never". That is where we started to follow the story when we returned to travel South.

We took a very refreshing dip in the river, were happy to see there were not many people around so hoped we would have a good night's sleep before continuing our exciting journey.

Chapter 45

KATHERINE TO DARWIN

On arriving at Katherine, we called for mail and found letters from members of our families, also one from my mother. Checked out the town, bought bread and milk at a terrible price. We also filled up with petrol then drove east out of town. There was a track that ran down to our left just beyond the hospital so we decided to investigate. To our joy we found a lovely shaded spot to back our van into, right alongside the Katherine River. Then went for a very refreshing dip in the river. We were not the only travellers to find this glorious spot, plus there were a few locals enjoying the cool river water. Just to the west of the swimming hole was a causeway. It turned out that this was one of the routes mentioned in "We of the Never Never" by Mrs. Aeneas Gunn. Both Vera and I had read the book while traveling and planned to visit places mentioned during our travels. And here we were at the causeway which had been flooded when Aeneas Gunn arrived with his new bride Jeannie in 1902 on their way to the homestead south of Katherine. Mine host, mentioned in the book, from the pub on the south side of the river came over in a small boat and brought them safely across. The remains of the pub was still there above the track which we had driven down, but no sign of the other buildings mentioned in the book

The water was only just over the causeway but to think during the wet season and the river running high, where we were parked would be completely under water. It was a wonderful location, I loved the amount of colourful birds there were. The very beautiful kingfisher with all its bright colours, being one of them. So unafraid of all the human activity below as they trilled and flew from tree to tree or swooped over the water in the swim hole.

We stayed a couple of nights relaxing, going for walks meeting people and enjoying the swimming hole. There was a very large bus parked a little way off from us. We wondered how they had managed to get tucked away

KATHERINE TO DARWIN

so neatly in the bush, we passed the time of the day and found they were a couple from near Sydney. Then we were off again, on the trail north to Darwin. The road was very good and we found ourselves approaching the outskirts of the city. As we drove into Darwin, we were amazed at how spread out the city was. There were many modern houses. Darwin was still recovering from the devastating cyclone which hit on Christmas day 1974.

Darwin the capital of the Northern Territory and here we were! First, we must find the house Lois shared with her boyfriend and two other guys. It was a great reunion with Vera and her daughter. We were made to feel quite at home and it was nice to have the facilities of a house once more. We both loved the bush life but it was a luxury to relax in comfort and enjoy a daily shower.

The old buildings that somehow survived the Japanese bombings during the 1939-45 war, the fibro and galvanized iron premises that sprung up soon after the war, before better building materials became available, looked in odd contrast with the fine new buildings. The city's business zone confined by the natural boundaries of the peninsula, with the harbour on three of its sides. There were many interesting places to visit while in Darwin.

A memorial near the Esplanade honouring the explorer Ludwig Leichardt, at East Point there were gun emplacements and a war museum, and along East Point Road a memorial to pioneer aviator Ross Smith. There was the Chinese temple which we only drove past, it displayed a very colourful facade. The Botanic Gardens overlooking Mindil Beach, a popular beach with the locals and visitors alike.

We were taken to the recently built Casino, one of the guys who shared with Lois managed it. We didn't gamble but took pleasure in a few cool drinks and a tasty meal. The sunsets at Fannie Bay were something to see, while on our visit we enjoyed several. Photos never seemed to do them justice.

Lois's boyfriend was the chef at Government House so we had a bit of a tour, in so far as where we could or would be allowed to visit. We were given a running commentary on the history of the place. The gardens were well manicured and a pleasant place to stroll.

We were surprised to see so many Jabirus walking around the streets in the residential area, where we were staying. Large black and white birds on legs like storks with long beaks, who made guttural noises.

The van was needing a good service after traveling such a distance, so we booked it in at a garage in Stuart Park. I drove it down early in the morning expecting it to be ready the same day but they found it needed a couple of parts replacing. I stayed with it during the day and wrote letters and read, then I was told they were not going to be able to complete the job. I phoned Vera and she got Lois to drive her down to pick me up. The next morning, we both returned to the garage and spent a further half day before we could drive away.

We spent a day sailing over to Perron Islands. The waters were quite calm and that beautiful colour tropical waters are noted for. Had a bit of an explore, a good meal and a swim before returning to Darwin. That evening we went in for a meal at the 'Don Hotel'. A real good atmosphere, there were so many backpackers of every nationality mixing with the locals. Great fun being with young people.

One day we took a run down to Berry Springs, an absolutely glorious spot surrounded by tropical rainforest. It seemed a popular place. The water tepid except under the small falls, but so refreshing. Visited Southport Historical ruins and Tumbling Waters, found a spot near Darwin River Dam and camped the night. The next morning decided to take a run out to Batchelor and Rum Jungle. As we drove along, we saw magnetic and cathedral anthills, this was a billabong area, crocodiles, wallabies, emus being some of the wild life to be seen. Rum Jungle was an abandoned uranium mine. The road was passable and the scenery interesting and certainly lush.

Then back on the Stuart highway, turned off at Adelaide River to Robin Falls a beaut spot for a swim and to drink in the scenery, spent the night near there then returned to Darwin calling in to Lake Bennett. We just lapped up all the water holes with their amazing terrain. So different to traveling across the top of Western Australia. It was fairly late when we got back so had showers and collapsed into bed.

One weekend there was a Rodeo just out of Darwin which we attended. Most there wore checked shirts and jeans with boots and large hats, we went in shorts and large hats. There were an enormous amount of 'tinnies' cans of beer, being drunk but there didn't seem to be any inebriated people around. The whole atmosphere was electric. The riders of bulls and bucking broncos came from far and near afield and were good. The clowns very colourful and clever as decoys.

Another day spent visiting Howard Springs, the landscape a varied rainforest with ghost gums and paper barks. An abundance of bird species. Animal life included rats, wallabies, flying foxes and echidnas. Had a very pleasant swim in the swimming area. On the Marrakai Plains, the magnificent jabiru, magpie geese and brolga that throng to the billabong. We also saw buffaloes. Called into Yarrawonga Zoo but decided just to return to Darwin as we had had a very tiring day. There had been so much to take in for one day.

We stayed in and around Darwin for a month then decided it was time we moved on. Our aim was to reach Adelaide before the rainy season set in.

Chapter 46

DARWIN TO KATHERINE

It was sad parting, we had fallen in love with Darwin. The hospitality incredible and the climate ideal. We drove out early in the morning intending to return to Katherine via Arnhem land and Kakadu Park. Turning off the Stuart Highway along the Arnhem Highway into Fogg Dam just past Humpty Doo. What an unusual name! But Fogg Dam, well that place, an absolute dream. We drove over a causeway out onto a wider bit of land, turned the van around and parked.

The waters covered in beautiful waterlilies and sedges, in spots one could barely see the water. Looking across the dam to the far bank, running around the edge of the water, the trees stood tall with their white trunks. White cypress, the Darwin stringy barks, the dense understory included ferns and palm like cycads.

Simply hundreds of water birds of varied breeds. The black and white Pied goose with a knob on its head, looked like someone had hit it with a hammer! The little grebe and horny-headed grebe, royal spoon bills and a golden looking yellow-billed spoon bills. The white ibis and glossy ibis with long curved beaks. The straw-necked ibis, a bluey colour with a rough bit below its beak which looked like a beard. A pretty little duck, the grass-whistling duck, with green colouring and a paler neck. The burdekin duck with a white head and looks like it's wearing a white apron. So many ducks and terns. The curlew sandpiper with a long, curved bill, the other sandpipers appeared to have straighter bills. The speckled-wood sandpiper walking with spindly legs over the broad leaves of the waterlily. Also, the lotus bird walking over the waterlilies, a funny looking bird with a red or orange comb on its forehead. When squatting on a leaf it looks like their legs are broken.

This spot would have to be one of the most exciting we have visited. There was so much to take in we decided to park and stay overnight, even though it would be fairly noisy. We were not disappointed there! The racket of water birds and frogs was incredible, but we were thrilled to be among all this wildlife, which just continued on its merry old way, seeming oblivious of our being there. Or were they objecting to our presence. Who knows!

We rose before the sun and sat at the front of the van, with a cup of tea, looking through the windscreen at such a dramatic sight. A fog lay over the dam, only the tops of the trees on the far bank stood out. But it did not lie as low as the water so *that* looked a dark grey colour. The mist an ashy grey and the tree tops a pastel olive green. As the sun rose the highest parts of the trees turned to gold. There was a slight breeze, and the leaves shone in the sunlight as they moved. The top of the fog cloud became flushed with pink and red-orange, below the grey turned to blue. The morning choir of birdsong seemed to be lifting the band of fog we were witnessing. We were joined by a busload of tourists who came out to enjoy the sights of nature at its best, only they had missed the best.

Many of the ducks flew off and we wondered where they were going and would they return. While having breakfast we watched the beautifully coloured dragonflies hovering over the water and the waterlilies. The spindly legged lotus birds feeding on insects that scurried across the broad leaves in an attempt to escape being gobbled up. Funny long-legged spiders, cobwebs stretched out between low shrubs on the shoreline. *So* much to see in this amazing Fogg Dam.

We moved out before it got too hot to continue our journey into this tropical and exciting countryside. Back on to Arnhem Highway soon crossing Adelaide River, seeing wild buffalo on the way. Passing grasslands, wetlands, there was still water lying in places left from the wet season. Arrived at Mary River where we turned off to the right on to a dirt track. Several hundred meters along the river the track became very rough. By now we could not be seen from the highway, we found a beaut spot to park and backed in. We locked the van and decided to take a walk to explore the layout. As we walked around a bend in the river, we spotted the large bus we had seen in Katherine. Another couple who enjoyed camping in the bush. Bill and Joan were very friendly, we stopped for a cup of coffee and compared traveling tales. Their bus was so well set up, they even had a plastic shower enclosure hanging from a branch. All the luxuries of home out here miles from any town!

During the day when it was too hot to wander the bush we relaxed in the shady cool of our van or a tree. We read or wrote to family and friends and I invariably tried to keep up with my diary. On our second night there, this happened to be Friday, at about 8 PM. We heard the roar of motorbike engines drawing close. And guess what? They all turned off into the area where we were. They were also accompanied by several panel vans. It was rather unsettling. Another panel van arrived and parked near us. By this time the bikies had torn down branches and small trees using chains and bumper bars. Being dark it was hard to see how many had arrived, but it sounded like too many. And we were about to experience a disruptive night's sleep.

Once they had built a huge fire which lit up the whole area, we could at least see roughly how many were there. Among them were many very noisy girls and it was rather disconcerting when a couple of them started screaming. The last arrival made a move to settle for the night and made it quite obvious he carried a rifle of a large bore. By this time, I was sitting in the passenger seat with our gun. As it turned out the crowd were harmless though extremely noisy. They thought it great fun to get on their bikes, rev their engines, hold the brakes and spin the back wheel until it dug a deep hole in the already rough track. We were soon enveloped in a cloud of dust.

Next morning there were bodies laying around in deep sleep. We didn't relish spending a second restless night so we walked up to Bill and Joan and told them we intended moving on. They said they had been worried about us as it sounded like a wild party.

We drove on, entering the Kakadu Aboriginal Land Trust. Only three years before the Governor General of the Commonwealth of Australia had proclaimed an area as Kakadu National Park.

We called into a place where they killed and butchered buffalo and we were given four pairs of horns. We'd seen these on our travels, cleaned up and carved into or used as lampshades. I wanted to give it a go. They told the easiest way to clean them was to boil them to soften the hard bone, then scrape all the rough surface off.

Back on the highway we drove to Jabiru where they were opening up a uranium mine. They were busy building houses to quarter workers and their families. Jabiru is the newest township in the Territory. The Ranger workforce and families were the first to be housed. There are two mine sites nearby, Boondjinnie and Coonjumba. Once the Ranger township is completed mining proper will get underway. We parked at the entrance to the Ranger consortium and were bused in for a tour of the mine site and some of the surrounding area. We were told the vegetation would be preserved, we have not been back so hope this is true.

We then drove on to East Alligator River where we found a shop "Boarder Store" which seemed to carry anything and everything one would require and if it didn't, they would have it there for the next day. The chap that ran it was very friendly and interested in what we were doing. He told us about a spot by the river where we could camp for the night. He even obliged us with a drum half the size of a forty-four drum, to boil our horns in! But he warned us "Do not sit around your van after dark as the tide will come in and the water will be practically level with the bank on which you are parked." The river was full of very large crocodiles!

We parked in a good position then looked around for some large rocks to sit the drum on, dug a shallow hole to set the fire in. In that way the fire was safer from being blown around and it also lasted longer. Then we went gathering fuel for the fire. Once that was all set and lit it was a question of how to get the water, as there was a good three-meter drop to the level of the river. The bank was very steep and there was no way we could get down and then climb back up. Near us was a tree with a branch hanging over the river. Vera volunteered to climb along it and drop a bucket on a length of rope. I agreed only if she tied a rope around her waist and then to the branch. After hauling up several buckets of water, which I climbed along the branch to retrieve, I emptied them into the drum, which we had sitting on the rocks. We got the offending horns in before the water became hot or they would not soften. We decided it would be a good idea to have several more buckets full to top up the level of the water once it started boiling.

It must have been a funny sight, Vera perched about two meters along the branch fetching the water up then I would climb along and retrieve the water and return with empty bucket being very careful not to get tangled in the rope. After all this palaver we had attracted some attention from the campers, but no one volunteered a better idea. All this done we set about getting something to eat. While that was cooking, we relaxed with a couple of cold shandies.

The horns were boiling merrily and we were about to retire when we noticed the river had risen at least two meters. We stoked up the fire, topped up the water level and moved into the van. We guessed that as long as there was a fire the crocodiles wouldn't come too close to us but wondered about the people in a couple of tents nearby! About 5 am. Next morning it was light enough to see the fire was nearly out. We had a good look around and saw no signs of movement so we hurriedly stoked up the fire and retreated to the van. We needn't have bothered, we hadn't noticed the tide had gone out and the river was low again.

When we fished one of the horns out it still needed a bit more softening so topped up the water and kept the fire going. We put the billy on and stuck some bread on a toasting fork and had breakfast. After the second cup of tea we locked the van and walked up the side of the East Alligator river to a causeway we had noticed the evening before. There were a couple of guys fishing for Barramundi. We could not cross to the other side of the river as it was an Aboriginal Reserve and we needed a permit. We asked about an Aboriginal man who had been in the army with Vera's husband, but he was not there at the time, he was in Darwin and would not be back for a week. So that was that.

We stayed a couple more days at this spot. Read, wrote letters, looked after our horns which we scraped with broken glass. This is very sharp and a good implement for scraping horns. We removed all the rough outside then rubbed them with wire wool and water. In fact, we made a pretty good job of them. They were a pearly, creamy colour with black tips and markings on them. Then we let them dry in the sun and put a bit of black shoe polish and spit and polished them up a treat.

DARWIN TO KATHERINE

Before we moved out, we stowed them in the storage space under the bed. Checked the engine, battery, water and tyres and we were on the move again.

Arnhem Land plateau is a source of many creeks and rivers which spread out over the flood plains. During the dry season water remains in several places which we stopped at in our travels. Beautiful billabongs surrounded by trees and inhabited by water birds and some with millions of flies and mosquitoes, like big black crows. We didn't stay at any that bred mosquitoes, that would make life too unpleasant!

After leaving East Alligator River we turned off on a track to visit Aboriginal rock paintings at Obiri. The road not the best as termites had decided to build mounds in the middle of the track and though not very big one dare not drive into one as it was like driving into a rock. We did not experience that but we met a couple who had and it put their steering right out of whack! Numbats eat the termites; they have very long tongues. There are several varieties of reptiles. The knobbed tailed gecko being one. The lizards we saw running around didn't seem to be affected by the heat of the day. All around there is bare rock with clumps of spinifex, this looks soft as it blows in the breeze but it is hard and very spiky even when you brush against it. The spinifex pigeons are very colourful and their call is quite different to other pigeons. Pink blood-wood trees interspersed in the grassland. They are a tall eucalypt, also there were many young smaller trees.

We climbed on a very tall rock formation and imagined in days gone by this being used as a lookout for game or possibly the enemy.

We had decided to return to Katherine using the back roads and visiting various billabongs, swimming holes and Aboriginal rock paintings we had been told about. Their art shows the internal anatomy of birds and fish, stylised stick figures of the Mimi spirits. In some there were scenes of animals and strange people, wallabies, handprints and even a ship! It was not an easy drive to reach many of these sites but with careful driving we succeeded.

The countryside varied so much as we drove down the road to Katherine. The surface of the road not too bad. Even the tracks we took to visit the various waterholes were passable. There is an abundance of bird life. The bright green colour of the leaves on the tropical pandanus palms. The mixture of colourful rocks in parts of the National Park quite breathtaking. I did several oil paintings of places we visited and sold them on our trip. Every little helped to cover our traveling expenses.

Some of the most unusual rock formations were along Baver Bird Creek, near the abandoned copper mine. The beauty of Rock Hole and the cascading waterfall. We stopped a night on the shores of South Alligator River, several others were camping nearby. One van near us left their dog chained to the back bumper of their vehicle for the night which attracted an alligator and there was a terrible din that night. They were very lucky they didn't lose their dog, we had seen signs saying, 'no dogs allowed in the Park'!!

We spent two nights at Jim Jim, on the Yellow Water Billabong. While there, a couple next to us had a small boat and he offered to take us out to do some Barramundi fishing. We saw crocodiles, water buffalo, some brolgas and many other species of birds. We caught a large catfish and a good-sized Barramundi which John sliced up into sections. We had some to put in our freezer, some for their freezer and enjoyed the rest for tea cooked on a campfire. Delicious.

Before leaving Darwin, we were told not to miss UDP Falls. So as soon as we saw the sign we turned off. It was certainly not disappointing and just what we needed at this stage of our journey. A very picturesque spot with a swimming hole, sandy beach, where we could enjoy a swim without the fear of crocodiles. Spectacular waterfalls. The scenery had changed so much since traveling from Jabiru, here we were under an escarpment of very high rock wall which we could climb. We did once we had parked and got into our bathers, grabbed some towels, a small backpack each with a bottle of drinking water, some fruit and the camera. Above the waterfall was another swimming hole with another waterfall beyond. What a panoramic view we had, both around us and below. We rested and had a dip in some icy water then made a rather slippery and difficult decent.

Several other vehicles had arrived while we had been exploring. Groups of young people from Darwin down for the weekend. We slept very well that night listening to the soothing sound of falling water. Next day we spent laying around enjoying our surroundings and watching young guys climbing the sides of the waterfall and plunging into the water. We hoped the water was deep enough them as some climbed fairly high before jumping off. But then they were probably used to visiting this spot. Some came over and were interested in our van, one had seen it in Darwin and they wanted to know about our travels.

We crossed the Mary River again on our travels before hitting bitumen once more. So we knew we were nearing Pine Creek turn off on the Stuart Highway. We had heard on the radio that busloads of objectors had arrived, from all over Australia, at an American base at Pine Creek. We hoped we wouldn't be held up on our trip by them.

In 1871 while digging post holes which were being sunk for the Overland Telegraph, gold was discovered. In 1882 there was a gold rush. Mines were opened. Then in 1888 a rail line was laid to connect Palmerston, Darwin, to the growing population at Pine Creek. The Pine Creek station still survives. The line was closed only four years ago and is now becoming overgrown. We joined the Stuart Highway once more and drove south to Edith River and found what we thought would be a cooling water hole. To get to the water we walked through muddy ground and rushes, the water was a bit murky but at the other end was a small waterfall. Once we felt refreshed and walked back to the van, where we had to wash the mud off our feet, we made for Katherine. We hoped we'd find a spot to park for the night down behind the hospital. We were in luck, backed the van in then went for a quick dip in the river. Had a couple of shandies and supper then flopped into bed.

The next day we drove out to Katherine Gorge National Park. The Katherine River flows between deep, canyon like rocks, through a series of gorges. We booked on a launch which took us down the river. There were Aboriginal rock paintings, Johnston crocodiles and tracks going into the wilderness areas. The colour of the rock wall varied in several shades of orange and browns depending on where the sunlight fell. There was a high-water mark on the rocks, which was a paler colour, white in places, this showed us how high the river rose during the wet season. Going up the river, in a further gorge, we were allowed out of the boat to walk along the rocky side of the river and saw something of the upper reaches. One can swim, fish and picnic as well as camp. We only spent the day there, walking and swimming, then returned to the position below the hospital. What a wonderful stay, it certainly is a diverse land this country of ours!

Chapter 47

LONG HAUL TO ALICE

We were lucky to find a spot, by the river, behind the hospital, and spent the night there. The next day we rose early, checked the van out. Then had a walk over the causeway, listened to the birds and watched the colourful Kingfishers. Some just sat on branches looking down at us and we were able to examine them through the binoculars. After breakfast we took a walk into town, bought milk and bread and some fruit then collected mail. We had letters from some of the families, also one from my mother, who could never believe it was so simple to send mail in such a large country 'post restante'. There was also one from Vera's Mum, who mentioned she was on a tour into the Northern Territory, she enclosed the itinerary. We worked it out that we could be at Mataranka when she arrived there.

Spent another night by the river, the next morning we drove into town and filled up with petrol then drove to Springvale Historic Homestead. This was a real tourist attraction with its old buildings and because they put on a Corroboree. Most of the buildings were ruins, the mortar used in between the bricks or stones was crushed termite hills, this was very strong as was seen with the parts of the building which were still standing. Most of the timbers had been eaten by the termites, so they were minus roofs. There was a little stream which ran out front of the restored homestead and we were told the water was radioactive and had been used a hundred years ago with no apparent ill effects.

We stayed to watch the Corroboree with all the Aboriginal men covered in their painted faces and bodies. Each dance told a story. Some were either a kangaroo, an emu or some other animal that was being hunted then killed. As they danced around, they stamped their feet so there was a considerable amount of dust flying around. For one of the dances one of the men came over and invited some of us to join them in their dance.

We drove to the Cutta Cutta Caves nature Park some 26 kms out of Katherine the next morning. Unfortunately, we had to wait an hour before the first guided tour. These are limestone caves with stalactites, stalagmites, frozen stone waterfalls and crystals on the bottom of pools. As we walked down to see all this, we were shown some very pale coloured snakes, they were a pinky white colour. They were not very big and were in the crevices in the limestone. The guide told us, though they were poisonous, we had nothing to fear as the venom was in the back teeth so we would have to stick our little finger into their mouths before we could be bitten. *None of us were about to do that.* Two of the other four people who were on the tour were reluctant to pass them. The sight that greeted us in the caves was spectacular. It was considerably cooler below ground compared to outside.

The scenery as we drove down the Stuart Highway was beginning to change. In parts we saw grass lands and very long stretches of road that shimmered in the heat. Very often we thought we were coming to a wooded spot but never seemed to reach it. We found a clump of trees to park under and stopped to cool the engine and ourselves. Had a cool drink and something to eat, a bit of a rest then pushed on to Mataranka. We were back in "We of the Never-Never" country again. Turning off the highway to our left to Mataranka Pool Nature Park where there was a caravan and camping area. At the reception area we asked if the tour Vera's Mum was on was due and were told not until the next day. We were given a spot where we could park. The Mataranka old Homestead, where we were, was surrounded by tropical rainforest and next to a clear thermal pool. Such a contrast to the countryside we had just driven down. The water in the pool was tepid and one felt like staying in it forever. Though clear the water was also a strange, rather eerie colour at times looking quite yellow to shades of green, the reflection of the limestone surrounding the bottom of the pool. We finally decided to get out of the pool and took a bit of a walk down a track which had a notice to warn us to 'stay on the path to avoid snakes and other protected reptiles.'

We had a good night's sleep and lazed around the pool until the time the bus was due. Then we hid behind some shrubs while all disembarked. We spotted Vera's Mum and noticed she was being assisted to a chair while all the others set about putting up their tents. We walked up behind and said, "Mrs. Giles we presume?" She was so surprised and pleased to see us. Her right leg was bandaged and she admitted she had injured herself when camping at Ayres Rock and it would not heal. We told her what we had been up to since we last saw her and she told us about her trip which she had been enjoying until she injured herself. We joined the group for the evening meal. Had a bit of a sing-song and then retired as we all had an early rise in the morning to continue our respective journeys. The tour went north and we drove about 24 kms south to the Original Elsey Homestead site used in Mrs. Aeneas Gunn's "We of The Never-Never," we also visited a couple of grave sites. The grave of 'The Maluca', that is what Aeneas Gunn was called, was very evident, in a clearing off the side of the road. Had a good scout around the old Elsey Historic Site and recalled a lot of what we had read in "We of the Never-Never." There was certainly a very strong atmosphere here at this spot. We continued our journey down to Newcastle Waters and found a place to park for the night.

By 4 am we were on our way again so we could travel in the cool of the day. We took it in turns to drive first while the other walked several kms. We would drive on and have breakfast ready when the other arrived. The countryside changing just about every fifty kms.

Hillocks built up with large flat sided rocks. Walls of rock with slits in them which looked like they had been cut in slabs. Spinifex growing in clumps, a pale olive gentle green. Interspersed with ghost gums, its upper branches, which are often knobbly, spread out and droop. Like other eucalypts, it does not provide much shade as the downward hanging leaves are incapable of shutting out the sun. The lower leaves eaten by cattle and kangaroos. When darkness is falling its white bark, which is slightly lustrous, can give off an eerie light. They can often be seen growing out of a bed of rock in arid regions. A grey-green vegetation, rocks the colour of terracotta and blue skies which stretch forever.

As we drove into Elliot what should we see but Bill and Joan's bus parked on the side of the road. We did a U-turn and parked beside it and knocked on the door. An Aboriginal man came across the road and told us "The man he proper sick, nurse man he drive him and missus to Katherine hospital. But them be back pretty late."

We called into the Nursing Station to be told Joan would be back that evening but Bill was being kept in hospital. So we decided to stay the night. Joan arrived about seven that evening and was she pleased to see us, she was so grateful for the company. Bill had pains in his chest and thought it better to get him checked out before continuing as Joan didn't drive and they still had a long way to go. Bill had thrombosis and would be getting treatment for several days. So we stayed another day with Joan. That night we ate together and then played cards in their bus, retiring about ten thirty. Joan gave us their address south of Sydney and invited us to call in on them during our travels and stay a while.

Next morning, we rose before sunrise to continue our journey. As we started up the van Joan popped out to wave us good-bye, though we had said our farewells the night before.

We were sad to leave her there on her own, but she was in good hands and she had the use of a telephone so she could keep in touch with the hospital and also with her family back home

There was a memorial to John Flynn near the Three Ways Roadhouse and the turn off to Barkly Highway, which would take us to Mount Isa, but we decided to continue down the Stuart Highway. That night we spent up

LONG HAUL TO ALICE

on a small hill just opposite Tennant Creek resuming our journey at a very early hour next morning.

About 80 km south of Tennant Creek as we came around a bend in the road, to our left we were surprised to see a strange pile of round rocks, easily thirty to forty foot high. Just plonked on the red, flat earth which surrounds them. These are called "The Devils Marbles." The Aboriginal legend claims they are the eggs of the 'Rainbow Serpent.' Of course, we had to get out and walk around them, they were so extraordinary.

The road seemed long, the land arid and we saw many a mirage on our travels. The appearance of a sheet of water, though we were traveling through desert. The road was straight, hot and shimmering. At times it looked as though we were approaching a lake surrounded by trees. We'd drive for miles and arrive at nothing but more red dirt and some shrubs which managed to survive this relentless land.

At a place called Ti-Tree we stopped as it was becoming too hot and we had found no where to shelter from the blistering sun. There was a small pub there so we parked in a position where the building afforded us some relief. While sitting enjoying a cold shandy, a road train pulled in and parked. There were some cattle on board. The poor things were half dead with heat exhaustion. The driver seemed to think they would survive until he reached Alice Springs. I had my doubts, I felt very sorry for the poor beasts. I could not understand why they could travel in the worst heat of the day instead of the cooler night!

We had a pie each and an ice cream plus a couple more shandies then decided to rest until three o'clock before moving on. It was at least a three-hour drive to Alice, where we were to park in the driveway of some friends of Vera's daughters. A school friend had gone to Alice to work, met and married a local chap and had just moved into a new house, on the other side of the Todd River.

As one approaches Alice Springs it looked like the road had been cut through a hill. And there was The Alice nestled among the hills. We phoned and announced our arrival and were given directions on how to find the house. The Alice was spreading out, so the only place to go was over the river. We were made very welcome, offered a shower, which was bliss, then Greg put on a BBQ and we sat around while Vera caught up on family history. Before going to bed we were told we were welcome to stay as long as we liked as there was an awful lot to see in and around The Alice.

Chapter 48

ALICE SPRINGS AND WESTERN COUNTRYSIDE

We drove in on a wide road, on the first corner and what seemed the outskirts of town, there was the John Ross Memorial on our left. Railway Terrace, over Stuart Terrace, to Telegraph Terrace were the widest roads. The two which led in from the North and exited via Telegraph Terrace to the South. The town seemed very compact, everything central and one could cover every street on foot quite easily.

A large oasis, nestled in the centre of Australia, surrounded by craggy hills. We had travelled 510 km, through arid country, from Tennant Creek and it was very refreshing to be here at last.

The Todd river runs through Alice Springs separating the main town from the residential area. It was a dry sandy riverbed when we arrived, but there was a storm one day while we were staying there. The streets were covered in hailstones, filling the curb as high as the pavement. Not long after the river was full of muddy water. Quite a spectacle not often seen by many during the dry season. All the Aboriginals who lived in the river and under the bridge, had to gather their belongings and find alternative places to settle. It did not take many days before they were back and the river was no longer flowing.

We hoped to get work while staying in 'The Alice'. Vera got a barmaid's job and I got to paint our friend's new house. They supplied the paint, brushes and any other materials required and for that we had the use of their shower and amenities, plus I got paid $1,500. The ceilings had already been done, so all I had to do were the walls, skirting, windows and doors. It was a three-bedroom house with open plan dining lounge area. Our friends continued to live in the large caravan they had occupied while the house was being built, until I had finished painting.

ALICE SPRINGS AND WESTERN COUNTRYSIDE

We shared meals and I baby sat their one-year old daughter a few evenings so they could have a night out. When I'd finished the painting job, I got a part time job at a takeaway place, run by a very rude Italian guy. He expected me to prepare and cook, clean and serve in the shop for very small wages, but at least it was a job.

In between working, when we had the same time off, we explored. We visited the Alice Springs Telegraph Station, built in the 1870s and the first European settlement in the area. It is actually a reconstruction of the original station. A combined Telegraph office and staff quarters, a stable and wagon shed plus a police hut on the bank of the waterhole. They had been built of stone. A separate telegraph office, telegraph master's house, and battery storage room and a small keeping cellar near the stables was built soon afterwards. Extensive alterations have been made, with the exception of the police hut and cellar. All the stone buildings are the original ones.

The Alice Springs repeater station worked south to Charlotte Waters and north to Barrow Creek and was in use until 1932. The present post office in town was then opened. The Telegraph Station is National Trust and is now a museum and National Park. Certainly a well set up place and extremely interesting. We were amazed how well kept the buildings and grounds were kept.

Alice Springs was named after Lady Alice Todd, the wife of the Superintendent of Telegraphs, Sir Charles Todd. The Todd River was named after him. The present town was surveyed in 1888, the township of Stuart was mapped out and gazetted, the name was changed in 1930. It is the administrative centre for the southern portion of the Northern Territory, a railhead for outlying cattle stations, mining projects and Aboriginal settlements. It appears to be quite self-sufficient in small industries such as engineering works, sheet metal, joinery, cabinet making, brick making, building and soft drink production. Dairying, growing citrus fruits, grapes and dates are ideal in this type of climate.

All the locals we met were very industrious and proud of their rather famous town. I must say it is a very attractive part of Australia. Had I not had family in Western Australia I would have felt tempted to settle there for some time.

One day we drove up Stuart Terrace and out on a well-made road to visit Simpson's Gap which was only 26 km out of town, the beginning of the western MacDonnell Ranges. A beautiful spot with its clear waters reflecting the orange rock face on either side. Beyond the water there's a gap between the rock, trees growing down near the water. The lower rock a white-grey colour. Among the lower rocks we spotted some black footed rock wallabies, they reminded me of mountain goats the way they managed to bound up the rock face. A tame colony of these rock wallabies can be seen here.

There is an echo among the rock walls, around there are some nature walks where one has the opportunity to glimpse local wildlife which include the rock wallabies, which were the most evident, dingoes, euros, and numerous reptiles. Some of the lizards looked as though they were doing push-ups. Eagles glided above. Nearby Euro Hill has central Australia's oldest rocks, millions of years old.

The MacDonnell Ranges are among the oldest mountains on earth and suggests a Biblical landscape. The drive along a bitumen road seems quite out of place to the surrounding countryside. It is an unusual terrain, rugged outcrops, the land rising in what appears to be terraced sections. We wondered if the land had been occupied by some unknown civilization, which had disappeared off the face of the earth, leaving this spectacular scene. All the terraces seemed so even, it was hard believe they *just happened*.

We carried on another 29 km to Iwupataka and turned off right on a very rough track which would take us to Standley Chasm. The track in parts was mainly rock and seemed to go down in steps, so I had to drive very carefully as we descended, so I wouldn't hit the exhaust pipe or any of the tanks at the rear of our van. At the Chasm there was a large parking and picnic area. There were some Aboriginals selling their hand made artefacts.

The Chasm in places was only a few meters wide and is formed by sheer quartzite walls some 75 m high. The walls are stained red by iron oxides that change colour as the sun passes over head. The direct rays of light for only a few brief moments each day. The floor was like a pebbled beach, at the end of the Chasm we were confronted by large rocks and further walls of coloured rock formation, an odd gum tree clinging to these walls. In a few places the wall stained where, in the wet season, water had flowed down the sides.

We managed to climb the track out without event and continued to Lizard Rock. Another unusual spot, to whet our appetite. Ellery Creek Big Hole Nature Park, red rock mirrored in the emerald water of a very deep pool, we walked down to it and threw a couple of stones in to see if we could see how deep! Then Serpentine Gorge Native Park, with more ghost gums silhouetted against coloured rock and earth. Purple walls reflected in a pair of waterholes. Veins of colour decorate the banks at Ochre Pit, ochre used by the Aboriginals to colour their paintings. We travelled from one beautiful spot to another mesmerized by colours and atmosphere of each new area.

Ormiston Gorge National Park was just breathtaking. So unexpected to arrive and find its blue rock structure. A colour we had never seen before. It was unreal and SO blue. It is supposed to be the most impressive gorge within the MacDonnell Ranges. Hundreds of meters of rugged walls tower over Ormiston Creek, which reflects the blue rock. A tributary of the Finke River, the water from the creek feeds into Ormiston Pound, a ten km enclosure. Virtually encircled by high ridges, like an amphitheatre. Sheltered in the moist, shady niches, where there appears to be constant water, one can find the rare cycads, probably the most primitive of all seed producing plants.

The Gorge is quite park-like, river red gums among the ghost gums and coolabahs. Spangled perch buried deep in mud during droughts, visible in the water after the wet season. There was sufficient water on our visit to sustain fish and small crustaceans.

To our great surprise and delight there was an ablution block, newly built, clean and supplied with hot water, solar heated. Quite bizarre in these surroundings! We decided to spend the night. While there we enjoyed the changing colours of our surroundings at twilight. Wildlife appearing, coming down to drink. Flocks of zebra finches and bright green budgerigars as well as a collection of screeching parrots swooping in to bathe and drink. During the night the sound of frogs and crickets and from the sound of it, larger animals cooling in the water. It is such an exciting place.

Next morning, we were up before the sun to witness the glorious colours of the sky, rocks and everything in the land around us, as the sun slowly rose. The rock wallabies were still around. We had hoped to see a dingo but fear they are too timid. While having a cuppa we sat and enjoyed our surroundings before moving out, that I might add very reluctantly, but we had to get on with our journey.

Not many kilometres and we were at Glen Helen Nature Park. The land here seemed flatter, a green valley, blue waters and lower escarpments. Some dwellings nestled bellow an escarpment, the land appearing to open out beyond. We did not linger long as there was a long journey back to Alice Springs where we had to return that day as both had to work the next day. Though the drive back was hurried we still noted the scenery around us as we drove and promised ourselves we would return but alas never did.

Chapter 49

ALICE SPRINGS VISITS

While in The Alice when we had a few spare hours, we visited places of interest. Panorama 'Guth' an art gallery like no other in the southern hemisphere, a must on our list. Artist Henk Guth, a Dutchman, moved to Alice Springs in 1966 and opened 'Art Studio Guth'. Gradually a museum of Aboriginal culture was built up. Having been inspired by the beauty of the Central Australian landscape, Henk decided to produce a circular painting on canvas, to be viewed from a central platform. The platform was reached by a spiral staircase giving the impression of a lookout. The canvas consists of thirty-three pieces of Irish linen joined together by aluminium strips. It is twenty-foot high and 200 ft. around, the diameter is sixty feet. The canvas hangs from a circular rail and is hooked at the lower end, hidden by red earth, rocks and flora which looks as though it is part of the painting. So cleverly done.

Special scaffolding was erected, a colleague from Holland came out and helped in the enormous task. The scaffolding was erected on wheels so it could be moved around. The painting depicts the many scenic attractions around Central Australia. Several Mounts, Gorges, the Undoolya Ranges, the Olgas, Ayers Rock (now Uluru) and out to Ross River, east of Alice Springs. Many of these places we had not yet visited but after seeing this painting were very enthusiastic to visit all, if possible.

While we were in the Alice, Princess Alexandria came up to Alice Springs on the first Ghan to run from Adelaide. So the rail line was opened once more for passenger trains to commute between both places, opening the Centre to tourism.

All the locals were dressed in their Sunday best. We joined the excited crowd to await the arrival of the train. When it arrived, it stopped outside the station and Princess Alexandria alighted, she walked to the front of the train, cut a ribbon and then got back on the train until it pulled up at the station. There was much cheering and waving of flags followed by speeches.

Everyone stood around, in the heat, with cool drink cans in their hands, children with icy-poles and ice cream dripping down their beautiful clothes. There was clapping and hoorays until the ceremony was over and the town absorbed everyone again.

The day it hailed and the Todd River flowed, just about everyone got their feet wet and many were soaked all over, but they relished the cooling rain. The river was completely dry when they ran the "Henley-on-Todd" boat races. Quite hilarious watching all the enthusiastic competitors running down the dry riverbed in all manner of homemade boats. They had rail tracks running the course and the boats were on wheels. But not all were like that, some were carried by the owners, they were in the boats which they held up around their waist height, then they ran as fast as they could, some falling over they were laughing so much. The distances varied according to what size the boat was that was being carried. You never heard *so* much laughter, the atmosphere was great. It was a real holiday for all, culminating with BBQs and much drinking of 'tinnies. All looking forward to next year's event.

When I wasn't working and Vera was, I parked the van in a park near the ablution block, on the outskirts of town and painted. One day while doing this a guy knocked on the door and introduced himself. He turned out to be a Jamaican, married to an Aboriginal lady. They were both teachers and were up from Sydney, visiting some of her relatives. He invited me to go with him to meet some of the Elders, who were sitting in the shade, under the Todd Bridge. I was made most welcome, we all sat in a circle and told tales of places we'd been, we talked about art and the situation the Aborigines found themselves living in the Alice. Many of them belonged to the Lutheran Church, this came about because Lutheran missionaries came into the area and converted a lot of the locals. They also supported them and educated as many as possible.

They were all very concerned about the drinking problem amongst them, especially the young, but then they didn't get much of an example. They were being exploited by some unscrupulous shop owners, who were buying their paintings for a pittance and then selling them at a terrific profit. Unfortunately, some of the painters were only interested in getting money to replenish their liquor.

The Old Stuart Goal has been restored and being kept as an historical building, dwarfed by modern buildings. There are many churches with quite modern architecture through the town. Green parks, where groups of locals sit under shady trees while their children play. One day we visited Pitchi Richi Sanctuary walking up several paths admiring carvings of gorgeous Aboriginal children by William Ricketts. The carving of the moon and a young child on top of it, nestled in rocks. Another amazing one was, five children's faces, so beautiful, out of the top, another child from the waist up, with one arm appearing to embrace the others.

Incredible Memories

As we walked around the paths there were impish indigenous faces looking at us so cleverly carved. All with different expressions. Pitchi Richi also contains open-air pioneer displays. Mr. Ricketts was not in residence in the colonial style house, sitting on the property. We hoped to catch up with him when we got to Melbourne.

The young Aboriginal children had a mop of blond hair. Even with their running noses, which attracted the insatiable flies, were very fascinating with their large twinkling eyes and winsome smiles. We had only been there four weeks and they were calling me 'Aunty' which I found presumptuous until I realized they were showing me true friendship. I could only presume word had spread among them that I was amiable when serving them at the delicatessen where I worked. When in town I often had a couple running along beside me chatting away and inviting me to "Come see my mum." Which I did one day. I joined them under a tree and was introduced. I found it difficult to understand them, they were all interested to know where I came from and did I 'pray to the Lord Jesus'. That I would be most welcome to visit their church. They were all genuinely friendly. While there I realized that the women ruled. This was very evident when, down a side street, one of the women was upbraiding her man in no uncertain manner. He was drunk and she was yelling and hitting him with a stick, telling him in their lingo how wicked he was. Or so I was told by one passing woman.

One day when I was taking a short cut through a car park, to my surprise, who should I meet but Joan and Bill our friends from Mary River. Their daughter and son-in-law had come up to drive the bus back to Sydney. We all ended up having a counter tea at the pub where Vera worked, and catching up with all the news. The doctors in Katherine had said they didn't think it a good idea for Bill to drive the bus until his health was better.

Another day when we both had a couple of days off, we visited the camel farm. We were shown how to ride a camel. First, we had to get on one, so the guy in charge got the camel down on its haunches and we climbed on. As it rose, we had to lie back or end up over its head, as it raises its hind legs first. I must admit the ride was more comfortable than I expected until it started to run quite fast. We hung on for dear life as we were a fair height from the ground. The descent to the ground was just as uncomfortable as the ascent. My legs were a wee bit wobbly when I got off, and stiff the next day.

Further south we visited a date farm where some men were up a ladder leaning against the tree. They told us they were pollinating the flowers as so far they did not have the particular beetle that pollinated date palms naturally. The palms were some thirty years old and starting their productive life.

We also visited a vineyard, this was also in the infant stages of production, the couple that owned it were very nice and as they were not busy the wife invited us to have a cup of coffee with them. At another place there was a lady making pottery and she offered me a job, it was very tempting! The land around seemed very fertile, to be able to grow fruit and vegetables to supply 'The Alice.'

Another day we drove out to Meyer Hill Flora Reserve, up a stony hill, we parked and walked around. It would have been nicer on a cooler day and possibly straight after the wet season. But there was still a variety of plants and lizards, also ants, which meant we had to keep moving or be bitten.

After nearly two months we had saved enough money to support ourselves for several more months and pay for a flight to Tasmania and also a return to New Zealand. Now we only had a couple more places to explore before leaving to journey south. In the next chapter we visit east of Alice Springs.

Chapter 50

EAST OF ALICE

We had been told it was worth a drive out east to Ross River Historic Homestead before departing "The Alice". So off we went. Not far from Alice was Emily and Jessie Gaps Nature Park, our first port of call. Beautiful ghost gums showed up in the landscape as we drove along, the earth red, and scraggy rock formations, plus the gentle looking spinifex. The road was not too bad.

At Emily Gap, the red rock stood out with the Witchetty Grub Token paintings. They were vertical lines painted at quite a height and then what looked like a pair of large eyes. The Gaps are carved into white quartzite and red sandstone. These gorges are smaller in scale than the western ones, never-the-less possess their own unique beauty. We found no water here but had been told there was water not far below the surface at any of these gorges when dry. Some of the ghost gums were lying on their trunks, new branches growing skyward. I presume they had been knocked down either by the force of flood waters or strong winds. We walked to the back of the Gap, there was a fairly strong breeze blowing between the high rock. The scenery very picturesque with the usual Central Australian colours. The background to all is red or orange during the day but changing to a blue-purple at dusk. We never found out why this spot was called Emily and Jessie Gap. We had our breakfast there as we had left very early. Then continuing east, the road suddenly turned to a dirt track. This was called a 'Scenic Drive' *and it was.*

To our right appeared this extraordinary rock formation, 'Corroboree Rock'. An upright stone which figures in Aboriginal lore. We had found so many of these unusual rock formations all through our journey. We drove on and turned up the track to Trephina Gorge National Park. This track was a bit dicey but we persevered. This is called lizard country because of the variety of lizards found around the area. There is the small freckled monitor and also Australia's biggest lizard, the perentie. We found them daunting though a wonderful creature which I am sure would not have attacked us.

EAST OF ALICE

But we were cautious of the one we came upon. It looked at us and then wandered slowly off into the bush. There were tiny geckos in comparison. They seemed to be constantly licking their eyes with their long tongues.

Native fig trees hung out of cracks in the gorge face. Fairy martins darted around. Eagles carried high into the sky by wind currents. The vegetation quite lush as there seemed to be sufficient water in the area. This amazing land with its umpteen oases.

We nearly became bogged on the way out. Just a bit of action to stimulate our adventurous spirit.

Back on the firm track we drove to Ross River Historic Homestead where the road turned to a four-wheel drive sort of track which led to N'Dhala Gorge Nature Park and the rock carvings. There was some work being done on a bridge and the road was closed anyway. So that was disappointing.

Around the homestead there were some wonderful large trees. The whole area was humid and tropical. Everything was closing up preparing for the wet season which was shortly due. By this time, we were getting quite tired and decided to return to Emily Gap where we thought we'd camp for the night and relish the dusk colours on the rock formation and maybe see some more wildlife during the evening. We witnessed a glorious sun set while we sat having our tea. The flies do not allow one much peace so we retired to the van and watched the changing scenery from there.

Rising early in the morning we delighted in the different colours of the rocks during the sunrise. From blues to purple, to oranges and reds, then shades of brown and all in a matter of one hour. These colours I have tried to capture in my paintings. My memory carries so many picturesque scenes. Fortunately, I am able to paint some of them from recollection.

We drove back into Alice to our friends and announced we intended to move on. They begged us to stay another couple of days, which we did. BBQing each evening and enjoying their company. We were sad to leave this magnetic town and promised ourselves we would endeavour to return one day.

Chapter 51

SOUTH TO ULURU

Once more on the Stuart Highway heading south from Alice Springs. What a long stretch of road! It must have been the longest without human occupation. Mulga country with tough shrubs which survive this relentless land. is humped camels, the most in the world, roam the deserts. There are over half a million of them, they are now a pest. These poor animals were let loose to fend for themselves when they were no longer being used as beasts of burden.

An occasional road train would hurtle towards us. When we saw one coming, either in our rear-view mirror or coming towards us, we pulled over to the side of the road for fear of them clipping us with the last trailer. Some of them pulled up to four trailers and when overtaking they swayed, plus they left so much dust in the air one could barely see the road.

We passed many a vehicle wreck off the side of the road. All wheels stripped off, some minus doors and motors. Anyone who broke down and left their car to get help would return to find half their vehicle left.

The road shimmered with the heat. Where there was a place we could pull off the road, we did, just to cool the engine. We were amazed at the amount of meat ants there were on the side of the road. They have a terrible bite. Bull ants even eat small reptiles alive. We were lucky to see a couple of thorny devils, hard spiky lizards, like tiny prehistoric animals. They are rather hard to see as they blend in with the sandy countryside. They would do well out in this wilderness as they eat ants and there were certainly plenty of them.

Finally, the landscape changed as we drove between the James Ranges on our right and Chandler's Range to our left. They formed rocky escarpments. We crossed the Finke River, quite dry, supposed to be the oldest in the world. It doesn't go to the sea but feeds beds of water holes for some 700 miles.

SOUTH TO ULURU

Then we saw the sign to Henbury Meteorite Conservation Reserve and turned to our right which took us off the bitumen. We did not have to drive too far. The Meteorite site consists of twelve craters formed by meteorite fragments which struck the ground several thousand years ago. The largest crater, which we visited, is 180 meters wide and fifteen deep. An extraordinary sight, all the rock around shattered and the hole was like a huge bomb crater. It was splattered with vegetation, growing out of this shale like ground. We followed a path down to halfway into the hole but it was becoming too hot to hang around for long. There were dirt roads leading off in various directions but we felt one crater was the same as another. We had seen the biggest, so found some shade and parked for a couple of hours to eat and rest ourselves and the van.

Back on the Stuart Highway we drove for about an hour and spotted a track going off, so we checked it out and found the remains of what must have been a camping spot for workers when building the highway. We decided to spend the night there. During the night we could hear trucks going down the highway. We also heard signs of fairly large animals moving around outside. So we had a bit of a restless night.

We started off before sunrise and carried on down the highway to the turn off to Ayers Rock (now called Uluru). The road was not very wide but had a good surface. We were surprised at how many abandoned cars there were on the way. I remember a small, what looked like a brand-new car, on its side down a bank on the side of the road. It looked like the driver had just driven it down the bank then walked away and left it.

We only drove until about ten that morning when it became too hot to continue. There was a spot just off to our right where there were three trees, so we stopped and found the ground to these trees, which were about thirty yards from the road, quite firm, so we drove off the road and parked between the trees so we could have some semblance of shade.

We took two folding chairs out of the van and sat in the shade of the van. A bird flew on to a branch of one of the trees and sat there with its beak open and its tongue out, the poor thing was so hot. I went in and fetched out a bowl of water in the hope it would come down and drink. It took nearly half an hour before it felt safe enough to fly down to drink, then it stood in the bowl.

We stayed there until about four o'clock then decided to move on till we came to the turn off to Agnes Downs, not far from there we could get off the road and park for the night.

Again, we started off before sunrise and drove to Curtin Springs where we stopped to have breakfast before driving on to what was the ranger's house where we had to stop. He took the number of our van and asked how long we intended staying, gave us some information about the rock and we drove on.

Incredible Memories

Ayers Rock was sticking up out of the ground in all it's glory. It was a brilliant orange, the few trees silhouetted in black against the Rock. As the sun climbed higher into the sky all the many crevices show up as brown streaks from the top to bottom of the rock. The formidable size of this monolithic, dwarfs all below at ground level. Ayers Rock (Uluru) part of a subterranean mountain range.

There were several tents and a few caravans parked in the camping area, there was also a small building there. We drove slowly around the Rock and found a spot where we parked. There was no shade for the van, we got out and locked it and decided to try and climb the Rock. We only got halfway up. It was very windy and we didn't feel safe as the lower half didn't have a rail to hold on to. In fact, it was easier climbing up, but coming down was a wee bit more difficult. In places we were more or less coming down on our bottoms.

Ayers Rock has always been held sacred by the Aboriginal people and has great Dream Time significance. There are caves covered in ancient paintings, these were fenced off and signs saying the public were not allowed to enter. Some are still used for traditional ceremonies. Like an iceberg the greater part of the Rock is buried beneath the sand. It rises very abruptly out of the ground to a height of over one thousand feet. This monolith is composed of a hard feldspar and quartz-rich sandstone called 'arkose'.

Deep furrows running down the sides shows that the rock has been upended and tilted by earth movements. This is very obvious in so many of the rock formations in the Northern Territory. The surface of the Rock is flaky and covered in thick sheets of rock. When parts of these flake off the rock, where exposed, looks a dull greenish-grey, it then turns to red as the iron in the rock oxidizes.

The most extraordinary thing we were told was that when rain fills depressions, on the top of the Rock, primitive shield shrimps appear. The fertilized eggs can survive years of drought and drastically varying temperatures of from below freezing to over fifty degrees centigrade.

We passed part of the Rock that had a huge flat piece of rock which looked as though it was hinged to the side of the Rock but was completely away from the surface. The scrub around the furrowed base is well watered by run-off from the Rock and is home to wallaroos, dingoes and rabbits. There were several native fig trees. Various kites and wedge-tailed eagle's nest on high ledges on the Rock. It is an exciting sight to see the handsome wedge-tail eagle glide around carried by the thermal airstream. Such an enormous bird, so weightless.

At sunset the shadows on the Rock are a purple lined by areas of pinks, blues and reds. The outline of the Rock very distinct against the yellow glow of the lower part of the blue expanse of sky, which gradually changes to dark blue. We looked west towards The Olgas and the colours of the changing light on the cluster of rock domes. The Aboriginals call it Katajuta which

SOUTH TO ULURU

means 'Many Heads'. These rocks are also sacred to the Aborigines. The colours of the rocks are an amazing purple, pinks and blues. They also are part of the subterranean mountain range. Out here with the expanse of sky at night it sparkles with millions of stars

We arrived not many weeks after a baby was reportedly taken, from a tent, by a dingo. So that was one of the main pieces of gossip.

There was a great feeling of peace and quiet around the Rock but at night felt a wee bit eerie. After spending two nights and days there we were on the move again. Leaving at the crack of dawn, we drove about fifty miles then had to stop as the sun rising from the east was making it hard to see the road. On the way out we had been told to look out for Mt. Conner. As we drove along there it was to our right. How had we not noticed it on our way in. An incongruous sight on the horizon, looking quite flat-topped in comparison to Ayers Rock and the Olgas. A cloud hovered on top. The left side quite orange as the rising sun shone on it. The right side appeared purple. Just below its flat top a rim, as though it had a pudding basin haircut. All shapes due to wind erosion, as it did in all the rock formations we had witnessed. The softer rock crumbling or being blown away.

Parts of the road were built much higher than the surrounding land, presumably to avoid it being flooded during the wet season. The drive out didn't seem to be as long as the drive in and we were soon at Eridunda, the junction with the Stuart Highway, where we turned south.

The Stuart Highway follows the footsteps of the early explorers. The overland telegraph line runs the same route, with repeater stations planted at intervals all the way up, near to the highway. The scene, sand dunes and in some parts stony desert, hummocks of spinifex and a scattering of trees and shrubs. The road not too bad, it shimmered in the heat of the day. The Simpson Desert lay to our left. We called into the roadhouse at Kulgera for a break and treated ourselves to a shower.

After leaving the roadhouse, we carried on down the road, much to our surprise the road was no longer tarmac. We travelled several miles on one of the worst roads we had come across in our entire journey. It was so terribly corrugated it was rattling the van to bits. At Granite Downs we met a guy who told us the road through to Oodnadatta had just been graded. So we turned back to the turn off.

Chapter 52

OODNADATTA TRACK & FURTHER SOUTH

The track to Oodnadatta was very much narrower, especially in some places, than the highway we had just left. We now had to look out for bull dust holes, which was a bit worrying. We prayed not too many trucks and road-trains used this route, as they and tour buses were the culprits that made the roads corrugated.

We were actually driving through a cattle station at one point and had to open and shut gates. We had driven several miles when we noticed a cloud of dust approaching us, some distance away but getting closer. It was a truck and by chance there happened to be a part of the road that divided as it came abreast. Well the next thing, as he rushed past, blowing his loud horn in acknowledgement, we were completely covered in a film of very fine red dust. It slid very slowly down our windscreen. Fortunately, we were stationary as we could see nothing. So, we just had to sit there until all the dust settled and we could clean the outside of the windscreen and windows. The rest we hoped would blow off as we drove along. The shower we had had was quite wasted; the fine red dirt permeates all!

We continued on our way, the scenery here different again. Numerous trees, some quite large, low shrubs and occasionally the dogged river gums, indicating the presence of underground water. Because in parts the trees lined both sides of the track, and the sand was so deep, we wondered if we were driving down a dry creek bed. The worst part of the journey was that we could hit a hole full of bull-dust, which usually was just over the crest of a mound or hump in the road. We checked the road for signs, like a dent in the track with a very smooth patch. We skirted these, driving in low gear until past them. It seemed to take forever to reach Oodnadatta. Then there it was, we arrived tired, hungry and very thirsty to find an old railway station, a general store, with a bowser outside, and a row of a few houses on the opposite side of the road.

We pulled in next to the bowser and filled one of our tanks with petrol. While doing this we noticed several inebriated indigenous people staggering across the street. The guy who served us said if we wanted to spend the night, we could pull into a driveway he pointed out to us and we would be undisturbed. The early part of the night was fairly noisy. As we didn't feel like cooking yellow greens, we opened a can of spaghetti in tomato sauce and laced it with garlic accompanied by a can of carrots and peas.

As we drove south from Oodnadatta, we witnessed the beauty of red sands of the plains. The winds leaving ridges and mounds, sandy rivulets throwing extraordinary shadows as the sun rose. In parts a carpet of rust coloured stones. The crest of some of the dunes devoid of vegetation. Other areas there were clumps of spindly cane grass, which grows in the gullies along with hummocks of spinifex or desert grass. There were scattered low woodlands of mulga and bloodwood, growing along the edges of dry riverbeds, presumably there still was underground water.

As we continued on what was more like a track than a road, though wider and firmer than the previous track we had travelled, the landscape free of vegetation and of a yellow colour. To our great surprise what was coming towards us but a Volkswagen beetle. We could hardly believe our eyes, it was only the second vehicle that we had met all the way from the highway, other than ones we had seen at Oodnadatta. We pulled over, it stopped, out stepped a French guy. He asked us how far the next town was and seemed quite surprised when we told him it was several hundred miles on. He was making for Alice Springs and was under the impression that it was like a day trip. He was completely unaware that this was not possible!

Travelling this countryside minus food or water a madness. We tried to persuade him to return to where he had come from and couldn't believe he intended to continue his journey. We supplied him with some water and a packet of sandwiches then watched him take off to goodness knows where!! Not long after this episode we arrived at Lake William Creek Hotel, this was at the turn off to Coober Pedy. We decided to give that a miss and continue down the Oodnadatta Track. We did not stop at William Creek as there seemed no reason to do so. The track took us south of Lake Eyre South, a massive stretch of dry salt-lake that seemed to go on forever. So absolutely white, like snow. We dare not look at it without dark glasses because of the glare. Looking at the map we noticed that north of the lake was Lake Eyre which was far greater but this was not visible on the route we were on.

The heat shimmering on its surface. Driftwood and rocks covered in dry salt look like they are covered in frost. As the sun was setting the surface around the shoreline turned to pink. Though the land was so barren around this area there was still a beauty about it. We found a spot to camp for the night not far off. There was an eerie feeling about the place it was so silent, the black sky shining with millions of stars and a wisp of a moon.

As we drove on toward Marree the landscape did not change much, we passed several desert spa mounds, the sky reflecting in them giving them a blue-pink colour, tuffs of desert grass growing around them. In parts for as far as the eye could see not a single tree, just an occasional ridge of low shrubs between stretches of what appeared to be pale crusty looking sand. Greenish-grey clumps of the needle-like spinifex, this extraordinary plant with its sharp tapered leaves surviving the extreme drought conditions. So painful to brush against!

The rail line ran close to the road as we drove on. Every now and again an old railway house still standing by, unoccupied. What a life it must have been to live out so far from any town. At some of these houses there were palm trees, bougainvillea's, a few trees and geraniums that were growing wild. A keen gardener in particular must have occupied one place. What may have been a vegetable garden or flowerbed outlined by rocks or railway sleepers. Overgrown pathways with dead vegetation and heaps of ants. Some of the fence posts hung from the stay wire, termites had eaten them. We spent a night at one of these deserted houses leaving very early next morning. We'd travelled about fifty miles; our engine and we were getting very hot so we pulled into the next house and parked along-side a shed for some shade.

Vera and I grabbed a cool drink and went for a bit of a wander. Then we noticed some clothes hanging on the verandah. The back door was ajar, had we seen some movement behind it? We called out but no one came out so we returned to the van, which was out of view from the house. As we sat listening, a man appeared. I said I would go out and talk and Vera stayed in the van. I called out that we had stopped for morning tea and hoped he did not mind. He looked at me with suspicion and returned to the house. There was no other vehicle visible and we didn't know how many were in the house. They could be escaped prisoners and were we at risk. We started the engine and moved out hoping we'd find some shade further down the road. The temperature by this time was 45°C and getting hotter. The sky cloudless and the sun relentless.

Luckily we found a spot where we could drive off the road and shelter under a few trees. The mulga wasn't much shelter but there was a line of dark green gum trees and a few saltbushes and blue bush. Several dead mulga, its irregular and straggly branches a subject very prominent in my paintings.

We finally arrived at Marree. Once a thriving mining town. A very hot place, lying below sea level. We were told that the town site sits above tunnels now devoid of coal, some of them flooded. It was a neat town with several well-kept fibro houses. In years gone by a stop-off for Afghans who travelled with their camels carrying goods to Alice Springs. It was very hot being so far inland and below sea level. We only stop to talk to a couple of the locals, have a cuppa and something to eat. Topped up on petrol then were on our way,

Going east from Marree was the famous road to Birdsville. A red dirt track. Not a track we wanted to attempt with our vehicle. By this time, we were looking forward to lands with more vegetation. We were now in South Australia, our third State in our travels. What lay ahead?

Chapter 53

SOUTH AUSTRALIA

From Marree we travelled south making for Port Augusta. We realized we would have to make a steady trip south before the wet season arrived. My cousin Ian and family lived just north of Adelaide and we had a date more or less arranged to visit them. The scenery changing again, the Stirling ranges began to appear to our left from the flattish land we travelled along to the distant peaks and hills in the distance.

The outback doesn't appear to have much animal life. But as night falls and one sits around the dying campfire, it is amazing what activity there is, all have been hiding in cool places, conserving fluids and keeping out of the fierce heat of the sun.

We were still rising at the crack of dawn; a quick breakfast and we were on our way again. Only traveling until late morning and then finding a nice shady spot to park for a few hours. This to cool the engine and tyres plus ourselves. We would relax until mid-afternoon then be on the road again making sure we found a suitable spot to park for the night. Our rations were running low so we would set three traps, rabbits were in abundance, a mixture of colours and sizes. It was not long before we heard the traps go we would fetch our gun as we did not only catch rabbits but often a fox or feral cat. The rabbits we would skin and clean and if more than one we would freeze the others.

By then we would have a nice fire going ready to prepare the evening meal. It was so peaceful sitting under the stars listening to whatever night life might emerge. Then out with the fire and if safe we would bury it so we had hot coals to start a fire in the morning to boil the billy. After making sure the fire was out and safe, the area cleaned we would be on our way again. We took it in turns to walk ahead while the other got the van ready to move. This was our form of exercise. It was amazing what we found on the side of the road as we walked along. We collected a variety of tools which had been left behind by other motorists.

SOUTH AUSTRALIA

Lyndhurst was the first town we came to. We were following the old rail track. Then we came to Leigh Creek, most of the towns if you blinked you'd miss, we found no need to stop. On the trip down, we passed several old railroad houses now unoccupied, all still showing signs of having been looked after. Geraniums and bougainvillea's still surviving as were much cared for garden paths and remains of flower or vegetable patches, also an odd broken cloths line.

At Parachilna the Flinders Ranges rose to our left. There was a turn off to the Ranges but we decided it would be too much stress on the van as we had travelled quite a distance. The Ranges were a bit of a disappointment as we expected more tree covering but the scenery was still spectacular with the colour of the hills a ruddy red to purple pyramid shaped rocky hill side. Here we found more signs of farming and the beginning of more population.

We always found a nice secluded place to camp for the night. There were more signs of kangaroos and wallabies, we crossed many a creek, some dry and others with a little water, so at least more vegetation.

At Hawker there were many more signs of sheep farming. It had been a wheat growing centre with a couple of flour mills but drought drove the farmers away. It even sported an airfield and an historical museum. The Cypress Pine seemed most common and the mallees evident as we drove south the landscape was less arid. Hawker was the rail centre for Alice Springs rail line. Quite a tourist centre now with access to the Flinders Ranges.

We continued to Kanyaka where there were ruins of Kanyaka homestead and outbuildings. Driving between the towns the road was good, the landscape flat and rather bare looking. We managed to get a good camping spot. More rabbits for dinner,

Then on to Quorn, a former rail centre. Dogs of German Shepard blood are not permitted in the pastoral areas north of Quorn. It was quite a busy town. We had a quick look around and stopped for the night near Woolshed Flat. The next town was Stirling North where we met the Princess Highway. We kept to the right and made for Port Augusta. This was a major rail and road junction. There were many historic buildings. Here we looked for a mechanic recommended by the RAC here we booked a service for the van. They were very accommodating and started work first thing in the morning.

I think they were quite amazed when they heard about our travels. We needed a new battery, sparkplugs and general grease up and oil change. The tyres were still good, this only because we had been careful drivers. We were soon on our way to Adelaide. The first big town was Port Perie, not far past we found a nice camping area, we had by-passed the town as wanted to keep going.

On reaching Adelaide, after a couple of nights on the road down, we called at the post office for mail and were redirected to another post office in another part of the city where we did find a quantity of mail. The drive

Incredible Memories

around we found slightly exhausting as were not used to being in a city traffic again! We did not hang around and decided to go back north as we would see Adelaide on our way east.

We made for Gawler from where we were to find our way to my cousin Ian and family at Heyshaw Cockatoo Valley. We arrived very tired and were shown a nice spot to park the van a bit away from the house. Ian and Ann his wife made us very welcome with a cup of tea and we met their three children Simon, Phillipa and Kate. Then they announced they were going out for the evening so I said I would get tea as had some fresh rabbit in the fridge. They immediately said, "Don't let the children know it's rabbit pretend it is chicken." Which I did, the whole meal went down a treat and they were none the wiser.

After the children were in bed Vera and I cleaned up and were just about to go out to the van when Ian and Ann got home. We sat a while with a drink, did a bit of catching up and then retired. Early next morning we got up and went for a bit of an explore. Their property was about 5 acres. Ann collected old buggies and restored them, so they were dotted around the yard. After breakfast the children came out to the van with a hundred and one questions. During our stay of a week we were taken around by Ian to show us the area. There were several orchards, they had trouble with birds attacking the fruit so the farmers had fixed up devises to frighten them off. In one there was like a gunshot which went off at intervals. A very pleasant visit getting to know my cousins and to catch up with Ian and Ann after several years. After farewells we returned to Adelaide to call for more mail before continuing on our journey,

Adelaide, we found to be a very well set out city, many churches and parks and some lovely old buildings on the roads. Ian had told us about an alternative route to Mount Barker a pleasant change with so much greenery but so much traffic. Followed the South Eastern Highway and turned off to Mount Barker, a small town not as big as we had expected. Then went over the bridge to Mt Barker Creek and continued to Murray Bridge which was also off the highway, did a loop and on to Princess Highway. Murray Bridge we were told has the smallest Cathedral in the world. The town had been known as Mobilong until 1924. There was a paddle steamer which left from the wharf, we neither had the time nor could we afford a trip. It would have been an experience.

Chapter 54

VICTORIA AND BEYOND

We then made for Tailem Bend, an old pioneer village where many heritage buildings had been relocated along the streets. We had a bit of a look around and a bit of a break, noticed some Clydesdale horse's, beautiful animals. Then continued our journey turning right to Princess Highway making for Meningie on Lake Albert. Drove for miles in rather lovely countryside along The Coorong which seemed to be one long waterway with salty water, ending in some swamp land. The highway was good to drive along but it was a long haul to Kingston. I have been to several Kingston's in my life and now Kingston in Victoria, there are three more to visit in my travels. The historic Red and White lighthouse stood out as we drove in. Fishing for crayfish is a major activity but as I am allergic to crayfish, I could not sample any. We decided to find a quiet spot to camp for the night, we turned off to the right on a small road to Lake Alexandrina. It was a freshwater lake and we found a lovely spot with lots of water birds. The highway turned inland about 20 miles out and we found a place for the night. Such a beautiful relaxing area secluded from the road. After a drink while our meal cooked, we decided an early bed was the order of the day, we slept well.

When we looked at the map, we saw we had a bit to go before going back down to the coast. We were still on Princess Highway towards Millicent on our way to Mount Gambier.

The city of Mount Gambier is built on the slopes of an extinct volcano, with three craters, the main one contains the Blue Lake, the city's water supply. A rather beautiful hilly town, Mount Gambier is the centre of the timber industry based on radiata pines. Lovely pine forests around reminds me of Scotland. Cave gardens around a cave in the city centre once supplied the town water.

We passed through Dartmoor, its main street lined with beautiful Atlantic cedars, a number of them have been lopped, the trunks carved to represent service men and women. We decided to give Portland a miss and turned just north of it. We went down to the coast again traveling due north then left to the coast, enjoying the large trees and countryside till we hit Port Fairy on the coast. A bit further on, we saw a small road to our left going into what looked like a forest and decided to investigate. Found a lovely clearing with level ground. It was a large area clear of trees. We parked facing the way out again and went for a bit of an explore. Came face to face with a huge lizard which decided it didn't want to have anything to do with us, much to our relief. It wandered off into the woods.

We both sat outside and decided to write to family and just relax. A sherry and some nibbles, the sound of bird song and the movement of the breeze blowing through the treetops and we were happy. We would have liked to spend a few days there but resisted the temptation as Vera was impatient to get to Melbourne where her eldest daughter lived and had just delivered a wee daughter.

Next day we called into Port Fairy which was right on the coast. There were many 19th century buildings, it had been a whaling and sealers port which then became a cargo and fishing port. Had a short stop then continued on Princess Highway and made for Warrnambool about 250 miles west of Melbourne, so not too far to go.

We had driven for most part from Adelaide through very green pastures, passed dairy farms, witnessing lovely eucalypt forests, mountain ash and massive tree ferns. The drive quite beautiful. The soil must have been very fertile, absolutely lovely passing all the different shades of greens.

There is a Maritime Village on Flag Hill, in the museum there are old ships, and lighthouses in Warrnambool. The highway then went inland, we decided to find a nice spot to spend the night. It had been a tiring day and we had done a lot of driving. We were always lucky to find a quiet spot. We enjoyed our usual sherry and a nice meal, then got an early bed. In the morning, we changed our minds and decided we'd like to see along Great Ocean Road. This would make the trip to Melbourne about another hundred miles. We didn't regret it.

The Great Ocean road follows the coast, passing some sheer drops to the sea. To our left the Otway Ranges, the road took us inland a bit but a picturesque drive. Then back down to the coast to Apollo Bay. Pretty rugged shore, there were many shipwrecks of old. Timberland and farming and very picturesque. We virtually followed the coast all the way to Lorne. There were lots of blue gums and beautiful tree ferns. It had a lovely surfing and swimming beach. We slept the night there listening to the sea lapping the shore.

We drove through Port Campbell National Park, a bit further on to our right the Twelve Apostles. The rock stacks offshore are no longer twelve as many have collapsed from sea erosion. A spectacular scenic drive passing through forests, skirting ocean views. It was not easy to hurry our trip as there were so many beautiful scenes to stop and admire. Just past the Apostles we found a nice spot to stop before we continued inland.

Geelong was the next big town where we again saw water. We decided to drive down to the waterfront to have lunch and stretch our legs where there was some nice parkland. Quite a busy town and we thought we'd come back another day as it seemed an interesting place. Drove on to Melbourne through a town called Werribee, not very big and flattish countryside on our way to Melbourne.

As we came into Melbourne, we were surprised to find we had to stop at a toll bridge. It was a bit confusing as we weren't sure which lane to stop at as we wanted to by-pass Melbourne proper and drive south to St Kilda. After leaving the toll bridge we seemed to be in an industrial area, then we saw a sign to St Kilda drove on till we found a phone box and phoned Vera's daughter. We told her where we were and she gave directions to their house. It was fairly easy to find, there was great excitement at the reunion.

By then we were ready for a cuppa, Di had made a pizza which we all enjoyed. Vera's granddaughter was a beauty, very blond with an olive complexion. She was a few months old but very responsive to all going around her. While there we met some of their Kiwi and Maori friends and relatives. One evening we enjoyed a hāngi out in the back garden. The weather was quite warm, in fact one day was really hot and little Desa was very distressed. I told Di to give her plenty of water and put her in a cool bath. This she quite enjoyed and perked up again. While there we were taken down to Torquay, did a bit of fishing and swimming. Another day we were taken out east up into the Dandenongs. A beaut drive, we visited the man who had sculpted aboriginal children on his property out of Alice Springs. He lived on a lovely property with sloping pathways down which he had more of his sculptures. We met him, he was very old but so interested in our travels and so pleased we had seen his work in Alice.

We had decided to go down to Tasmania, left our van in the driveway of some friends and flew over for three weeks.

On returning from Tasmania we stayed a few days then started our trip to Sydney. Had an introduction to some friends in Bega for when we got there. Sad farewells and we made our way to Nepean Highway which ran down Port Philips Bay to Frankston then cut across to Cranbourne to the South Gippsland Highway making for Tooradin, then Korumburra. Lovely lush countryside, we hoped to reach Wilsons Promontory National park. Arrived about 4pm only to be told we were too late to enter and stay for the night. Very disappointing so just found a place to stay the night. It had been a long haul and we were good and ready to batten down.

Early in the morning, we drove north to Foster, turned right and continued along South Gippsland Highway to a place called Yarram where we stopped for lunch. As we drove along, we were amazed at the tall gum

Incredible Memories

trees or mountain ash, a canopy over smaller trees and tree ferns. So different to the arid lands we had left behind in the central parts of Australia.

Very refreshing scenery as we drove towards Sale. This was more inland than I had imagined. Long before we reached Sale we decided to stop and enjoy our surroundings. The weather was very pleasant and kind to us, Holey Plains State Park to our left just the right spot. Next morning, we drove to Sale where we would again meet up with Princess Highway, on to Bairnsdale where we drove south to Lakes Entrance the eastern end of Ninety Mile Beach. Much of Gippsland is low lying farmland. There are large areas of swamp land. The land has been cleared with only corridors of eucalypts along the roadside. Lakes Entrance is Australia's largest fishing port. A very busy town. We visited a museum dealing with the culture of the Bindi Bindi Aboriginals. East of Lakes Entrance it became wetter, with rain supposed to fall all year round from a moist subtropical air blown in from the Tasman sea. Tall trees crowd in on both sides of Princess Highway. A line of forested hills lining the horizon. Among the trees white stringy bark and several varieties of tree ferns. Absolutely beautiful.

We continued inland to Nowa Nowa, the highway crossing over several creeks to Orbost. Giant eucalypts surround this riverside town. We continued to Cann River. Nearly twenty miles beyond at Alfred National Park, we decided to stop as on looking at the map, Bega was too far to travel. As usual parked in a lovely spot, our daily sherry and a good meal and we were ready for bed. Next morning, we were up early and off. A couple of hours later we crossed the border from Victoria to New South Wales. We stopped at a picnic area on the Wallaga river and enjoyed our surroundings.

Chapter 55

TASMANIA

We flew from Melbourne to Devonport and were staying one night in a camping ground while having a counter tea in a pub when we got talking to a couple of guys a bit older than us. They were interested in us seeing as much of Tasmania as possible. They offered to pick us up the next day and drive us out along the north coast to a town called Burnie and another Somerset. We had a good night's sleep and were picked up at 8:30. Both men were very full of knowledge about all the places we drove through. There was so much information I found it very difficult to write about it that night on return.

I remember Burnie being a very attractive town, on the coast of Bass Straight. The water was calm on the shores of Emu Bay. It was a paper manufacturing town, the paper was handmade using traditional methods. Somerset sat at the mouth of Cam River. It seemed greener than Burnie, there was a big wooden boat in one of the parks, a reminder that it had been a ship building town and a busy port. The guys had very thoughtfully brought a picnic basket with flasks of tea and sandwiches which we enjoyed in one of the parks on the beach front.

Bill (I'll call him that) said that he lived in a large house and invited us to stay at his place. Which we accepted for one night. The next day after a hearty breakfast he had prepared, he drove us to Burnie again so we could hitch a ride down the Murchison Highway. A car pulled up and we climbed in, made ourselves comfy, the driver was not very talkative but we enjoyed the scenery which was mainly pine forest. We drove several miles and then he pulled up in the middle of dense forest and said he was turning off! There we were, not a building in sight just pine trees all around. While we were wondering what to do a huge furniture truck pulled up. The driver said, "What are you doing out here?" When we told him, he couldn't believe anyone would do that to us. We climbed up into the cab and the driver chucked our backpacks in behind the seat. It was rather hilly countryside and

Incredible Memories

at times a steep drop to my left. From where I was sitting, I seemed to be overhanging the steep drop on the left of the road. After a rather hairy drive we were dropped off at the turn off to Zeehan on Henty Road.

We soon got a lift into Strahan. We walked around to the campsite and put up our tent then went to get a bite to eat returning and collapsing in the tent and slept soundly. Next morning, we got up early and went and booked a trip around the harbour. The waters were black, apparently stained by tannin from the logging of Huon pine. In the nineteenth century Strahan was a major port for the booming mining in the area and export of Huon pine. We were told and shown Huon pine logs being floated down the Franklin River. During our visit there was a lot of controversy about the river being dammed. It was a beautiful sight cruising around the harbour surrounded by the magnificent forest. Strahan's historic Customs House and Union Steamship buildings were quite impressive.

We stayed another night after a feed of fresh fish for tea. In the morning we hitched a ride to Queenstown some 35 miles away. The scenery quite changed, bare hillsides of white and purplish earth, colourful but sad looking. The result of past mining days. The forests stripped to supply wood for the smelters. Toxic sulphur fumes and bush fires killed off the remaining vegetation. We decided to have a comfortable night and booked into the hotel which was packed with busloads of people on tour. Here again Queenstown was surrounded by hillsides stripped and stained by pollution.

Next day we caught a bus and travelled down Lyell Highway through Franklin Gordon Wild River National Park. The scenery more beautiful. Stopping at King William Saddle to admire the view. The scenery was more pleasing as we continued down the Highway stopping at a town called New Norfolk reputed to being one of the oldest towns in Australia. With various historic buildings and oast houses built in a variety of shapes, these dot the countryside around New Norfolk. As we drove towards Hobart to our left the splendid jagged peaks of Cradle Mountain, then on into Hobart. We were glad we had chosen to travel by bus as we managed to see more.

Hobart a neat, tidy township nestled down on the shores of the Derwent. We could see it was starting to spread out with houses dotted in the surrounding hilly terrain to the right. We had booked into the caravan site for a few days. From there we took daily trips in various directions. One day we visited the old buildings of the notorious Port Arthur, a former penal settlement. Rather spooky place where convict chain gangs worked in silence from dawn to dusk. There were many restored buildings one being the Model Prison where the worst offenders were isolated in small dark cells. Not a pleasant place to visit when told the past history of so much suffering.

We also visited Richmond, a well-preserved Georgian village with many historic buildings. Convicts built many including Richmond Gaol which once held prisoners in transit to Port Arthur. A very attractive bridge, the oldest bridge still in use in Australia, another thing built by chain gangs.

TASMANIA

In the background St John's church, the oldest Catholic church in the country. Hobart, the second oldest city after Sydney, lies between Mount Wellington and the Derwent. The East and West are joined by the Tasman Bridge. The buildings a mixture of convict, colonial and the maritime past, one the sandstone warehouse. Constitution Dock is dotted around with types of fishing and pleasure boats. Altogether a very likable city.

We made our way to Sorrel, where we hitched a ride to Swansea where we decided to spend the night at the caravan site with views across blue waters to Great Oyster Bay. A lovely seaside town where black wattle bark was processed, the main ingredient for tanning leather in years gone by. While in the communal kitchen we met two young fellows who were going to Launceston in the morning and said they were going a quick way up. We accepted a lift as felt we had explored enough and had a plane to catch. We seemed to be traveling along an escarpment looking down into valleys. They were pleasant company, good drivers and beautiful scenery. After our farewells we had to find our way to Devonport to catch our return to Melbourne.

On our arrival we picked up our van and drove down To St Kilda, spent the night with Di, Willy and Desa before starting our journey to Sydney.

Chapter 56

NEW SOUTH WALES

We were at last in New South Wales. I would say maybe three quarters of the way through our trip, at least of Australia. We travelled another couple of hours and we saw the Tasman Sea. Stopped for lunch at Eden. The road was good as we drove up down hilly parts to Merimbula where the highway turned in land to Bega. We arrived at Bill and Sandra's place just after four o'clock and were made very welcome. A lovely friendly young couple. Their house was on a slope but luckily they had a nice level part where we could park. We had driven past several paddocks with Jersey cows, Bega being a dairy district. We felt we had known them all our lives, such an easy couple to get on with. We spent a lovely evening with them over a BBQ. It was nice again to have the use of a bathroom and have a nice warm shower before bed. Sandra suggested we stay a couple of days but we said we were trying to fit in stopping with other friends on the way to Sydney. As Vera's youngest was expecting her second sometime this month, we were pushed for time.

Sandra called out to us early the next morning, she knew we wanted an early start, and said breakfast was ready. So sweet of her. Bill had gone to work

The Princess Highway runs between the hills on our left and the Tasman Sea to our right, then inland for a spell. We saw the sea again when we reached a small town called Narooma. We drove on till we reached Bateman's Bay where we stopped in a parking spot near the beach and had lunch. Decided to stretch our legs and explore a bit on a road going along the ocean to a little place called Batehaven. It was a lovely refreshing walk where we could breathe in the sea air, the weather was nice too.

We drove on till we got to Ulladulla, drove around and found a beaut spot across a stretch of green away from houses with a handy ablution block, parked up behind it. An ideal spot to relax and catch up on letter writing. There were a couple of small trees where we put a line across, did a bit of washing. We'd just hung the washing out when a guy with a German Shepard dog arrived and was trying to be very officious. Turned out he had been a security guy, retired. He wanted to know what we were doing. As the clothesline was well hidden and there didn't seem to be any reason why we shouldn't be there for the night. After a bit he simmered down and became quite friendly. His dog took a liking to me and he said we must be okay as Shep doesn't usually take to strangers. Good old Shep, what an original name, ha ha! I will never forget the spot, except for that guy we were left in peace. Ulladulla, the town was quite big with an attractive harbor full of fishing boats. It was a lovely day the next day so we sat around writing and relaxing. After another night there, we drove through acres full of trees.

The highway was hilly to drive along and went inland till we reached Nowra, it had been a long drive. It was another big town, we drove around and found a lovely spot with a car park near a rose garden, set out in the middle of a sort of oval. So we parked there and decided we had driven enough for the day. Next morning, I went for an early morning walk around this well set out rose garden and found a patch of mushrooms coming up in the lawn pathway. So picked enough for breakfast. Returned to the van and we had mushrooms on toast, yum. Not far out of Nowra, we went over a big river, Shoalhaven River. Still on Princess Highway past a couple of interesting villages, after about 50 miles of a windy road, we reached Kiama. We drove through and just passed it, turned right towards Shellharbour and made for Windang, a strip of land between the ocean and Lake Illawarra where we were to meet up with Bill and Joan. We had first met them at Katherine then again at Mataranka and the third time at Alice Springs. We went up Shellharbour Road over a bridge, the entrance to Lake Illawarra from the Tasman Sea strait into Windang. We found them quite easily from a mud map they had previously given us when they invited us to stay.

They lived in a lovely cottage as we pulled up outside their place, there in the driveway was their big bus. It was a great reunion. During the few days we stayed there Vera and I used to go for long walks along the beautiful beach which was right on their doorstep. One day Bill took us up in a small plane, we had a marvellous flight up the coast as far as Sydney. While going along we had a running commentary on the places we were flying over. We visited some of their relatives in Port Kembla, one day Vera and I nearly walked that far.

Bill and Joan took us for a lovely drive up to the Illawarra Range. They bought one of my paintings, they said it reminded them of the Northern Territory. Joan said I was not asking enough for my paintings and payed me what she felt was a more realistic price I should ask, which was very kind of her as I felt I should be giving it to them for all their kindness. We visited some of their grownup children and Joan's Mum who lived across the road. All together it was a very happy reunion. Such nice folk. It was sad to say goodbye.

Incredible Memories

As we had driven up the coast, we missed a lot of places inland that we had planned to visit. From Shellharbour we cut inland to join Illawarra Highway and drive west to Mossvale. From there, we turned left to join Hume Highway and turned south to Goulburn. Goulburn seemed a big town with several historic buildings. We didn't stay too long as still had a long journey to Canberra.

On our way around Australia, we used to listen to an ABC program on a Sunday morning. This guy interviewed people from all parts and also would talk about the farmlet he and his family had just out of Canberra. When we got up in the morning, we took the Federal Highway to Canberra. At the end of Federal Highway, we turned left into Barton Highway and had about three miles to the capital.

It had been the capital since 1913, the High Court Building had not long been completed. We explored the streets around the Capital Hill, there were umpteen embassy houses along some of the tree lined streets. All the properties with beautifully kept gardens, green lawn sloping down to the road. Lake Burly Griffin which one crosses to get to Capital Hill, looked refreshing. We found it too much to take in in one day, we found few friendly so did not explore too much. We decided to drive out and find somewhere to camp for the night. In the morning we went to find the farmlet in a small village. Finally found it down a narrow sandy lane. It was nothing like we expected from what we had been led to believe. Here was a small cottage in need of repair and a spot of paint, sitting on a quarter acre block. Some sort of vine partly covering the front left side of the house.

We knocked to ask if we had found the right place. We were made very welcome and offered a cup of tea. Out the back down some rundown steps we were greeted to barren sandy soil. A very friendly, large nanny goat came running toward us. To the right there was a wooden platform where said nanny goat stood to be milked twice a day. From her milk they made cheese and used it in many other ways besides drinking it themselves. They had a small son who ran around in bare feet and half naked. The couple were extremely interesting. Such a happy family, so down to earth in the way they lived. We found it hard to leave their company. Of course, we left with a bottle of milk and some homemade cheese.

We drove back to Yass keeping left on the main road and started going south. Lovely hilly countryside then started to descend down this wide steep road to Gundagai. We had read about the dog on the tucker box, now there it was as a statue on our right as we arrived. This being one of the places we planned to visit. So, what was an extra 200 miles after all we had already travelled? We had not realized there was so much hill climbing but it was worth it. The road was good and we were rewarded as we drove into Gundagai. Not a big place but certainly a very welcoming town. There was a gravel parking area cut into the hillside just behind the dog, handy to park.

We read again the story about the faithful dog who sat on the tucker box of his dead owner and refused to leave, as I recall the story. It was time to leave and retrace our way up the steep hill, this after having something to eat at a small general store opposite the carpark.

Up the Hume Highway back through Yass and on through Gunning and Goulburn and decided to find somewhere for the night as we had had a tiring day. Found a nice spot in a picnic area about 14 miles out and were looking forward to a sherry a nice meal and early bed. It was a bit noisy, more than some of the places we had found as it was too near to the highway.

In the morning we made for Moss Valley a market town, passing dairy farms, lovely paddocks. In the town itself quite a few historic buildings. Cut across on Illawarra Highway to meet up with Princess Highway for the long haul to Sydney. Stopped at a place called Figtree at a picnic area, there was an old fig tree hence the name. We could tell we were getting to a more built up area. Not long after we crossed with Southern Highway, we found a spot and parked for the night as we decided to take it easy approaching Sydney. We were just north of Wollongong. Next morning, we continued on Princess Highway through Royal National Park, a lovely treed area. When we hit Rochdale, we knew we were near Sydney. When we got to Sydney, we followed signs to Pacific Highway. Once on the Highway we followed signs to Balmoral and Manly. We were told to turn off to Dee Why, after that signs to Narrabeen where Vera's youngest daughter Nola and her husband Gavin lived, they already had a little boy and were expecting their second, due any day. When we got to Narrabeen, we phoned to find out how to get to their place.

We had to climb out of the town. Luckily there was a level spot outside their house. Terrific reunion, we had a cuppa then said we'd have a rest before joining them again. They hadn't been there for long and the backyard was all overgrown. So the next day, I got stuck in with my machete but had to be careful of funnel web spiders and snakes.

We had promised another couple we had met on our travels, we would visit them, so phoned them and asked if we could visit, they were so pleased we had made it to Sydney safely and asked us to lunch. They gave us directions to their house. Take the road to Collaroy then make for Dee Why turn left towards the coast keep left and come to a lifesaving complex and they were opposite. Their house looked as if it was built into the hillside and went up three stories hugging the face of the hill. They were looking out for us and came down the steps to the road before we even got out of the van. We spent a lovely day with them catching up on our travels since we had last seen them. We met their youngest son too.

They used to fossick for precious stones during their travels, take them home, cut and facet them, polish them and put them in an album. These they used to pay their way while traveling. We were fascinated by all their tales and what they knew about places to find stones. They had studied how to

Incredible Memories

cut the stones and had all the tools. It was something that interested me greatly and keen try myself some day.

Nola gave birth to a little girl and we were glad we were there for the birth and were able to enjoy the new arrival. We had booked a flight to New Zealand and were to spend two months back-packing, visiting friends and relatives of Vera's son-in-law. We were driven to the airport and who should we bump into but the two Martins and their partners who we had met months before in our travels! They were also flying to New Zealand but they were going to the South Island and we to the North. But each were spending a month in each island. Swiss Martin gave us his address in Switzerland in case we wanted to visit them at a later date and travels. We agreed to meet in Picton on the South Island on a certain date, they left for their flight and we waited for ours.

Chapter 57

NEW ZEALAND

We flew into Auckland, then found our way to Willie's (Vera's son-in-law) sister's house on the outskirts of Auckland. Were very warmly welcomed by her and her young family. We met her brother who said he had tickets to a Maori gathering at the sports stadium, to which he was taking us. What an experience, I think I had goose bumps through the whole show.

It was entirely Maori with the most moving singing and music, the Haka being performed and the women in their traditional get up (costume), dancing and singing.

There were sport events in between. Just too much to remember and relate but I am sure I will never forget it.

We were then taken to a hāngi (food cooked in the ground) on such large proportions, also something never to forget. Delicious was all I could say for the result.

While staying at Janice's house, which was across the road from the local cemetery, I witnessed a funeral procession. How joyful everyone who followed the coffin seemed to be. As usual their singing was a joy to listen to. Janice explained that they were joyful and happy, the departed was released and going to a happier place.

Vera and I paid several trips into Auckland. Then it was time for us to start our hitchhiking around the North Island.

The first place we were making for, was the town that Janice's mother and sister lived in, Whangarei. Again, so welcoming. I helped in the garden, they had homegrown vegetables and also showed me edible weeds, not considered weeds in New Zealand.

We were introduced to other relatives and friends and given the history of the family and how they had land further North, which was enjoyed by all relatives to enjoy, whenever they go there. A huge rock, called St Paul, rises above the town.

Incredible Memories

After a few days we put on our back packs, said our farewells and hitched to the Bay of Islands on the West Coast. There are over 100 islands in the bay. We met up with a young Kiwi (white man) guy, we had known in Fremantle. He and his mates and family took us to a lovely beach, where we went on a launch around the bay. Then were shown how to dig for Pipi's (small shells with an animal inside). These shells living not very deep in the shore. They are quite delicious eaten raw, with a taste of the sea. My fingernails were quite sore after digging in the sand, as usual we were well feasted and toured around the area. All the while being given history and interesting information.

It is a very volcanic area and then we were taken to Waitangi one day, the town where the signing of the treaty took place. The treaty house is set on beautiful sweeping lawns, running down to the bay. Across the lawn was the detailed Maori Whan Runanga, a meeting place.

Down at the cove was the largest canoe in the world. Ngātokimatawhaorua, a replica of the canoe, the legendary Polynesian Kupa, who discovered New Zealand.

Just nearly too much to take in when listening to the history but all very impressive. Then to Paihia, the main town in the area, where the first Rapuo hut was built. Rapuo or bull rush.

The treaty granted the Maori citizenship and land rites. While there we saw some amazing Hei Tiki (carved figures, worn around the neck) a representation of an ancestor.

We were fortunate to be present at a Hakau (feast) where there were several hangi to feed the crowd. These had been started several hours before. When the steaming meats and vegetables were unearthed, the smell made my mouth water. Then after a few days on with the backpacks, we decided to get a bus. The top end was quite tropical, at the Bay of Islands we saw various coloured Hibiscus growing in gardens as hedges, I couldn't get over the size of the flowers and colours I had never seen before.

There are organised bus tours to Cape Reinga and Ninety Mile Beach from the Bay of Islands. This we thought would be more interesting, hitching would not take us to some of the places. On the bus we had many stops with a running commentary on history at points of interest such as the meeting of two seas of the west coast. Cape Reinga the most northern point with a very impressive lighthouse. The meeting of the Tasman sea and the Pacific was an awesome sight. It looked like a long wave which seemed to be continuous is the only way I can describe it.

We were told they only drove on the Ninety Mile beach when the tide was out. We had several stops along the beach. This is on the Aupouri Peninsula. Huge sand dunes plus large a pine forest, scattered with Kauri which had been the previous forest before most was cleared. We were also told that there were parts of the beach that was quicksand. After the long drive we ended up at Kaitaia where we found camping grounds. We were

NEW ZEALAND

pleased we didn't have to put up our tent but could choose little one room huts with basin and toilet. They had communal kitchens which were wonderful as we met up with other travellers from all over the world. They were always so friendly and wanted us to share their meal. Here we met Dennis, probably in his early twenties, while chatting he offered us a lift in his station wagon, all the way to Rotorua. How could we refuse!

So off we went with two other girls who were backpacking. A bit of a squeeze but good fun until while driving down a very hilly area Dennis announced he didn't have any brakes. So until we reached another town he drove using gears and hand brake. Veering from one side of the road to the other, luckily in those days hardly any traffic used the route he chose to take. He seemed to know his way around. When we got to the next town the other two girls decided to part company. Dennis drove to a mechanic and got him to fix said brakes. This meant staying the night but as usual there was always a camping ground. The next day we were off again. In return we paid for a lunch each day we were with Dennis. We drove through Opononi, Dargaville, Wellsford and Huntly and then skirted Auckland proper. Dennis seemed to know all the short cuts and streets.

'The hiking grannie', backpacking around New Zealand, Whakatane by ginger lilies, North Island February 1981

Incredible Memories

Absolutely beautiful countryside and he was very informative with so much knowledge and history. Just too much to take in plus he was very amusing. From Auckland we made for Hamilton and the Rotorua where his parents owned a guesthouse. They were so kind and put us up as guests with B and B and the first night's meal. Dennis told us that all their radiators were heated by steam from hot springs. This we found hard to believe but then while Dennis was taking us around, we realized how warm it was everywhere. He took us to see the bubbling mud pools, gurgling hot springs and gushing geysers. The sulphur smell was overwhelming. Rotorua is actually 280 m above sea level and sits on the edge of Lake Rotorua. We were now in the area called Bay of Plenty. After a couple of glorious days with Dennis and family we thought it was time to move on. Dennis drove us about 15 miles out to Hell's Gate a highly active thermal area full of steamy vents. This was on the way to Whakatane. He dropped us off outside the town where we started to hitch again.

It started to rain so we at up on a bank at the side of the road under our raincoats, when a ute pulled up and said they could take us to Gisborne. So we climbed into the back and sat on our back packs. While there we hurtled up and down a very windy wet road. We hung on for dear life. It stopped raining just before we reached Gisborne. They dropped us off outside a camping site. Boy, were we glad to be back on terra firma again! We pitched our tent and decided we would treat ourselves to a counter tea at the pub nearly right cross the road. While we were waiting to be served two Maori guys started to talk to us one said we were welcome to stay with his family but we had already paid and were settled to sleep in our tent. Then another guy came in for a drink, he had a small box full of mushrooms he was taking home to his family when these two guys said he was to give us some which he did! Next morning, we cooked them up for breakfast and enough for us to have at our next stop.

Hitched about 90 miles south of Gisborne to Wairoa, a very twisty drive, up and down through very wooded state forest. We were lucky to get a lift in a spacious grey car with a gentleman who travelled around on business. At one point, he said he had to call into his home and we were welcome. It was a short way from the main road. A lovely home, he did a lot of fishing and had large stuffed fish on the wall. His big catch. He made sandwiches for lunch with a cuppa which went down very well. Then off to Napier, he was a very interesting person and seemed to enjoy our company with tales of our travels.

Napier lies on Hawke Bay, it was a lovely day with a Mediterranean warmth and feeling. It looked like a very fertile area. We found a camping ground and crashed early. Quite an exhausting day.

We were told it wasn't easy to hitchhike further so we took a bus to Hastings. The bus stopped several times and at each stop there was a pole at the side of the road with a bag hanging on a large hook, these were mail bags.

NEW ZEALAND

As you took one off you replaced it with another, which was mail for that area. As I didn't have a seat, the bus was that full, I had to sit on the step of the bus. The driver said I could do the job if I liked, I had to get up every time he got up to do the job. What fun!

While traveling we got a running commentary, he even stopped if there was a place of interest and we could stretch our legs. Time flew and before we knew it we were at Palmerston North. Then on down the West to Wellington where we slept the night. We took the ferry which would take us across Cool Straight to the South Island and Picton. It was a long journey, as we wandered around the top deck, we were befriended by this lovely young Canadian couple who asked us what we intended doing. They said they knew the way to the camping grounds when we got to Picton and to stick with them.

Traveling across it's like going to a different country, the landscape quite different. The Ferry entered Marlborough Sounds through the Tory Channel to Picton. Beautiful scenery. Don led the way, it was a long trek to the camping area. We were very amused as his wife only carried a handbag. They travelled light because Don had one pack on his back and the other on his front. We walked for what seemed miles, our packs being larger got heavier and heavier.

After getting settled we wandered around the large area in case the German and Swiss couples had arrived before us but there was no sign of them so we joined the Canadian couple in the communal kitchen and got ourselves something to eat. Early in the morning we left, walked a distance and started to hitch again. A car pulled up and said if we walked another mile to the next crossroad, we had a better chance to get a lift. We just got there when a station wagon passed us with the German and Swiss couples, they yelled out "See you in Switzerland!"

Finally, a car pulled up and off we went at quite a speed hardly seeing anything but trees, going up and down hilly roads. Then he stopped and said that was as far as he went. Out we climbed to find we were in the wilderness. To our right forest and to our left a steep valley. It was getting dark so we thought we'd better find somewhere to pitch our tent. As we walked trying to find a flat clearing, along came a huge furniture removal truck. It pulled up and the driver asked, 'what were two ladies doing walking along here?' so we told him we just got dropped off. "Come on then you'll have to come with me." He chucked our bags in the back of the truck and we climbed up into the cab. Vera got in first and I sat next to the door

Off we went starting to descend this windy road, when I looked out it looked as though my part of the cab was hanging over the steep fall into the valley. Finally, we came to a small town where he dropped us off at a camping site. We were most grateful and relieved to be somewhere where people lived as we had seen little or none on the long journey here. The next morning, we walked into Rupton and booked two seats on the bus to

Incredible Memories

Greymouth. When the bus arrived it didn't stop, the guy where we got the tickets phoned the company and told them what had happened. Next thing we knew a car pulled up and asked if we were the two ticket holders, "Jump in and I'll take you to Greymouth where we had to spend the night as there wasn't another bus until the next day. He gave us tickets that would take us to a few places south which was nice of him. The drive was much more comfortable, we drove through Opawa National Park, the scenery beautiful, such lovely trees and shrubs. We stopped at a place called Pancake Rocks we walked down and onto these limestone rocks which looked just like a pile of pancakes stacked on top of each other. We were told when the tide was in the water surged into caverns below the rocks and squirted out in geyser-like blowholes, but we were not there in time to witness that. Our driver dropped us off at a camping area where we spent the night.

Greymouth with a gold mining history is the largest town on the west coast. It sits at the mouth of the Grey River with a large sweep of beach culminating in the faint outlines of Mts Cook and Tasman looking south west, to the north a rocky promontory to Big Rock. The next morning, we got up and caught the bus and who should be on the bus but Don and his wife. It was nice catching up with them again, they said that they were on the bus that didn't stop for us and had wondered why and what had happened to us. We travelled about 40 miles south of Greymouth through beautiful countryside all the while catching up on where the couple had been. We swapped news. The bus stopped at Hokitika where we stretched our legs and got something to eat and drink. It is an old gold mining town and produces green stone which is carved in all forms. Our next stop was Franz Josef Glacier which we were looking forward too as never having seen a glacier before.

We booked into a camping area just off the road and set up our tent. That evening the four of us walked a wee bit up the road where we found a bank on the side of the road aglow with blinking fire-flies, they lit up the road. Franz Josef is named after the Austrian Emperor in the 19th century. Mighty rivers of ice descending at about 15 feet a day, ten times faster than any glacier in Switzerland. They tumble down to the Tasman sea. The west coast is subject to prevailing Westerlies, the rains fall as snow and fuses to form clear ice at a depth of around 60 foot. Both Fox and Franz Josef are very steep so the ice can get a long way before it melts. What a wonderful sight of shining blues and greys topped by the white snow.

We were so fortunate to have visited these spots before they became so controlled. The four of us walked across the road and a short way up the glacier. There was a sort of inspiring silence with at intervals a slight cracking sound, such beauty we hardly spoke. Certainly an experience never to forget. Franz Josef is the fastest, steepest moving glacier in the world, it flows into a temperate forest before entering the sea.

NEW ZEALAND

We spent two nights then caught the bus. Drove through Haast Pass surrounded by the National Park to Wanaka. About 90 miles to Queenstown which Vera and I wanted to see but Don and his wife didn't want to stop as they wanted to visit somewhere further south. We parted company, exchanged addresses so we could keep in touch as we had an invitation to visit them should we go to Canada. We went on to Queenstown.

Queenstown on the shores of Lake Wakatipu, quite breath-taking as we drove in. It was a mining town in the 19th century but by the 20th century the population dropped considerably. It is a very compact town sloping up from the lake. We promised ourselves we would stay at a hotel and enjoy a few comforts. We felt a wee bit out of place arriving with backpacks but it was so nice to relax and enjoy the luxury of a hot bath and being able to sleep in a bed, eat at a table where the food was served to us. A tour bus arrived and a poor woman who we guessed had been touring for some time at a terrible rate, proceeded to collapse on arrival. It was nice for us to travel at a leisurely rate and enjoy all the wonderful places.

After a good night's sleep and a wholesome breakfast, we got on a bus to Te Anau, on with our backpacks to start hiking again. We were so lucky a young man in a ute pulled up and said he was going to Milford Sound, our bags in the back and we hopped in. As he hurtled along we had a most scenic drive through undulating farmland. Not far along we entered a patch of forest then a bit further along at Fiordland National Park some beautiful trees and meadows. We came to two interesting places; Avenue of the Disappearing Mountains and the Mirror Lakes. Further on the road rose and we went through a tunnel called Homer Tunnel, not long after that we were at Milford Sound. What a sight greeted us, the 22km long fiord dominated by the 1690m high Mitre Peak. The calm waters reflected the sheer peaks that rise around it. The young man who brought us said the Captain on one of the cruise boats "owed him, just hang about and I'll get you on board". Were we lucky or what! We could never have enjoyed this luxury. He said he was going back to Te Anau later in the day and would take us back as there was no where we could camp cheaply.

The cruise around the sound was magic, saw several waterfalls and we backed under one and got pretty wet. But we were so fortunate that we struck a day which apparently was unusual, bright sunshine and fairly warm. After about two glorious hours where we spent a lot of time saying, "Wow look at that", the young man was waiting for us. Before we knew it, we were back at Te Anau and he dropped us at a camping area. The friendliness, kindness and hospitality we found incredible. We took a cabin for the night and in the morning caught another bus which would take us to Invercargill. The drive through many hilly places with odd lakes here and there, which we flew past, there didn't seem to be many towns or villages. When we got to Invercargill, we found out about a camping area and made for it. There was a steady rain so again we did not tent it that night.

Incredible Memories

In the morning we made for Bluff where we would get a ferry to Stewart Island. After a long journey we pulled into Halfmoon Bay and asked the way for a backpacker's to stay. We had quite a long walk along a well-worn path to a chalet which we shared with several other ladies. An A-framed very compact but comfortable place sitting in a glorious spot of bush. A couple of ladies seemed to be in charge. We all shared meals, had storytelling and sing-alongs in the evening. The Maoris have such lovely voices and songs. The next day Vera and I took small packs with sandwiched and water and we walked around to Butterfield Beach and Bragg Bay.

Halfmoon Bay was the only town or village on the island. The distinctive plant life is a product of the lovely rich soil. That evening after a shared meal, one lady told us where we could sit quietly to spot a Kiwi, we were lucky and saw two brown Kiwis. The island was full of bird life. On one of our walks, we met a young Irish couple with a one-year old girl who backpacked on her father's back, a small potty hung also on his back. We walked with them for a while then they stopped and sat the little one year old on the potty by the side of the path, she sat quite happily while we chatted and she performed. What a life, eh!

We stayed three days and really didn't want to leave but time was passing quickly and we had to get to Christchurch to catch our plane back to Sydney. The long ferry ride back to Bluff was a calm journey. Bluff back to Invercargill, bought a couple of paua shells, and spent another night there. In the morning we caught the bus to Dunedin via Gore and Balclutha. It was a long but pleasant journey.

Dunedin is the 2nd largest city of the South Island, home of the first University. It was founded by Scottish settlers. Dunedin is Celtic for Edinburgh. Much of the Victorian architecture has survived. There is an eight-sided Octagon in the centre of the city. The steepest street in Dunedin, Baldwin Street, was very close to the family we were staying with so of course we had to see how far we could walk up it. It was steep and very tiring though we did not go too far up it.

The family we stayed with was related to a priest we had met on our travels. Though the city seemed quite hilly where they were was relatively flat. Such a nice homely couple and two young children. One of the days there I went to the library and on the wall high up were some large framed photos of some pioneers and important people. When I looked up I thought I was looking at my mother-in-law. I made some enquiries and the lady in question had the same name as Ma's maiden name. This made me wonder as she had told me she sailed to NZ when she was 18 to visit relatives. I visited the museum too, very interesting. It's the only place in NZ to sport a castle. Being so Scottish it has a statue of Robert Burns in the city centre. We stayed a couple of days then started our long journey to Christchurch.

We managed to get a lift to Oamaru, the seventh largest city in NZ. The local sandstone is soft enough to saw but when exposed, it hardens making it ideal for buildings. It boasts the best preserved historic commercial buildings. Refrigerated meat shipping made it prosperous. It is noted for its beautiful Public Gardens, some dating back to the 19th century. One can enjoy the little blue penguins and the yellow eyed penguins which are among the rarest in the world. We saw them at sunset, the yellow eyes are very shy.

The next morning, we got a good lift to Timaru which is halfway between Dunedin and Christchurch. We were enjoying NZ so much we were quite sad our visit was coming to an end. Timaru is a thriving small port city, it used to export whale oil. After more than 20 shipwrecks attempting to berth near Timaru, an artificial harbour was built in the 19th century, today it's an excellent port. Stayed the night at a small camping area. We were so lucky with the weather, our tent had a chance to dry out. The next day a lady picked us up and said she was going to Rolleston, not far from Christchurch. We thought that would be good so we could spend more time in Christchurch. It was company for her and we had a comfortable ride and a free guide. We stopped at Ashburton and were treated to a coffee and toasted sandwich. Again, the hospitality incredible, she would not accept that we pay. Her home was just the other side of Rolleston.

We sat for some time and no one stopped, then her husband came out and said he would take us into Christchurch. It was not too far to go and he dropped us off at a camping spot just on the outskirts of the city. He said the bus service was very good. We booked into a cabin for our last two nights.

Most of the drive up to Christchurch had been fairly flat, it had been easily a six-hour drive and we were pretty tired. We had driven through mostly farming country. Passing several hills but always looking to the inland mountains as a backdrop. After Timaru we didn't call into any towns on the Pacific Ocean.

Christchurch is mostly flat and sits at the base of Port Hills. In the 19th century it was considered to be a model class-structured 'England in the South Pacific'. Churches rather than pubs were built. When we went into the city we were confronted by all the Gothic style buildings, the centre looked grey and white, impressive building which struck us the most was the railway station. The Avon River winds through the city, the centre very compact and easy to walk around. The weather was very British in my eyes, so we wore rain coats all day. But there were so many interesting buildings to visit we were under cover most of the time.

Places we visited: art centre, Canterbury museum, the Cathedral, excellent book shops, even a Smiths bookstore. Then South City centre, a statue of Captain Cook in Victoria Square and some beautiful spots along the river.

The next morning, we caught a bus in Cathedral Square for the nine-mile drive to the airport.

Incredible Memories

And so ended our memorable visit to New Zealand. When I look back on it, I am so grateful we did the trip when we did as it was less crowded and a lot cheaper.

Chapter 58

SYDNEY

We had a good flight from New Zealand. With very many wonderful memories of a beautiful country and people. Were met at the airport by Gavin and taken back to Narrabeen. It was a happy sight to see our van sitting on the side of the road, waiting for us to occupy it again. We had a lot to recall of our recent journey but said we would not be staying long as still had quite a journey in front of us.

While there we took a trip just north of Narrabeen, to Mona Vale up a narrow strip of land to Palm Beach, a very unspoilt area. We took Vera's young grandson with us and had a picnic and a bit of an explore. Nathan, then three year's old, was so thrilled with his ride in such a big vehicle. He was interested in all we showed him as we walked around. He collected some small stones and different shaped leaves, also some nuts off trees around us that had fallen on the ground.

While in Sydney we had promised ourselves a visit to "Old Sydney Town" near Gosford. A Frank Fox developed it, the staff all dressed in costumes of the day. They re-enacted life between 1788-1810. A re-creation of Sydney Cove. All the labour was by convicts. The lifestyle reflected in the buildings. There are many shops selling candles, barrels, leather goods, pottery, and sweets of the day. There is a white-washed cottage with a thatched roof. Bullock teams and covered wagons were in the streets, with a driver. An odd soldier, with a musket, keeping an eye on the convicts at work cutting and splitting timber. The re-enactment in a court room and public punishments. The white-washed buildings and gravel roads so realistic. This took up a whole day, including the traveling back and forth.

A ferry from Manley through Port Jackson to Circular Quay. As we travelled the last few miles we enjoyed the views of the Harbour Bridge, completed in 1932. The most massive single span steel arched bridge in the world. Then the Opera House, Sydney's most famous building. It stands out with its unusual architecture, overlooking Circular Quay.

Incredible Memories

Once there we went to The Rocks, one of the first areas settled in Sydney. Many of the buildings are restored. We enjoyed walking around this high point in Sydney. That day we walked around the city, I wanted to find a shop in Pitt Street which sold glass funnels for kerosene lamps, as mine had broken and was told before leaving Perth that this shop was the only one that carried anything like that.

We took our leave and started for our climb over the Blue Mountains. First, we made for Parramatta on the Western Freeway, a mostly built up area, very busy trying to make for Penrith via Great Western Highway. Luckily all well signposted and with the mountains in our sight.

We passed through several small towns on our winding road from Penrith to Springwood. By the time we reached Katoomba the van needed a rest, and we did too. It was a lovely scenic surrounding, because the road was so twisty it seemed like we had been driving for ages but according to the map we were not too far from Sydney and still a long way to go. We sort of skirted Blue Mountain National Park, climbing through scenic uplands. The road varies from two to four lanes. Heading across the tableland, the highway was mainly three lanes it then narrowed to a single carriageway with overtaking lanes. Usually many vehicles passed us on these over taking lanes some giving us a friendly toot as they passed. The awesome mountain scenery makes it a very enjoyable drive.

We met a few interesting and interested people while we found a spot to rest up. There seemed to be a lot to explore around Katoomba but we wanted to get on. Once we had something to eat, a cuppa and several interesting conversations with people who were interested in our van and what we planned to do and had already done.

We made for Mt Victoria via Blackheath, this all the way in second gear, it was a steep climb. On the way up we saw a semi-trailer on its side. Blackheath is a sort of country-village town with interesting crafts and antique shops. Mt Victoria is also an interesting village with shops and eateries along the main road occupying many of the heritage buildings. The Heritage listed Railway Station houses the Mount Victoria Historical Society Museum which features artefacts recovered from Cox's River convict stockade.

Then on to Bathurst, Australia's oldest inland settlement, dating back to 1815. It became a boom town following the discovery of gold. Cobb and Co moved their headquarters here in the late 1800's, one of their few remaining coaches is on display at the visitors' centre. From Bathurst we took the Mitchell Highway to Orange. Found a nice place to spend the night before continuing. Our usual sherry, a nice meal and a good night's sleep. Left early next morning and had a pleasant drive to Orange.

Passed several orchards of apples and pears, No oranges! Looked like well-kept farmlands, lush green paddocks. It had been raining off and on for a couple of days. Orange besides growing fruit is also the location of the highest wine region. It produces lamb and beef too. There were beautiful very large old trees, we were very impressed with the whole town. After the long haul from Sydney we thought we would hang around for a day or two. Found a nice spot to park on the outskirts.

Woke early, Vera did some washing and I scouted around. We pottered around all day, still raining off and on. A farmer guy came up to shift his cows and stood talking to Vera for quite a while. Vera thought she would like to get a few day's work as she felt she was getting low on cash. The guy told her she would probably get work in Bathurst, so next morning we drove there but no luck.

Chapter 59

WEST OF SYDNEY

Now we were over the Blue Mountains we were quite west of Sydney. Vera read up on Mumbil and Dunedoo and all around that area. We went back to Orange and parked for the night near Kerr's Creek, it was still wet. In the morning we backed the van over a slope and emptied the toilet and wastewater storage, then we covered it up. The ground was a bit soft so got on firmer ground, had breakfast and tidied the van then went into Kerr's Creek. Had a wee look around, went on to Euchareena, got a few litres of petrol then on to Stuart Town, originally called Iron Bark, we drove over quite a lot of dirt road. Then continued to Mumbil to Vera's son-in-law Gavin's folk's, Enid and Wilson.

We found the house very easily as Mumbil is so small. Enid welcomed us and made tomato sandwiches with a cuppa. We showed her family photos, Wilson got home from out looking to buy a car, had a drink then got ready and went over to Stuart Town pub. Met a couple of friends and we sat drinking and talking till about 7pm, went back to Apsley Crescent and enjoyed a roast dinner. Went to bed 9pm, rather exhausted.

The next day we went for a walk around town with Enid, met Aunty Eva and Ivy and Pat from the pub. When we got back, we all got into Glen's (Gavin's brother) panel van and went to Dubbo to visit Bev and Les (Enid's brother), on the way we went to see about a car. Played Canasta with Nickie, their daughter, she was very like Alison my daughter. Had very nice spaghetti dish with salad for lunch. Then went with Wilson to see a car which he bought. Back to Bev's played more Canasta then I drove the car to Wellington as Enid was a bit nervous after having an accident, then she took over and we drove back to Mumbil. Had a drink while Enid cooked tea, went to bed about 10:30.

Wherever we stayed we'd help out to 'pay' for staying with all the lovely people who put us up. I always loved gardening so I was happy to help Enid mow the lawn and do a bit of tidying in the garden. That night we went into Iron Bark pub in Stuart Town.

Ivy's mum turned up, then we rushed home as Enid had tea ready then had a quick wash and went up to Nora's to an Avon Party. We met Pam, a quiet person and Pat a funny little stout thing, Nancy was there too. The evening was quite hilarious with little town small talk and back biting.

Whilst at Enid's, I primed eight boards ready to paint and started with a small painting of Franz Josef and the water fall at Milford sound as I remembered them from our recent visit to New Zealand.

We went into Wellington with Enid the following day, had counter lunch at The Grand and met Nancy there. I went to the bank, Enid went for haircut. One of the situations where Vera and I differed was that I was receiving a pension which meant I didn't have to find work. But Vera needed to top up every now and then. So when we stopped somewhere for a while she would try to find work, and so Vera saw proprietor about a job.

The next morning, Glen dropped me over at the old family homestead. I spent nearly all day drawing the Amyville homestead, I was rather pleased with the result. It had been a nice peaceful day without interruption, I had taken water and sandwiches, Glen picked me up about five when we all sat outside and had the usual couple of drinks before tea.

Next day Vera and I decided to go to Dubbo, Vera went to CES and went on the dole as she was determined to get a job. Afterwards we drove out to the open-air zoo. It was so nice that we could drive around in certain parts and see all the animals out in the open. They were in areas below us but able to roam around without being penned in and still not a danger to us. The weather was ideal and we spent a lovely day before returning to Mumbil. Western Plain Zoo houses about 1000 animals from all over the world, they all looked so happy in their surroundings and it was nice to be able to drive around the 6 km loop road. Dubbo is actually on the Macquarie River, the town looks very refreshing with trees lining the streets. It was settled in the 19th century like so many other towns the result of discovering gold.

On Good Friday 17th April 1981, we were woken 6:45am by Willie (Vera's son-in-law) knocking on our door. He, Di and Desa had driven up from Melbourne to spend Easter with us! We put the kettle on and all had breakfast. They had arrived at 4am and stayed in the car so were pretty cold by the time they knocked. Enid came out and took Desa in. We sat chatting and catching up on news till I went up to the school about 8:30 to tidy the garden for the Centenary celebrations. Vera and Di walked up about 10, Di had cut Vera's hair. We all went back to the house, Stephen and Judy turned up and we all sat around with a drink. Enid cooked some fish which we had with salad and hot-X-buns. After lunch, Stephen and Judy took Di and Willie for a drive to Burrendong Dam. Glen went too then they went up to the farm. Enid had a rest. When they got back Stephen, Judy and Glen went back to the farm for tea. Di bathed Desa and got her settled for the night, Wilson got Willie some tea then Di, Vera and I had a snack and were deciding to go to bed when Stephen, Judy and Glen came in. Glen, Stephen and Willie played cards at the table and Di showed Vera and I how to play Last Card.

The next day, Saturday, all the Peacocks went off to the school for roll call for the Centenary Celebrations. Di cut my hair then Willie drove us into Wellington, had a bit of a look around. Wellington is on the Mitchell Highway and lies at the junction of Macquarie and Bell Rivers. Landscaped gardens run alongside the main street and down to Bell River, a popular picnic area in the heart of the town. There's a suspension bridge over the river. Early on, around 1820, Wellington was a short-lived convict station. There were some nice heritage buildings, again a town with a history of a bit of a gold rush.

When we got back the Peacocks had returned. Enid and Vera fixed some lunch, after lunch Di and Willie decided to get going. Vera and I set our hair, had a bath then got ready to attend the dinner dance at the C.W.A hall. It was very crowded and noisy, nobody extra-friendly. Quite a nice meal of mince in pastry as entrée, chicken and salad followed by pavlova and cheesecake for sweets, a very sour wine with the meal. Then we all went over to the ball in the Town Hall. A good band sat out in the marquee with Jude and Stephen, Wilson's sister Clare, nice very chatty comes from Forbes. Del Fields came over and joined us for a while. Vera and I got up and did a quick step together, had a barn dance with Stephen then about 12:30, Wilson got me up for an old fashioned dance, then we decided to leave with Judy and Stephen as we were getting cold and it was a bit boring. They dropped us off and we went straight to bed.

Easter Sunday up about 8 had breakfast Stephen and Jude came over with Glen, Wilson was not looking too good, he had finally got Enid to bed at 6:30am! We all stood around outside talking, then Clare and Ben, Naomi and Jim and son arrived, Wilson's brother Tim and Bev, Nickie, Jackie and Steven arrived. Jude and Stephen decided to leave and go and visit Hilton's mum. Enid was in a very cranky mood, they all went up to school for Easter Service except Bev and the girls. We showed them photos of our trip and talked, then the Peacocks came back and got into the grog! We ate some hot-X-buns and lunch, then went over to the Oval for sports day. Vera and I entered the obstacle race and 'chase the chook', Vera caught it! Then went into tug of war twice. We had the cheapest hamburgers; only $1 each and quite good too! It started to get a bit chilly so we went home with Wilson who had also had enough. I had a bath and tidied up before everyone returned. Enid was still very grumpy but still played Canasta with us then went off to bed when everything wasn't going her way. Nickie and I stayed up and played King in the Corner till Enid yelled out to turn the light out and go to bed!

WEST OF SYDNEY

Things with Enid were going a bit downhill, so we decided to leave for a few days. We left for Orange at 4:30pm and arrived about 7pm, parked off the road in Council Park for the night. We got up early as usual and after breakfast we drove into town and Vera called at several hotels to try and get a job. We then went to the Visitor's Centre, had a coffee and watched a film on the district. It was the best tourist centre we have seen yet. We had a shower up in Cook's Park then drove out 6 miles to Lake Canobolas and found a beaut spot with poplar trees and BBQ's also a caravan park and a deer park. We drove around and stopped to walk and enjoy the scenery. Then we drove on to John William Park another 3 miles and found a level place to park for the night. Very nice and peaceful with beautiful trees and bush in autumn dress. Had a fairly early tea cooked on a campfire and retired after the 7pm news.

After breakfast I wandered around then went up the road to sketch a tree while Vera wrote a long letter to Di, then we drove to Pinnacle Picnic area, these are all places we saw on the film. We walked up a very steep hill to the lookout with wonderful view of Orange and surrounding countryside. Then we drove into Orange having completed a circle. Vera posted parcel to Di while I did some shopping. Then we went to Cook's Park and had a nice hot shower and washed our hairs. At 4pm we drove out to Bathurst bought petrol and drove out to Georges Plains arriving at Jude and Stephen's place about 5:30. Jude was really happy to see us, had a cuppa and told her what we had done since we saw them in Mumbil.

Stephen came home and we had a glass of wine while Jude cooked pepper steak and salad for tea, talked to 9pm then all went to bed. Stephen had to leave for work at 3am and we had filled quite a lot in the day.

Early start to Bathurst. We called at the cauliflower fields looking for work and ended up with a couple of caulies and pumpkins, went on into town. Vera did the Hotels and clubs looking for work and made an appointment with two. We went back to van for lunch then drove back out to Georges Plains. I prepared a chicken dish and vegies. Chatted after the meal then had cup of Milo and we all retired at 9:30pm after trying to phone Gavin several times.

The next morning was foggy and cold. Stephen went to work and Judy went with him. We repaired the exhaust pipe then phoned Nola and Gavin and found out they did not intend coming to Mumbil for another seven weeks or so. We had sandwiches and cuppa with Stephen and Jude, then the four of us went in the ute about fifteen miles away to get wood at Stephen's uncle Bill and Kaye, they had two girls and a boy. Stephen and Bill went off to get wood and the girls sat around chatting and sinking a couple of cans. Got back to Georges Plains about 5pm and I made a vegie curry and rice, Stephen got a beaut fire going in the lounge. We had a glass of wine, Jude prepared some flounder. Lovely tea. Jude and Stephen are a real nice couple. Had a cuppa and at 9:30pm went out into the cold to bed.

Incredible Memories

We spent a lovely few days with them and then decided to go back to Mumbil to prepare for the next leg and say goodbye properly to Enid.

On the way we got gas bottles filled, made an appointment to have an oil change and grease up and to have exhaust fixed. Drove around outskirts of town and found a nice spot down on Macquarie River east of town, about three miles out.

We went to a garage at 8:30 to have the exhaust fixed, job finished at 10:30, went to another garage and had oil change and grease up. Then drove out to river again and set up a fire, had lunch then went through cloths and discarded a few things. Repacked everything underneath the bed.

On May 1st our Avon delivery arrived, and with the van serviced and ready it was only left to say our farewells. We drove out to Mumbil and stopped at the Peacocks. Vera did a big wash while I went to P.O and paid for our Avon goods. Then we both had baths and washed our hairs. Vera spent afternoon writing to Loise. We called at the Post Office but no telegram or mail so left for Wellington, arriving at 5pm.

After breakfast went into town to pick up photos and bought a few groceries and headed out of town, headed North East to Gulgong. The photos taken at the peak of the gold boom are the basis for the illustration on the $10 note. The old buildings on the note are still standing. We spent three hours looking around, a quaint little town; busy with auction, clothing market and CWS hall. We left about 2:30pm and drove towards Coolah. Turned off east about 31 miles north and found a quiet reserve and made camp. Made a nice fireplace with an old tin sheet we found and used it like a hot plate

Got up at 7:30 had eggs and bacon, spent the day writing letters, I wrote a long letter to Sister Emmanuel my old Guide Captain in Jamaica. Vera put some photos together and got tea ready then she set three rabbit traps.

The next morning, Vera went and collected one rabbit from the trap but it had also caught a large white cat which we had a bit of difficulty letting loose. Vera skinned and cleaned the rabbit then I cut it up and put it on to stew. I spent the morning stewing the rabbit and some apples. I did a sketch of our campfire. At midday we travelled to Coolah. We found parking area near bowling club under a shady tree, had lunch then walked down the street, not much to see.

Vera phoned Dubbo CES but still no word. Drove 14 miles east to find a place to park, the road was terrible and no nice spots so we returned to about one mile from town and parked in a gravel hill among the trees for the night.

I checked the van and Vera washed inside of van. About ten we moved out, got some petrol and drove north and stopped 19 miles out at the Black Stump rest centre. Took some photos then went on through a dirt road, through Binnaway to Coonabarabran, arrived about 1pm. We parked up a quiet street, had lunch then changed and went for a walk found a nice shady park with toilets near a river where we moved the van. We walked around looking at things, Vera phoned Dubbo, no joy. Called at PO for mail, nil. Drove west out of town found a nice reserve to stay, gathered wood found tin to make up a fireplace.

When I looked towards the creek, I saw a small animal about the size of a large rat but it wasn't a rat as it was sort of hopping, it went down to have a drink then disappeared into the rushes. I never saw another so don't think there were many around.

We decided to take a trip further west to the Warrumbungle Ranges. We called into Lee Miller's studio and had a look at some of his paintings and pottery. He had an ex-chef bloke, who was crippled, who helped Lee by making the picture frames. We found out Lee and family had lived in Fremantle before moving here. We then drove on to Miniland, a dinosaur theme park which was quite nicely set out with prehistoric animals out front and through the shop area. There was a small museum area with some really interesting items from the pioneer days. There were pathways through trees to a wildlife sanctuary, then down a hill to a castle and moat area with drawbridge and a chain raft. A BBQ area and playground with manmade stream and waterfall.

We drove a couple of miles to a picnic park and had lunch. I did a sketch of Timor Rock. Vera wandered around collecting wood. Drove several miles further on to a parking spot, 750 metres below a lookout and parked van and walked up. Took a distant photo of Breadknife Rock. We decided not to go on as it was very steep and the road further on was not too good. Took photo of the Conservatory Dome, then drove back to campsite after 3pm.

For Mother's Day Vera gave me a "Little Boy" Avon perfume and I gave her picture soap. We thought about our girls who were mothers for the first time and wondered what they had got. I sat down front in the van and did a brush painting of the road into Lake Argyle and a brush and palette knife painting of Lightning Ridge. Vera sorted photos and put them together in concertina way. The nights were cold so we usually went to bed early.

The next day, we drove over a bridge north for a few miles then turned around. Parked in a park on the river and walked to the PO finally got mail sent on from Mumbil. Vera got cheque, at last, from CES $36 dollars! She raved on about it for a while. Drove back to campsite had homemade soup which warmed us up nicely.

Next, we drove south to Hickory Falls and had a look around, talked to a couple from Goondiwindi. Left at noon and drove to Gilgandra. Called into BP garage and had brakes adjusted.

Then on to Coonamble where we bought petrol, drove till late afternoon looking for a likely place to camp. Very barren and dry here. We saw SEC road veering to the left so drove up a short distance found some bush and parked near a tree and set up camp. Rather hard to find decent wood.

Incredible Memories

Got up early, Vera took a photo of the sunrise. We broke camp and hit the road at 8am. Stopped several times and collected what we called telephone domes. These were coloured glass domes of different shapes that were used on telephone lines as insulators. These we could sell as they were quite valuable collectors' items. We found many scattered in the bush on the sides of the road. They are quite beautiful, purple, blue and clear.

We arrived at Lightning Ridge 11:30am parked in Opal Street, had lunch then went for a wander. Checked out about all the Opal shops and tried to get as much info as possible. At 3pm drove out to Spectrum Mine and saw a film on the development of mines and places to see in the town. Then put helmets on and went down into part of the mine to see opal in its original state. We drove on another 3 miles to another mine, went down three levels and saw more opals and a young fellow told us the method of mining opals. We then drove out of town, east, to see if we could find a spot to camp. The road was very rough and all fenced so drove back towards town to a mining site and drove in to see if we could find a place there. No success so drove out and went south, branched out on a side road a hundred meters or so and turned into some bush and set up camp.

The next morning, we drove 3 miles out to Opal Bazaar then on to Bird of Paradise Art Gallery. It was a terrible road, then back into town and visited a house made entirely of empty beer bottles, then went to a museum there was a good rock collection, got a few opal samples. We filled up with petrol and water and drove out east at 3pm for about two hours on rough dirt road then pulled off into some bush and made camp.

I fossicked around and found a few stones. We had a coffee and broke camp about 11am. Drove to Collarenebri and parked near a river and walked up main street. There were more Aboriginals than whites which was something we hadn't seen since we left Alice Springs, they were very friendly. Bought some fruit and then headed off. Travelled another 70 miles east, mostly dirt road but not too bad. Pulled off on a track to the right, down under some trees about half a mile off the road by Gwydir River. Wandered around picking up wood and found the top of a 40-gallon drum and made a campfire sitting the top of cans. It was a good spot so we decided to hang around there for a couple of days, enjoying the nature.

Next stop was Moree twenty miles away. Moree is noted for its mineral waters. We parked in a quiet street and went into town. Called at the tourist centre then went to Coles and bought a few stores, went back to the van had lunch, then went to rest centre and had lovely hot showers, washed our hairs. We then drove south over a bridge, got petrol looked at artesian baths, skirted around for a while then headed north on the Newell Highway at 3pm. We drove about 50 miles and found a nice secluded place off the road near Croppa Creek, hidden from the highway.

The next morning, we headed off to Goondiwindi, 20 miles away the border of Queensland and New South Wales.

WEST OF SYDNEY

Our Days

Most of our days followed a similar routine. We started the day with a jog before breakfast. If we were out in the bush, we lit a fire every morning so time was also spent collecting wood.

Every few days we would check our post and most days we would write letters. We took it in turns to handwash our clothes. If we had the luxury of staying with friends, we used their machine and luxuriated in hot showers or baths.

In the evening, we'd wind down with a couple of drinks. We alternated between Ginger Wine, sherry, brandy or beer. This would be followed by dinner. If we hadn't caught a rabbit in our traps or roo, we'd have tomatoes on toast, curried vegies and rice, sausages, rissoles, onions, pineapple and baked potatoes with salad and garlic bread. Or silver beet and eggs, cauliflower and cheese, grilled tomatoes and bacon with spinach, cold stewed apple and custard, grilled bacon and tomatoes, apple and creamed rice or the vegetable chocho with gravy, lamb chops and mashed potato and peas with gravy, poached eggs and tomatoes, cheese fritters to name a few dishes. We cooked on the open fire.

Our evening entertainment was reading a good book or playing cards. We loved Canasta and King in the Corner. During the day I'd sketch often, which would allow me to get away on my own and just watch and listen to the birds and wildlife. Sometimes we'd do a jigsaw puzzle.

We always left the campsite as if we had never been there.

Chapter 60

QUEENSLAND

Goondiwindi is on the border of New South Wales and Queensland. A bridge over Macintyre River, originally Gundwanda the term for local Aboriginal "Resting place of wild ducks". It is the site of a customs house where they collected duties on goods transported to or from New South Wales. The building is now a museum. It is a major cotton wool and cattle centre. We drove over the bridge and took photos of each other under the Queensland sign. We drove up street to our left through the shopping centre to find a garage to check our brakes, but they couldn't do it so we drove further on to a park and got more water into our tank. Then headed off north. Stopped at Moonie and got petrol, some 56 miles onward, then on for a few more miles and stopped by the roadside to get a few purple telephone dome insulators, had lunch then off again at 1:30 pm. We drove for about two hours before turning off and parking about 18 miles west of Condamine, found a rest area just west of Dogwood Creek, drove well off the road and set up camp.

Went for a walk and collected stones, an old drum top and wood and made a nice fireplace. Made a roast and vegies with some sliced beef I'd bought. After tea it started to rain. We played cards then bed.

Got up at 8am still raining so had breakfast in the van. Vera did some mending while I knitted a dilly bag to hold cigarettes, Vera wrote her diary. Pretty cold and bleak. Fortified with hot coffee several times during the day. Had Green Ginger wine to warm up before tea of hot soup. Still raining and on the news it is to continue.

Got up about 6:30 had breakfast and stowed everything away. The road very wet so had to be careful not to get off onto soft sides. Had to drive around a fallen tree but luckily not off the road. Drove for two hours on not very good road on the way to Roma. Stopped at a nice rest area just out of town. Still raining. In Roma got petrol and filled gas bottles. Stopped and had lunch by the side of the road and found exhaust pipe had come loose did a patch up job and continued to Mitchell along the Warrego Highway. We arrived at Mitchell about 12:30, stopped in main street, changed clothes and went over to a garage to see if they could fix the exhaust pipe. Two hours later we had the exhaust pipe altered and a new muffler fitted.

Vera walked to PO and collected six letters which was nice, she also got a chocolate cake from a stall. Then drove round and visited Gwen and Bill Rush, parents of Cowboy from Wagin WA. We were made very welcome and stayed until about 5pm.

We had planned to stay with Keryn and her husband Errol, the daughter of friends of Vera, the couple she had worked for at the caravan park in Bunbury. We phoned Keryn but she suggested we stay in town for the night as the road into the station was bad from recent rain. We went back to the Rush's to park outside their house. Gwen insisted we stay for a meal. We had a beautiful hot bath before tea. While at the table another son, Garry came home from 80 miles away where he works with cattle and horses. Garry took us down to the hotel for a drink, after an hour we went back and sat in the lounge and watched TV before bed about 11:30.

The following morning, we headed into town to get the brakes looked at and do some shopping when Keryn around looking for us. We sat in the van catching up with her as we hadn't seen her for about two years. We said say goodbye to the Rush's. and at 1:30 we started for the station. We drove about ten miles back towards Roma then turned off onto a dirt road, not very good. Had to do the last three or four miles in first gear as it was rather boggy but got through okay, the back wheels were coated in black mud; our introduction to Well Gully.

Well Gully was a station owned by the parents of Keryn's husband Errol. Keryn and Errol managed the station which was struggling through a drought. To repay them for letting us stay there we offered to repaint the homestead. We had a coffee and talked for ages. We then went for a tour of the farm buildings, thank goodness the rain stopped. We had showers, then a rum and orange while waiting for Errol to come home. We had a lovely steak dinner and talked well into the night.

Over the course of the next few days we were busy around the farm. It was so interesting learning about the workings of the property. The first morning we went down the yard and gave Keryn a hand cleaning up the scrap heap. I cooked a roast and met Craig the jackaroo and made them lunch. The next morning, we were up early to start work. I got gear together to start cleaning the verandah in preparation for painting. I stopped for lunch then did a bit more. I then went in to start tea, made pumpkin scones, but they weren't very good as I didn't know how to regulate the oven.

Each day when we stayed at Well Gully, we rose early and went for our runs before starting our daily activities. We shared the cooking, Keryn cooked tuna casserole and vegies, lamb chops, chicken done in fried onions and apricot nectar, crumbed chops. We would have lunch then spend

Incredible Memories

another couple of hours cleaning, have a coffee and call it a day. We'd often have a couple of drinks after showers and before dinner.

The second day we continued to clean all the woodwork, I took broken glass out of dining room door, Keryn started painting windows and Vera continued washing down walls. Keryn went over to the shed and helped unload hay.

The following day, we went into Roma with Keryn. We did some shopping then went for coffee and sandwiches before driving around to the school, show grounds, paint shop and hardware store to buy glass for the door. At 1pm we went to the club where we enjoyed a couple of brandies each and a very nice lunch. Then went with Keryn to buy groceries. We left Roma and drove into Mitchell to call for mail. On the way back to Well Gully we saw 18 roos. When we got home around 5:30 we found their dog had got out and rounded up all the sheep and had them by the house! What a clever dog but all were very thirsty and hot. Got the sheep back down the paddock, I prepared vegies, Vera lit the fire and Keryn went down and fed the hungry sheep. When all the chores were done, we sat down with a drink and played a few games of cards. Then Errol went out and worked a bit longer we sat around talking till late.

On day four, I fitted glass in the door, Vera sat in the van and caught up with her diary. After breakfast, we got the paint rollers ready and Keryn and I started painting while Vera continued cleaning. Soon after got a phone call from Errol saying he wanted Keryn to go over to Tree View (Errol's parents' property) to meet some ram buyers. Vera finished off Keryn's painting. After lunch I continued painting and Vera stayed inside cleaning, then she came out and continued painting and cleaning beams. We stopped about four had a coffee and I started tea while Vera got in wood and set three rabbit traps. Keryn came home at sunset after showers we sat and enjoyed a wine and lemonade, a new experience.

The next morning, we got up early and Vera found one of her rabbits eaten but had caught another one behind shearing shed which she skinned. Vera cleaned up, Keryn did a wash, I painted. Then Vera and Keryn fenced the vegie patch. Vera cleaned beams, Keryn joined me painting. Vera got coconut milk ready, got washing in and fetched in wood. She then made a fire outside to boil chillies to make insect spray, then she set traps again. I made meat patties and prepared vegies, Keryn fed sheep. When Errol came home, we had kidney beans, rice, cooked in coconut milk and chocho and peas, a taste of Jamaican dish. Errol went out to plough paddocks, we made fruit cakes, played a few games of cards while the cakes cooked, had coffee, bed at midnight.

Once again Vera checked the traps in the morning but this time there was nothing. We had planned to go horse riding but there was a storm brewing and before we finished breakfast, it started to pour. Errol's brother Nigel and Craig the Jackaroo came over and filled the ute with grain, they went down to the paddock and joined Errol, it was raining too hard so they came back. By lunchtime Errol went to bed, he had been ploughing nearly all night.

We had been at Well Gully a week and there was still plenty of work to so. That morning, Vera went to cut wood and raked up a heap, I caught up on my diary then it started to pour again. When it stopped raining, Vera trimmed a pine tree and I went back to the van. Keryn put a big leg of lamb on for lunch. Had nice roast and vegies, had a shandy with lunch. Errol went down to see if he could plant but the soil was too wet so he did office work instead, then went out to make bullets.

The next day, Errol took us down to the shed and showed us the huge Chamberlain tractor, I had a go driving it, great fun. Vera dug a trench to let water out of the dog yard, Keryn and I painted walls and Vera painted beams. Errol stayed home doing odd jobs, all stopped to have a cuppa, Keryn and I on the porch and Vera and Errol in the kitchen. Played cards and had a Milo then another midnight bed.

After breakfast Errol and Keryn fed sheep close to the house, then Vera joined them and they went to collect three sick sheep and went to feed the sheep in the paddocks. I warmed pasties up for lunch. Errol did book work, then he went to town with Vera. I painted for a couple of hours. Errol shot an emu on the way to town.

Each day was a different experience. One day, Errol, Keryn and I were away all morning feeding sheep. But we got good and properly bogged in the black mud. When we got out we went scrub cutting. I found some petrified wood. Later, Keryn and Vera sifted stock feed and bagged 20 bags of it.

We were luck to be there when the sheep shearing happened. I got up at 6am, took photos of the sunrise. After breakfast I cut sandwiches and prepared hot drinks. We left in the Suzuki for Tree view, I sat in front with Errol and the other two sat on the back, it was rather cold. We loaded on the gear and left for Eastland; Heather and Ruben, Errol's parents, and Craig followed in the Toyota. Errol shot a couple of emus and a kangaroo, he baited them all. We continued but then found the others were not following us. The next thing Craig arrived on horseback leading another. He said the weight of the horses on the Toyota were too heavy in boggy conditions. When we arrived, Errol and Craig went off on the horses to fetch in the sheep. In the meantime, we women cleaned up the shearing shed, then helped to get the sheep into yards. We all had a coffee, then sorted and drenched the sheep. We stopped for lunch and all sat around on drums and logs. I travelled back with Heather and Ruben, Vera and Keryn rode back on top of the Toyota with the dogs. When we got back to Tree View, we helped load the sheep-spraying gear on to the truck then went down to the house and had a very welcome coffee while we waited for Errol. We were taken on a tour of the farm and helped pick tomatoes. Errol got there about seven and we returned to Well Gully tired and cold. Keryn started to get food packed for the following day, I made coleslaw, had a drink with the delicious salmon and cheese bake. Early bed as we had very early start in the morning.

We were up just before 5am, ate then packed up the gear, tidied up and were on the road by 6:15. We sat on the back of the Suzuki and watched the sunrise. We called into Tree View but Ruben, Craig and the shearers had already left so we followed. They had already started shearing. Vera and I made a nice fireplace and put the billy on for morning tea. We served five men, Vera and I had tea, crackers and cheese and cake. Our job was to keep the fire going and billy hot. Keryn mostly helped in the shed, I swept the boards for a while. Vera caught up on her diary and I did a sketch of the shed and an old harvester just outside. They all stopped for lunch which I had prepared on the open fire. After the last smoko, Vera saddled the horses and she and Keryn rode off while we packed up. I went with Errol and Craig went on the back. We shot a couple of emus and a roo, Errol baited them. When we got back to Tree View, Heather and I had a cuppa while Errol killed a couple of sheep. The riders returned and unsaddled the horses and put them in the paddock. Then we drove nine miles back to Well Gully we all had much needed showers.

It was quite an experience watching the shearing and the speed each shearer went as if they were trying to shear more sheep than the next. They crutch them up the stomach then clean around the ears and head before the long blow, which is the rest of the sheep. Before 'down the long blow' all the wool is on the floor and that is what one sweeps up when sweeping the board. They have to shear so the whole fleece comes off in one piece. Then it is scooped up and thrown on to a table and all the edges are tidied up before bagging it. Then the sheep is pushed down a chute to the holding yard.

We didn't get up quite so early the next day. We all decided to go with Errol to Mount Ascot to check the fences in that area. It gave us an opportunity to see the rest of the property. Packed lunch again. First Vera and I went with Errol to feed sheep, the ground is still very wet, black soil is terrible stuff. Shot a roo and baited it to kill eagles and wild pigs. Checked a paddock with a crop coming up, returned to the house and decided to have lunch before going to Ascot. We travelled along the fence line and mended a few places then drove right up to Mount Ascot and saw the remains of a house. What an isolated place to live but it was beautiful up there. Shot another roo and cut off its tail and some good pieces off the back to hang. When we got to Tree View Homestead, Heather gave us tea, Errol's eldest sister Amy was there with her boyfriend. Errol went to the shed and blade sheared some rams for the show. I watched for a while but it was too cold. We headed home about 7:30, when we got back and prepared lambs fry and bacon and sliced up the roo to freeze. Another full and tiring day, but interesting.

We started the day with Vera doing hand washing while I got breakfast. After that Keryn and Vera did a big wash and I got on with painting. Then Keryn spent about two hours baking cakes. I painted all day, Vera did odd jobs and Errol went ploughing in the east paddock. Nerada, Errol's sister, and Julian brought the two jackaroos over to screen and bag grain. Errol and Keryn went into Mitchel to see a sheep feeder at the rail station. Vera and I had showers and got tea ready, when Errol and Keryn got back we sat and had a drink and talked about what we had all done during the day. Had rice and cabbage with kangaroo steak also rice pudding, always a yummy meal.

During the last two days of our stay, we continued painting and helped screen and bag grain. Keryn got the ute out and drove around picking up rubbish. I helped with the heavy stuff then took it down the paddock to the rubbish dump.

On our final day, we had an early rise, Vera packed up things in the van while I got breakfast, Vera did some ironing and after breakfast we said our goodbyes to Errol. We helped Keryn put new wire around fruit trees and took old wire down the paddock to tip. Had a cup of coffee took a few photos and departed at 10:30. Keryn followed us into Mitchell PO, it was sad to say goodbye. Then we went to the Rush's to wish them farewell.

It certainly had been such a busy few days with Errol and Keryn, but what fun and we sure learnt a lot about farming under the difficult situations they lived in. It was a treat catching up with them, such a nice couple, and all made us feel like family.

After breakfast we drove into the garage had brakes adjusted and bled. Posted letters and headed east to Miles, the commercial centre of the Darling Downs, a sprawling beef and grain producing area. We then drove north on the Leichhardt Highway and travelled until it was nearly dark and parked off the road. Had fried eggs and tomatoes and honey and cream on brown bread for tea. Were in bed by 8:30.

After a good night's sleep and breakfast, we drove into nearest town and got petrol and blew up the tyres. Continued north and turned off into Isla Gorge with panoramic views. Then drove on to Theodore with its lovely palm lined main road, a very neat town. Then we went back on to the highway, an hour later we reached Banana Road we veered right and stopped at the sales yards, it was then 1:30 so had lunch. Drove on to Biloela stopped to get petrol and I drew out $100, we drove till 5pm and found a gravel hill and parked for the night. Had a Cherry Brandy and lemonade after tea we read for a bit before lights out.

After breakfast did hand washing, emptied the toilet and for the first time for ages, it was warm enough to get into shorts. By 11am we were off to Gladstone, only 5 miles away. We saw Rocky Glen Hotel so we drove into the car park and walked to the Beer Gardens and there was Jan Chay, a friend of Di's, sitting with some friends Robert, Les and Tricia. She was very surprised to see us. We had a couple of drinks then went around to her place.

Incredible Memories

Had a nice lunch then we went for a drive around in the van with Jan directing us.

Gladstone a fast-growing industrial area and port. It has a bauxite refinery, coal and grain exporting facilities, a powerhouse and new aluminium smelter. The harbour is considered to be the best natural harbour in Queensland. When we got back, Vera and I relaxed and Jan did some cooking. Then she got on her bike and took her dog Ralph to go down to the wharf to meet her boyfriend Greg. We both had showers had a drink and relaxed in front of the TV. It was almost dark when Greg's mum, Joan came to tell Jan the boat wasn't coming in till Monday. She went looking for Jan, they both came back had a cup of coffee then we had tea and played 500 till bed.

Had breakfast with Jan 8:30 then some friends picked her up to go to a Christening and we said goodbye. Headed north to Rockhampton arrived about 11:39 and called into tourist information, very friendly staff. Vera tried to phone Sue Kirk's mum. Drove to Botanical Gardens and sat in the van overlooking a lake and had lunch. Parked near the entrance and walked around the attractive grounds, the Botanical Gardens feature very colourful tropical plants. Rockhampton sits on the Tropic of Capricorn, there are some fine Colonial buildings. The Customs House stands out with its copper dome.

We drove around the outskirts of the city west of Fitzroy River and went over a bridge on to Bruce Highway about two miles before turning left at the sign to Yeppoon. We travelled 20 odd miles to the beach, then drove north to Byfield, then 23 miles through pine forest to a lovely picnic area called Water Park Creek arriving about 5pm. Luckily several campers left for town and we had the place to ourselves. We had a drink while our tea was cooking after we played cards till bed.

There are wide beaches and rocky headlands with many tropical islands a few miles offshore in the sparkling blue waters. We enjoyed the warmth and spectacular landscape. First thing in the morning we grabbed our fishing gear and walked through a tropical forest to a river. After spending two and a half hours trying, we caught nothing. I fished for a bit longer and Vera wrote up her diary. Walked back had lunch, got fire going and wandered around. We split some big pieces of wood and carried them back to our camp. I cooked tea of chops and vegies and made some scones while Vera mended the fly wire on the hatch. After coffee we went for a walk down to the river and over a crossing and up a hill and took photos of the sunset. Came back and warmed the lamb stew while we had a drink. After tea played cards, always found it relaxing before bed.

Got up and got fire going, after breakfast we went for a walk on a road east of our camp. On the way back we collected firewood, had a coffee, then Vera stuck stickers on the van. I prepared to paint a name on the front of the van. Vera wrote to her mother, we had a coffee and I did small wash. Vera wrote to Lois, Malcolm and Dot in New Zealand. Had a drink then tea, macaroni and tomatoes in a cheese sauce, yum, had the last of the honey and cream on toast. Played a few games of cards then it turned cold so called it a day.

After breakfast we packed up made sure we left camp sight clean, we left about 11am to return to Yeppoon then on to Rosslyn Bay. We then drove along the coast, attractive surroundings. We stopped by a beach and collected a few shells and took some photos. We drove on to another beach and stopped for lunch. Drove back to Rockhampton via Emu Park, about 23 miles, stopped to get petrol, went over Fitzroy River bridge and parked. Went to the PO and posted cards and parcel to Marie-Therese then drove west along the river and parked opposite the Bowling club under some huge trees. Had eggs and tomatoes for tea, played cards before retiring.

Up by 6am put everything away and left for Mackay. It was very cold till the sun came up. We stopped about 8am and had breakfast then travelled till 11am when we had to stop at bridge over Funnel Creek for an hour while bridge was being repaired. About fifty cars and caravans lined up on either side of the bridge. Met a couple from Melbourne called Margaret and Cliff Carver. When bridge was finished, we drove to next small town and bought a few things before continuing to Mackay.

We called into Tourist Information, which was a Vietnamese fishing boat which had been confiscated, this was parked about 2 miles south of the city. We arrived about 3pm and parked near the PO; got letter from Marie-Therese and Di and a telegram from Alison. Drove east of the city to Queens Park, found a nice tree near some toilets and parked. Had a drink, warmed up chops and vegies, played cards, Vera had an aching jaw so we retired 7pm.

Mackay was very touristy, the sugar city of central Queensland. The manmade harbour is not only designed for the large sugar and general cargo shops but special wharves have been designed and built for small ships which cater for the tourists.

Went for a jog around the park, had breakfast and sat writing letters. I wrote to family via Marie-Therese and to mum. Beautiful sunny day. Walked around to the shopping centre, at 4pm drove out over bridge north to Blacks Beach. Had a drink, tea was rice tomatoes and sardines, played cards till 9pm.

Went for a run, had breakfast, tidied up and went back on to Bruce Highway and headed for Seaforth, turned right towards the coast and drove through sugar cane fields to Holiday Bay, arriving about noon. We booked into caravan park. Cliff and Margaret who we'd met earlier came out to meet us and invited us for a cuppa. We caught up on what each of us had done since we last saw each other. Had showers and washed our hairs and also did a big wash. Had a late lunch then went for a long walk along the beach. Met three people from Melbourne stopped and had a chat. We have met so

Incredible Memories

many lovely people on our travels. Cooked a roast in the electric frying pan and sat talking with the Carvers in their annex while it cooked. Had tea then went over to Carvers and played Back Gammon and Canasta till 10:30 had a cup of tea and homemade cake. It was almost midnight when we went back to the van. It was a most enjoyable evening.

When we got up we went for a jog along the beach right to the end then climbed over some rocks to the point where there was a good view of the Bay. After breakfast the couple from the van next to us came over to look at the van and brought us some fish. Left the park 10:15 and parked down at the beach. We went back to the Carvers and had a cuppa with them and chatted till noon then left. Stopped along the way and had lunch then drove to Shute Harbour. Called into the Information Centre and bought tickets for a cruise to the Islands for the next day. Drove out to harbour along a very windy hilly road. Parked in the car park and decided to spend the night there. We wandered around the jetty and watched tourists coming and going. Cold meat and salad early bed.

Monday June 22nd 1981, we have been traveling for just over one year. It has been an incredible experience. And we still have some way to go. Today is to be something we have both wanted to do. After breakfast we got ready to leave on "The Challenger", it had been made in Fremantle WA. We sailed past Day Dream, South Nole and Hook Islands. We stopped at Hook for a very nice lunch and drinks in a beer garden, a lovely tropical jsland. We were treated to a glass dome where we could view the underwater life as if we were diving. Then we sailed around Whit Sunday, Dent, and Long Islands, past Palm Bay, Happy and Day Dream again and returned to Shute at 4:30.

We had excellent weather, the trip was very smooth. The waters breathtakingly clear with those marvellous blues and greens one experiences in the tropics. The beaches on each Island so attractive with palm trees on the fringes of the white sands.

When we got back had a drink and relaxed recalling our day. We met a young couple from Sydney. The man had just caught a large flathead off the jetty. We had spaghetti on toast and retired early, quite an exhausting day, luckily it was a nice quiet spot when all had left.

Got up at 6am and were on our way by 7am. Rather cold and foggy drove back on Bruce Highway, going north. We drove till 9am until we found a nice sunny warm spot. We parked on the side of the road and had breakfast. Drove on to Bowen but just before the town there was a caravan on the side of the road; the Information Centre. Met the two ladies who ran it, Daphne and Doreen, who invited us to coffee and biscuits, we chatted for an hour and they gave us their addresses. We then drove into Bowen, down Herbert Street, the main one, down to the waterfront and parked next to The Lyon's. Met a couple with their four kid who hailed from Carnarvon WA. We walked out onto the jetty and took deep breaths of fresh sea air. We went

QUEENSLAND

back and had lunch in a good spot under a shady tree. Watched school kids playing on the grass and down on the beach. Bowen is a lovely little town enclosed by hills and fields full of fruit and vegies. Vera wrote to Nola and posted a 21st birthday card to her. We walked around the shops and I got my glasses fixed. When we got back to the van there was a young couple looking at it, Keith and Kathy from Sydney. Keith is Canadian and Kathy from New Zealand, when they left it was quite late so we just stayed where we were. Had a rum and orange each then rice mutton and gravy for tea, played cards and fairly early bed.

After breakfast went to RAC to see about the brakes. The rep sent us to BP Better Brakes made an appointment for after lunch. We went out to beaches and met Keith and Kathy again, then drove to Greys Beach parked under a shady tree and had lunch. I fossicked for shells while Vera caught up on her diary. Then we drove back to Ron Perin's garage. They took front wheels off and found the bearings were worn and they suggested we get new brake shoes, also to renew bearings on back wheels. They didn't have any in stock so had to send for some from Townsville.

We sat reading while we waited. As the van was jacked up we had to stay there the night. Went for a walk down to the beach, a very nice one. Had a Green Ginger wine, rice tomatoes and lamb for tea followed by fruit salad and ice cream. Ron had put us on power, so we played cards then went to bed and read as we had good light.

Up at 6:30 walked down to the toilet then went for a long walk along the boat harbour, on return had breakfast. I did some sketching while Vera sorted some paperwork, had a cup of coffee, Vera put her photos together. Finally, at 11:30 they started to work on the van. By 5pm they had all done, bled the brakes but air still getting into line. Ron drove around then came back and bled brakes again. Just couldn't get them as good as they should be. Paid and left at 6:30, it was dark by now we went around to see if we could find Doreen's house. She was not home, we spoke to Barbara her neighbour, she asked us to drive in and wait but we decided to stay on the road and had tea.

Doreen didn't come so we drove back down to the beach parked and decided to retire as we were both pretty tired.

Got up about 7am with the intentions of continuing to Townsville but while we were having breakfast Doreen drove up and joined us, she asked us to stay at her place for the weekend. We followed her around and parked alongside her unit and plugged into power. We helped clean her unit as she is crippled with arthritis. Had lunch then Doreen took us on a tour out to farms to look for work; got a heap of corn and honey but no work. The corn was huge and delicious eaten raw, with juicy white milk when we bit into them. We went all along the beaches and went up to a lookout and witnessed a panoramic view. Went into town and got our gas bottle filled. Then went around to her friend Don's place. What a dump! He was a huge ocker bloke, had a coffee, helped hang his clean curtains up, then he drove us back to Doreen's as we had to leave the car for Garry, Doreen's son.

Prepared vegies for roo stew, had rice, tomatoes and herrings. Doreen came out and we talked till 11pm washed up had a Milo and bed, rather exhausted.

Decided to get up after the seven o'clock news, we walked down to the phone and phoned four farmers asking for work but no luck. Had breakfast about 9:30, had showers and washed our hairs. I talked to Doreen and Barbara while Vera did our washing and hung out Doreen's washing. Then the three of us went to Woolworths and did shopping. Went around to another friend, Norm, had a coffee and looked at some of his wife's pottery. I got a couple of green coconuts off one of their trees. Had a late lunch then went in and showed Doreen some of my paintings, she was also a painter. Doreen and I sat in the lounge painting, she had a go at palette knife painting. Vera sat outside catching up on her diary. Then we had to get ready as Don was picking us up to have tea at his place 6:30. Had a delicious oxtail and vegetable stew. After tea we watched films about different holidays they'd had and also their farm. Finished with a Milo and he drove us home about 11pm.

Up at 6am had breakfast, packed lunch and thermoses of tea and coffee. Don came at 7am and took us to Grays Bay, we put the boat in and away we went to Middle Island about three miles offshore. We pulled onto a nice beach and had a coffee and admired the view. Got on board again and went around to a calm spot and sat fishing. Don said none of mine were big enough to keep. Vera caught one and Don caught two. We then went right around the Island. The tide was going out so we stopped near reefs and got out and fossicked among the reefs.

When we got back to Don's he had a shower and we had a cup of tea, then he took us back to Doreen's. He has taken a shine to Vera, quite amusing. Vera had a shower while I cleaned the fish, then I had a shower and Vera prepared tea. Don called back and gave us tomatoes and zucchinis, had tea then went into the house and met Doreen's mother and sister who had arrived from Gosford for a holiday. Garry came out and had a look at the van he was quite impressed.

After breakfast packed away paintings, shells and left at 9:30 and drove down to Field Street to visit Daphne, she was very pleased to see us. Had a coffee and talked for about an hour, she gave us a couple of paw paws. We drove for about an hour then pulled into a rest area and had lunch. Then drove to Townsville arrived at 4:30, drove to north end of a beach to a parking area and decided to stay the night there. We went for a walk along the beach. Had a drink when we got back, had roo stew and tinned fruit for tea, played a couple of games of cards. We were woken at 9:30 when a Combi pulled in beside us.

QUEENSLAND

Townsville is the departure point for the cruises to the reefs and the ferry to Magnetic Island. Considered the Capital of North Queensland. It has beautiful beaches, the largest arts and crafts market. The Strand is lined with restaurants, cafes and bars. It is surrounded by hills, a very attractive town.

Vera went for a run along the beach while I got breakfast, then we went and talked to the Dutch couple in the Combi. Vera went over and talked to three young fellows from Hamilton Hill, WA who were doing more or less what we were doing, but not as comfortable as we were as they were in a station wagon, a bit of a squash but they were having fun and enjoying the experience. We drove down the Strand and parked under a massive tree across from the TV Station, by Centenary Park. We walked into town to the Mall, bought some cards and Vera bought a pair of Army trousers and a couple of books. Then we treated ourselves to lunch which we had sitting under umbrella tables watching the world go by down the Mall; a very Continental atmosphere. We decided to go out of town to Better Brakes, they bled the brakes again, they had improved a bit. Got petrol and drove for a couple of hours till we found a rest centre 20 miles north of Cardwell, it was almost dark. We downed a couple of Shandies, had rice tomatoes and zucchini for tea, played cards then bed. It was rather noisy as we were close to the main road.

July 1st. After breakfast we chatted to a guy named Roy who had parked his caravan and white Toyota in front of us. While traveling we found people tended to park near other travellers, so we were not often on our own. We set off, drove through Tully then turned east towards the coast into Mission Bay. It was a lovely drive through rain forest and arrived at a tropical beach with coconut palms and heaps of sea gulls. Went for a walk along the beach, got some lemons someone had left in a box with a sign "Help Yourself", We then travelled on to Clump Point. We enquired about the boat to Dunk Island.

Bought nice hot pies, parked a wee bit down the road by the beach, had a cup of tea and the pies. I went for a walk along the beach and collected shells while Vera caught up on her diary. We then drove around the Bay to O'Conner's store. Vera phoned Sue Kirk and told her we were coning over, another friend we had met on our travels.

Drove back down the road and turned off to North Bingal Camp site in Bingal Bay. Found a site with a fire already going so tidied it up a bit and put the billy on. Vera spent the afternoon reading and sewing, I cleaned up some shells. Cooked fish for tea with rice and tomatoes. Met a couple of young fellows from Brisbane so sat chatting to them for a spell, played cards and called it a day at 9pm.

Backed out of our spot and drove to Clump Point, parked and had breakfast, bought our tickets and went aboard. Left soon after 9am had a really good crossing and arrived on Dunk Island at eleven. We walked up to the hotel and coffee shop bought a couple of oranges and went for a walk through some forest, and across a swinging bridge. There were some beautiful trees with weird roots and big tropical vines growing up them. Walked up winding path practically to the top of Mount. When we got back down, we asked directions to the farm, as we arrived Sue came out to greet us, met her two work mates Jenny and Annie. We had a cuppa, sausage rolls and chocolate the Sue showed us around. She took us down to the cow shed and gave us a milk shake, and she called her little calf over, a little beauty. She then showed us the way to Art Village. We walked for about a mile through paddocks and down a track, over a stream and into forest. There was a sign on a cowbell hanging off a post which said, "Ring Loudly". Then we walked into a cleared area where the potter, Henry, came out in raggedy shorts. He had built his house out of mud bricks and had built his own kiln. He showed us his work, not bad. We then went on to another clearing to Bruce's place, they had built a circular art gallery with paintings and tapestries hanging all around it. Two ladies and Bruce live there. Further in the forest a sculptor called Dennis lives. Time was too short to really enjoy this ideal living situation. We were shown another path which led down through thick forest over a couple of little bridges and finally out into the open at the far end of the air strip. We had to run part of the way as it was a long way back to the boat.

Sue was down at the wharf and she gave us a big bag of lemons, we said our farewells and hoped to meet again some time. We only just got on the boat before it sailed. Dunk was such a beautiful island, we just wished we had spent more time to enjoy it. It would have been so much more of a pleasure had we been able to spend the time more relaxed. We stopped to talk with a couple from Swanbourne WA when we went ashore. From Clump Point we drove to El Anish via a dirt road, filled the petrol tank, drove about four miles and turned off on to South Johnston Road looking for a decent parking spot. We drove about 30 miles and finally pulled off onto the side of the road and parked opposite a sugar cane field. Feeling very tired we warmed up the stew had good washes and collapsed into bed.

One thing we enjoyed in our travels was the variety of birds and their calls which we do not have in Western Australia. The cockatiel which we do have and called a weero, found inland in New South Wales and Queensland with their warbling call, mainly while in flight. The King Parrot we saw all up the East coast, with their green head and brilliant red under body, has a shrill call while in flight but more of a piping bell-like call when perched. Towards Cairns way and the tablelands in the west, the pretty red-winged parrot. Then the bigger yellow-tailed black cockatoo we saw through Victoria, New South Wales and lower Queensland. The sulphur crested cockatoo similar to the one seldom seen around Perth, we saw all through our travels in the east. Plus, the very colourful lorikeets. Several types of cuckoos which we heard through the night, their calls differing. The owls tended to have more of a scream which we wondered what it was when we first heard it. Of course, sounds at night so much louder to us while parked in a quiet camp. Kingfishers, varied in size and colour, we saw at various points in our travels, also the little yellow rainbow-bee-eaters with their high pitched chitter-chitter. The noisy pitta we saw more in the northern Queensland forest, with its loud melodious whistle which we heard frequently in forest areas. The sounds of most of the Eastern birds were quite new to us. Some very noisy but still a thrill to hear them. All swallows no stranger to us, but always present, but their whistle more strident in the east. We spotted several red-capped robins, also found in Western Australia, while in lower Queensland. The black-faced monarch with its blue head and back with a russet underside. There were so many varieties of small brown and grey feathered friends flitting around wherever we camped, with all their different songs and whistles. Just a delight to pause and enjoy.

Colourful finches, the scarlet honey eater, the white-breasted wood swallow, always several of them perched together on a branch, chattering together. We witnessed several types of pigeons. While camping in the Gem fields I would sit quietly by the campfire and these little red-chested button quails would join me, so exciting. When they came out of the scrub, they mad a weird 'OOM' sound, very softly. It wasn't really red it was more of a russet chest.

In the Tablelands out of Cairns I spotted a bush turkey with its naked head, very red, it reminded me of the John Crows in Jamaica. We saw several hawks in flight plus a wedge-tailed eagle perched on a branch watching us drive past. We were most fortunate to spot a cassowary up at the point we got to just out of Daintree, North East Queensland. During our travels we encountered umpteen water birds, in billabongs, lakes and by the sea. So many birds we heard but never saw. I loved the sound of the curlew. To enjoy what we saw and heard, we had to pause, look and listen.

We are surely a fortunate nation to have such numbers of our feathered friends the width and breadth of Australia. Some of which we share with other continents.

Already July, time flew and we still had many miles to cover. We hit the tracks after breakfast, got back on the Highway, pulled into a Rest Centre at Babinda, met a couple from Port Lincoln, South Australia, chatted with them for a while. Always interesting to hear of others travels as quite often they tell us of good camping areas. They left and we went over and talked to an older couple, they were in a camper with a trailer, Teresa and Bob. They have spent years living in the out-back, she was German, a little tiny lady, and we compared notes. We then moved on and stopped at a really nice rest centre just south of Gordonvale. There were nice BBQ's and grassed areas, had a cuppa and tomatoes on toast, the headed for Cairns.

Drove right through the city to the Esplanade and parked, got changed and walked to the PO. And who should be standing two in front of Vera but Bev from Canada, what a lovely surprise! We had last seen her in Lumsden

Incredible Memories

South Island, New Zealand on the 11th of March according to our diaries. We collected mail then went and had a coffee, talked and did some shopping, then all piled into the van and drove around to Beer Mart and bought some booze. Then drove north of the city to Lake Street to Don and Bev's place A neat little house, Bev made us some lunch we sat talking and Don came in about 5pm, we had a couple of drinks then Don and Bev got ready to be picked up by Gale and Peter they were going to a BBQ. We got ourselves tea had showers. We watched TV until 10:30.

We got up early and went for a walk, when we got back Don opened the door and invited us in for breakfast. Then we all went to 'Rusty's Markets', bought vegies and I bought some Picture frames. We had a look around, after that they took us to meet their New Zealand friends, Nyle and Cynthia. They had a huge home with a large swimming pool, nice couple. When we got back to Lake Street it was time for Bev to go to work, got lunch ready and Bev went to work. Don went crabbing, we went to shops on Bruce Highway and phoned Margaret's mother, Margaret and Martin were there so chatted to them as well.

When we returned, we had showers and washed our hairs, so much easier when we have the luxury of showers in a home. I prepared soup and kangaroo stew then we had tea and watched TV till Don got home about 3pm with a few crabs legs which Vera sampled, don't know what happened to the rest of the crabs, I suspect don and his mates had them for lunch. Don and I played Back Gammon then about 10:30 Don walked to meet Bev from work. And we retired.

Our usual early rise, Don left for a day's fishing. We went for a long walk along the Esplanade, bought papers and cards, when we got back Bev was busy hanging out washing. Had a coffee together, then I brought out my paintings to show Bev. Vera went out and tidied the van. Had lunch then Bev got ready for work. At about 3pm Margaret Jones came over with Rhys. We talked and showed her photos of family, after an hour we went down to Martin's ship, H.A.M.S Warrnambool. We went into the Mess and had a couple of beers then Martin showed us all over the ship.

When we got back to the mess Martin made us a cup of coffee, we stayed for a couple of hours then walked back to Don and Bev's. Don was home, we had soup and sweet corn and salad, then the three of us played Scrabble and Back Gammon until Don had to meet Bev from work. We retired about 11pm.

Up by 7am had breakfast then drove to Southside of City to have our van serviced. We had a puncture so drove along Bruce Highway to Tyre Service and had it mended, we were lucky the rare wheels were dual so we could still drive. I walked miles to find a PO so I could draw some money. When we got back to town centre, we found a nice park and a lovely shady tree to park under, had lunch. After lunch I wrote to family via Alison and Vera wrote to Di, walked to PO around 4:30, I got a letter from Marie-

QUEENSLAND

Therese. We then drove back to Don and Bev's. Bev was still at work, Don came in soon after while we were having a drink and wondering if we should get tea when Bev got home. She made savoury mince, tomato paste in pasta. At 7:30 Don drove us to the phone, Vera phoned Di to speak to Nola as it was her birthday but they had already left Sydney. Got back and had tea and I made some pumpkin scones. We all played Scrabble. We played Speedy with Bev. Bed at 11pm after a happy evening, they are such a lovely couple.

Rose about 6:30 had breakfast then prepared to leave. Bev went to work and Don left soon after. Had quick showers and left about 8:30. Posted letters then headed North, drove past several beaches, such nice tropical vegetation as we drove towards Mossman.

Cairns is the most northerly city in Queensland, and being a tropical holiday resort many cruises leave from here for the Great Barrier Reef. It overlooks Trinity Bay, and it has an underwater observatory and was an old gold port. On the shoreline in parts there are swamps, good for crabbing. Macalister Range closely follows the coast between Cairns and Mossman forming a high blue-green rainforest behind the town. Mossman is the most northerly sugar town.

Arrived at Mossman and wandered around, not a very big town, bought some 4X beer. Drove out along a nice tree-lined road and continued North. Found a nice secluded spot on the beach north of Port Douglas. Had lunch about 1:30 then both had a snooze. I got up and went for a walk along the beach collecting shells. We had a cup of coffee and decided to stay. Backed the van further in for better parking. Lit a campfire and cooked some pumpkin which I added to the soup already made. I had a rum and Vera had Ginger Wine while tea cooked, ate about 6pm, sat and talked about our nice stay in Cairns, we read for a bit and had an early bed for a change.

Got up went for a run then we had breakfast and we decided to spend the day, I did some painting, Vera cleaned shoes, shells and pottered around. We had a coffee and Vera read then went for a walk. Vera cooked fish and we had potatoes and peas, after tea we played cards and another early bed. It was nice being on our own again in a quiet colourful countryside enjoying the lapping of the waves on shore.

Went for a run along the beach then we had breakfast, packed up and took off for Daintree. This is a very small place, drove through to the end of town where there was a caravan park overlooking a wide river, across from that there was a small shop come hotel. Quite a lovely spot. Went for a walk down to the river and were about to take off when there was a knock on the door and there was Gwen, a lady we'd met down at the rest area out of Gordonvale, they are from Port Lincoln South, Australia. Chatted for a while then drove around to the PO posted a card from Vera to Margaret. Got talking to the lady in the PO and she took me through and showed me her shell collection. Met her husband then we went out into her garden and I told her all about the achee tree (which we had in Jamaica) which she had but didn't know much about the fruit then she presented us with some delicious tangerines and a pawpaw.

We then drove to some tearooms south of Daintree and treated ourselves to a cheese, tomato and onion omelette with salad, sat overlooking their lovely garden. Drove back to Mossman and posted a letter to Marie-Therese, then we turned right and drove a couple of miles to Mossman Gorge. Walked along a narrow path to the Waterfall where I took a photo of Vera on some rocks. Drove south about 16 miles to Turtle Creek Beach and found a lovely parking spot and decided to spend the night, had a couple of shandies then had toast and peanut paste and honey and jam on toast for tea. Played Coon Can 500 and bed about 8pm.

When I got up, I went for a run along the beach and Vera joined me. Had breakfast, washed and tidied up then drove out heading south again to Ellis Beach. Bought bread, found a nice secluded spot just south of Ellis and parked. We got into our bathers and lay on the beach reading and sunbathing for about an hour, returned to the van and had lunch. At 1pm we decided to leave for Cairns and arrived at 2pm, walked to the PO. Vera received a parcel from Loise with two tee-shirts and a couple of cards for her birthday also a card and letter from her mother plus a long letter from Di. I got a letter from Alison and one enclosed from Mum and my sister Teresa. We sat outside the PO and read our mail then went shopping.

We drove south to Bayview to visit Martin and Margaret Jones, sat talking over a beer. Soon after Margaret's parents arrived. Then we drove back to Lake Street. Don came home soon after we arrived, he had bought a hamburger for tea, Bev was at work. We cooked zucchini, tomatoes and rice in the van as the power was off. Later we went in and played Coon Can 500, had showers and watched TV. Four young friends of Don's came in, they were from New Zealand. We sat around drinking and talking till Bev came home at 11pm. We watched the end of the film and off to bed at midnight.

Up early Bev went to work. Don took us into town and we went to the markets and spent about two hours looking around, bought a few vegies then walked back to Lake Street. Made Don and ourselves salad rolls and a cuppa then Don drove us to the Cascades, went for a long very pleasant walk. Got back about 2:30 had showers and washed our hairs. I did some washing and Bev got home and started to cook a meal. Don, Vera and I played cards. Had fish, vegies and salad then Don and Bev got ready and went to a film we went to bed and read. Bev woke us to get the key to get in.

Sunday July 12th. Bev went to work, Don, Vera and I went down to the wharf and watched the Blessing of the Fleet. As the ships were filing out of the harbour it started to rain. When we got home, I cooked bacon, eggs and tomatoes, Vera hung the washing in the shed. Don went visiting, I started a painting and Vera went out to the van and wrote to Loise. When Don got back, he and Vera repaired a window, I prepared a chicken and put it on to cook. When Bev got home, we went for a drive up into the hills to visit the Electric Turbo Plant. Very interesting and a lovely spot with impressive views. When we drove back, we saw a field of sugar cane burning.

Went for drive to Holloway Beach, got out and stretched our legs. Called into Cynthia and Nyle's on the way home. Put vegies on to bake, Vera collected washing. Then we all had a drink and played Coon Can 500 while we waited for the tea to cook. Just sat down to eat when Peter, Gayle and Dean arrived. When we finished eating all had a cuppa, then Peter, Gayle, Don and Bev played cards, Vera and I watched a film. Peter and Gayle went home at 10:30 and we sat talking for a while bed 11pm, we read for a while.

Up at 7am after breakfast we prepared to move out. Left about 8:30 and drove south to Brake Specialist, when we finally found it we made an appointment for 8am Tuesday. Drove back into city parked and walked to the PO, Vera went to Shell House, I went to try and get prints done of sketches. We met up back at the van, had lunch, Vera caught up on her diary and sorted letters and did some mending. I walked back to the PO, got a letter from Di and one from Bill and Joan, from Windang. Met Bev and Gayle at the PO, drove back with them to Lake Street. We all had a cuppa, Vera went out to the van and finished writing to Larry and Gloria, Port Headland. I sat in the lounge and painted. Vera and Bev had showers, Vera made rice for curry and I had a shower. Don came home and we had a drink, had tea then played Scrabble till 19:30.

Got up at 6:30am, had breakfast and got down to Knight's Brake Service by 8am and sat around till workers arrived. They replaced master cylinder and adjusted the brakes. One and a half hours later we drove to Water Street and filled up with discount petrol and drove out of town to Kuranda. Stunning views looking back over the valley to Cairns as we climbed high into the mountains.

Stopped at a park in Kuranda had lunch then drove to the railway station with all its tropical plants and flowers. Then drove to Mareeba, quite a big town. Drove into Tolga and turned right about a mile or so, up a hill to visit Margaret's parents, Gwen and Bryne, her sister Cathie was there too, also met Gwen's parents from Brisbane. Had some tea and chatted for an hour then left and drove to Tinaroo Dam. Gwen and Bryne's house was a huge double story beautifully designed place sitting on five acres with immaculately mowed lawns going down to the road. It was up on a hill overlooking miles of countryside all around.

We drove about a mile and parked down near the yacht club. Very cold with gusty winds, had a couple of brandies to warm ourselves. Made zucchini, tomatoes onion and rice for tea and played a few games of cards before retiring.

Still very blowy when we got up but a spectacular view overlooking the dam. Went for a brisk walk before breakfast. We moved out to Tinaroo looked at the spillway, drove over a bridge and up the other side of the spillway got out and had a look around. On the way back we drove up to lookout, rather a rough road but a lovely view. We drove on to Atherton via a back road, quite a large touristy place, maize producing and is dominated by giant silos. We drove through slowly, then went on south and called into Crater National Park; terrible facilities but quite a striking spot. Met two couples from Western Australia doing the same as us so we had quite a chat. Had lunch and walked around the crater returning a different way and saw three breathtaking waterfalls.

Drove on to Milla Milla Falls and I did a sketch of the rocks below the falls. Milla Milla town is noted for its cheese making. Very hilly being in the Great Dividing Range, nice tree -full scenery. We drove on to Malanda branched off to view a huge Curtain Fig Tree its roots hang down from the trunk metres high. Huge trunks on the trees hold aloft a canopy of various green excluding all but a few rays of sunshine, below a variety of orchids, ferns and mosses flourishing in the rich compost produced from the leaf drop.

There are vast areas that have been cleared for agriculture, Malanda is noted for its biggest milk run. While at the Fig tree we took a couple of photos then drove to Yungaburra turned right had a bit of a look around then drove east another six miles and turned off to Lake Eacham. Parked in a nice spot to stay the night. We walked around paths along the lake, the water in the lake was a most unusual colour, nice and peaceful after all the tourists had left. It is a volcanic crater lake with lush forest encircling it. Had a drink when we got back to the van. Rice and tomatoes with soup for tea, played cards for a couple of hours. Lay in bed recalling our day's travels.

Rained a bit in the early hours. We had just had washes and got dressed when two Rangers knocked on the door. They were quite rude about us staying the night, apparently we were supposed to get a permit from them but there was no sign that said we did.

After breakfast I did a painting and Vera wrote diary and finished a letter to Di. Had lunch 1pm and at 2pm decided to pack up and head for town down the Gillies Highway. The first two miles were a fairly steep climb and there was a lot of road works in progress. Then we began the longest windiest decent I have ever experienced for about twelve miles. Glorious views down into the valley and beyond. I had to keep on pulling off to the side of the road to let cars pass as I was driving in first gear. Iwas very relieved when we arrived at Gordonvale and stopped to stretch our legs and do a spot of shopping then raced back into Cairns to catch the PO before it closed.

Went back to the van, had washes and changed then drove out to the Jonses'. Had a couple of drinks while Margaret got tea. Had lasagne, salad and garlic bread and a very delicious wine, chatted until about 10:30 then

QUEENSLAND

drove to Lake Street and went in to see Don, Bev was at work. I think he was quite glad to see us back in one piece. Fell into bed very tired.

We had a bit of a sleep in, while I got breakfast Vera got a load of washing into Bev's washing machine. Don and Bev were at work, I started to prepare a meal for the evening. Vera was fixing their letter box. Then we trimmed each other's hair and I put a rinse through Vera's hair. Had lunch about 2:30, walked into town to the PO, Vera posted a letter to Di and then we shopped around, bought car stickers for the van and some cards then walked back to 256 and I started to get the tea on. Bev got home about 5pm, Don came in soon after. Had rissoles in tomato sauce, pumpkin, potatoes, peas and carrots followed by rice pudding. We then went around to Gayle and Peter's to watch Dallas in colour on the TV. Had wine and biscuits, cheese olives, and pickled onions. Stayed a couple of hours then home by 11pm.

It was Saturday, Bev, Vera and I walked into town went to Rusty's Markets and wandered around for an hour. Bought some vegies and walked back with all the shopping, our arms were aching, I got back before Vera and Bev, Don was home and Peter had come around for lunch break. Had salad rolls for lunch, Peter and Don went back to work, Vera hosed the van down then we fixed the back of the van as a few rivets had come loose in our travels. Cynthia and Noel came around for a while, then I helped Vera finish mending the letter box and we put it on the stand out in the driveway.

Vera helped me gather my paintings and return them to the van. We had a couple of drinks then Don came home, we played Canasta, had to leave the game while Bev dished up tea, steak casserole and vegies. Finished the Canasta after tea then Don and Bev went over to Gayle and Peter's, we watched a film on TV and bed 11pm.

Up at 8:30 Vera and I went for a walk when we got back Bev was up washing, I rinsed out a couple of blouses then we joined Bev who cooked us up egg, bacon and tomatoes. Don came home from work and Bev cooked up the same for him. Peter, Gayle and Dean came around and asked if we'd like to go for a run in their new boat. So we all drove down to the wharf, launched the boat and we all climbed aboard and went up the estuary to try our luck in crabbing. Then Peter took us for a run. About an hour or so later went back to the crab pots but no luck. Tried fishing but kept pulling up crabs so we reckoned someone emptied the pots while we were away, we weren't quick enough to get the crabs off the line, but it was fun. Bev made a cuppa when we returned Peter and Gayle left. We had showers and Bev made tea - chicken, mushrooms and vegies.

Peter and Gayle returned with their game of Monopoly we all played for a couple of hours, Don won. We had a coffee and Peter and Gayle left and we went out to the van at 11pm. They all are such fun to be around, they all treat us like family.

Incredible Memories

We got up at 7:30 and went in to say good-bye to Don before he went to work. Had breakfast and packed up the van ready to move out. We went into town after Bev woke and did some shopping

Vera got a letter from Di, I bought some canvases to paint on, went back to Lake Street and Bev made salad rolls for lunch. I potted some plants for Bev and Vera hemmed a couple of trousers for Don. Bev got ready for work and when she left we said our sad good-byes. We headed south about 2:30 called in to see Margaret for about an hour. Gave Don a wave as we passed where he works.

Chapter 61

THE FINAL LEG

It had been hard to leave all our kind friends in Cairns. It being a tropical tourist resort, it didn't seem as crowded as other resorts. there was always so much to do and see and most people seem to be on the go. We headed back down south and drove for about an hour and a half then stopped at Diggers Creek rest centre near El Arish. It was only a small rest area, it was raining so we parked near the ablution block. Had a brandy each and a light tea, tomatoes on toast then played cards till 9pm.

After the usual chores we were on the road again by 9am. We drove through Tully turned off to Balgal Beach and found a nice parking strip near toilets. We were very disappointed with the water off the beach, it was very cloudy, but a pleasant spot so we decided to spend the night there listening to the lapping of the small waves. That evening when I went to the toilets, I was surprised to see so many green frogs in the toilet and the cistern. Not easy to perform! The area was not yet developed for tourists so it was nice and quiet.

When we drove on to Ingham, we drove through expansive cane fields, it had a strong Mediterranean flavour. Labour in the early days was provided by Italian migrants. Ingham was surrounded by hills, we got petrol when we arrived then parked in the main street and went for a walk, I called in to the bank. We drove out about twenty miles and turned West into Jourama Falls, found an ideal camping area by a creek, had lunch and decided to stay the night. We set up camp then went for a long walk, crossed a river, clambered over rocks and up windy path to see the falls. Took some photos.

On the way back stopped to talk to a few people camping there. It took ages to get the fire going as the wood was wet and green. Had rissoles, mashed potato and peas for tea the played Coon Can 500 till 9pm.

Rose to find it rather wet, it had been raining overnight, we decided to stay. I started a painting and Vera caught up on her diary. Had lunch, still

Incredible Memories

raining, Vera cleaned the battery terminals. I wrote a couple of letters, had an early tea bacon, eggs and tomatoes. Played cards for a couple of hours.

After breakfast we got ready to move out we arrived at Townsville about mid-day called into CIG to get gas bottle filled and the bottle tested. We left the bottle and headed into town. We parked near the TV station and walked into town. We wandered around the mall, called at the PO and went to the bank then checked out the shops. At four o'clock we drove out to pick up the gas bottle.

Then drove North to Cape Pallarenda along the beach to a picnic area but thought we had seen another better one on the way so decided to drive halfway back to that one. Parked for the night, sat drinking a couple of beers looking out to sea. Had tea, played cards till 8:30.

Got up early had breakfast, tidied up to leave for town. Talked to a young couple from New Zealand who had also spent the night near us. They were on their way to Darwin so we were able to give them some good spots to camp. Drove back towards town then turned right into Town Common Wildlife Sanctuary for a spot of bird watching. Did not see as many as we thought we would, drove on into town and parked under a huge fig tree, walked to the mall, I sold some coins for $96, Vera browsed around a book shop and we met up at Kelly's Kitchen. Bought sandwiches and iced coffee and sat under umbrellas and had lunch. Then shopped for groceries and walked back to the van heavily laden. Three thirty we left town and headed south again on Bruce Highway.

Drove about 25 miles to Mt Elliot National Park which was about three miles in off the highway, parked the van in the picnic area, walked over a bridge to get a permit from the Ranger. We lit a fire when we got back and were about to start tea when Keith and Kathy turned up. We last met them at Bowen. They sat and ate takeaway while we cooked bacon, tomatoes and eggs. Sat talking over a cup of tea and after two hours they took off back to tomato farm south of Bowen. Tidied up, played cards till 9:30.

We lit the fire as soon as we got up, had breakfast then moved out on the road south. Drove to Ayr then over the Burdekin River into Home Hill. We continued till we arrived at Bowen, we were at Doreen's by noon. She wasn't home so we had lunch and a short nap. It was pretty warm, decided to call on Daphne, we parked under a nice shady tree. Daphne was very pleased to see us, we met her husband, Alan. Had a cuppa and stayed chatting till about 5pm, real nice people. We promised to call again next afternoon.

We drove back to Doreen's and as we drove in the back way we were greeted by Don. Doreen was going to Don's for tea and they wanted us to join them but as we were tired we decided not to. Had showers, cooked tea and did some washing and went to bed and read, lights out at 10:30. It's so nice being allowed to feel right at home and being able to use washing

THE FINAL LEG

machines and have nice warm showers, and also somewhere to park and enjoy the friendship of such lovely people.

Got up at 6:30. We were supposed to be going to Gray's Beach swimming and skiing with friends of Don's. Doreen had breakfast with us. I unpacked my paintings and took them into the house, sat around talking and pottering around as Don didn't turn up. He finally arrived at noon, we all decided to go to Queen's Beach with a picnic. We followed Doreen and Don down and spent a very pleasant two and a half hours under a shady tree then at about 3:30 bade them good-bye and drove around to Daphne and Alan's. Had a cuppa and Alan marked some good spots for camping on our map. I helped Daphne cook a chicken with Spanish rice which all enjoyed.

We introduced them to Stone's Ginger and lemonade which they enjoyed. Then did washing up and Vera made lemon lime and bitters for Daphne; she thought it was rather good. They decided to stay home with us instead of going to dancing lessons. We taught them King in the Corner, also Last Card, then Alan fell asleep so we played Coon Can 500 till eleven we had a cuppa and Alan went to bed. Daphne enjoyed having company, we played cards to the small hours of the morning. We returned to our van, which was parked in the road. It was a really good night.

Got up at 7:30 and said good-bye to Alan when he went to work. Had breakfast and then went in to say good-bye to Daphne, Doreen turned up to take us to the Handycraft Centre so we followed her. She showed us all the work the disabled do. Took our leave and went to Woolworths and bought a few things, went and bought petrol and some vegies and headed out of town. We drove south to Rilet's Tomato Farm, called at the big packing sheds, met Cathy and the foreman "One-armed-bandit Gordon". No luck with getting a job but he gave us a box of tomatoes and one of capsicums. When driving out we met Keith he was very surprised we didn't get work.

Stopped down the road at 1:30 and had lunch. Called into several farms to ask for work it was very disappointing not to get work. We drove through Proserpine, about 35 miles north of Mackay we turned west into Marion. Six miles on to Eton then south west to Nebo, 18 miles near Mt Spence on the Park Downs Highway we parked for the night next to a PWD metal dump. Had a beer and a quick tea and early bed somewhat exhausted.

Got up early after a good night's sleep, after breakfast we continued towards Clermont. It was a good highway passed unusual peeked rocks and hills. Turned on to Gregory Highway, stopped and had lunch of yoghurt and mango juice, then drove on to Capella. Stopped at a rest centre and had a hot shower and washed our hairs, such a good feeling. Drove on to Emerald arrived about 3pm, called into Woolies, the bakers and PO, no mail. Posted letter to Di then drove out of town and camped about nine miles out. Had a couple of drinks, wrote letters and cards, tea and we decided to go back to Emerald. Bed about 9pm.

Incredible Memories

    Got up early had breakfast then drove into town. It was cold. Called at PO still no mail. Vera registered with CES then went for an interview at Woolworths. We then checked caravan sites, had lunch and decided to go out to Rubyvale and Goanna Flats. We stopped at Sapphire and sold the tomatoes and capsicums at caravan parks and houses, made $16 dollars. Drove through Rubyvale and on about two miles on a rather bad road and found the Birk's Villa Nova parked on a rise. We caught up with them last in Sydney. They were quite surprised to see us as we were too, they were there with their son Jeff and his lovely part Aboriginal wife. They were there to see a couple of gem cutters, Carlos and Joe, they showed us different sapphires, Jeff bought two stones.

    We walked back and Ol, one of the people staying at the camp, had a big pot of stew going we all had a good tea then sat around listening to Prince Charles and Diana's wedding. Ol made a huge damper which we all enjoyed with Golden Syrup and a cup of tea. Johansen Borge joined us, what lovely company, we spent a most enjoyable evening but it was getting cold outside and all decided to call it a day at 11pm. Rather tired.

    Got up early after a cold night, got a fire going and set up our camping gear, then had breakfast with the Birks. Then they showed us how to find sapphires. Vera and I started digging near the van. Wal lent us some tools and suggested places to try. Vera caught up on her diary. All stopped for lunch. Returned to digging Vera went exploring and brought back some wood. Stopped at 4pm, Wal and Jeff had a swim in the dam which was down from where we were parked. We had washes and changed into clean cloths. Cooked broccoli, silver beet and a curry stew, had a couple of drinks sitting around the campfire. After tea we all sat around the fire talking till 9pm then had a cup of Milo and went to bed, as it was still so cold.

    Ol and I got two fires going after we got up had breakfast and then we all got stuck into work. I was determined to find some precious stones but Vera preferred the idea of a job to fund her travels. She started to walk to Rubyvale and got a lift. When she got back (a lift in a 4wd this time) we had a cup of coffee when she got back then went on fossicking. Finished at 4pm and cleaned up, had a drink then tea of zucchini, tomatoes and rice. After tea we all sat around talking till the fire was nearly out bed 10pm.

    Saturday August the 1st. Up early had breakfast with the Birks, took a couple of photos. Did some digging while the Birks broke camp. They left some gear with us, a pick and sieve which we were to return when we back in Sydney and the rest to drop off at friends in Emerald. They left about 10am. Did lots more digging and knocked off at 4pm, had a wash and an early tea. It was still a bit chilly so we played cards till 8:30 and then to bed to get warm.

    We spent the next couple of weeks trying our luck at digging. Most mornings we got up early and lit the fire. We'd fossick then sift and wash the stones, chatting to the others there, then break for lunch with a shandy. A rest in the afternoon would be followed a coffee and more fossicking. Evening were spent around the fire, sharing food, chatting, playing cards or reading by gaslight.

There was quite a community at Russian Gully; Joe a permanent, a Romanian, Anne Sutton a New Zealander and a guy called Gerald. Gerald camped near us and slept in a station wagon. Then Johansen a Norwegian who had a tent near Gerald. Bill and Ann, an elderly couple in their 70s showed us some sapphires, opals and other stones they had dug from other fields. Everyone was very friendly. It was a quiet and peaceful spot.

One day Vera went into Emerald with Joe and Joanne. She called for post and posted cards and got 1st Day covers of the wedding. Vera went to CES and then went to buy a lamp for Gerald. When Vera returned from Emerald, she gave me a telegram from Alison to phone Marie-Therese. After tea Gerald took us into the PO and I phoned Marie-Therese and was told they are expecting another baby in March! Also got all family news while talking to her.

A couple pulled up in a Toyota, Joe and Amy from Western Australia, we chatted for a while. Gerald came up and we drove through Rubyvale to Reward Cut to check it out but decided it was better to stay at Russian Gully.

One day I went for a walk to check out the windmills and found signs of rabbits down at the creek, and also found the road didn't go past the windmill. Vera set a couple of traps. Johansen came up and joined us and we played cards. We tried some of his Southern Comfort, not bad. Vera checked the traps and got a nice big one, skinned it and cleaned it and left it in saltwater over night.

I went for a walk to try my luck at specking, interesting but no luck. Later that day Vera, Gerald and I walked up to Joanne and Fred's with some bread for the pet Kangaroos. We met Don the publican from Anakie, also the yardman George. We joined them with a glass of homemade beer, a strong brew! Got back at 5:30, changed into trousers and boots, borrowed Gerald's gun and walked about 2 miles with Johansen to Policeman's Knob. We saw a few roos but they were out of range so returned at sunset.

Vera had finally got a job at The Pastoral College. Gerald came up and put her gear in the car plus water containers and drove into Emerald. At 4:30 we went to the caravan park and put the tent up for Vera then went to Emerald Hotel and had a couple of drinks.

some quals came visiting out of the scrub. Very exciting.

The days went by and I kept on digging, sieving and washing and was finally rewarded in finding my first blue sapphire. Very exciting!

Friday August 14th, my George's birthday. I had lain awake since 5:30 so decided to get up and write a letter to the family via George. At six we were deciding to drive into Rubyvale or further to pick up Vera, when she arrived with Paddy and his wife. Vera was all dressed up in her uniform which looked quite out of place in the bush surroundings! Got her a drink

Incredible Memories

while she changed then we had tea, very nice soup. However, Vera and Gerald always ended up arguing about something. He was a bit of a bore and seemed to enjoy stirring Vera and she always bit back. The lads stayed till 8pm, by this time Vera was very annoyed. A couple of days later, Gerald and Vera were at loggerheads. After he left Vera went off her brain about him. Then she washed the van down and painted the wheels silver. Johansen came up, sat talking to him for a while, I think he realized Vera was upset. He said a few words to Vera and then left. Vera was in a terrible mood all day and succeeded in upsetting me too. We didn't say much for the rest of the day. I have told her I can't handle her going off the deep end over such trivial things. All of Rubyvale must have heard her. She spoke to a couple who were out specking and managed to get a lift with them into Cross Roads. Both of us were pretty upset by the time she left, but it was a relief as it was peaceful again.

I lay and read for a while and had a little snooze. I got up at 5pm, had a wash and lit the fire. Gerald and Johansen came up with some beer and Claret. Gerald had already had enough to drink. He said he heard Vera going off and wondered if I was alright. He said all of Russian Gully would have heard her. I told him it was none of his business and didn't want to discuss it anymore and with that he got up and left. Johansen stayed, I had tea he said he had already eaten. He was quite concerned and hoped the quarrel was not too serious, I told him I could handle it. We spent the rest of the evening discussing music and he told me about his home. He left at 8:30 and I went to bed and read for a while and fell asleep about 11pm.

The next morning, I walked down to Anne and Bill's spot and fossicked around then sat watching the birds have a bath and fly about. When I returned Anne Sutton was wandering down with a book called "Gem Fields" by Glen Gillard; a sketch book on Anakie and surrounds. We talked for a long time then she went off to her sieving up the road.

The following day, I dug on a corner behind the van and found a nice little blue, this spurred me on to work all afternoon but found nothing else.

A couple of days later, Johansen came up and said he was going to Rubyvale, I went with him and drew out $20, still no mail, funny how much one looks for contact with friends and family. When we got back, I finished cleaning the van and did a bit of sieving and found a big Star Bomb then a Bronze Star. These are semi-precious stones which are not transparent but it felt so good when one finds something (even if it's not quite a sapphire!) I continued digging sieving and washing until 4:30. Quite a nice breeze sprung up as the weather had warmed up.

The next day I found another Blue Bomb and a little Bronze ball. That night I listened to the radio till 10pm news, biggest Green gem found on Poverty Hill, 113 grams they reported. That would be nice. Then again the next day I worked till 5pm, rewarded with a very small Party, another semi-precious brown stone.

THE FINAL LEG

One day I walked up to 'Rangi' to visit Nick and Anne Sutton, quite a distance away. Anne took me down a mine where Nick was sitting and talked for a spell, then walked back to their shack. It was a very comfortably set up abode with almost every mod con. I had lunch with them and a very nice home-made Sherry. Nick went back to digging and Anne and I talked until 4:50. They were such a nice couple, they made me feel like family.

On Monday August 24th it started to rain at 5am. It cleared enough so we planned to cook the remainder of the kangaroo the hangi way. Johansen and I collected wood and dug hole in old fireplace, Wal and Ol had covered it with a bit of tin. We kept the fire going nearly all day. Johansen stayed in the van and played my accordion. Had lunch and we talked then he played the accordion again. At 2pm we buried the roo and vegies in the hot hole and put the fire on top. As it had been raining all day Nick came over and said I should maybe go into Emerald while the road was still good as the forecast was for more days of rain. After tea I packed up and broke camp and made for Emerald. My reception from Vera was not too warm, but she moved out of the tent into the van.

The next day it rained most of the day, Vera went to work and I wrote letters and my diary and read for a while then got tea ready for Vera's return. We had some of the rest of the roo with more vegies. We played cards until bed at 8:30. The next day was dry. Vera went to work and when the tent had dried out, I took it down and stowed it under the bed. It wasn't very long before the spot had another tent on it. A young Canadian couple Ann and Ron, a real nice pair from a small town in the Rocky Mountain north of Vancouver. Had the rest of the roo for tea when Vera came home from work. Then I introduced her to the new couple we sat and talked till bed at 8:30.

The next morning after Vera went to work, I decided mid-morning to drive into town and parked across the road from The Commonwealth bank. When it opened, I withdrew some money and did a bit of grocery shopping. Then I sat in the van painting, it seemed to attract a few people so I pinned a couple of my paintings on the open door of the van and managed to sell one. This was very satisfying. I sat there till Vera joined me after work and we drove back to the caravan park. Anne came over and said someone had tried to park in our spot till she said we were already there.

Emerald is regarded as the capitol of the Central Highlands, it lies in from Rockhampton. The industries include coal, cotton, grain and beef products. The town is located in one of the biggest gem fields. Most of the original buildings were lost in several huge fires that occurred. The railway station is considered one of the first in Australia, it survived. Outside the town hall stands a huge fossilised tree. We found it a very friendly town and the surrounding countryside quite attractive bar the coal mining area.

It was getting close to the time when I would be sending my overseas Christmas cards, so during the day I sat outside the van and painted Australian scenery as I remembered it on my travels. I had brought blank

Incredible Memories

cards and envelopes with me so decided to paint in water colours. As I sat painting, people wandered past to see what I was doing, I no sooner painted half a dozen then I would have a buyer. So for a week that is what I spent my time doing, this after completing my mundane chores. On the Thursday I would drive into town and park opposite the Bank painting on canvas and also painting cards, again no sooner than I painted something I would sell it.

The weather had cleared so at the weekend of the second week, Vera and I returned to Russian Gully as I had dug a heap before I left which needed sieving and washing. On the Saturday we arrived back in the gem fields called for mail and arrived at our old spot to find someone had gone through my heap. We went around saying good-bye to the Suttons and any that we knew that were still there.

On returning to the caravan park we found that all around us had kept it empty for our return, which was good of them as it was a good spot serving us with electricity and close to the ablutions and overlooking a nice grassed area with a clump of very mature trees beyond. Anne and Ron were staying on for a few days so we caught up with them again. They gave us their address in Canada and invited us to visit them if we travelled to their neck of the woods. They bought one of my oil paintings because it reminded them of places they had visited while traveling in the Northern Territory. One evening Vera never got home from work till10pm. I was worried sick as she used to walk in from the College to town after work but it turned out she had met a guy from the mines and spent the evening him at some pub drinking. She was pretty well under the weather by the time she returned to the van. I had a few words with her and she couldn't see why I was so worried.

As I was not going back to the gem fields I went and visited Wal and Ol's friends and returned the tools. The lady, Jan, had rescued some joeys that had lost their mums in road accidents, so they had a few kangaroos wandering around their large property. I asked if I could go around one day to sketch some of them, she said I was welcome any time. One morning I was sitting trying to do some sketches and this kangaroo with one of its front legs missing, kept coming over and trying to get my pencil!

I spent several days over at Jan's, sometimes we would have a cup of tea together and she told me a lot about Emerald and how she started rescuing and looking after the joes, that at times she had to feed them every four hours and look after their wounds if they had any. A full-time job, but she felt she was getting too old to continue so only kept the few she had as they would find it hard to survive out in the wild.

All together for the month we stayed in Emerald I sold several oil paintings. One a German couple liked so much they bought it before it was completely dry, and went wandering of down the road holding it out till they got back to their hotel, they were staying a few more days so it would by dry enough for them to travel with.

THE FINAL LEG

I missed my bush life with an open fire and the peace and quiet. I must have painted at least 200 cards all together. I even had my photo taken by a traveling journalist from Brisbane. He ordered six cards, paid for them and I posted them to him. By return he sent the photo and a bit he had written about me. Vera and I had boosted our bank accounts and decided to move on.

Emerald to Rockhampton via Black Water, a big coal mining area. There was a delightful Japanese Garden there with little bridges, amazing that one finds these huge surprises in the most unlikely townships. This of course makes our travels amazing and so interesting. It reminded us that life must be lived to the full with just so much to enjoy and of course learn about in this wonderful country of ours

Duaringa, with historical buildings, former sawmill and because of so much felling no longer a timber industry. Mackenzie Park with a lovely picnic area, tall stringy bark trees shading it. The Aboriginal people used the bark to make rope and various other things like baskets. We had lunch enjoying the surrounds and bird life.

Then on to Mount Hay Tourist Park, where we fossicked for thunder eggs. We were given a bucket for $6 and told that we could fill it then return and have some stones cut and polished for a price. We spent all afternoon examining these rough but interesting stones of all shapes and sizes. A large one we had cut had an extraordinary centre, it even had a small pocket of liquid, like water. So exciting to think that it was probably captured steam millions of years ago which when it cooled turned to water. Around this were formations like fine coral and green fern formations all encased in jasper which was in shades of pale grey with blue streaks.

The manager said he had never in all the years he had cut stones seen anything quite like it. If we let him have half of it, he would cut and polish six others for no payment. The eggs are formed as molten lava blasted into the air, falls then cools and crystals form inside gas bubbles. It was so exciting to witness the various shapes in the ones we had cut and then to see the result when polished. One of the smaller eggs had what looked like a blue dolphin swimming in this greyish jasper.

Back on the road with our treasure, just past Gracemere we turned right onto Bruce Highway south of Rockhampton. We drove through farmlands full of cane, taller than the van. When we reached Gin Gin, we turned east again towards Bundaberg. Gin Gin is a small town with many historical buildings. We filled up with petrol then on to the city renowned for its rum, an historic town centre at the heart of Burnett River. The sugar city of the Central Queensland. Set among tall green cane fields. There are several sugar mills, it is the only port with sugar bulk-loading facilities in Central Queensland. Had a bit of a look around but as it was getting late, we left and found a place to camp for the night between Eliot Heads and Eliot River.

Incredible Memories

After a good night's sleep we made for Childers on the Bruce Highway. The plains again such a flourishing sugar industry. Headed for Maryborough at the mouth of Mary River, with many colonial buildings. There is an historic gun just near the swimming baths. One looks out to Fraser Island. From there we continued on Bruce Highway and turned left, not many miles and we arrived at Gympie. The town arose around the miners' camp during a gold rush in the late 19th century. Today's crooked road follows the original wagon track that had run between the tents.

Gympie from the Aboriginal gimpi-gimpi for the stinging nettle that once grew in the area. It had been a great forest area before all the tree cutting and milling. There is a section of two-hundred-year-old Kauri. One could cry at the thought of what we have missed.

Only 20 miles down to Cooloola Rocks and Minerals, just off the highway, but we decided to carry on a bit further to find a camping spot. We turned off to the left on a side road to Pomona and not far in from Bruce Highway found a lovely quiet area. It was raining so we cooked tea in the van, played a few games of cards then went to bed and read.

We were woken by very noisy bird song. It was still wet so we went back to Bruce Highway at about 9am, turned left at the highway. We drove through farmlands until we reached the Big Pineapple. And it is big. Of course the pineapples are much shorter than the cane but quite a sight to witness. The giant fibre glass icon marks the entrance to a theme park which we did not go to. The drive took us through some forest, found a spot to drive onto and stopped for lunch. Drove further on and decided to turn east to Caloundra to get near the ocean again. The beaches were sandy and very inviting but for the crowds and having to pay for everything, so did not stay for long. We bought petrol and left looking for a spot to spend the night.

We drove toward the Glass House Mountains, a spectacular sight. Oddly shaped, jutting abruptly upward from a landscape of farmland, forests and fields. No longer active volcanic mountains. We found a place about three miles away but it was a busy road until quite late that night. After tea we played cards for a spell then went to bed and read.

We returned to Bruce Highway and continued south. Looking at the map it looked like we had a long stretch with most of the townships off the highway. After about 40 miles, we saw a sign to Caboolture Historical Village. That sounded interesting. A pleasant surprise, the museum has more than 70 historic buildings that have been relocated. They are restored and range from PO, police station, sawmill, church and village pub. A fascinating town which one could spend a full day to see all, as all housed period furniture and trappings. We had lunch at a small café, a ploughman's dinner and coffee, a pleasant venue but coffee not too good.

We left about 3:30 and returned to the highway via another route as on the map it looked like it would be a quieter road. Crossed Caboolture River and found a lovely wooded area to camp for the night. The night was full of

THE FINAL LEG

wildlife sounds with quite a lot of nocturnal movement accompanied by a loud call from a bird I could not identify. We rose early as usual and had a bit of a walk before breakfast then continued to Bruce Highway.

We drove south for about four miles and saw a sign to Deception Bay, turned left and east another four miles. It turned out to be a picturesque bay and we were again near the water and change of scenery. We stopped and had a bit of a wander, enjoyed listening to sea gulls cry. We drove south along the bay for a couple of miles then turned west to re-join Bruce Highway. Turned south and drove through mostly farmlands till we reached Apsley where we stopped for lunch. We still had 12 miles to Brisbane.

While in Emerald we got to know a young couple who had won a new house on a winning lottery ticket. They invited us to visit them and as their house was in a new suburb in northern Brisbane, we phoned them. They were very pleased to hear from us and gave us further directions on how to find them. They had originally given us a mud map. So off we went and made a beeline to them, parked outside this massive home of theirs, which was worth about a million dollars. They and the two children gave us a warm welcome when we arrived at 4:30.

They invited us to stay in the house which had ample room but as they were in a cul-de-sac we chose to stay in the van. Particularly as we were early risers and liked to go for an early morning walk. We were treated to a delicious Chinese takeaway which gave us a choice of several different dishes. Jess didn't enjoy cooking so it appeared they lived mostly on takeaways! Her husband, Len, was a mechanic by trade and said he would give us a service while we were there. They wanted us to spend a few days with them. While there they showed us around a few places but after a couple of days we were on the move again.

Jess told us of a supermarket near them where we could stock up on groceries. So after farewells we hit the road at 10am. When we got to the complex it was sort of up on a hill and the parking bays were so small we took up two bays parking at an angle. We had several complaints from other shoppers. Bought our goods and were soon on the road again.

There seemed to be so many roads and the traffic constant we decided to give Brisbane a miss and look for a sign which said, "Express Way". Brisbane is about 29 miles from the coast, there is a port on the banks of Brisbane River. It is Queensland's Capital City and the 3rd largest in Australia. It is a very busy prosperous and very rapidly developing commercial and industrial centre and lies 104 miles north of the border with New South Wales.

It has been called the City of the Seven Hills having as a backdrop hills to the west of the city. As we drove through a maze of streets passing many park areas and driving down tree-lined streets, we finally came to a sign to the Express Way which we knew would lead us to the Pacific Highway. In

Incredible Memories

a way it was a relief to be out of the hustle and bustle of the city but a shame we did not enjoy some of the interesting parts of Brisbane.

We followed signs to Beenleigh and Southport and the Pacific Highway. The scenery still very tropical with farmlands growing fruit, avocados, vegetables and banana plantations. About five miles past Oxenford we turned east on the Gold Coast Highway making for the coast again. Southport to Burleigh Heads we passed high-rise buildings and lots of places to visit like Sea-world at Southport and the largest walk-through aviary in Australia, Andalucian Park with Spanish dancing horses. Lovely lakes and picnic areas, very inviting but too expensive for our pockets.

Then on to Surfers Paradise with a 32-kilometre chain of beaches stretching to Coolangatta, offering many types of entertainments, eateries, hotels of all sizes, but the beaches being the biggest attraction. We drove through to Burleigh Heads where we joined the Pacific Highway again. We were able to enjoy the scenery but unable to afford visiting the venues offered, there was enough to see during our drive.

We stopped at a picnic area near Burleigh Heads and had lunch while watching the world go by, a fauna reserve at Burleigh National Park where we stopped. Always nice to relax among trees which invariably house birds, always a delight.

The next 16 miles to Coolangatta where we crossed from Queensland into New South Wales was a very picturesque drive with sugar cane fields and banana plantations. This being the southern end of the Gold Coast. Out on the point a lighthouse and memorial to Captain Cook. We left the views of the Coral Sea when the highway turns west and inland to Murwillumbah with blue hills surrounding the town which sits on the Tweed River. It is the centre district growing bananas and sugar cane and supports a flourishing dairy industry. It lies 32 miles in from the mouth of the river. The surroundings were very attractive so we thought it would be nice to find a spot to camp for the night. A couple of miles on we found a creek so drove off the highway and as the weather was dry we made a fire and cooked tea outside. Played cards before bed.

In the morning we went for a lovely walk along the creek, it was a bit chilly but enjoyed being in the bush again. Interesting to see different scenery nearly every day and to meet fellow travellers. The sugar cane with its feathery pale purple flowers above a mass of greenery, the broad green leaves of the banana plant which grow in such neat rows or even to glimpse green pastures dotted with cattle grazing happily or just laying there chewing their cud. Admiring the wildflowers along the roadside, something to stop, at times, to get a closer look. But one of the most enjoyable things while traveling is to stop and camp for a night or two amongst the unique Australian trees observing all around us. Something that always amazed me was the bright green regrowth on trees black trunks that had been in a bush fire.

THE FINAL LEG

After our interesting walk and breakfast and tidying up the sight we left about 8:30 and were back on the highway making for Brunswick Heads. There were several minor roads leading east out to the coast but we stuck to the highway till we came to Ewingsdale where we turned east to Byron Bay. Cape Byron is the most easterly point on mainland Australia, the land seemed very low. Byron Bay used to be a whaling station, the lighthouse stands up on a rocky mound, and there is a sign which says it is the most easterly point and was erected by the Byron Bay Progress Association.

It boasts of its excellent holiday climate. The lighthouse is the most powerful in the southern hemisphere. Needless to say, it was a very busy town with interested visitors. We decided to stay the night as we were pretty tired so drove out a wee way to a side road. Next morning took a road west just before The Everglades with a sign to Bangalow and joined the Pacific Highway again and turned south.

The Richmond Range was to our right, the landscape a stunning picture outlined by a very blue sky and on to Ballina in the Richmond River Valley at the mouth of the of the Richmond River. It is a prosperous dairying, tropical fruit and cane growing district. The highway ran east of Maclean, we turned west on a side road and found a quiet spot to have lunch, we also stretched our legs. We had thought about going further west to Lismore to catch up a couple of George, my son's, friends but changed our minds. We phoned friends of Bev and Don in Grafton to say we were on our way and could we call in. They said they had heard we on the road so were expecting us.

So once back on the Pacific Highway and going south driving through farms growing tropical and sub-tropical fruit, avocados, bananas and sugar cane we entered Grafton. What a stunning sight greeted us, the streets lined with Jacaranda trees in full, bloom, their beautiful blue flowers, some already falling and covering the pavements. We had been given directions to Dot and Glen's place arriving just after four, Glen was still at work. As usual such a warm welcome. We went in and enjoyed a cup of tea with some homemade cake before Glen came in.

Dot had made a very tasty stew with baked potatoes, in their skin, plus a fresh salad. They were originally from Canada and reminded us very much of Bev and Don. They offered us their driveway for the night. We declined a night of games as we were so tired. Next morning Dot took us for a drive around Grafton, what a pretty town. The Clarence River runs down into Grafton from the Dividing Range. This region of green countryside, lush forests and almost tropical climate makes for very comfortable living. The river flats make for good pastures and grazing for cattle.

Honey eaters and lorikeets are seen in abundance and make a colourful sight among the blue Jacaranda. We stopped at a quaint little café on the way and had soup of the day, pumpkin, and homemade bread rolls and a nice cup of coffee. Drove back through the picturesque square with Dot and all had a siesta before joining Dot for a cup of tea and more homemade cake.

I offered to help Dot prepare the evening meal and Vera borrowed their washing machine and did our washing. We had a BBQ out in the back garden, sausages, steak with potato salad and a salad of tomatoes, cucumber, and capsicum all from the garden, with a nice homemade dressing. It was a gorgeous evening and we spent a very pleasant chatty time with such a lovely couple. We thanked them for their hospitality and invited them to visit us should they travel west.

Next morning Glen knocked on our door and said goodbye before he went to work. Dot asked us in to join her for breakfast. We left at 8:30 and on looking at the map there weren't any big towns, about 24 miles south of Graton we came to Halfway Creek found a spot and had an early lunch.

The drive through to Woolgoolga was mainly banana plantations and the odd forest area. Woolgoolga with uncrowded beaches and rocky headlands backed by forest. A prominent feature being the gleaming white onion-shaped dome of the temple on top of the highest hill. It is a Sikh temple built by the descendants of Sikhs from the Punjab. We felt we were in little India, such a friendly town, they developed the growth of bananas.

We had seen on the map Emerald Beach so thought we would make for that to spend the night. It was about seven miles further on. A nice quiet beach where we could park. We enjoyed listening to the waves splashing onto the beach from the South Pacific Ocean. We went for a walk along the beach letting the sea water wash over our feet. Had an early night after tea, we had treated ourselves to an Indian take-away.

Back on the Pacific Highway in the morning, our next aim was for Coffs Harbour, which appeared to be just off the highway. It is the biggest sea boarder between Newcastle and the Queensland border. It is a sheltered inlet, had been a dairying town but then the farmers grew fruit and vegetables and later bananas won out and the hillsides are covered with banana plantations. The famous Big Banana outside the farm and theme parks confronts one. It is a real tourist resort. We drove through and did a loop back to the highway. On the way out spotted a place to park and have lunch.

We thought we would make it to Nambucca Heads and get off the highway near the ocean again, and here spend the night.

It was a very pleasant drive down through farmlands and many areas of forest. We have been fortunate in having good weather and being not too far from the ocean there were very cooling breezes. Arriving at Nambucca Heads, which was only a couple of miles off the highway. We were greeted by a picturesque vista of the Pacific Ocean. The town is divided by the Nambucca River. The name apparently originated from the Aboriginal word meaning 'Crooked' which well describes the river which winds its way through the Nambucca Valley.

THE FINAL LEG

We drove down to the beach and found a spot to park but thought better of staying there as there seemed to be a set up caravan park and thought we would be moved on by a Ranger. So after walking around the beach area we drove up another road leading down to the river, which we took and there was an ideal level spot to back into. But we couldn't sit outside as the mosquitoes came out to greet us. We sprayed repellent around the door and driver's window which had a flyscreen but didn't trust it was sufficient, also did the sleeping area. Cooked tea in the van and sat playing cards till bed 9pm.

The sun rose early and woke us to the sound of many birds. After breakfast thought we would go for a walk along the river but found the mosquitoes too friendly, so took to the road again hoping to reach Kempsey for lunch. Back on the Highway, which is very busy. The road was winding as we followed the river then we seemed to be driving west till we reached Macksville when we went south again. Nine miles past a small town called Warrell Creek, there was a picnic area where we pulled into it was surrounded by trees which gave us shade as it was a hot day. We followed a path and stretched our legs for half an hour, had lunch accompanied by lots of flies then carried on as there were still many miles to Kempsey. We wound our way through farmlands and rain forests, although they are small they don't have as many kinds of plants and animals as the rain forests farther inland. But each is a mini rainforest with strangler figs with thick vines and a variety of ferns and orchids. These mainly fringing the dunes and giving a delightful change as we came to them. Especially as they attracted so many birds.

When we crossed the Macleay River we knew we were close to Kempsey. Kempsey is the centre of the Macleay Valley, great dairy farming. There are factories engaged in making butter, cheese and producing milk. There are also piggeries where bacon is processed. The area is a large producer of maize. A very busy town, we parked and had a wander, bought groceries and then drove to a petrol station and filled up, before moving out to find our spot for the night. Re-joined the highway and about 10 miles south of Kempsey found a lovely picnic area by Maria River, again among forest trees. A couple in a Combi were the only other ones occupying the area but we never saw them and when we got up in the morning they were gone.

Back on the highway, drove through Pipers Creek and another small town, Telegraph Point and just beyond crossed over Wilson River. Then about another ten miles the turn off to Port Macquarie. Quite a picturesque drive and the road not too bad but of course narrower than the highway. On the north side was the Hastings River, which goes into the Tasman Sea, so Port Macquarie juts into the sea. It is a coastal resort offering a warm climate and beautiful beaches. Pacific Drive traveling south of the town offers access to the beaches and halfway along there was a surf club. On the drive out on

Incredible Memories

the main road, there were scrubby forest of Banksia, honey eaters and lorikeets were in abundance.

Back on the Pacific Highway and drove south through hill country and forest. At Herons Creek we pulled into a picnic area for lunch and a bit of a wander. Then carried on towards Taree went through small towns called Kew and John's River, Moorland, and Coopernook and arrived at Taree on the Manning River, we walked around and got some groceries. Then out just south to a small place called Purfleet and found a picnic area on a side road to Old Bar. Here we relaxed with a drink and made a pasta dish with mince done in a tomato sauce with carrots and peas. Played a few games of cards and bed.

Next morning, we set of for Newcastle. The road again among hills and forest, crossing a few creeks to the small town of Nabiac, most of the towns are State forest, then on to Bulahdelah through rolling hills and State forests. Over the Myall River, Nerong State Forest, the about 40 odd miles to Karuah on Port Stephens Great Lakes. This is a large deep inlet more than double the size of Sydney Harbour. Despite residents along the shores, it is relatively unspoilt, with a backdrop to the west of Karuah State Forest. It was a delightful spot. We drove nine miles further south and camped in a picnic area by Twelve Mile Creek surrounded by cool forest.

We enjoyed a quiet evening drink listening to the breeze blowing through the tops of the trees and the bird calls. Heated the rest of the mince and pasta and had another drink, played some cards and retired.

Next morning, we left early, just down the Highway we crossed Pipeclay Creek and a sign announcing a lion safari off on a side road to our right. We soon came to Raymond Terrace which was settled by Cedar cutters. It had a large nature park, besides several animals it also housed lions. About ten mile down the highway we crossed Hunter River, over Hexham Bridge. It seemed quite a large river. At Hexham we met up with New England Highway to our right. The Pacific Highway turned east, not far from Hexham the river that divided and formed an island, Kooragang Island. Not far down the highway we had the river running close to the highway.

Thirteen miles further on we branched off to Newcastle just past a railway line. The Hunter River was just like a huge inlet, Newcastle being down at the mouth. It is the second largest city in New South Wales, and third largest port in Australia, exporting coal, steel and iron products and general manufacturing. Besides wool and farming products all to various parts of the of the Commonwealth and other parts of the world. It began as a convict outpost, its main industry was coal mining but now has heavy industry. It has many beaches, the Civic Centre precinct had a Captain Cook Memorial fountain. To the north is Newcastle Bight and the Tasman Sea to the east.

THE FINAL LEG

We left by Memorial Drive with many beaches. At Merewether we found a camping area to spend the night. We saw on the map it was still a day's drive to Sydney.

In the morning we drove along Scenic Drive which went east through hills and trees and away from the beaches. We had gone in a big loop around King Edward Park, very well kept with several picnic areas. On re-joining the Pacific Highway, we turned south after a few miles through a town called Belmont. About two miles on, to our right was Lake Macquarie, a scenic drive to Lakes Entrance over the Bridge, Lake Macquarie's water goes into the Tasman Sea at Blacksmiths, where we stopped for lunch. Then continued to Ourimbah where we turned off to Gosford, in Woy Woy district on the southern shore of the Hawkesbury River mouth inlet with its amazing views. We drove through and back out to the Highway through Brisbane Water National Park.

On the Highway, and on a bit further over a bridge, beneath the Hawksbury River, Marramarra National Park on our right then on our left Chase National Park. Some trees showing signs of having been in a bush fire but with renewed green shoots up their blackened trunks. After we reached Hornsby, we started to look for signs to Narrabeen.

We arrived back at Nola's about 5pm rather exhausted. We were greeted with great excitement. And so completed our trip of many exciting and wonderful experiences. After a bit of a rest we went in, had a drink and caught up on all the latest news and found some mail which had caught up with us. Had a lovely meal with the family enjoying the two grandchildren who had grown so much since we left.

We were glad to get an early night. Then in the morning Vera did a big wash and I got into the garden which needed a bit of attention. Nathan, 3 years old, tried to give me a hand but wanted to kick a football with him most of the time. Later that day we learnt that Di and Willie had decided to move to Sydney. Nola said she would put them up till they found a place.

The weekend was to be the big move so I went down with Gavin in his 4 wheel drive, a small truck as we were told they didn't have much to move. We left very early and got to St Kilda at noon. Had a coffee and a sandwich then started loading. Di and Willie had already piled stuff into their car and we all took off back to Sydney by 4pm. They drove ahead and while driving back we stopped halfway for a break, I offered to have a spell at driving but Gavin said he was alright as he had taken a pill to keep him awake. I did not feel very safe about this. But we arrived in one piece about 9pm, quite an exhausting day. I left them to the unloading. Of course, it was a great reunion for Vera and her family.

All went well for a few days though the house was very crowded. Then the girls started to argue and disagree over certain things, so I suggested to Vera that we move on but she decided to stay. I had enough and went into town and booked a seat on Greyhound to return to Perth. Things did quieten

Incredible Memories

down once they realized I was taking off. I had a rather tearful farewell from all when I left for the long journey back home. This also meant that I was not completing the full circle of The Around Australia Trip.

It was an interesting trip home as we called into several towns we had not visited during our journey. We would stop and pick up more passengers or drop some off at various stops. At some we had a twenty-minute break to stretch our legs and buy something to eat and drink. I was surprised to see I was he only one that didn't spend the time sitting for a meal in the cafe. We took a detour off the Eyre Highway across to see the Bight which was an experience to witness the high cliffs and bubbling Southern Ocean below. Then we were off again. I had a nap and when I woke, I realized the driver was nodding off so I got out of my seat and sat on the step next to the driver talking to him to keep him awake. Luck would have it we changed drivers at our next stop.

The Nullarbor is a long straight stretch of road To my surprise there was a lot of vegetation and it was an interesting journey, first thing in the morning we were given the pleasure of a brilliant sunrise with all its yellows and red, oranges melding with the wider blue skies.

We had several stops, some only a petrol station with truck bays and hot food available and much needed toilet facilities with showers. I did not find the crossing boring as some had told me it would be. I expected a barren desert land for most of the drive, it was a long journey but with interesting vegetation. More shrub like than forest, many in flower. Then we were at BP Travellers Village the border between South Australia and Western Australia where we were searched for contraband, no fruit, seeds or vegetables allowed over the border.

The first town in WA as we turned north after the lengthy east to west where we joined the Esperance Highway at Norseman. Then on to Widgiemooltha then to Kambalda, dropping passengers off at each town and on to Kalgoorlie, originally called Hannons. It sports one of the longest railway platforms. A very old mining town with a one-hour drive through the old mine, this Vera and I did when we visited a few years before. We also went down into a real gold mine riding down in a cage facing the wall of the mine shaft, rather frightening experience but worth it when we got to the bottom. We were shown all the workings.

From Kalgoorlie we went to Coolgardie once a bustling gold town. As we drove out of town to our left was the supply pipe for water all the way from Mundaring Weir in the hills just out of Perth. The longest water pipe in Australia. We were now on the Great Eastern Highway, Perth being several hours away. When we reached John Forrest National Park to our right I knew we had not far to go. The sight of familiar Perth came into view as we descended the steep drop from Greenmount to Midvale where we joined the Great Northern Highway and drove into Guildford over the Swan River to Bassendean, Bayswater, Maylands, and Highgate and into East

THE FINAL LEG

Perth Train station. All the towns from Guildford very busy and well populated. At the station I was met by George, Bernadette, Margaret and Marie-Therese so had a very warm welcome, we all went back to my unit in East Fremantle where Alison had breakfast ready. Had a lot of mail from abroad and we sat over breakfast talking nine to the dozen and catching up on all the family news and my travels since leaving Sydney

It was good to be home and be with family again. To get to know my grand-son Joel and I would be home for Marie-Therese's second arrival. I caught up with my many friends and the next chapter of my life.

Back home, I realized I should have written my journal in more detail. But having written about daily incidents to my family and my Mum and asked for the letters to be kept I missed out on so many funny and not so funny occasions that we experienced. Humorous sayings, and they differed from State to State. After such a length of time I have forgotten so much. I am so grateful I had the opportunity to travel and enjoy this wonderful and diverse country of ours. Needless to say, there are no letters that I can refer too.

The photos and rocks we collected on the way remained in the van. Vera stayed in Sydney for a month then travelled back on her own. I was already planning a trip around the world to visit my umpteen relatives and friends so did not return to Sydney. In the meantime, I got several cleaning and gardening jobs. On several weekends I drove to visit friends who lived in a beach-house just south of Mandurah, south of Perth. We spent the time fishing and surfing, it was a lovely spot and was a reminder of the beaches Vera and I visited during our travels.

I would join many of our friends and attend dances run by the Feminist Group, always good fun and good music. Men seemed to feel we craved their company and presumed we could not live without the sexual side of life. Many of us had not experienced any need to repeat some not too pleasant relationships.

My mother was to celebrate her 80th birthday in England in September 1983. All my siblings and their partners planned a reunion, so it would be an ideal time to travel to each country to visit them and their families and catch up with friends and cousins who were scattered around the world.

On making enquiries one could purchase a return ticket around the world, so long as one travelled in one direction, for the same fare as a return to London. So I saved, saved, and saved and planned and replanned a route to make this happen.

It was very easy to get cleaning jobs and was given referrals from jobs I already had. What with gardening jobs as well I was working practically all week, but mainly in the mornings. Except for two jobs where I did the garden in the morning had a break for lunch then did the cleaning in the afternoon.

After Vera had been back for a few weeks, she moved into my flat. On hearing I wanted to make a trip around the world she asked if she could join

Incredible Memories

me as she also knew the various people we had met on our travels. And so it was we were off on our next adventure together.

14th October 1982

Chapter 62

AROUND THE WORLD ON A SHOESTRING

My best friend Vera and I held monthly stalls at various venues selling superfluous items in order to make money to do a World Tour. We both had cleaning jobs as well and saving like crazy for our trip of a lifetime.

We had backpacks weighing about thirty-six pounds and we planned to see as much of the world as we could. On our around Australia trip and while backpacking around New Zealand and Tasmania we had met Germans, Swiss, Canadians and Americans who had given us their addresses and asked us to call on them on our way around.

In New Zealand we had been dubbed "The Hitching Grannies". It took six months to work out an itinerary. Write to umpteen people asking if it was convenient to call on them, giving approximate dates we would be in their neck of the woods. Then we awaited replies.

On May 31st 1983 at 2:30 PM we said tearful farewells to our families, then took our first flight on Singapore Airlines from Perth airport, the first leg of our four and a half months trip on an open ticket around the world going east to west.

This was the first time Vera had taken such a long trip. We changed planes at Singapore then flew to Taipei where we found our movements very restricted. While the plane refuelled and staff were changed we disembarked and walked around the airport. The place was very clean, we walked along a corridor looking through windows down onto the rest of the inside of the building. All the while we had suspicious glances from armed security guards. We were happy to leave that atmosphere. After two hours we boarded our plane on our way to Honolulu. Flying across the Pacific was the longest non-stop flight of our whole journey. At the point of no return the captain announced we were halfway to our next destination, he hoped we were enjoying our flight and thanked us for flying with them. The service on the plane was excellent though we were flying 'economy'. Our seats were good, the food very substantial. We both indulged in a sherry before each meal and a glass of wine with the meal. All drinks being on the house. We slept well and, on the whole, enjoyed our trip. By the time we reached Honolulu we had crossed the International Dateline and gained a day.

It was daylight when we arrived so we had an aerial view of the city and surrounding eight islands with beautiful beaches and turquoise waters. A hurried change of staff and a refuel, Polynesian music entertaining us as we waited. Then we were on our way to Los Angeles arriving on the 1st of June. By the time we had gone through customs, boy were they thorough! They wanted to know everything about us and why we wanted to visit the US of A, how long and who were we visiting and why. Most important seemed to be that we had a return ticket!

Making for the exit was very confusing as a lot of building and reorganizing of the airport was in progress. The next thing we knew we were out of the airport in a rather busy area where there were stalls that sold souvenirs and take away foods. Neither of which we were interested in. As we stood discussing our next move, we were approached by two African American gentlemen who asked what we planned to do. I suspect they were plain clothes police. We told them we had just arrived and hoped to find a youth hostel or YWCA. Their reply was "No way Jose" not safe to go into the city and suggested we try and get back into the airport and sleep there the night. They showed us a way we could re-enter part of the airport. We found a lounge in the lady's rest room and spent the night there. At about 5 AM we were woken by some very noisy cleaners who told us we could not stay.

Fortunately, we found a food stall where we could sit, we grabbed a coffee and an egg and bacon sandwich. Then we were told which bus to take into the city. The youth hostel was a ridiculous distance out of town, so we hiked the few miles up the hill to a very nice and friendly hostel out at Long Beach. Booked in for two nights and met some other travellers who gave us a few hints.

We had a good look around the city, we took a bus out to Beverly Hills and viewed the most glamorous movie star homes, built along tree lined boulevards, they all had manicured gardens. Most surrounded by high railed fences. The buildings in the city were many and tall. The streets in most parts not clean. We found the people helpful and friendly and felt no threat until someone suggested "Watch your backs."

On 3rd June we checked out early after a hearty breakfast, also managed to score some bread and cheese with which we made sandwiches and departed. Hiked into town booked an overnight trip on a Greyhound bus to Flagstaff via Phoenix. At Flagstaff we had a meal in a very interesting restaurant where all the servers were dressed in cowboy outfits. They made us welcome even announced on the loudspeaker that there were two ladies from Western Australia. Several people came over to speak with us and offered to buy our meal. We had to cut this time with pleasant company as we had to catch a connecting bus to the Grand Canyon. We were both able to sleep quite comfortably while we travelled. Spent the next day at the Canyon on shuttle buses seeing the east rim of the Canyon, visitors centre etc.

The Grand Canyon was carved out over millions of years by the Colorado River. The unique landscape is painted in breathtaking colours that change with the movement of the sun. We found the whole experience fascinating. To think that Ayers Rock-now called Uluru- turned upside down would fit quite easily into the Canyon. The Colorado River at the bottom of the Canyon looked like a creek it was so far down. So much to see from so many vantage points. Looking down the side of the Canyon one is confronted with layers of different coloured rock, some white and others going into various shades of browns and oranges.

By going around in the shuttle bus, we could alight and walk and explore a substantial area before catching the next bus. These buses were like motorized trams, open on either side so one could view the scenery as we drove along. At various stops there were small shops or Indian vendors selling jewellery and souvenirs or cool drinks, food, coffee or tea. As we were traveling on a very tight budget, we were limited to what we could purchase. Our daily limit was $11 each per day, our Greyhound travel was prepaid so that amount had to cover food and accommodation. Of course, on some days we spent more than that but we made it up when we were staying where we didn't have to pay accommodation, like the nights we spent traveling on buses that were prepaid.

That evening we caught a bus back to LA via Williams, Kingman and Barstow. We were very impressed with the scenery in all the areas we covered. Not unlike the countryside in Western Australia. The Mojave Desert with its arid barrenness reminded me of traveling through the centre of Australia. Then there were scenes not unlike Kalbarri in Western Australia, and the surrounding country with tree clad gorges.

Our round trip was over 1,000 miles. We had an excellent conductor-driver on both legs of the trip, very handsome African Americans who were full of information. In fact, I wrote to the company and told them how impressed we were with the service.

We arrived in LA at 6:30 AM. Went to a downtown eating joint and had for breakfast, two fried eggs, bacon, toast butter and marmalade with as much coffee as we could drink. All for $1.50, as soon as we sat at the table a jug of cold water and glasses were put on the table, then we'd order.

Well satisfied we caught a bus to Disney Land and spent the better part of the day looking around. Quite an experience there was SO much to see and do though we didn't go on many of the rides, too expensive. We just enjoyed watching everyone else enjoying themselves. We visited the wax museum, the figures so real looking of the stars of yesteryear, Knott's Berry

Incredible Memories

Farm with its re-created Western Ghost Towns. There were several historical exhibitions which were included in the price of our $14 entry ticket. We watched the daily parade of Disney characters led by small bands. Even shook hands with Mickey Mouse!

At 7:00 PM June 5th we checked in at the airport for our next 1,500-mile trip to St. Louis. Had a light snack and forty winks on one of their lounges before boarding our flight on a TWA at 11:30 PM. We arrived at St. Louis at 6:30 Am after a good flight, we slept most of the way.

While waiting for a bus to take us into town, a gentleman approached us, he had just seen his daughter off on a flight to New York. He offered us a lift into town. We were driven to the youth hostel which turned out to be a dump of a place with several people stoned out of their brains, we were not enamoured by the place or its occupants. So Larry Thomas asked us to stay at his place. Vera and I looked at each other, we decided it was probably quite safe. The hour we had spent with Larry convinced us he was genuine.

We arrived at an enormous three-story house. On the 1st floor we were introduced to LaRonna, Larry's partner, then shown into the daughter's room where we dumped our gear. Had a quick shower and change of clothes. The ones we had worn since we left Perth were good and ready for the washing machine of which we were offered a loan. LaRonna told us breakfast was ready. The first time we had eaten 'Hash Browns and gravy,' the gravy made from a roux using the bacon fat and flour, these were accompanied by bacon and tomatoes, toast and jam and freshly made coffee.

Larry and LaRonna, St Louis June 1983

While there we learned a lot about the 'Gateway to the West,' as St. Louis is known. Saw the city from the dizzy heights of the Archway; 630 ft. high, which we reached by a lift. Larry and LaRonna paid for everything including a slap-up lunch at one of their favorite restaurants. They drove us over to the state of Illinois, north to Hannibal. We crossed back to Missouri, the side of the Mississippi, into Mark Twain country. Up the Mississippi we watched the locks being closed to lower long barges, loaded with goods, to the next level down the river. They were on their way down south. The whole procedure very well managed and an excellent way of transportation of goods from the far south as well as from the north.

The Mississippi hails from Lake Itasca, it starts as the spill over a small dam, the stream so narrow one can leap over it. It then enters a chain of lakes, meanders through woodlands. From Minnesota to Minneapolis it becomes a powerful river. At St. Anthony Falls it rushes through the first of twenty-nine locks and dams that stretch to just south of St. Louis. At St. Louis the Mississippi is joined by the Missouri River to make it even mightier.

Larry was a paramedic so naturally we had to be introduced to the crew down at the fire station. We were shown around then presented with badges and made honorary members. Had to try on their regalia and needless to say we could barely walk, it was so weighty.

We met LaRonna's charming Grandma. She had the ground floor of the house. Beyond the house was a massive shed. Grandma's incredible second-hand shop. We feasted our eyes on all the interesting items she had collected from the pioneer days. Spent a whole morning examining everything and being told what some of the items were. People were very ingenious and creative in those hard days. We wished we had more money to spend as we would dearly have liked to have purchased a couple of things, especially some of the homemade toys or gadgets like an apple peeler and corer.

After lunch we were taken on yet another drive to show us the hospital, LaRonna nursed there, the museum and the University. The streets were lined with beautiful trees and the gardens ran down to the sidewalks (as they call pavements), all were so well kept. Unlike the poor section of the city we had visited where the hostel was. Showing the contrast between the rich and the poor side of the city.

We had already spent three very full days with Larry and LaRonna and were finding it very hard to convince them that we were only just starting our journey and still had a lot of ground to cover. We were taken down to the fire station to say our farewells. I was presented with a bottle of rum and Vera with a bottle of Bourbon, both had labels reading "Only for medicinal purposes."

Larry drove us to the Greyhound depot where we boarded a bus, destination Chicago. On this bus we met children and their grandmothers who were traveling from Florida and places on route to Chicago where they were spending their school holidays with relatives. During the trip we were plied with sweets (lollies), sandwiches and pieces of cake which they wanted to share with us. What hospitality and friendship we were shown since arriving in the United States. We found the children so well mannered,

Incredible Memories

always seemed to end their sentences with 'Mam' and always a thank you and please.

We arrived in Chicago on June 9th, found a locker for our bac packs then spent the day admiring the old buildings around Michigan Avenue. We were impressed with what we saw especially the beautiful old-fashioned brass lamp posts.

Took a night ride to Rochester, Minnesota where we were met by my cousin Maimo. I had not seen her for twenty years. She and her husband Jack had booked us into Pine Lodge motel about five miles from their home in Oronoco. They had very thoughtfully brought a picnic basket with food and ample drink to soothe our weary bones.

We had showers, ate and drank then had a very relaxed afternoon. I had a very amusing incident at the motel. After performing in the toilet, I spent a considerable time endeavouring to find a button, chain or some way I could flush the toilet. As soon as I lowered the seat there was a sudden rush of water. Relief, with a giggle.

Maimo picked us up at 6pm and took us back to their lovely Colonial, two-story house to meet Jack and family, those who still lived at home, and share the evening meal. We returned to the motel for the night and the next day Maimo picked us up with all our gear to stay with them as they now had a vacant room for us to sleep in.

With cousin Maimo outside her craft shop, Oronoco, Minnesota

They had such a beautiful spot to live in, away from the noise and bustle of the city. We had a very relaxed, interesting three day stay. Visiting friends, meeting family, seven offspring they had, we met five. I did a bit of gardening, we swam and visited Maimo's little craft shop. We went for several lovely walks, the weather being ideal.

Monday 13th went to Rochester with Maimo to visit Carol, the eldest daughter, at the public radio station. We were shown around and presented with tee shirts. Took a drive around Rochester then said our farewells, and left on the 2:30pm bus to Minneapolis, one of the twin cities. When we arrived, we had a cup of tea and changed buses to start our trek west across the top of the States going via Fargo.

It was raining so hard when we arrived at Fargo we decided to continue to Billings arriving at 11:30am the next day. We travelled miles of grasslands, some parts very bare and rocky but none the less interesting country. We saw our first bison grazing near the roadside. The road followed the Yellow Stone river in many places from Glendive to Billings. The countryside became even more varied, very flat in many places, stretching for as far as the eye could see, then small hillocks which were a bit greener than what we had just passed.

We met very amusing and friendly people on the buses so far. Some a bit difficult to understand, especially those from way down south.

At Livingstone we had to change buses to go into Yellow Stone National Park. Unfortunately, there was no connection for two hours. We kicked our heels in a very dingy roadhouse in between taking short walks with our back packs, as did not feel safe leaving them unattended. It was very hot so did not walk too far.

Yellowstone National Park

We had travelled for twenty-four hours by bus and were feeling very tired. It was a relief to arrive at Mammoth hot springs, but very disappointing to find no cheap accommodation was available. There was a German guy by the name of Franz also trying to book in. Tough luck, as there were no more buses for the day! We ended up sharing a one room hut with Franz so we could cut expenses. We booked a further night, also with Franz, down at "Old Faithful" the other end of the park. We all had a good night's sleep. Franz being a perfect gentleman, he turned his back while we got ready for bed. We booked a tour down the east side of the park, for the following day. All around our hut and surrounding accommodations, the ground was covered with burrows and every now and again a small animal, a prairie cat would pop up, stand on its hind legs and look around with its beady eyes. They reminded me of a weasel. There were dozens of them scurrying around, always one appeared to be standing guard.

Yellowstone is the first National Park to have been developed in the US. It is nestled in the Absaroka Range, part of it in Montana, another in Wyoming and yet another in Idaho. We had reached the Rocky Mountains and all its beauty. It might have been better had we had our own transport. There is so much to see, traveling on a tour which only stopped at certain points we felt we missed a lot. But the other side of the coin was that the guide gave a running commentary as we travelled the whole of the East side. There are sky piercing mountains, spectacular falls and geysers, magnificent canyons, bubbling hot springs and so much wildlife.

We saw elk, moose and bison while traveling through unreal countryside. Up into snow covered mountains, fir covered hilly country, in parts similar to that we had seen at the Grand Canyon. There were waterfalls rushing down beside the road through beautiful coloured rock scenery, down to grassy woodlands. Eagles gliding high in the sky, the large American robin hopping around on the ground, all new to us. Being woken by unusual bird song before sunrise, making this trip something we were glad we had done.

In the evening light we saw "Old Faithful Geyser" rise some sixty feet in the air. Quite spectacular as everything is lit up at night. The huge hotel building built like a massive log cabin. The tourist information on the ground floor in a huge entrance hall with accommodation on the first floor with a balcony looking down to the hall from all sides. One could purchase very expensive souvenirs. After a very heavy downfall of rain it turned very cold, so that night we slept in jumpers and woolly socks.

June 16th got up at 6am and got ourselves over to the hotel to catch the bus out of Yellowstone West. Then on to Bozeman traveling through some of the famous 'Wild West' country. We passed marmots, ground squirrels and bubbling hot springs, accompanied by the smell of sulphur. Saw more moose, bison and steam rising in several places along the road.

At Bozeman we made our connection to Seattle. On the way we climbed the Rocky Mountains through to Spokane via Butte, Drummond, Missoula and very interesting Coeur d' Alene, where the houses differed to those in the other towns. Very European. Just before that there was a place called Kellogg! On the way we noticed how the buildings differed depending on what European pioneer group settled. A German settlement so very German in their architecture, and the streets had German names.

Over the Rocky Mountains we travelled through Spokane to Wenatchee, now in the State of Washington. Down through Leavenworth Pass in the Cascade Ranges to Everett and south to Seattle. The roads were winding through lush countryside, woodlands in many places.

We arrived in Seattle at 11:30am booked into the youth hostel, nothing to write home about. The hostel a multi-story building where we shared a room with several other women, it was rather dingy. It was near the waterfront. We spent a good deal of time exploring yet another multi-story building, the very interesting markets, part of which was over the water. We managed to get some cheap fruit, bread rolls and cheese so we wouldn't go hungry. The best way to see a city on the cheap is to ride the street cars and cover as much ground as possible. The bus drivers were usually friendly and quite willing to act as guides. We liked the place. In the surrounding suburbs we found neat houses and gardens. It was quite hilly in places out of the city.

AROUND THE WORLD ON A SHOESTRING

Next day we left on the 1pm bus for our trip into Canada. We drove back through Everett and Mount Vernon sighting water on several occasions on our left. At Bellingham there was a sort of bay with lots of small boats. On to Blaine and the border to Canada where we had to produce our passports and declare goods before proceeding to Vancouver. We were met by my youngest sister Christine, her husband Shanti and eldest son Rahoul. They took us to a Greek restaurant where we talked endlessly about the seventeen years since we had seen each other.

Tina, Shanti and boys, Vancouver

They live in a neat suburb in Vancouver called Richmond. Very nice being in a home again. While in Vancouver we caught up on a niece of mine, on Tom's side of the family, Margaret, and her husband John and three children, Sorcha, Sarah and Johnathan. One day we spent with a friend of my youngest daughter Alison, Cathy Kershaw. We walked over the longest suspension bridge in the world, went up the Grouse Mountain in a sort of cabin lift. Cathy drove us around and were generally shown all over the city of Vancouver with its tall buildings. A modern looking city.

We crossed the Strait of Georgia by ferry to Victoria on Vancouver Island, the capitol of British Columbia. Spent a day with Christine. Visited the beautiful Butchart Gardens with its magnificent collection of flowers, trees and shrubs from all corners of the world. Tina took us to the Museum of Indian artefacts, also the University of Vancouver set in lovely gardens. Very impressive buildings. Also visited the underwater world with its performing whales.

It was so nice to get to know my two nephews, Rahoul and Kunal. We spent evenings pouring over photo albums after a delicious Indian curry. Having completed a very happy week we took the Greyhound and headed

Incredible Memories

north on yet another leg of our trip. To visit new and exciting places and catch up with friends.

Canadian Rocky Mountains

Sunday June 26th arrived in Quesnel at 7am. We were met by Anne Baker, a Canadian friend we had met in Queensland during our Australian trip in 1981.

She took us around to her Mum's, Barbara, for breakfast. Later we caught up with Ron, Anne's husband, a sister and brother of his and his mother. They all made us very welcome. Another 175 miles and we were at Lake Fraser. Anne and Ron's house overlooks this Lake. Absolutely breathtaking scenery, a lawn ran down hill to the vegetable garden before one reached the shore of the lake. We spent a very full week being shown around, travelled for miles. We saw bears, one mum with three very active cubs, chipmunks, some beautiful birds, a beaver and several deer, also a woodpecker on a tree just outside of the dining area. It was busy banging away at the tree with its beak. Ron and Anne owned a motorboat, they took us for a spin around the lake. Around the edge of the lake were narrow stony beaches leading into dense woodland. As we sat quietly admiring the scenery a deer came down to the water to drink.

Vera, Ron and self, Lake Fraser June 1983

On a drive to another lake we met an old couple who were fishing for trout then smoking them in an old fridge they had set up on the bank near their caravan. They gave us a couple of jars full of smoked trout to eat while we travelled across Canada. They were so delicious they did not last very long. They had been smoked with pinecones and twigs.

AROUND THE WORLD ON A SHOESTRING

One evening Ron and Anne took us on a long ride to a cinema in Prince George to see the brilliant film "Ghandi." As in Australia they thought nothing of traveling twenty miles to see a film.

While gardening in Anne's vegie patch I got badly bitten by some little black flies and ended up with welts all over my head. A most uncomfortable experience. We celebrated Vera's birthday with the Bakers, cake and all on July 3rd. That evening we started east very sorry to leave this peaceful spot but we had to get on the move again and had been fortunate to see so much of that part of Canada.

In Ron and Anne's vegie patch, Fraser Lake June 1983

Had a good run through some incredible scenic areas, the summer nights being light until late. Arrived at the heart of the Rocky Mountains and the resort town of Jasper at 6am. A picturesque town set high in the Rockies. Had breakfast and a look around the township set in its own National Park. Later catching a bus down through the Canadian Rockies to Banff and Calgary. The road was very good with breathtaking scenery all around us. We had cat naps in between stops to admire views or bears close to the roadside. We were warned not to approach them as many had young with them.

We called into Lake Louise, in the Yoho National Park, Where the elegant Chateau Lake Louis sits on the edge of the magnificent lake. Then drove through Banff National Park to Banff only a short distance away, where we stopped again. Finally arriving in Calgary where we were met by Mrs. Ritchie a friend of the Baker's and taken home to spend a very comfortable night in her lovely home. It makes such a difference to our survival visiting homes where we can have a comfortable sleep in a bed! Next day we met her daughter Donna and Donna's fiancé Carl, who showed us around Calgary. We were shown the grounds where they were about to hold the world-famous stampede in their huge Rodeo Grounds. Saw Fort McLeod, the first headquarters of the Canadian Mounted Police. Had some good fun with them that day. They drove us to the bus depot to catch the

Incredible Memories

7:30pm to Winnipeg. We left well rested and pleased to have met such nice people.

It was a very long drag over the prairie land, from Alberta via Medicine Hat, Moose Jaw, Regina and Brandon. Wonderful names! We arrived in Winnipeg at 3:30 am, not a soul in sight and nowhere open, in a strange city. Never been in such a quiet town or city, we wondered what to do next. We wandered around for a while and then decided to find somewhere we could have forty winks before finding an eatery where we could get breakfast. It was a long wait. That day we were very hot and tired. We went and booked into the youth hostel, a large two-story cream and dark green building. Here again having to share with several other women, we were warned not to leave anything lying around like towels as they had a habit of disappearing! A rather difficult task if we wanted to explore the area! Phoned an old friend, Roy, from Jamaica days. That night Roy Kartzmarks picked us up to go and meet his wife Olga. I had not seen Roy for forty years. He was one of the handsome soldiers I'd fallen for when they stayed with our family. It was a great reunion though he said it was quite a shock to get my phone call. It was very amusing as Roy did not know what to expect, we had not corresponded for years and he was surprised we were staying in a hostel. After the evening meal which we enjoyed with them they invited us to stay with them the following night.

We spent the next day with the Kartzmarks getting to know them and learning a bit about the years in between for both families. Roy was very interested to hear about my siblings as he had often wondered how we all had turned out since we were all children when he last saw us on his visit to Jamaica during the war when he was in the army as a young eighteen year old. We had some good laughs about the past. Roy took us for a drive around Winnipeg then we left on the 11:30am bus for Toronto, it was July the 8th.

Self with Roy Kartzmark and his wife after 39 years, Winnipeg July 1983

AROUND THE WORLD ON A SHOESTRING

We went via Dryden, Thunder Bay and along Lake Superior. Next morning, we stopped at Sault Ste. Marie and had breakfast. We had a bit of time to go for a walk and stretch our legs also get some fresh air. The scenery was not very exciting as the depot was alongside a big railway yard, but still wherever one is, there is always something interesting or new to see and invariably someone keen to tell us something about their town. Back on the bus with Lake Huron on our right, past Blind River, on North Channel to Webbwood to Sudbury then we travelled south, Georgian Bay on our right and finally Toronto on Lake Ontario.

East Canada & USA

The countryside had been a mixture of hills, pine forests and lakes. It has been comfortable riding in the buses, the scenery has certainly been very varied.

On arriving in Toronto, we spent the first night at a youth hostel. Next morning our friends Don and Bev and little Grant came over to pick us up. We had met Don and Bev while hitch hiking around South Island, New Zealand.

They took us on a tour of Toronto and up into the CN tower, all 1815 ft. of it. What a magnificent view we had overlooking the city. We walked up the mountain side to a restaurant as none of us felt like going up in the chair lift. There again we saw for miles around, looked across Lake Ontario, had a nice meal, then walked down again. Bev and Vera kept getting impatient with me because I would stop to examine a plant or flower or even watch an insect moving in the undergrowth by the side of the path.

We spent a week meeting family and friends and getting to know something of Toronto but also enjoying their company. One day we spent on a visit a short drive away to Niagara Falls and Marine Land. Went down Niagara Parkway and looked out at the falls. I thought it would have been a lot noisier because of the volume of water that was falling, but then I suppose it was because we were quite a height from the base of the waterfall. There were people down there in boats going under the spray. Then we took a walk along Rainbow Bridge as far as the customs house so we were practically on US soil and had walked over Niagara River. We walked around and saw a huge floral clock, Brock's Monument, the power plant, Fort George and several other tourist attractions which we avoided because of cost. The Skylon stood high above all the other buildings. Marine Land was like a massive fairground come Disney Land. The water way from Lake Ontario running through the centre of it. A very enjoyable day but too much to take in!

Went for a meal and a swim at Don's folks place. The weather was very hot while we were in Toronto. We all went up to the village of Tweed for the weekend to meet Bev's parents, Vick and Mary. All making us *so* welcome, found Tweed a delightful village with such friendly people. Spent all the time outdoors, even had our meals in the garden, the weather was ideal. Mary and Vick's house was set high from the road surrounded by large trees, a very green lawn spread out across the back of their home.

On July 17th we bid all a sad goodbye and were on our way to Ottawa with a farewell gift of a bottle of Brandy, the label read, "For medicinal purposes only." We arrived in Ottawa at noon. We slept most of the way so missed the scenery. Spent the time in Ottawa looking around the very old and the new Capitol of Canada. Never seen so many copper roofed and ornate buildings before.

After another bus drive through rather flat farming land with their red roofed sheds, we arrived at Montreal. We were met by Don's aunt Louise and partner Bernard. They gave us a marvellous run around the city. Took us up the Mount with a good view of the city, saw some really nice homes as we drove around. After tea we were taken in to see a bit of the night life, it was strange hearing French being spoken everywhere. Montreal being the second largest French speaking city in the world. The sidewalks were on two different levels and the restaurant and shop fronts very European looking in architecture. The streets are cobbled. We saw Chateau de Ramezay, the fine French building that was the headquarters of the invading American army in 1775. A square called Place d'Armes overlooked by Notre Dame de Montreal, the second largest church in North America, with it's beautiful stained-glass windows.

When we got back to the house while having a night cap, we compared our two countries. They had a very nice double story house. We were fascinated by a false window on the wall below the stair way which made one feel as though we were looking out into the garden.

Had a comfortable night's sleep and feeling refreshed, Bernard drove us to the bus station where we deposited our backpacks. Bernard and Louise had to go to work. We walked into the older part of Montreal and had a look around before catching the Greyhound for our journey to New York via Vermont and Boston. The New Hampshire countryside is some of the most beautiful one can drive through. We were too early for the spectacular autumn tree colours, but the leaves were beginning to turn. The bus flew along at great speed, we slept most of the trip.

We arrived in New York at about 4:30AM. It was light enough for us to see some of the suburbs like the Bronx and Queens as we drove through. A bit of an eye opener. We were surprised to see so much activity at that hour of the morning. Garbage trucks noisily collecting garbage in bags that lay in heaps on the sidewalk. We heard there had been a strike so the bad smell was because the bags had lain there for days. Delivery vans at various points, newspaper deliveries. But there were also a lot of people just walking around. This looked to be the poorer suburbs of New York.

The bus depot seemed to be very far underground. We arrived in a very busy area which was full of people of every race and description awaiting buses, arriving on buses or just seeking shelter. We had arrived earlier than expected so decided to remain in that area. A jolly African American beckoned us to join her and her children on a bench. She told us to be careful of our back packs and that it was not safe to leave that part of the building until later. We sat there taking in the scene, it was a real education. there were a few stoned out of their brains while others tried to care for them. Some were obviously trying to pick up business either as prostitutes, homosexuals and guys trying to pick up girls.

I asked our new friend why there weren't any police. She told us there probably were some plain clothed police milling around but they would do nothing unless someone started a fight or were making a nuisance of themselves.

By six o'clock the place was getting pretty crowded so we decided to move up a level or two and found ourselves in an area where it seemed safe. We were waiting around to see who could spot my sister Pat first. A voice behind me asked, "Is this the way to Perth?"

It was the first we'd seen each other for just over twenty-eight years, so it was quite a reunion. Then we went up another level where we tried to get a cab. The drive to Astoria, where Pat lived, was very interesting too. This suburb was quite a bit cleaner than the suburbs we had driven through on arrival to New York. There were overhead rail lines running down the centre of the streets. We felt more at home here probably because we were with Pat.

Needless to say, we had plenty of catching up to do. Pat took a couple of days off work. We spent one day on the Circle Line going around Manhattan Island, passed Stanton Island. A great way to see New York from the Hudson River. It was also an education! We saw where all the garbage from New York was dumped, into barges which were towed by tugs out to sea to be disposed of. As we passed the Statue of Liberty, I was surprised it wasn't bigger. It always looks so huge in pictures. We were told over a tannoy what all the buildings were as we passed, and even who lived in some of them. Some had flat roofs with gardens on top, some even had trees growing on top of them.

Another day we went by foot around Manhattan. We visited the United Nations building with Pat where we saw some of the conference rooms. There were some unusual shops which sold souvenirs and goods from all member nations. We sent postcards to our families from the Post Office there, I bought some First Day covers which were only sold in this building. Visited St. Patrick's cathedral. Pat also took us to where she worked. On other days Vera and I explored various parts, we visited the 'Village', had a drink and something to eat at a quaint little pub and met some nice folk who were interested to meet two ladies from Australia. Had a few remarks made about us having just won the American Cup!

We also walked through Central Park. There were people skating around, some dancing on skates, others figure skating, there were buskers

Incredible Memories

and for the first time we saw guys spinning around on their heads on pieces of cardboard on the ground. They were doing all sorts of things with their arms and legs and seemed to be competing to see who had a new trick. We bought some hot dogs and a cup of coffee and sat watching them. We heard the clip clop of horses as top-hatted drivers took riders through the park in a hansom. On a street going down to the Circle Line we found some very cheap shops and bought a few things to send home to the family and grandchildren. Walked back up to the business centre, saw the world Trade Centre, the Empire State Building, but did not go up it.

Pat was horrified when we told her where we had been. She told us it was asking to be mugged. We met her at her office, were introduced to her work mates then went home with her on one of the overhead trains.

Living with Pat were my nephews Bertrand and Gilbert and niece Pascal. It was strange meeting them for the first time and they grown-up or nearly so, Gilbert was still at high school. We all fitted in very neatly, Vera and I shared a pullout lounge converted into a double bed which was in their sitting room in the centre of the flat. Bertrand was studying engineering and Pascal worked at a clinic.

After a very happy week with Pat and her family we were on yet another flight, New York to London. Pat saw us off at the airport, we went by a New York Yellow cab that Pat's company used so Pat was quite familiar with the trip. We could not understand the cab driver, Pat said it was New York lingo.

With backpack at Pat's apartment, Astoria New York July 1983

AROUND THE WORLD ON A SHOESTRING

Our Stay in the UK

On July 27th we landed at Heathrow Airport. The flight over had been a bit bumpy and we were both suffering jetlag.

We were met at the airport by my mother who I had not seen for seven years, and my brother David who I had not seen for fifteen years. Getting through customs had been a nightmare and took ages as we were both holding Australian passports and we had to join the queue marked "All Others." This queue meant everyone from all over the world who did not hold a British passport!

I noticed a lot of changes on the journey to peaceful Woodley where David and Marianne, his wife, live. After a rest we all caught up on family news. The next day Vera and I took a run into London to meet up with Sister Marie Emmanuel from Jamaica. She was the Captain of the 21st St. Andrew Girl Guide Company which I belonged to. I had not seen Sister since 1947. It is extraordinary how the years fall away when one starts to recall things of the past. Sister belonged to the Order of St. Francis. Being a nun did not prevent her from taking an active part in Guiding.

Meeting Sister Emmanuel at President Hotel, Russel Square London July 1983

Also met Sister Ruth from Kansas, who was traveling with Sister Emmanuel. Two Gibraltarian sisters I had not seen for some thirty years and who I had known in Jamaica, Pili and Lourdes. We all had tea and sandwiches at the hotel Sister was staying at, recalled all manner of stories that had happened to us during the stay in Jamaica. Sister was very interested to hear about my family. Before I knew it, my youngest brother Chris was there to pick us up. Could not believe we had been there for five hours. Sister had not seen Chris since he was five years old! It was a shock to her to be confronted with this tall, terribly English man. As she said, "One sees in

Incredible Memories

one's mind's eye what we last saw. And that was a little blonde boy two and a half feet tall, man you have grown into one big man!"

It was very sad saying our goodbyes. But it had been a happy reunion and was providential we both were in London at the same time and had the opportunity to meet.

I had not seen Chris for fifteen years so we had a lot to catch up on. Basia, Chris's wife, had a delicious supper waiting for us on our return. The night went far too quickly, the next day we were rushing around London trying to fit in as much as possible before returning to Woodley that evening. As we both needed more funds, we called into the Commonwealth Bank at Australia House. Walked across the road to a shop that sold 'Vegemite' then took a double decker bus from the Strand to Marble Arch. We walked past 'Speakers Corner' into Hyde Park and across to the Serpentine where several boys were sailing model boats. Then to Hyde Park Corner on into Green Park, up Constitution Hill where we saw several people on horses on the Horse Ride. Finally arriving at Queen Victoria Memorial and Buckingham Palace where we stopped and watched the Buzzbies in their bright uniforms, change guard. Then on up the Mall under all those beautiful trees alongside St. James's Park, through Admiralty Arch to Charing Cross where we bought something to eat and drink and also some souvenirs.

Vera couldn't get over how many parks there were and how big they were, right in the centre of London. After retrieving our bags from Victoria station, we took a bus to Woodley. We spent a couple of days trying to unwind and relax before starting our twenty-eight day 'Brit Rail' trip around the UK. Woodley being a quiet town with lovely parks and woods, so enjoyed some peaceful walks and catching up with family and friends.

On August 1st we took a bus into Reading and a train to Portsmouth to meet up with Vera's friends the Philips. They had not seen each other for seventeen years. Their home was a few miles out of the city near Waterlooville which was overlooking Portsmouth and the Solent. Driving past Havant brought back memories of my Navy days. I was stationed at Havant while I did my Petty Officers course.

We were introduced to their local pub, met a few dart players and spent a couple of pleasant hours there. Fred and Audrey hired a car and took us sightseeing around the south coast as far east as Bognor Regis, where I visited my Uncle Anthony and his wife Mary John. I had lunch with them, showed family photos and caught up on the years that had passed us by, some thirty-three years since we last saw each other.

AROUND THE WORLD ON A SHOESTRING

Aunt Mary and Uncle Antony, Bognor Regis

Vera was down on the beach doing the same with her friends. After about four hours we drove back via Chichester. Visited the Giles family in Fareham, who are distant relatives of Vera's family. We then called into Porchester Castle, ruins, also some of my old haunts in Southsea. Another day we went to visit an excavation site where an old Roman settlement had been discovered. Had a nice but rather exhausting four days before taking the train to Bath. We toured Bath and surrounding countryside by bus. Up steep hilly lanes with very attractive old buildings.

We caught a bus to Holcombe, the trip was along twelve-mile winding narrow country lanes, passed a pub called "Ring a Roses" halfway to the village of Holcombe where we were met by my Aunt Alice. We spent a very happy restful weekend in her lovely little cottage. Had some very relaxed walks with her over fields to neighbouring villages. The weather was ideal and we would have liked to have stayed longer, we so enjoyed Alice's garden setting where we had most of our meals. Because her garden was surrounded by lovely trees the bird song was a joy to listen too. As we sat eating and talking, starlings, robins, black birds and tits hopped around the lawn and in Alice's vegetable garden.

Incredible Memories

Self with Aunt Alice, Holcombe

On the Monday we got a lift with Alice's neighbour Chris, into Bath. Took a train to Stratford upon Avon arriving at lunch time. We spent a couple of hours going around in a tour bus and a short walk along the Avon. A quaint township with beautiful gardens and buildings.

William Shakespeare produced his plays here. We saw Anne Hathaway's cottage, the Church of the Holy Trinity where both are buried also the memorial theatre and a garden which was where Shakespeare lived but the house is no longer there

That evening we caught a train to Stoke on Trent via Birmingham where we were met by Pauline, Barry and Lisa Davenport who I had not seen since they left Australia thirteen years before. After a delighted reunion, we drove to Kidsgrove where they live.

Aunt Alice, Uncle Tom and Mummy

AROUND THE WORLD ON A SHOESTRING

Self with Pauline and Barry Davenport, Stoke on Trent July 1983

We spent five happy days with them being driven around for miles, into Peak District National Park. We saw castles, moors and were taken to the highest pub in England, I think it was called "The Cat and the Fiddle." The countryside was so green and we drove through some very beautiful wooded areas. We drove through Leek and places like Brindley Ford, Biddulph Moor, Chapel en le Frith, Fawfieldhead, Hollinsclough, Alstonefield, what wonderful names. The National Park was between Manchester and Sheffield. One day we drove to Tamworth to visit Paula, Pauline and Barrie's daughter, and her husband John, spent a very hilarious day with them in their new home which they were busy renovating. Barry drove back an alternative route so we could see more of the country. Another time we visited the Mersey Canal and watched houseboats going through the locks. What a way to go! The houseboats were so brightly coloured. Some people had their cats and dogs with them, they had pot plants decorating the decks. One of the ones traveling on one of these houseboats would hop off and work the lock gates at either end then off they'd go again, slowly enjoying the countryside.

Mark and his wife Gill had just returned from a holiday in Spain, we spent the last evening with them up in a pub called "The Ash". Mark was only twelve and Paula ten when they left Australia, Lisa was a baby. While with the Davenports Lisa took Vera and I up to the stables where she helped out so she could get some rides. It was very hilly in this area. When we looked out of the bedroom window, we could see the ruins of a Castle over the valley.

We were driven to Crewe to catch our train to Scotland. When it arrived, it was packed and we had to stand or sit on our backpacks for half the journey. When we arrived in Scotland and were traveling toward Aviemore, the train was stopped as it had caught fire. We were delayed for

Incredible Memories

three quarters of an hour. It was very mountainous country around, quite beautiful.

In all our travels Vera has been very impressed with the greenery of the countryside also with the closeness of the houses, villages and towns. How the fields are sectioned off with dry stone walls or thick hedges.

The colouring in Scotland was tinted with purple heather, the sheep looked a lot whiter and cleaner looking for being on the moors in nice clean air minus the red dust we are used to in Australia.

We arrived in Inverness about 8:30 that night and were met by my sister-in-law Sal, her two sons Derrick and John and John's fiancée Karen. It was seventeen years since I'd been to Scotland. Sandy, Sal's husband was waiting at home when we got there.

As we sat having supper, we caught up on some of the family news. We were made to feel so welcome, the boys had given up their bedroom for us to spread ourselves and baggage.

During the nine days we spent in Scotland I met up with about thirty in-laws. We were taken on many a trip around the countryside. To Lock Ness to check out the monster. No luck there! My brother-in-law Andrew drove us over to the Black Isle, over a new bridge which went from the Kessock, bringing back so many memories of when I lived in Inverness and surrounding Glens. We were taken as far south as Fort Augustus, visited Cromarty, Elgin and Forres, where another sister-in-law, Rose lived. One day Sal drove us out to the old battlefield of Culloden. Drove through Drumnadrochit to Glen Affric, where my son George was born, then on to Glen Cannich where my daughter Margaret was born and Bernadette went to school and we went to church. Where we lived in a cute wooden cottage made of Canadian pine shingles, among a group of Forestry houses.

I was amazed at how the pine forests had changed. In some parts, where, when we lived in the Glens, were saplings, now large trees, to where the larger trees had been felled and then been replanted into new plantations. While in Cannich I called into the local shop to visit the Duncan's who owned the shop, they were very surprised but pleased to see me. They gave me news of various friends we had known while living there.

The family put on a reunion party for us at my sister-in-law Babs and her husband Arthur's home. Young nephews and nieces now adults and married, some with children, were all there. What a spread there was, it was certainly a very happy evening with much laughter.

Derrick (pushing Sandy in his wheelchair, he had been crippled from polio as a boy) Sal, Vera and I went for a long walk one evening. We walked through the west side of Inverness to the river and crossed a bridge onto an island in the middle of the river. On this island there are some beautiful paths to walk along. In a clearing we sat and listened to a pipe band and watched some Scottish dancing.

AROUND THE WORLD ON A SHOESTRING

The time flew as it always seems to, especially when one is enjoying everything. Before we knew it we were saying more sad farewells.

Tuesday August 23rd came all too quickly. We took the train down to Edinburgh. On the way south we stopped at Aviemore and saw people skiing down the grass slopes. Then on through Kingussie, Pitlochry, having passed through Glen Garry. Through Craigvinean Forest, Perth, stopping at all these places to take on or let off passengers. To Dunfermline, over the rail bridge with Forth bridge on our right, and finally Edinburgh.

We arrived very early in the morning, put our backpacks into lockers and spent the day walking around this truly beautiful city. After a look around the Castle we walked the Royal Mile down to Holyrood Palace admiring several ancient buildings of interest on the way including Canongate Tollbooth with a projecting clock, very handy to tell the time when walking down the street.

The Castle stands high above the City, built on Castle Rock. It commands a fine view over the Firth of Forth and is the ancient seat of the Scottish Kings. The Palace of Holyrood was first lived in by James IV, Mary Queen of Scots stayed there also. Bonnie Prince Charlie held court there.

In the evening we watched a couple hundred people doing Highland dancing in a huge park. After having high tea and being played to by a piper we caught a night train to travel back into England. We slept soundly until we reached Nottingham to call on some friends of Vera's. Connie Sester and her son Les met us. Here again we were shown around, visited the oldest pub in England "Ye Olde Trip to Jerusalem." Les took us to the castle, drove us one day to visit Robin Hood country, walking through Sherwood Forest and re-living the history of those times.

We met several of the Seton's relatives and friends. Again had excellent weather. On the 28th we were heading south once more, for London. There was a bitter cold wind to greet us, just a taste of what it could have been like most of our trip. An east wind in London is something else, goes straight through you.

We stayed with my niece Clare and her husband Rob and son James for five days. They had recently moved into a large semi-detached house in East London which they were in the throes of renovating. I had never met Rob or three-year-old James, a real little character. Clare and I had not seen since 1968 when she was fifteen.

While there we saw quite a bit of London. This time we went to the east end of London and saw St. Paul's visited the Tower of London and saw the 'Beefeaters' and the famous ravens. As we left, we noticed a large crowd which we joined, in the centre of the ring stood a man in shabby clothes singing, very out of tune, "Pennies From Heaven" and people were chucking pennies into a hat on the ground. Wonder how much he would make in a day! We went down to Wimbledon to spend a day with my mother. While there we went for a walk on Wimbledon Common then had a delicious counter lunch at a typical English pub, "The Crooked Billet" just off the Ridgeway near the common.

Another day Clare drove us around to visit my niece, her sister, Rachel, her two daughters Kylie and Carmen Nina. After that we went to my niece Sarah, had a look at some of her beaut paintings. Sarah illustrates books. Finally, around to visit my nephew Simon and his girlfriend Sally, where we were joined by my other nephew Matthew.

Yet another day while still in London we went to see Vera's cousin Graeme whom she had not seen for twenty years, had lunch with him while he and Vera caught up on family news.

Rob and James drove us and our back packs to Arsenal Station where we got a train to Heathrow airport to start the next leg of our journey.

A Visit to Europe

We had a good flight to Zurich arriving at 8pm on September 2nd. Took a train ride into the city where we had to purchase tickets to Freiburg in Germany via Basel.

At this point we found it very difficult to make ourselves understood. The station staff were very uncooperative and at times quite rude. We finally found someone who could help us. After making a phone call to our friends in Ettenheim to let them know the late hour of our arrival we made our way to the right platform, the train was packed. We were helped in by Ferdinand, a guy from the Philippines who was studying in Europe. We had met him on the station platform while waiting for the train. The train was full of Italians who were returning to Belgium where they worked. They had been home on holiday.

When we got to Freiburg, much to our surprise we were met by Gisbert and his girlfriend Tina. Gisbert is the brother of Demaris and Beate friends of ours in Fremantle who we had met on our trip around Australia. They had asked us to visit their mother, Doris, in Germany. By coincidence Demaris was also visiting with her two-year-old daughter Maya. A pleasant surprise to see Demaris there. We found Doris a charming person and were so happy to be staying with her in Ettenheim, an interesting town with pastel coloured double-story houses. Everything looked clean, green and fresh, and it seemed so very quiet.

One day Doris drove us across the Rhine over the border into France to visit the ancient city of Strasbourg. We walked the cobbled streets and admired the unreal architecture and we visited the Cathedral in all its glory with its magnificent stained-glass windows. While in Strasbourg Doris took us to sample some French cuisine after which we went for a drive to see a bit more of the countryside. It was nearly too much to take in.

Another day Doris took us up into the Black Forest, Schwarzwald as it is known in Germany, so we were told. There we were shown some very beautiful scenery, an ancient castle ruins looking down the Rhine valley.

Many of the fir trees are suffering from the acid rains they are experiencing in Europe. We were taken to the town where they make cuckoo clocks, very interesting but the clocks were too expensive to purchase.

The towns and villages quite lovely with so many window boxes filled with flowers, nearly all the houses made of wood. The mountainside covered in fir trees and every now and then a different colour green, an elm or large oak tree. Doris took us to lunch to sample a fresh river trout. Then one evening to a beer parlour where everyone sits around drinking large mugs of beer, singing and dancing to a small band. Everyone very happy and friendly. Another day we had a hair-raising drive down the autobahn. Demaris had taken us to visit a third sister and her husband in another town and on the way home Maya kicked up a shindy and wanted to sit on Demaris' lap, she pulled off the road and asked me to drive. I had never driven on the right side of the road, never mind on the autobahn where cars rush past at about 200 Ks an hour. It was certainly an experience I don't relish repeating and shall never forget.

Again, we found it sad to say goodbye. This time the train was to take us south again, back into Switzerland to a town called Thun to visit more friends we had met on our Australia trip 1980-81.

Suzanne, a German girl and Martin, Swiss, Suzanne's sister Sebeya, her husband Gerd and their two-year-old son Timmie, met us off the train. Within an hour we were whisked off on a sightseeing tour. Up the mountain side by very narrow, windy roads then Martin pulled into a dirt parking area. Out we all got and climbed goodness knows how many hundreds of feet. As we got to one summit there was yet another hill to climb. Finally, at the top Vera and I just collapsed and lay there looking up into the clear blue sky. After resting a while and getting our breath back, we looked around us, in front were some snowcapped mountains like we'd never seen before.

Incredible Memories

On top of a mountain out of Thun looking across to the Matterhorn

There were the Eiger, Monch and the Jungfrau and bellow us the constant ringing of cow bells, each with its own note, as they ate or were being taken down the mountain to the farms to be housed for the winter months. The animals are housed below farmhouses so when one visits there is a decided farm smell wafting up through the floor. Martin and Suzanne took us to visit friends of theirs at a farm. We were shown how they run a farm in Switzerland then invited to partake a meal with them. What a spread with Swiss cheeses, sausages and delicious home baked bread plus home grown salads. By that time, we were quite used to the farm smells so enjoyed the meal as well as the company.

Again we found the towns and villages so lovely and colourful with their painted wooden houses, window boxes and hanging baskets full of an assortment of geraniums. We were shown how they make the mountain cheese and saw how it was carried down the mountain to be sold. Everyone works so hard to cultivate all the steep ground. Tractors winched up the mountainside while they till the land. Cow manure watered down and put in tankers then sprayed over the ploughed fields. A noisy, smelly exercise but obviously very fruitful.

AROUND THE WORLD ON A SHOESTRING

With Suzanne, Martin and Eva, Switzerland September 1983

Our other friends Eva, Swiss, and Martin, German, it was a bit confusing having two Martins, also met on our Australian trip as they had been traveling together, lived six kms away. They took us for a day trip in a mini minor, to Bern where we found the city was holding a festival which turned out to be very interesting. There were all sorts of stalls and exhibitions. While there we visited the Cathedral and walked around all day so covered quite a bit of ground. Even saw the famous bears in the pit performing, poor things.

We were very amused at the public toilets. Along the side of the road were some walls divided into cubicles where men just stood and performed. The ladies was not much better but we were at least hidden by a curtain, and we had a toilet. The drive home was a bit hair-raising as Martin hurtled along doing over a hundred km an hour in such a tiny car, Vera and I sitting in the back pretending we weren't worried.

Suzanne and Martin lived in a farmhouse just under the mountains, this is where we stayed. There was a beautiful view down a valley. We had some sunny days while there but on no day were we able to see the tops of the mountains, so we were very fortunate that Martin had decided to take us up the mountainside on our arrival. We saw snow fall while there and what it was like when the clouds came down and covered all the surrounding countryside. When we got up in the morning a very heavy mist hung down in the valley and clouds covered the mountains making it look as though we were in a framed picture.

Thun was rather beautiful, the town nestled down in the valley at the head of the Lake of Thun. The lake extended to Interlachen, it was a glorious blue colour, a low wall surrounding it along the roadside. As we drove the length of it, we saw all manner of boats sailing on it.

Incredible Memories

We found things in Switzerland very expensive. One day we met Swiss Martin in Thun for morning coffee, I was horrified at the price of coffee and pastries. We had a very happy and interesting, and extremely full week with our friends before we got moving again.

Tuesday 13th, on yet another train, this time going still further south to Ascoli Piceno in Italy. The first part of the journey through the mountains of Switzerland and northern Italy with beautiful scenes in between long tunnels.

We left the snow-capped peaks and moved down to flatter ground where the Italian architecture was so different to the Swiss. We changed trains at Milan, a very busy noisy station, then again at Bologna. We found both stations huge and rather confusing places but were lucky to find someone who could understand us and point us in the right direction as well as the right end of the train, as the trains unhitched to send one half one way and the other half another way.

We left Bologna in a very crowded train but did manage to get two seats in a compartment. The Italian occupants showing considerable interest in these two Australian ladies. I managed to get past with my limited knowledge of Spanish. We stopped at Remini, Ancona, the line running down the Adriatic Sea, Ancona looked a lovely little seaside town. Finally arrived in San Benedetto del Tronto, also on the Adriatic Sea, and stepped straight off the train into my sister Teresa's arms, what a coincidence our carriage stopped exactly where she stood!

I had not seen Teresa for twenty-six years. It was quite a reunion. With Teresa was her friend from work, Giovana, who seemed just as excited to see us. We piled into Giovana's small car and drove some thirty odd miles to Ascoli where Teresa and family live.

Ascoli is an ancient city with narrow streets and a hundred and one people and all their relations dashing through the streets in tiny little cars or motor scooters. Italian driving is something to be seen to be believed. Scooters speeding through one-way streets going the wrong way. Incessant horns blowing, a pedestrian taking their lives in their own hands, having to be constantly vigilant.

We arrived at where Teresa lived, we piled out and were confronted by a massive wooden door which led into a cobbled yard with stairs going up into several living units. At the top of one of these stairways Teresa opened a large door into her unit, first a long hallway off which several rooms went, all with very high ceilings. The walls were at least two feet thick. The building about two thousand years old had been modernized in the interior. A couple of the rooms overlooked the narrow street with the fire station and firemen's quarters directly opposite.

We met Teresa's three children, Angela Maria, married to Roberto, who very cleverly timed, produced Danielle for me to meet while on my visit. Giuseppe, doing his conscription with the fire brigade and Vincenzino, her youngest, about to join the Caribiniero. Neither of the boys speak English but we managed to communicate with many a laugh when we tried to make ourselves understood with sign language.

One day Vincenzino drove us to visit Assisi with Teresa and Vincenzo's girlfriend, Latizia. We hurtled along winding mountain roads. It was not easy to see much as he drove at such a speed. Returning by a different rout so we could see more of the countryside. Assisi was very interesting, built on a mountainside, the streets very steep the buildings and monastery had a decided orange colour or so it seemed to me. We walked through the monastery where St. Francis lived, there were several white pigeons cooing as they perched on some of the pillars. We sat on a garden bench for a while looking down the valley, this was the most peaceful part of the day.

That day I got to know my nephew a bit better, he was a delightful young man, always smiling.

Teresa and I had a lot of catching up to do and spent most of the time talking, when she wasn't at work. When she was at work Vera and I went for long walks out of the city walls and up into some terraced gardens. Ascoli is an ancient city divided in two by a river, the old on one side and the newer buildings on the other side of the river.

I visited the hospital with Teresa the day Angela was to have Danielle. It was easier communicating with Angela as she spoke English, a very sweet young lady. She produced a lovely blonde son. We met a lot of the relatives, none of whom spoke English.

Teresa put on an English-speaking tea party where we met a few of her English, American and Australian friends, all married to Italians! So we spoke English all afternoon. Vera and I found it a bit of a strain not being able to speak the language as even at mealtimes Teresa spoke Italian to the family, even to Angela.

I was very happy to at last meet my lovely niece and her husband and my nephews. Vera's visit was slightly marred by a wretched cold she caught just after we arrived.

Again, it was time to move on but this time we were to travel with Teresa. We had managed to book seats on the same plane which was taking us to London. We all set off on a coach early in the morning of September 22nd. A very comfortable run on a fairly good road, though very windy round the mountainside which meant the driver sounded his clarion at every corner, if it was a big corner, he played a sort of tune! It was mountainous until we reached Rieti where we had a halfway stop. I was in a hurry, trotted through the restaurant to the ladies, opened one door, 'no toilet', into the next, the same. By the third I closed the door behind me and all I was confronted with was a hole in one corner which I stooped over. What an experience! I still have dreams of trying to find a toilet in the ladies. Wondered how the nun who was on the coach would manage with her long habit. But then she was probably used to the situation!

Incredible Memories

Teresa had bought us each a cool drink, we sat on a low wall just outside until we boarded the coach for the second half of our journey. As we approached Rome the land was decidedly flatter and the towns very much closer, some beautiful tall shady trees lined the streets. The trip was very much slower as we neared Rome central where we were met by our cousin Heather and driven to her home on the outskirts of Rome. We had lunch and met her two sons, Aldo and Luca. Heather returned to work and Luca went out with a friend. The three of us spent the afternoon relaxing. Heather rushed home from work and drove us out to the airport showing us a bit of the city as we went.

Self with cousin Heather and sister Teresa, Ciampino Airport, Rome

Saw a beautiful sunset from the plane. We arrived rather late at Victoria Station after a long wait to get through customs, we went by train from Gatwick airport. Took a taxi to our brother Chris's place and it wasn't too long before we were all in bed.

Back in England

After a restful night and a good breakfast, we were joined by my mother who had come down from Wimbledon. Chris drove us all down to our other brother David's place in Woodley where the family were gathering. Chris returned to London after lunch. The following day was a pretty full day. My mother and I left early in the morning and travelled by train back to Gatwick to meet my youngest sister from Vancouver, Canada. Meanwhile David and his wife Marianne drove to Heathrow Airport to meet my sister Pat from New York. Imagine the reunion at lunch.

After lunch David and I took Vera into Reading where she caught a train to Portsmouth for another visit with her friends there.

When we returned to Woodley everyone was busy catching up on the latest news from their part of the world.

On Sunday September 25th all of David and Marianne's six children, their husbands and the grandchildren turned up. It was the first time I had seen Helen, David and Marianne's second daughter, since leaving England in 1968 so that was fifteen years and the first time I had ever met Les her husband, Christopher and Johnathan, her two sons.

It was a beautiful day as we were experiencing an Indian Summer. We had been extremely lucky with the weather since we started our trip.

We all had a sit-down lunch, seventeen adults and five children celebrating a birthday in honour of my mother's 80th year which was actually on the 27th September.

Self with Mum and siblings (David, Tina, Chris, Teresa) at Woodley, 27th September 1983

A very happy day was had by all. Trestle tables had been set up in the garden under a large apple tree. We all enjoyed cold meats and salads followed by fruit and ice-cream, and of course a birthday cake. We had bonbons and party hats. Mother was very happy to have all of us there. During the afternoon David and Marianne's children left to return to their various homes.

On the Monday, David took Pat and I down to Sonning and we walked along the banks of the Thames under some very large shady trees. It was so peaceful and quite beautiful with a gentle breeze blowing up the river on which were several boathouses, some were tied up alongside while others were slowly put putting down the river. A damp earthen smell hung in the air, a couple of squirrels scurried around and the bird song was thrilling.

Incredible Memories

On Tuesday 27th September my brother Chris and his wife Basia joined the rest of us at Woodley for the birthday. This was to be the first time in twenty-eight years that my mother had all six of her children together.

This time we celebrated with a lunch inside, the weather was not as kind as it had been on the Sunday. As a family usually does when gathered together, we talked of our childhood memories, which at times had us all laughing hysterically. Some recalling scenes my mother knew nothing of. Just as well parents do not know all their offspring get up to at the time but can join in the laughter at the incident recalled.

At the end of the day, Pat and I returned to London with Chris and Basia to spend a few days with them. While in London we relaxed and enjoyed each other's company. On the Friday Vera joined us. Pat, Vera and I visited Portobello Road markets with its cosmopolitan atmosphere, its marvelous antiques, clothes, and bric-a-brac and the flea market. Then we walked about two miles back to Chris's. As we walked along, we noticed the trees in the parks and gardens were starting to turn into their autumn colours

On the Sunday the rest of the family came up from Woodley for lunch. That evening Pat and I swapped places with Teresa and Christine, Vera and I returned to Woodley with David, Marianne, Pat and my mother. During the week we visited places near Reading, spent another day up in London. David lent me his car and we drove over to Windsor Castle. David kept on insisting I drive on the left-hand side of the road presuming that we drove on the right side out in Australia.

We were a bit disappointed as parts of the Castle were closed due to restorations, but we had very good weather once more and what we did see we enjoyed. I did not find it taxing driving on English roads and found my way around quite easily.

Friday October 7th another big day. All at Woodley travelled up to London. My Uncle Tom and Aunt Mabel put on a party for all relatives who could make it. I think there were twenty-five there, a reunion of my generation, Aunt Alice was there and her son Ian, from Australia. The last time Vera and I had seen Ian was when we visited his family on our around Australia trip.

Cousins and siblings' reunion at Tom and Mabel's

It was really great meeting up with so many of my cousins that I hadn't seen for so many years, also to meet a couple I had never had the opportunity to meet before. Tom and Mabel and their daughter Marie-Belen put on a terrific meal and the hospitality was unreal.

They lived in a large flat in Victoria which lent itself nicely for such a crowd. Another happy memory to add to our many. After the party we went back to Chris and Basia's to have a farewell drink and to thank them again for their hospitality.

The next day we were once more on the move, this time on the first leg homeward bound. Time flies too quickly when one is enjoying oneself. But Vera and I were also looking forward to returning home to our families.

After saying our farewells to David, Pat and Teresa, Marianne drove us into Reading to catch a train to Gatwick airport. We were met there by my mother who had gone there earlier to see Christine off. Vera's friends from Portsmouth, the McPhilips, were there also to see us off. We checked our bags in and had time for a cuppa before sad farewells

We took off for our flight to Rome. The trip was good and our rout took us over the beautiful Alps.

Homeward Bound

At Ciampino Airport we were met by my cousin Heather and her youngest son Luca. When we got to her house, we were met by her husband Angelo. The last time I had seen him was seventeen years before when we were both visiting my Aunt Alice, Heather's mother, and Uncle Bill when they lived in Scotland.

Incredible Memories

The next day being Sunday, Heather was not at work so she took us and Luca on a sightseeing tour of Rome and the Vatican City. Heather is a very good driver, I would never attempt to drive in Rome, the traffic was quite incredible. It was a wonder there wasn't an accident on every corner, never mind in between. *Everyone just goes,* horns blowing, police on point duty blowing whistles, motor scooters and those small Italian three-wheeler vans and cars darting in all directions. I found it hard at times to take my eyes off the road to look at the ancient buildings we were passing.

Heather drove around a large area but we also went by foot. We visited the famous Pantheon and walked several piazzas with their fountains and sculptures, saw where Bernini lived. The Basilica Massenzio, the Basilica of St. Paul, the Colosseum, Constantine Arch, and we crossed the river Tevere several times. Some of the bridges being only for pedestrians, they were beautifully built bridges with wrought iron balustrades, with ornamental lamps at either end and at intervals along the bridge. We also walked along the streets which ran alongside of the river. Heather drove us around to see the FAO buildings where she worked.

We drove down Bargo Santo Spirito and up some side streets where Heather found somewhere to park then we walked to the Vatican. Along all the high walls that lined the streets there were capers growing and hanging down all over them. We walked around the Piazza S. Pietro and looked at all the statues up on the pillars which were on either side of the piazza. The Basilica was very impressive, Heather showed us where the Pope stood to bless the crowds in the Piazza. We saw only a small part of inside St. Peters, the Swiss guards looked very smart in their colourful uniforms. The floors were all marble, in the hall we went into. There were small enclosed chapels with rows of candle holders out front with money boxes to drop your money in if you purchased a candle. We also saw the famous Pieta. Any statues that could be reached had shiny spots where they had been constantly touched by millions of people as they passed over the years.

Then we walked up Via della Conciliazione to Castel Angelo. All up the via there are people trying to sell souvenirs of the Vatican. The crowds were incredible.

We were made to feel very welcome and I was happy to get to know Heather and Angielo's sons, it was also a pleasure seeing them again. Both Aldo and Angielo spoke English which made it easier.

On the 10th we said our farewells and took a taxi to Fiumicino airport. The traffic was terrible, cars and trucks were bumper to bumper. The taxi driver took a detour and sped up and down so many different streets we were sure we would miss our flight. As it turned out our plane was an hour and a half late in leaving.

Next stop Bahrain where we were held up again. A short stop at Bangkok, those not disembarking had to stay on the plane. Cleaners came on and cleaned around us. More food was brought on board and the smell of fuel was very overpowering.

Finally, Singapore, we were glad we were stopping off here as the trip had been long and tiring. We arrived at our hotel about 9:30 PM. Ready for a shower and bed. We spent the two days we were in Singapore sightseeing and shopping for the family and purchasing some duty-free items for ourselves. Breakfast was inclusive at the hotel so we'd have a hearty one, then snack through the day and having a Chinese meal at the restaurant in the hotel in the evening. The time was getting closer for our return home to our families.

It was a rather bumpy trip from Singapore. We had been booked on an evening flight arriving at Perth at 1:30 AM. We spent hours getting through customs, having to open bags and declare all we were bringing home. What a way to end our trip of a lifetime.

We finally got to see our family who had come to meet us at 4 AM. They were beginning to wonder if we had missed our flight. There were the smiling faces of Bernadette, George, Alison, Lois, Guido and Tara. All drove back to my unit. After a lot of talking and breakfast, Marie-Therese, Claude, Joel and Matthew arrived.

The whole trip was beginning to feel like an unreal dream. But then we had heaps of photographs to prove we'd actually been to all those wonderful places and met up with so many who had helped to make our trip such a happy one and making it possible to achieve. On a rough count we had met up with 115 friends and relations.

Chapter 63

BOONDARABI, MOORA

Not long after returning from our trip around the World, Vera and I could not see eye to eye. She decided to go and live just down the coast at a caravan village. We met on occasions but then I got a phone call from one of her daughters to say sadly she had taken her own life. This was a real shock to all that knew her.

I often went up the coast to stay with a friend who lived right on the beach front. We used to go down to the water's edge early in the morning and catch herring for breakfast and then we would either go for a long walkalong the cliffs or visit local friends and either play card games or Scrabble.

Sometime after that, I decided I would like to get a place and live in the bush. An opportunity came up and I was offered to go and stay up in Three Springs, about a four-hour drive north of Perth, to see if I liked it. That is when I moved in with Sue, she had a son and a boarder living in her house and I took over the housekeeping. Not long after I moved up there Marie-Therese, Claude and my two grandsons came up for the weekend. They brought a large tent which we set up on the back lawn. We had a lovely weekend, drove around and showed them what Three Springs had to offer.

Sue used to take her weekends off in the middle of the week as the hospital she was in charge of could be quite busy at weekends. Each time she took days off we would go on either a fishing day at the coast or just explored the countryside. At times we would camp over-night. On one occasion on one of our explores we discovered the remains of a small town. Most of the buildings had crumbled but it was interesting to explore and imagine what it would be like to have lived there in the last century. That night we lay under the stars in our sleeping bags, on top of a brick floor which was all that remained of the building.

Another time we drove out east to a place called Camel Soak which at the time was very dry. We witnessed a father emu and his three young ones

BOONDARABI, MOORA

cross the dry creek. That evening we saw many more emus. We also saw a falling star as we drove back to Three Springs that night. Of course, when we went on these outings, we took food and plenty of drinking water. It was quite exciting driving along so many dirt roads experiencing, discovering new fauna, a few foxes and many species of birds, mainly various types of parrots. We drove past several deserted farmhouses, a shame to see them in the process of slow destruction.

Whenever Sue went down to Perth on a refresher course, I would go with her and visited the family. Sometimes she would be down for a week so I had the time to myself and I would catch up with family and friends. On one of these trips we called in to visit Alison and Carl who lived in Padbury a suburb in north Perth. We arrived about 4:30, Alison was due to have her first child. After we bought Chinese take-away and continued down to East Fremantle to my flat. After eating and enjoying a few wines had an early night. About 4am we were woken and told Alison was in labour, so I got dressed and drove back to Padbury. Shortly after I arrived the mid-wife came in and I assisted in the delivery of a lovely little girl, my first granddaughter.

Another trip to Perth we stopped at Moora to have lunch. I had mentioned to Sue that I would like to find a nice five-acre block and move to the country. We bought a couple of hamburgers and some take away coffee, Sue drove out of town and up a dirt road, a no-through road, where we pulled up by a gate to have lunch. I looked across the block and thought it was an ideal spot as there was a creek running through it. Then she announced she owned it and wanted to sell it! But it was 20 acres; much too big for me.

Any way over a matter of months while we talked of our futures, which were similar in ideas, I suggested buying half the property and we could share the whole and develop it with a few sheep. These would supply the wool we planned to spin and develop it into a business.

By this time Sue had decided to move on. She had been under the strain of being in charge at the hospital and without a resident doctor. She applied at several hospitals in a large area near enough to Moora and got one as a registered nurse and midwife, only 35 miles from Moora.

In the mean time we pitched a tent, made a bush toilet surrounded by hessian, and so started our dream of developing the land. On Sue's days off we would go down to the block and plant trees and do a bit of fencing to divide up the property. We planted over 1,000 trees all around the perimeter of the block. I found a man who built sheds at a very reasonable price. Next thing we had a 20 x 40-foot tin shed with a high roof, a double sized door at one end and a single door the other end. Got a concrete floor poured and when the concrete was set started to move in.

Incredible Memories

Living in a tent for several months, March 1986

Outdoor loo and first shed

At the back half we stored Sue's gear, we used wardrobes and high bookshelves to separate the middle of the shed into two bedrooms, using curtains as doors. The other end set up a pot-belly stove for heating and keeping a hot kettle going. With two lounge chairs and a rug on the floor in front of the fire made for a very comfortable and cosy area. Then I cut a hole in the wall near the single door and fitted a window, below this I put a sink and bench-top with cupboards below.

While Sue was at work, I built a patio area outside the single door. The tall farmer down the road helped me put the two-by-fours across for the roof. This was to be our out-door area till we got a house. I also built a small shed as the bathroom, with basin and shower recess. Hot water for the shower was a black plastic bag filled with water and hung on the clothesline to be solar heated. This had a shower head attached to have a shower just added some cold water as the bag would get very hot.

I made us two fireplaces at the far end of the patio and this is what I cooked on. I got a 2,000-gallon tank put against one end of the shed to catch water when it rained on the shed. In the meantime, we had bought a small truck, on the back we put a 44-gallon drum which we would fill with water from town. One weekend Alison, Carl and Carl's uncle out from England came up. The guys and I put up a 10 x 10 shed to store all the garden tools and wheelbarrow. Then I built a greenhouse butting on to it and made a flower bed along the front where I grew Chrysanthemums to sell as cut flowers on Mother's Day.

Placed another 2,000-gallon tank placed close to where the house was to go. When Sue came over, we separated the block into six sections, so we had heaps of fencing to do. Previously Sue had fenced the whole perimeter, and a mighty job she did of it. With three gates onto the property from the dirt road and a cockies gate from the property next door. There were only nine trees on the block so planting trees was a major project. All together we planted two rows of trees along the fence line up the road and across the back of the block bordered by a lane. We also planted Lucerne trees which we could feed the sheep with during the dry season. Having planted young trees, they needed watering during the dry season so I would put a drum on the trailer and fill it with water form this I would bucket the water and walk around watering the trees.

A neighbour had used the block for several years without permission, to run horses, therefore the banks to the creek were badly damaged by their hoofs when they went down to drink. We levelled the banks as best we could. Grass soon grew on the banks, one water hole down by the front gate always had water in it being fed by a spring, so we planted some native shrubs near it. When Sue was home, we planted trees on both sides of the driveway, put lengths of pipe down the side of each tree to pour the water in so the tap root of the tree would grow straight down and the tree didn't form surface roots.

Life was very exciting experiencing all we were achieving. One doesn't have to have heaps of money. All one has to do is use a little imagination. There are those who recycle houses. For a considerably low price one can purchase a second-hand house and have it relocated. First, we had to get in touch with a firm that removes houses from one area to another. After viewing a few houses, imagining what can be done to enhance them. When

Incredible Memories

we decided on a likely possibility, pay a small deposit, sign some contracts and leave the rest to the guys who will remove, transport and deposit said house. I paid $ 1,500 for the house, Number 7 1st Avenue Bicton. They arranged with council re conditions, fees and inspections while the house is being rebuilt.

The entire roof was removed; this being a tiled house, the tiles are removed and neatly stashed in the house. Then the pitch of the roof was taken to pieces, each timber numbered and marked, also put inside the house. Then the house was raised on stilts, lifted by large jacks leaving behind all concrete floors, i.e. kitchen, bathroom and laundry and verandas. Any brick fireplaces and chimneys left were demolished. None of these were included in the purchase of the house but the guys were to replace with floorboards and plaster board for walls. Any breakages while in transport were replaced.

The house was then cut straight down the middle, each half loaded on to a semi-trailer. We were informed on the date and approximate time of arrival. Having decided where the house would be and which direction the front door would face. The said house arrived. It had to be taken through the next property as there was a large tree down by the front gate which I didn't want destroyed. The semi-trailers drove across two paddocks and through the cockies gate giving access to a lower paddock on our side.

As they arrived, I told the first driver to miss the centre of the paddock as it was a bit sandy. "She'll be right" says he and drove on and of course became bogged with half a house on board. To cut a long story short, after two hours it was mobile again. All were amazed we had not chosen to have the house facing our front gate, in the distance. The property was not aligned direct south, north and one had to consider sun rise and setting in both winter and summer for heating and cooling the house.

Both halves of the house were expertly lifted off the trucks on to raised jacks. The trucks drove off and the jacks were lowered very slowly until the two halves came together perfectly and sat on stumps already in position. I had asked them to raise the stumps another six inches as it made it easier to get under the house to treat the stumps for white ants.

The three guys who were to replace all missing parts over a period of three weeks, chose to sleep in their swags in the house. This was to cut costs to me. I had to give them three meals a day plus morning and afternoon tea. All this I managed on the two open fires set outside the shed I was living in. I had arranged for the men to have showers at the caravan site in town, only a mile away. They did a marvellous job replacing the tiles, tying down every 5th tile.

BOONDARABI, MOORA

Two halves of the house on jacks, February 1987

For breakfast they would have porridge one morning and a choice of cereals the next with several pieces of toast with homemade marmalade or vegemite washed down with copious cups of tea Every fourth day they had bacon and eggs, Morning tea cake and tea, afternoon tea they had homemade scones. For lunch I made a variety of sandwiches followed by cake and choice of tea or coffee. The evening meal could be anything like cauliflower au gratin, meat, jacket potatoes and carrots and peas or a pot roast boiled potatoes and greens of some sort followed by apple crumble and custard or fruit salad and ice-cream. My Guiding days stood me in good stead as did my Navy cooking.

They were very appreciative of my cooking, said it was 'better tucker than they would have got at the hotel'. They were jolly good company and we had heaps of good laughs, and I never heard a single swear word. The whole cost was $14,000.

Then there was the painting and cleaning up to do when they finally left they said they hadn't had such fun doing the job for a long time. Steps to make going in and out of the house as it was now a metre above ground, and of course electricity and water connections to be considered. An exciting project!

To renovate the house, where does one start? First get two bedrooms ready. While doing this we could still live in the shed and use the existing facilities. I started to make the sleep-out into the bathroom. Being a large room, I could have both bath and separate shower, a basin and large linen cupboard. We would continue to have the toilet just outside back door, between the house and the laundry which were on ground level. Had a small water tank put on a stand just behind the toilet I put a pipe through to serve the toilet, gravity feed.

Incredible Memories

The original bathroom was in the centre of the house facing the front door. I blocked off the door into the hall and cut a hole in the wall behind where the bath had been. This opened into the kitchen and now became a walk-in pantry.

When next in Perth, we went to WA Salvage, a marvellous hardware outlet, very cheap slightly damaged new stuff. Here we bought a fibre-glass bath and a shower recess, plus tiles for shower and surrounding walls. They also had second hand kitchen sinks, cupboards and bench tops all at a ridiculously low price. The truck was loaded for our trip back home. Then we remembered we needed to get paints, oh well, that meant another trip sometime, there was enough to get on with.

Front of the house before the extensions

Once we were able to move into the house, we had to start thinking about getting some sheep. A friend of Sue's had said we could have ten of her coloured lambs when we were ready. We made arrangements to go up to Three Springs to collect them off a farm just outside the town. When we got there, we found that Elizabeth had gone into hospital but her husband said he would help us pick some and load them onto the back of the ute in a cage we had borrowed for the job. When he pointed out a couple we could have we got quite a shock, they were not little lambs as we had thought but huge sheep. We were told they were classed as lambs until they were just over a year old. He assured us they would fit in the cage, better to have a tight fit for traveling!

Then we remembered we had promised a farm hand we would pick up two lambs from his home which he had saved from being killed as farmers don't like having coloured sheep among their white ones. At the farm this brown very, quiet sheep with sad eyes had followed me up and down the raise, I felt she was asking to be picked so I said we'd have her, little did we know she was one of Elizabeth's favourites. But she was happy that Ma Baa as we called her was going to a good home. When we were loaded, we drove into town to Dave's place only to find that the lambs he had told us about were wee lambs as we had expected all the others to be.

Self with Ma Baa 1992

They were in a small pen at the side of the house. Our worry was that they would be trampled when put in with the others. Well they were nice and small and we could carry them to the ute. They were quiet till we got near them, I know, we'll tempt them with some grass. No that didn't work, maybe if we made the area a bit smaller they would be easy to catch. What a laugh they could jump as high as the six-foot fence and just ran straight past us. If I could corner them even if they managed to get past me, Sue could catch them as they went past. That didn't work and we both ended up in the mud, it had rained the night before and as there wasn't even a blade of grass in the enclosure it was very slippery mud. after some length of time we managed to catch them and fit them into the back of the ute. While all this was going on all the sheep in the ute had been baaing their heads off in reply to these two little imps who were also baaing. For all we knew they were having a good laugh at us and also telling the lambs how to get away from us. Both of us were pretty exhausted and very muddy. By this time, we were quite hungry but didn't want to go into town looking like we did so left down a backstreet and stopped some distance from Three Springs at a roadside shop and hoped we wouldn't meet someone we knew.

On the trip home I remarked that the one metre fence I had so cleverly made for the little lambs we were picking up was absolutely useless. The big lambs would just walk over it, so we had a good laugh over it. When we arrived back, I backed the ute up to a mound of sand so they didn't have too far to jump off the ute. I opened the back of the cage and they all started jumping out all except one very large grey one who stayed at the back stamping down very noisily on the metal floor and looking very annoyed. So we had enough and decided to leave him, as we walked away he jumped

Incredible Memories

off and raced down the paddock with all the other "lambs" following. We named him Flash. We went inside and left them to sort themselves out.

In the morning I went out to check on our wee lambs when I noticed one of the big ones lying off by itself, on looking a bit closer I noticed a little round black ball beside it. This turned out to be Ma Baa with a baby who we named Georgie as it was born on my son's birthday. So now we had thirteen. We wondered how many more were pregnant. The next day we found out, for there was another but this time the baby was white. So they became Uda, Mum and August. Now there were fourteen.

Being winter there was plenty of feed so we didn't worry about them all too much. We thought we would let them settle down a bit before we decided what we were going to do with them. Ma Baa Was very friendly and came to me quite easily but didn't want me to touch her baby. A couple of weeks went by and we got on with what we had to do, then I noticed one of the big ones lying off by itself and twin white babies beside her but they were baaing a lot so thought I better check on them. The mother had died and the wee ones were probably hungry. So I went down the road to see the farmer who followed me back and caught the babies and showed me how to feed them. He said the mother had been 'fly struck'. That was a new one for us, apparently this time of the year was when the flies strike so he told me all about it and how to spot it and then treat it. WOW! Did we have a lot to learn and a lot of work to do. Not so easy raising sheep, but we would cross the bridges when we came to them.

Rome wasn't built in a day and it looked like we were going to be busy for a few years to get the property running and giving us a return. We live in a wasteful world, the exciting things I found at the local tip introduced Sue and I to a Tip Crawl. We knew all the tips in a radius of 30 miles. Most were some distance from the towns so very quiet and undisturbed while we explored the contents. After Christmas or a wedding was a good time to make the rounds. The amount of unopened and unused articles thrown out was incredible. Presents still in their containers, there were Pyrex dishes, vases, glass dishes, even a whole dinner set. One trip we scored a set of sheets and towels still in their plastic covers.

Shell Oil had closed their depot and dumped all their timber flooring and 4x4 timber all, well-seasoned so into our ute it went, all would be of some use in the future. One day I backed up to unload our rubbish when right beside the back wheel someone had neatly piled up a set of windows with small panes. Only one pane was cracked, so onto the ute they went. The front veranda was open to all weather so I planned to extend it another five foot and enclose it. So I designed it to suit the windows and made the extension in a half circle. Before finishing the structure, I took another trip down to the tip and low and behold there were 8 cut off sheets of corrugated roofing just the right length to reach the guttering. I put down the flooring, mended the cracked pane, when complete we had a lovely breakfast room overlooking my rose garden and we could be out of the weather.

House with enclosed breakfast room and start of extension on side

With a round table and chairs we now had an extra room. Along the side of the house we had a bull-nosed tin roof built onto the house. I made some stone steps going down onto the newly poured concrete floor. One weekend we went to Perth and stayed at a Guest House which was in the throes of being renovated and what should be in the skip bin but a huge window which would probably be just the thing for what we hoped to make the new covered area into a work room and extra bedroom. So onto the ute it went. By making a brick wall topped by windows along the length of the house, with a door at the far end and the large window at the other end we had another cosy enclosed area.

It looked like we would be continually thinking up some sort of building. The creek ran through the middle of the 20-acre block. Dry during the summer months but ran in abundance through the winter wet months. By this time, we were feeding 40 sheep in the western half, shearing being during the wet season it was impossible to bring the sheep across for shearing. It meant a trek out the far gate down the road and in the front gate, not an easy exercise.

The solution was to build a bridge. Material gathered mostly from the tip and kind farmers. There was no problem finding discarded 7ft pipes from road signs that had been renewed. A farmer offered all the floorboards from an old farmhouse, we had to recover them. After removing thousands of rusty nails, I had well-seasoned jarrah floorboards. At the tip old wooden bed frames, this gave us well seasoned double bed sized Oregon pine, 4 by 2 planks. After dismantling the bed springs, sometimes a bit dicey if well

Incredible Memories

sprung as they tended to give way very suddenly. The only thing purchased from the hardware store was, cement, nuts and bolts and nails.

Summer arrived, the bed of the creek dried and turned as hard as concrete so I had to use a long crow bar to dig the holes to drop the poles in . Then pour a base of concrete, make sure all pipes measured correctly in distance and were perfectly straight, and the same height. Before dropping them in, I took them to the blacksmith and had him weld L shaped lugs on to take the 4x2 timber for the edge of the bridge and to hold the pipes at the right angle. While the concrete was setting, I checked with the spirit level that they were straight. The bridge was 60ft long by a metre and a half wide.

Completing the bridge 1988

BOONDARABI, MOORA

Creek flowing under the hand built 60ft bridge

Not having built a bridge before and having no drawings, an idea in my head and an exercise of "As you go, what next". Any way I had it completed by the time the rains came, I <u>always</u> had a month's notice as the frogs would start their 'Gloop, Gloop' mating call as they emerged from the side walls of the creek. Once out of their tombs they deflated with a sound similar to letting a balloon down while one held the opening.

Now I was able to lead the sheep across and up to the holding yard, another project. The first crossing was quite comical, as some of the sheep just stood at the gate looking at my beautiful bridge. Then they did their little leap and twist, landed on the floor of the bridge and looked surprised and a bit spooked by the sound they made when their hooves hit the timber. Such a wonderful feeling of satisfaction as I watched the water flow beneath my bridge It stood the force of the running water which proved the farmer down the road quite wrong with his prediction it would wash away the first winter heavy rains.

A shearer gave me an old motor to drive the shears and said I could have it if I could get it going and he would come and shear the sheep. Well I took it all to pieces and cleaned and oiled it. It went like a song so I made a stand for it and away we went with our first shearing. Then I had to learn how to pick up the fleece and throw it correctly to clean the skirting, we got nearly a bail of very fine wool for which we got top price. We felt so proud to have achieved so much in our first year of farming. I even was able to whistle the sheep to follow certain commands, I had a special whistle to call them over from the far paddock so I didn't have to go over and fetch them.

Once the wool had been sorted, we kept a certain amount for ourselves so we could start spinning. We both had spinning wheels and it didn't take too long to get the wool into skeins ready to knit and to sell beanies and make jumpers. From one of the jumpers we sold to a sailor, we got our first order from a lady in Boston USA who had seen it and tried it found it ideal for

Incredible Memories

sailing in. All the wool still had lanolin in it and therefore was quite waterproof. We had got a very good price for the rest of the wool.

Now we had a means to get the sheep across the property, so the next thing was to build a causeway to drive a vehicle across. We had a very large concrete pipe dropped into the dry creek for the water to run through when the rains came. Then we went down to the tip to collect a dozen large tyres, this also saved them from being burnt, we put them three at either end of the pipe running away from the pipe, had a load of sand delivered then we started the task of filling each tyre. Once that was done, we got another load dropped to fill in either side of the pipe. We had just done that when the first rains came but luckily only enough for the water to run through the pipe so the next dry day, we had two loads of concrete poured to level off and make a substantial cause way. After a few dry days the concrete was set and we were able to walk across, push the wheelbarrow over, a couple more days we drove over and cheered.

Self and George 1987

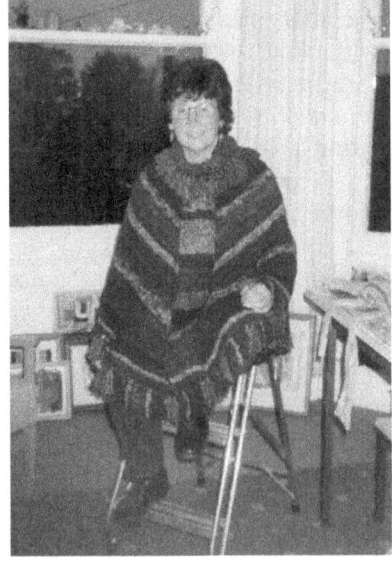

Poncho knitted with different shades of wool we spun from our sheep, 1994

BOONDARABI, MOORA

Beanies knitted from our sheep's wool

Never a dull moment with so much to do. With the wet comes fly-strike so daily I would go among the sheep to check. If I found any struck, I would have to get the mob over into a small pen, separate the one struck and get it into a race I had made at the back of a hay shed Sue and I had built. Once up the race, I had to grab and throw the sheep over, put a front leg under my left arm and a knee to hold it down would start the horrible job of cutting away the wool around the damp spot till I came across the fly maggots which I would douse with a mixture to kill them Often the sheep were so relieved they became quite relaxed. Then for the next one and hopefully no more as by then I was exhausted. This was usually a daily job.

One summer holiday my two grandsons Joel and Matthew came for school holidays and they helped me make a walk over stone causeway where the creek ran at the west end of the property. This entailed going for a drive to an old quarry to collect rocks, load them on to the ute then unload them and barrow them across to the creek. Then we had lunch and were straight into the job of fitting the rocks in place across the creek, then mixing a batch of concrete and barrowing that down to the spot where we filled in all around the rocks. The rocks were various colours so after cleaning the excess cement off them it turned out to be a very attractive causeway. The eight and nine-year-olds seemed to really enjoy all the farming exercises we achieved. While there we would go for a drive to a small seldom used track and I would take the boys for driving lessons in my Suzuki.

One day I had an urgent phone call from Alison my youngest, to say she wanted somewhere to stay as she no longer had a job. Sue and I discussed it and decided I would take the ute and drive south to Denmark to pick Alison and her two-year-old daughter Jessica and their belongings up and bring them back to the property. I phoned Margaret, another daughter

Incredible Memories

who owned a house in Bridgetown nearly half-way, asked if we could stop there overnight. That arranged, I drove down stopping over at a motorhome for a break, picked Alison and belongings up and started the long, slow drive home. We called into Bridgetown, rather tired and ready for the break. Started off early the next day for the second part of the journey having several stops on the way to stretch our legs and have something to eat and drink.

Before Sue went back to work, she had made beds and left a welcoming note. We arrived too tired to unload the ute, had a bite to eat and retired to bed. Jessica was amazing how she settled in and seemed to love the move. It was nice having them stay and Alison was a great help on the farm. When Sue came over from work we often went on an explore and took a picnic, Jessica used to enjoy these. After a short stay, Alison and Jessica moved to Fremantle.

Not long after that Sue managed to get a job at Moora Hospital doing mainly night duty. We always did jobs where it was easier for two, we built a forty-by-twenty open shed to park the vehicles in and it had a work bench to the back left-hand. We had a dam made in the middle of the property to take run off when the wet weather came. We planted trees along the mounds on either side and it wasn't long before it was inhabited by yabbies, they seemed to find their own way over from the creek and gave us several meals. They were large freshwater shrimps, which I used to bait and set baskets to catch them in. Word must have got around that we had them because when I went to set my traps someone else had also set one. Of course, we had to build a fence around all of this to keep the sheep out, just another job to keep us busy.

We also got a small dam dug in the creek just below the house. When it filled a pair of wood ducks brought their family to swim in it. At that time, we had a swarm of locusts go through the property stripping nearly every leaf they came across, the ducklings had a feast and when the locusts moved on, they would come up to the back door expecting me to feed them. They must have thought I had supplied the locusts. So I started to feed them, as they became adults, the ones the foxes hadn't got flew away to start their own families!

In the meantime, we had planted several fruit trees, we grew nearly all the vegetables for our use and also supplied the town superstore with bunches of silver-beet and flowers besides strawberries when in season. We were being overrun by rabbits, in one month I shot over forty plus six foxes and three feral cats. Some of the cats were nearly the size of a medium sized dog. I would skin the rabbits and freeze some and also gave them away to families in town. Always a regular supply and were welcomed by those who ate rabbit.

Another big job was to make the end of the shed we lived in into a double bedroom and an area with double bunks plus a small kitchen. We lined the ceiling and the walls to help to make it a bit cooler in the summer, also had running water at the sink fed from the 2,000-gallon tank at the end of the shed. So now we had a more comfortable place for visitors to stay. Like I said there was a never-ending job just waiting for us.

Sue bought an old tractor which needed a big job to get it going. So I stripped the engine down, got a new set of pistons and put it all together again and it worked! I had seen an old horse drawn harvester half buried in sand in a friend's back yard and asked if I could have it, the answer was yes if I found a way to move it. Which I did. I cleaned and stripped it all down cleaned all the sand out of the workings, found an old seat at one of the tips we frequented, greased all the cogwheels thoroughly and put it all together. The only thing I couldn't find was a long enough timber arm to rake in the hay. I made it so it could be pulled by a tractor as we didn't have a horse.

My days were always full, growing fruit and vegetables, the sheep to attend to plus all the mundane chores, they started very early and ended late but I always had a siesta to break the day. Over the eight years we owned the property we achieved quite a lot, I could relate many more stories but feel this book would never end.

I celebrated my 65th birthday there and then our friendship deteriorated, and Sue bought me out and I moved to Northam, bought a house and started renovating all over again. Life is never dull and certainly never boring.

Enclosure 100 x 36 ft to keep possums, parrots and rabbits out of orchard

Incredible Memories

Exploring the bush *Visiting Wilgie Mia ochre Mine*

Poona, an emerald mine in the Weld Ranges join *Oxer's Lookout where the 4 gorges*

Chapter 64

JAMAICA RE-UNION 1984

It was April the 22nd when I left Perth, Western Australia bound for Jamaica in the West Indies. My first port of call being Singapore. I was on my way for a reunion to celebrate the 50 years since Sr. Emmanuel started 21st St Andrew Girl Guide Company of which I had been a member. I stayed overnight in Singapore before the next leg of my journey to the UK where I spent a few days with my mother and two brothers and their families. Then on to Bermuda to refuel and finally Jamaica where I was met by Sr. Emmanuel and several of my old classmates who had also been members of the 21st. I recognized a couple of them, they like myself had not changed that much.

After 37 years some people change quite a bit but I soon found out their warmth and friendship had not. I was to stay at the convent of The Immaculate Conception High School, my old high school. All who met me at the airport congregated in Sister's office where we sat drinking tea, recalling events of the past. My room was large with an ensuite, there was no hot water which meant I had to have a freezing cold shower every morning or rather the mornings that there was water. It was sad to see how run down the building had become.

On the second day I was invited by Sister's cousin to stay with them in the coolness of the mountains. Here I caught up with the latest Guiding news, we were to go to the reunion dinner from there. I was much more comfortable and was able to have hot showers also I was free to go for walks quite safely.

While there I was taken to another friend who I had been at school with. She invited several other friends who had been my family's friends including our last neighbour, who had also been our landlady. This was a lovely surprise; my visit was not only a school reunion but a meeting of old friends and neighbours.

Incredible Memories

The great reunion to celebrate the 50th anniversary finally arrived and what a reunion that was, there were girls now ladies, old class and schoolmates who had travelled from USA Canada, the Cayman Islands and the Bahamas. All of us having left Jamaica and led very full lives since graduating from the ICHS. Most had married and had families like myself. Others had become Doctors and a dentist, another a Headmistress at a high school in the States. I was overwhelmed. Most had kept up with each other and had regularly met up in Jamaica over the years. Where they lived was of course so much nearer than Australia.

One day after the reunion Sister Emmanuel organized a picnic which we were to celebrate at Port Antonio situated on the north coast of Jamaica. To get there we travelled in convoy with several cars up over the mountain. I had forgotten a lot of the Booter talk which is what Jamaican slang was called. I was very amused listening to remarks made when recalling a certain teacher one lady said, "She was a real quarrelsome person." Then another saying, "Cha man that is something else." Then another telling a story about a maid getting caught stealing and her retort, "Me no teef teef me just take take."

Sister to a boarder who claimed she was feeling unwell she said, "she'd have no sympathy if they wanted sympathy to look it up in the dictionary. Don't be such a boderation". So the trip to Port Antonio was quite lively and amusing.

On the way over there were several roadside stalls selling beef jerky. We stopped and purchased some. I had never eaten it before so it was a new experience chewing away at the jerky which I found quite dry but very hot. My lips were burning and my gums felt as if I had scrubbed them with a very hard toothbrush. We had also bought some coconut grater which was one of my favourites when at school. It is coconut coarsely grated and boiled in molasses and soft brown sugar in tablet form and cut into squares when cool.

When I was at school a lady sat at the school gates at lunchtime and sold beef patties and coconut grater. The patties were very hot but delicious, they cost tuppence each and a square of grater cost a penny to cool the tongue!

On the trip north we stopped at fruit stalls, which were many on the side of the road. I also had fresh coconut water straight out of the coconut. The coconut was then chopped in half with one swipe of a machete, a slither of the outside of the nut was used to scoop out the lovely jelly inside.

We had a lovely day at a very sandy beach with calm clear azure water in fact it was so tepid and great to swim in, I didn't want to get out. Several of the ladies brought a plate of delicious food, salads and cold meats and fresh bread rolls which they purchased when we arrived at Port Antonio. There was also fruit salad and ice cream and Sister had brought us each a chocolate bar to finish off with.

JAMAICA RE-UNION 1984

Things in the country had not changed but I found the city very dirty. There were goats wandering around eating a lot of the rubbish lying around in the streets. It was less friendly and there were parts too dangerous to walk through. This made me very unhappy to see how changed things were in all the places I had lived in. All the gardens bare from shrubbery, to make living there safer, the verandahs were enclosed with metal shutters, all windows barred, those who could afford it had guards and fierce dogs.

Gone were the days of freedom to roam as I had in my youth. But it was so lovely to catch up with my school friends, teachers, friends and neighbours and to celebrate a wonderful reunion.

Cooling off

On following page:
Photo a: In Sister Marie Emmanual's office, I.C.H, Kingston Jamaica April 1984
Photo b: Girl guide reunion with old classmates
Photo c: Garfield and Judith Thomas (nee Troman) and two sons, Mandaville
Photo d: Reunion with old friends
Photo e: Port Antonio, North East Jamaica
Photo f: Roadside fruit stand

Incredible Memories

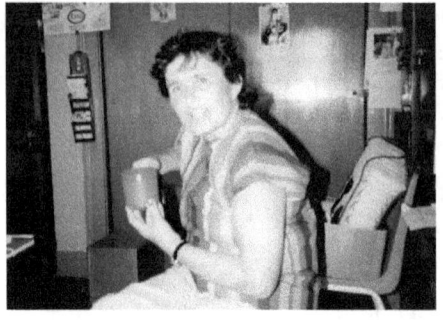

Photo a

Photo b

Photo c

Photo d

Photo e

Photo f

JAMAICA RE-UNION 1984

Picnic and trip to Port Antonio, guides past and present

Chapter 65

UK BY CAR

The next time I visited England I went with Sue in 1989, she had never travelled abroad so it was quite an experience for her. Before our trip, we drove down to Denmark to share in Alison and her new partner, Keith's affirmation. That evening when we returned to our cottage where we were to sleep, I slipped and hurt my foot. No, I had not had too much to drink! The next day after our farewells we drove to Bridgetown where we were breaking our journey at Margaret and Peter's house. The following day we drove to Marie-Therese and Claude's and the next day we were to start our trip. We flew to Singapore where we changed planes. By this time my foot was quite swollen. Then on to Italy landing in Rome to find our luggage had gone on to Holland!!! We had been met by my cousin Heather who took us to their unit where we were staying. The next morning, Heather took us to collect our lost bags as we were promised they would be at the lost property. That was an experience, we were shown into a large room with rows of shelves full of bags and told to help ourselves. We found our bags and thought we would have to check they were the right ones, but no one was interested and we could have helped ourselves to a couple of other bags if we were so inclined.

Heather gave us a tour of all the interesting parts of Rome, she was full of information. The traffic was quite frightening but Heather was used to driving around. That night Angielo and Heather took us out for a meal and we had an hilarious enjoyable evening with them. We related stories about our farming life and when we told the story about catching two small lambs, Angielo burst out laughing. He said that it was the first time he had laughed since the day they had lost their youngest son in a tragic accident a year ago. We had a very enjoyable two days with them before catching the bus to Ascoli Piceno to stay with my sister

UK BY CAR

Teresa. Had an exciting ride with the driver sounding the clarion horn at each corner as we sped up the mountain side. It was also sounded when approaching an oncoming vehicle the driver recognised.

There were small villages perched on top of any area that availed itself to several buildings across valleys. Terraced vegetable gardens running down the hillside. The road ran along shear rock held together by heavy wire mesh to prevent landslides. Then all of a sudden, we would arrive at a town where some of the passengers disembarked. At one of these towns we stopped for a twenty-minute break, presumably the halfway mark.

We were met by a smiling and relieved Teresa; happy we had arrived safely. We walked to where her car was parked. A very small car unable barely to fit us and our luggage, but we squeezed in. We ascended to Teresa's flat doing several trips in a very small rickety lift to the floor below hers. By then we were tired and very hungry. Teresa had ready a delicious cold meal, potato salad, cold meats and salad followed by fruit and a welcome mug of coffee. Then it was siesta time after catching up on a heap of family news.

The next day we met most of the family over a nice meal then Sue showed a film of family and Alison and Keith's wedding, Spent a couple of days wandering all over Ascoli and visiting villages by bus, Then it was time to return to Rome which we did by bus, Sue took a film as we travelled along. Found our own way to Heather and Angielo's, Aldo their eldest son had just returned from Aden. He had some very interesting tales to tell of his travels and he also showed us how the Arabs of Yemen pot their head gear on. The next day we took a taxi to the airport, saw three accidents, the worst caused us to find an alternative route.

We had a good flight, took a bus to Reading then a train to Swindon where a nice porter helped us with our bags and put us on to a small train to Stroud where we were met by my brother David who was very excited to see us. Sarah, David's youngest was living with them and made a delicious supper. We chatted for a while but were very tired and went to bed at 9:30 so missed my Sister-in-law Marianne and my nephew Matthew who returned from London at 11:30.

Sue and I got up early but couldn't find the kettle, so when David came down, we all had breakfast. The camera had been playing up so Sue and I went into town, Dixons sold us some head cleaning gear but it got jammed. Matthew took it next door to Bryan who said his brother-in-law would be able to fix it. Matthew took Sue into town but Philip said we needed a different part for the UK. The next day up early, laid the table and all had breakfast. Bryan came over and took camera to get it fixed, Marianne started to get lunch, David took Sue and me for a lovely walk along and old Canal and up through a beautiful village. That evening Matthew and Sarah went back to London.

The next day went into town and gave back chewed up tape and were refunded. Asked everywhere and could not get part. Got a three-pound fine

Incredible Memories

for parking! Got money out from Nation Wide. David Sue and I left for Gloucester to pick up the car we had hired, but David's car started to play up so went home and phoned to say we would be there in the morning. David took his car to his mechanic. David took us and left us in Gloucester the next morning, after filling all the papers and paying our deposit we went out to drive away when a truck that had taken off in front of the car had left a nasty greasy mess on the windscreen. Was this what we had to breath in when driving behind a diesel truck, we were horrified. We drove around to get used to the car, visited the Cathedral and some lovely spots around the city. It was getting late, phoned Stroud and were told Bryan was coming over to watch the video so we drove back to Bisley Road. The video wouldn't work, Sue phoned Phil he said we needed another part for it to work in the UK. We went for a walk with Mum down by a church, it was high up so we had a lovely view down over the rail line to the Severn River, Sarah and Marian had made a delicious supper which we had after gin and tonic and nibbles.

Next day drove into Stroud with Mum, she bought Sue a book and gave me some money to spend. Got part for the video for 35 pounds from Phil. When we got back David and Marianne were getting ready to go on a visit to Wales, I watered the garden and then drove Mum to the station. Then went down the back block to say good-bye to John, Irene and Ian, neighbours.

Up early and took off to Stratford on Avon, we took a tour bus, Sue filmed places of interest. Then we drove to Wolverhampton and took the M6, it took us 1 hour to drive 3 miles, finally got to Kidsgrove, asked the way to Pennyfield. Found Barrie and Pauline's house and had a very emotional reunion. We had met this couple at the very first place I'd stayed when we arrived in Australia all those years ago, the dreadful 'hostel'. That evening we looked at photos and caught up on family news. Went to bed very tired.

Next morning, we got up and Barrie made his favourite egg, tomato and a sort of pancake dish which is so filling it does for 'Brunch'. Then they took us for a lovely drive through the hills and dales of that area. We stopped at a quaint village pub and had a couple of drinks and a counter tea. On the way back we stopped near where a couple of men were fishing in a river, watched then for a while and then returned home. All very tired so had an early night. We visited their children the next day at their homes. It was strange to see them grown up married and with their own children. All well settled in their own homes and happily married to really nice partners. A very full day and all tired, retired early and said we wanted to get on the road early.

Sue and I got up early and got ourselves breakfast, got our gear into the car and still no signs of Barrie and Pauline, Sue wanted to get going and started to get a bit annoyed when they came down , we said a hurried

UK BY CAR

farewell and finally left at 10:30. Made for the M6 and then the A6 to Kendal then Penrith to Carlisle where we decided to turn west to Windemere and the Lake District. The scenery was beautiful, we drove around but found it was so busy with tourists, nowhere to park, drove on a bit and discovered a lovely building with plenty of parking, This turned out to be a sort of college, we sat on a lawn and had a picnic lunch talked to a couple of young folk who told us they were students there but were on two weeks break. We continued north on the A704 and made for Gretna Green hoping to make it early evening, we were fortunate to find a nice B and B. Up early next morning had a look around the town, very interesting then took off to Glasgow. Had a drive around and stopped at a couple of places on the way, nice countryside. We didn't stay long in Glasgow, found our way out on the road to Lock Lomond. Very industrial area on the way through to the Lock. Breathtaking scenery, we drove into a parking area close to a large building which we were told was going to be turned into an hotel. Ideal spot for anyone to stay. We wandered around admiring the views up the Lock and across to distant hills.

We continued north on the A82, hilly country running more or less alongside the Lock then turned into the Black Mountains to Glen Coe, the Three Sisters to our left, along Lock Lever to Kinlochly where we discussed whether to continue to Fort William. We decided we would spend the night there and look around as there was an Abbey that I thought would be interesting. But when we got there, we found great celebrations going on, everywhere was booked out so we had to continue to Spean Bridge where we found a delightful B and B with such a nice couple, very homely and they made us so welcome. We had a delicious evening meal for very little extra, then a huge breakfast of mouth-watering pork sausages, eggs and tomatoes and fresh buttery rolls the likes one can only find in Scotland.

When we climbed into the beautiful Westcountry Scottish countryside, we came across a well-kept area with plaques commemorating different events during WW II when it was a training area for the army. We stopped for a break and wandered around reading up the History of the place, something I had never heard of. The hilly position ideal for combat training, the conditions being rather difficult in spots to take cover, but also in other areas a vantage spot to attack or take cover.

We continued up A82 up the side of Loch Lochy and Loch Oich, to Fort Augustus and the beginning of Loch Ness to Invermorrison, Strone and to Drumnadrochit where we stopped to take a walk around Glen Urquhart Castle, an old stamping ground of mine. Since last visiting the Castle, the building, or what was left of it, had been made safe for tourists to walk among the parts of the building and the beautifully kept surrounds. The view looked straight up the Ness, we looked as many did, to see if the monster might appear. Leslie's grocery shop was still there in Drumnadrochit, a few more houses than I remembered.

Incredible Memories

We continued our journey along the side of Lock Ness until we reached Inverness, met up with my in-laws. Everyone so welcoming as usual and so much to catch up on. We were invited to tea at Mrs Duncan's, now widowed, they owned the shop at Glen Cannich when we lived there when my children were small. In fact, my daughter Margaret was born there and Bill Duncan helped us to move down to England. Mrs Duncan gave me the Millar's phone number, a couple of friends from the old days at Glen Cannich, we arranged to stay with them for a couple of days.

We drove back out along Loch Ness to Drumnadrochit, the scenery looking just as beautiful and interesting each time viewed. We turned into Glen Urquhart, the road still narrow as I remembered, through a couple of small villages until we came to Shenval where we had lived in Forestry house back in 1957. The pine trees had grown to a great height since then. We drove in over the old bridge, past our house which looked the same, then drove out again as didn't know anyone. Drove on to Glen Cannich to find our old house was no longer there and things quite changed. The school and Church were still there, so was the shop and the houses behind it. We drove on past the hydroelectric pump house, and the swinging bridge to Tomich where we were warmly greeted by the Millar's, shown our room then settled down with a welcome cup of tea and lots to catch up on.

Their house was built of stone, grey granite, at the bottom of a steep hill on which they had a terraced vegetable garden. We sat out in the garden for high tea as the evenings were still long and light plus we were enjoying perfect weather. In the morning after a good night's sleep, Sue and I went for a walk up the road to visit a couple who had made a shepherd's shelter built off the hillside. They had made an extraordinary living room into their home. Everything made from re-cycled material, their double bed folded away to become their living room, that was divided from the kitchen area by two-sided cupboards under a work bench. The stove, a wood-burner was made up from recycled material the hinges on the oven door made by the guy from a piece of stainless steel he found at the tip and beat it out to look like an old-fashioned hinge. The bathroom, tiny, with only a shower recess and an old-fashioned toilet, the pull chain type; only this worked by a stuffed mouse running down the arm thus weighing it down and flushing the water. The whole room was unbelievable and so well thought out.

The roof was flat with herbs growing and lettuce and vegetables like radishes, turnips and beetroot, Then a wee bit away from their home a timber mill where they cut their own planks, the like I can hardly describe as it entailed using a ladder, somehow, to run the tree under the saw. Then the planks were carefully stacked to season. Just amazing and the couple so nice, an experience never to be forgotten.

After a couple of glorious days, we returned to Inverness, a different route via Beauly, which hadn't changed much. While there we visited the Castle. For the last days we drove around, over the new bridge to the Black

UK BY CAR

Isle, down to Kessock Ferry and around the streets where the Aitken family grew up and I first stayed at. Most of the houses were boarded up and looked uninhabited.

We visited Forres where Tom's youngest sister lived but she was off on holiday so drove back through to a community at Find Horn. Quite interesting but didn't find anyone very helpful. Then drove back to Inverness via Nairn. Visited in-laws to say farewell before starting on our return South via another route.

From Inverness we drove to Daviot, down the A9 Tomatin, Carrbridge and took the road to Aviemore all very mountainous. At Kingussie we stopped and had lunch, then still on the A9 through Glen Truin as far as Dalwhinnie Hotel where we booked in for the night, by then we needed to get a good night's sleep. The Scottish countryside so green, hill upon hill through Glen Garry, Calvin, Blair Atholl then Pitlochry. Mountains on either side, they ski in the winter and grass slide in the summer. We drove through all these places, slowly and looking as we went but didn't have time to stop at too many places. Dunkeld, over the Tay and driving through so many small villages on the way to Perth which meant we were back to busy cities.

Still on the A9 out of Perth on to Stirling but at Causeway Head took the A907 to Dunfermline and A873 to get on A90 and make for Forth Road Bridge where we stayed on A90. Quite an experience driving on the bridge over the Firth of Forth. Not a long journey to Edinburgh where we booked into a B and B absolutely exhausted but hungry, so after freshening up we went for a walk to find some food.

After a hearty Scottish breakfast, we made for the Castle. At the entrance went into a building and looked up the name of my uncle David who had been killed at the end of WW1. Found it with all details having served in the Black Watch Regiment. We walked up the Mile Walk to the castle visiting several shops on the way. The Castle is quite impressive, we wandered through it all then it was time for it to close. We found something to eat then sat on a lawn area listening to bag pipes and watching Scottish dancing. This was just below the Castle silhouetted against the night sky. What a lovely city.

On our way out of Scotland, we took a wrong turn and ended up driving through hilly but rather nice countryside. We were amazed at how white the sheep were compared to Australian sheep. We finally found our way to Whitby Robinhood Bay and Scarborough via the Moors all on the east coast of north England. Parking in the parking bays was way past our budget but at Scarborough a very kind gentleman gave us his ticket which still had an hour on it. It was a very mild day so we enjoyed wandering around and breathing in the fresh sea breeze.

From Scarborough we made our way to Pickering, Hemsley and Sproxton on our journey to visit my cousin Mark at Ampleforth, then to find

Incredible Memories

the house. When we arrived, Mark was not home but the lady who does for him came across and said Mark was not yet back from London but she knew we were coming so let us in. We had got freshened up when Mark arrived. I volunteered to do dinner that night, Mark went and got food in. Two other cousins of mine turned up, both Monks at Ampleforth College. We spent an hilarious evening catching up and Sue showed videos getting up to date while we enjoyed very good wine and food.

The next day we helped Mark in the large garden of his and he took us on a tour of interesting places around, had a good night's sleep and left early to make for York. Followed a mud map Mark made for us to get on to B 1363 which would take us to A19 which took us into York. On the way out, we drove onto high ground and looked down on to Ampleforth College and took photos.

We drove around the beautiful City of York admiring all the buildings then made our way to Lincoln where we stopped to have lunch and visit the Castle where we roamed around the grounds and climbed up on the ramparts of the Castle giving us a lovely view of the city. From there we made for Aisthorpe where Sue wanted to look up any history on her husband's family who hailed from there. We spent a lot of time looking up records at the church and the Council Building but found little information. We decided to continue our journey and find a nice B and B to spend the night before continuing to Clare to visit my niece Helen. After driving for an hour, we found a nice Motor Lodge where we booked in for the night. The sleeping area has parking, then across a forecourt there was a large petrol station with mechanic available, and a restaurant plus a takeaway section. We got take away and ate in our very comfortable room where we could make tea or coffee.

After a good night's sleep, (it was surprisingly quiet considering the amount of traffic coming and goings), we breakfasted over at the eatery and continued south to Clare. Drove through very flat country with market gardens on either side. Saw a sign to a Saxon Village but when we arrived, we saw tour buses so decided against it. We found a lovely little wood just off the road so we drove in where we had sandwiches and coffee and a nice quiet walk. Saw some squirrels, studied them quietly for a spell, and enjoyed the scent of a wood.

Went on via Bury St Edmund, then through nice rolling hills into Clare. We had to ask directions a couple of times before finding the house and were greeted by Helen and her eldest son Christopher. Soon after Helen went to pick up her other son, Johnathan. While we got our gear in and were having a cuppa Les arrived (Helen's husband) he seemed surprised to see us. Sue set up the camera and filmed the boys before they left for Cubs. We had supper when the boys got home. All had early night.

Les had already left for work when we got up and the boys were ready to go to school. Helen had things to do so Sue and I wandered around Clare.

We found some very interesting shops and also a two-story second-hand building where we spent a couple of hours. So much we would have liked to buy but would never have been able to cart around with us. We spent a very enjoyable evening with the family showing them film we had taken and telling all about our trip and family back in Australia.

We left early next morning and made our way across country to Stroud. Next day went shopping, Marianne did a portrait of Sue, my niece Clare arrived and a friend of David's from Greece also arrived for lunch. Clare showed us some of her jewellery and Marianne showed some of her paintings. Clare packed her jewellery, Marianne and Sarah went to Cheltenham. On their return Sue showed film of our trip so far while I made supper. I phoned my aunt Alice to say about what time we would be with her the next day and wrote a thank you note to Helen.

Next day we had a lovely drive down to my aunt's, stopping at Bath and exploring around the city before continuing up some narrow windy roads to the village where she lived. We passed a pub called Ring of Roses and finally found the cottage where we were warmly greeted by Alice. The village of Holcombe had many narrow lanes, a post office come grocery shop and some lovely walking paths to the next village. Alice had a picturesque garden where we sat and ate our meals, it was so nice having long sunny days, we had been very lucky with good weather during our travels. After a couple of relaxed days, we continued to my aunt Margaret's.

We arrived at Well after driving through beautiful English countryside drove down the main street till I found the car park behind Margaret's house where we had to park. Margaret walked up her very colourful, narrow garden to welcome us. On arrival and after taking our gear inside we sat and had a sherry and nibbles while we caught up. Well was interesting as nearly all the buildings were old grey looking and very interesting. We then went for a walk with Margaret all the time giving us a run-down on all the places of interest in the town. Her house was a semi-detached and the front door opened straight on to the pavement. A small but very warm comfortable two-story house, with a lot of old furnishings she had brought with her. We had a delicious evening meal of a roast followed by chocolate mouse and home ground coffee. After the meal Sue showed some film and by ten thirty, we were ready for bed. In the morning we took a stroll to the library. Then back for a coffee before we were on the road again returning to Stroud.

When we got back to David and Marianne's, we had a big wash to do so we had clean cloths again for the rest of our visit before our long voyage back to Australia. Spent a couple of days enjoying Stroud and the John family. We went for some lovely walks, and I did a bit of gardening while Sue did things with Marianne. Then it was time for farewells, David and Marianne took us to catch the 9:05 to Waterloo. David ran along beside the train to the end of the platform.

Incredible Memories

From Waterloo got a train to Wimbledon then took a taxi to the convent where my mother lived, she had made a lovely pasta salad for lunch, we all had a siesta. After the rest, Sue and I went for a walk up to Cannizaro Park at the edge of Wimbledon Common, a very well-kept park with a variety of summer flowers. Saw a coot's nest on a little island in a pond at the bottom of a lawn which I remembered my children used to roll down whenever we visited or stayed in Wimbledon. When we got back, we had drinks with Mum and told her all about our travels and showed her films.

Next day we went up to London and bought silver to take back to a friend who made jewellery. We walked from Oxford St through to Buckingham Palace via Shaftsbury Avenue and Soho, up the Mall and got to my uncle Tom's in time for lunch. They lived just behind the Palace. Sue went and had a rest while aunt Mabel and I caught up. Then we left for my nephew Simon and his wife Jane's, got to J and S at 7pm then watched their first baby Dominic having a bath. Had a fresh salmon dish for supper and Sue showed video. Simon ordered a taxi to take us back to Wimbledon, got back very tired.

All had a late rise, had breakfast then Mum went to Mass, Sue and I went for a walk around Wimbledon and I showed her where we used to live and also the Darleston Road where my grandparents lived then we went to the church just up the road to meet Mum. Showed Sue around the church then we walked back to The Downs. Had a drink then Sue set up the video. Had a very nice lunch and a rest then a sherry and nibbles before a light meal before we took a taxi to the airport where we were to catch a plane at 10pm for Singapore.

Arrived at Singapore at 5:50pm after a good flight where we slept most of the time. Were taken to the Phoenix Hotel, had showers and got an early bed. The next day we walked to a huge shopping complex to do some shopping but found the prices similar to those in Australia so window shopped. Took a bus tour which took us further than we would have gone walking and more comfortable as it was so humid. That evening we discovered a Deli that was open 24\7 and decided to buy our evening meal there and eat it quietly in our room. The next day we had to pack our things as we had to vacate our room by 10 am. We didn't venture far during the day mostly stayed at the hotel keeping cool and drinking lots of cold drinks. We were picked up at 5:30 for the long drive to the airport, our flight to Perth was at 8:45. The airport is quite large with many duty-Free shops which we browsed about and bought a few gifts for the family. We arrived back in Perth at 1:30am and after lengthy passing through customs were greeted by many members of the family, were driven back to my unit and sat for a couple of hours over cups of coffee and toast relating stories of our trip.

Chapter 66

LONE TRIP AROUND THE WORLD

Every two years I would borrow $2,000 and with what I'd managed to save would take a trip over to visit my mother, aunts and uncles and my brother David and his family. It was a treat to enjoy the English countryside, my sister in law, Marianne would always take me some where new like Slimbridge, to wander among so many different types of birds. David often took me with him when he was having a statue cast or when he went shopping at wonderful hardware stores. When visiting my mother in Wimbledon we would go for walks on Wimbledon common or visit an aunt and uncle in London, there was always so much to do that my six weeks would fly. On the way back to Australia, I would go via Italy and visit my sister Teresa and her family, spend a couple of nights there before continuing to Singapore where I would spend a night or two to break the journey and relax.

On one of my trips, I decided to do a round the world trip again and visit a sister in Canada and a sister in America and caught up with their families as well as visiting a couple of friends then on to England to catch up with family and friends there.

On this trip, I made for Vancouver first to visit my youngest sister, Tina, and her husband, Shanti, they had moved to a unit since my last visit, it was on the opposite side of the harbour to the main part of the city. Very handy to a shopping complex and also with some lovely streets to walk along which I enjoyed on my daily walks admiring the houses and their gardens. One day we went across to the city by a funny little ferry where people commuted with their bicycles, we stood and could wonder at all around as well as some interesting people on the ferry. Another day I caught up with my old friend, Anne who Vera and I met on our travels around Australia, we had lunch together and it was like old times, both of us had done so much since we last saw each other on my previous visit.

Incredible Memories

After a lovely but too short a visit I took a plane to visit my sister, Pat, in Miami, going via Fort Knox. When at the airport I wondered why so many people were munching away on hamburgers then I realized no food or drinks were served on the flight unless one bought something at a terrible price. When I landed at Miami, I was met by my sister Pat, her daughter Genevieve, who I had not met before, and my grand-nephew Adam, a lovely boy of about five. It was quite a drive to Pat's unit where I was glad to enjoy some of Pat's good cooking. And to have met Pat's ex-husband Jean-Marie for the first time. After enjoying some of Pat's good West Indian cooking I was good and ready for bed.

While there I met the rest of Pat's family, went for a BBQ at Gilbert and Sandra's, that was Pat's youngest son and their two girls. Another day we went over to Pascale, her youngest daughter, and Robert and his son by first marriage and Bianca. Pascale's daughter. A few days before I was to leave there was a cyclone warning so we went over to Pascale's to help board up the windows. When the cyclone arrived, it was a very noisy affair but luckily no damage. Then I was to fly out, Tony, Pascale's first husband drove me to the airport, He was a very nice guy.

The cyclone had decided to turn around and make for the coast again so the pilot announced he would be flying very low which was quite a frightening experience as when I looked out the window there seemed to be lots of little planes flying here, there and everywhere. I wondered how we managed to miss them all. The next thing as I looked out of the window, I seemed to be looking straight down the middle of the cyclone, off to our left as we flew up the East coast. Like looking down a tunnel of different colours.

I was pleased when we arrived safely at Philadelphia airport where I was to be met by Bertran, Pat's eldest son. I was to stay with him, his wife Christine and their three children, Christopher, Jonathan and baby sister Michele. They lived in a huge house out of the city, the basement was in the throes of being made into a playroom come room for the boys to have their computers and desks to do their homework. Bertran was only twenty last time I had met him in New York on my first visit to the States. I was made very welcome and got on well with Christine when she took days off to entertain me. One weekend, Bertran drove us all down the coast on a scenic drive, calling in to a couple of beaches on the way to Mayne. I was to go on to New Jersey to stay with Keith's mother, Carol. It was arranged that Bertran would drive me to a point along the Highway going north, he spoke to Carol as I didn't know what and where. Every now and then we had to pay a toll, then Bertran said we should be pretty close and to look out for a black station wagon on the other side of the road when I spotted it we drove on a bit further and he did an illegal U turn and drove into a huge car park and there was Carol standing by her car. After introductions and a wee chat, we parted company and Carol drove to her daughter Linda's place where there was a gathering of musicians enjoying a delicious spread, we joined in.

LONE TRIP AROUND THE WORLD

Everyone was very interested in hearing what I was about and were very friendly, then they got on with their musical evening. That was great fun.

Linda offered us a bed to stay the night but we decided to drive on to New Jersey as we didn't think we would get much sleep with all the noise, said our farewells and drove north out of Philadelphia. Paid a few more tolls and arrived at Carol's in New Jersey at about 2am, had some fruit and a cup of tea and I was shown to my bedroom on the third floor of her huge muddly house. I slept like a log got up about 8 o'clock and wandered down to the ground floor and tried to remember where the bathroom was. Carol heard me and came out said she would get breakfast while I did my ablutions. We sat at a large table in this vast room which was rather dark then we went for a bit of a walk around the area where she lived, there seemed to be a lot of old large houses with rather untidy gardens with squirrels darting around. Carol said she hoped I hadn't been disturbed during the night as they get in under the roof off a tree close to the house.

Carol drove me around to an old army pier on the Hudson, then up to a look-out where we did a bit of bird watching. I looked up and saw a white-headed eagle sailing with the wind and it had a fish in its claws, one of the other bird watchers lent me some strong binoculars which was marvellous. Another day Carol drove to a park overlooking Manhattan, there were some very nice walks and it was so peaceful listening to strange bird song which I did not recognise. We then went down into the outskirts of New York city and stopped by a hot-dog van where she bought me a special hot-dog which had sauerkraut in it, rather delicious.

After a very pleasant visit, I left New York For London where I was met by a taxi man holding a card with my name, who drove me to Wimbledon to the convent where my mother lived. It was good to see my mother looking so well after my brother saying she was very frail. We sat and had a sherry and nibbles before my mother produced a yummy salad and cold cuts for lunch, while I had been freshening up. After eating we both retired for a siesta. When we got up we went for a long walk up to the Common while we caught up on family news. The next day we went by train to Woodley to stay with my eldest brother my mother only stayed a couple of days then returned to Wimbledon.

The countryside around was always lovely to explore, my sister in law took me on several long walks which we thoroughly enjoyed as there were always such colourful gardens. One day we walked to a railway bridge and looked down into one of the deepest cuttings surrounded by lush woodlands. I went for many walks when I wasn't catching up with friends and family. From there I went and visited my Aunt Alice and stayed a couple of nights in her quaint cottage and lovely garden where we spent many an hour talking and enjoying all our meals in the garden as had fine weather and long evenings. From there I went to visit my niece Rachel, one of David my brother's daughters and her two daughters who were nearly grown up since

Incredible Memories

I had last seen them. After two nights I went to visit my Aunt Margaret, it was nice to be able to get to know her a bit better as she was one relative I had not seen much of. We got on like a house on fire and had a most enjoyable visit. I then returned to Wimbledon as it was getting close to the time I should be moving on. From there I went up to stay with my nephew Matthew and his partner. While there, I had a tour of London east down by The Tower of London. Very interesting walking from St Pauls all around that part of London quite new to me. I was taken on a tour of the Stock exchange where Matthew worked. Not long after it was closed to the public who did not have business there.

Then I flew to Poland to visit my youngest brother Christopher and his wife Barbara. It snowed while I was there so I found it very cold. While there they took me out to dinner and Chris was quite surprised when I asked if there was a non-smoking part of the building, I found everywhere I went everyone smoked and I found it distressing as I was not used to so much smoke in fact I ended up with a terrible cough and spent a couple of days in bed. Though their house was well heated, I couldn't handle not having a window open and also not being able to get out and have a walk. One day they took me into Warsaw which had been completely rebuilt, the buildings were beautiful but the city so crowded. Another day Barbara took me to an amazing market, I have never seen such a variety of sausages, delighted in the smell of their cheeses and general smell of food that was available. It was not exactly a happy experience as my brother felt he had a right to criticize the way I lived as I no longer practiced the Catholic Religion, nevertheless we parted on good terms and I was grateful that I had got the opportunity to visit them. From there I flew across to Italy.

I landed at Bologna where I was met by Mariarosa, Vincenzo's wife, and my sister Teresa's daughter-in-law, and her sister who spoke more English than Mariarosa. We drove to the Palermi's flat where I was glad to freshen up before being whisked off to their parents' house where we were to have the evening meal. They are all night owls so by the time I took off to Ascoli I was pretty exhausted. But nevertheless, appreciated all they did to show me around. Even spent a very interesting day in Florence visiting art centres and museums and crossing a quaint enclosed bridge across the river.

Most of that visit was a bit of a blank as I was feeling a lot worse with being unwell. I was glad to reach Ascoli where I was met by my sister Teresa and all I wanted to do was have a shower and go to bed with a couple of aspirins. Had a good night's sleep, felt a bit better but told Teresa I wanted to have a quiet day, she got some horrible cough mixture which helped a bit. Met up with the family at a restaurant where we had pizza. After spending a few days there, went by bus to Rome where I caught up with my cousin Heather and Angielo, her husband, had a quiet visit then caught the plane for Singapore where I stayed with a friend who took me all over the place and we also enjoyed some delicious Chinese dishes. We spent a very interesting day over at Sentosa, all the visit being taken around most of Singapore. So much nicer going around with someone who actually lives in a place but always happy to be back in the wide-open skies and climate of Western Australia.

Over the years, I made three more trips to the UK via Italy. While in England stayed mainly in Stroud as my mother was at a nursing home just out of Stroud, so visited her most days and stayed over a couple of nights at the cottage for guests, We went for walks or just enjoyed the lovely grounds where she stayed being looked after by very kind nuns, many were from India. Stayed a few days with my sister in Ascoli and Piceno and visited my cousin Heather in Rome before returning to Perth. My last trip to visit my mother was 1998, she died eighteen months later.

Chapter 67

LASTLY

I have found it difficult to decide how much more I should write about. My life has been so full, fortunate and full of exciting and interesting events. When I think about it there are possibly another two chapters. My move to Northam faced me with a new beginning having bought another house which filled my mind with all the new ideas to do with renovating. Many were similar to the work done on the other house in Moora. My block being much smaller I didn't run sheep, I didn't have a creek running through the property and my neighbours were closer and many more. I was made to feel very welcome, I had a river one block away so I had some wonderful walks along it. I was closer to Perth and often had family visit and grandchildren to stay during school holidays.

My days were always full with the renovating, starting a vegetable garden, planting a few trees and making crazy-paving paths and building a small pond. Northam was a busy little town with always an event at weekends. Once a year a boat race to Perth down the Avon River, there was a very good racecourse which attracted racers from near and far. It was one of the main towns on the way east and of course an interesting tip. I soon made many friends and found my life very busy but a wee bit more leisurely.

I spent eight happy years there before my final move to Spearwood where I was closer to the family but I missed the country life for a long time.

After Tom died, I made another trip back to Scotland with Bernadette and Marie-Therese, to take half his ashes back to his homeland and visit family. This was to be my last trip overseas.

So having joined a couple of writers groups I decided to write a book, and have ended up with this my third and final book

I hope all find it interesting and enjoy it.

ACKNOWLEDGEMENTS

While back-packing around the world in 1983 to catch up with siblings, cousins, uncles and aunts I was being asked about my childhood days in the West Indies. One of my cousins said "You have to write a book." Twenty years later I started. During the time I was writing I found out I could self-publish. At least this meant I could afford to have a book published. Though now I realized the benefit of having my work edited as I have repeated myself through the books.

The main purpose of writing after all was for family and extended family. The cover of the book is a print of a scarf my eldest daughter, Bernadette, made for me for my sixtieth birthday. Some thirty years ago. On it she has printed photos of five generations, so felt it appropriate. The title "Incredible Memories" was what my cousin called them after I had related my stories to her. Several people have said I ended too abruptly, they wanted to read more hence my reason to continue writing.

The second book being from 1947 to 1968, the beginnings of my adult life. Leading to my third book. I have decided to combine all three as my first books are no longer in the Libraries.

My grateful thanks to all who have made this possible and to all who have encouraged me to continue writing. To Luba Kambourakis for editing and arranging my first two books to be published, Kendra Lindsay for typing and corrections in several chapters. To my daughter Shona (previously Alison) Hutchings who helped with photos and endless hours helping me to try and master my laptop, to get some order in setting out titles and to put all on the thumb-drive. My thanks to Karen Peradon-Alaga for editing and proof reading.

Incredible Memories

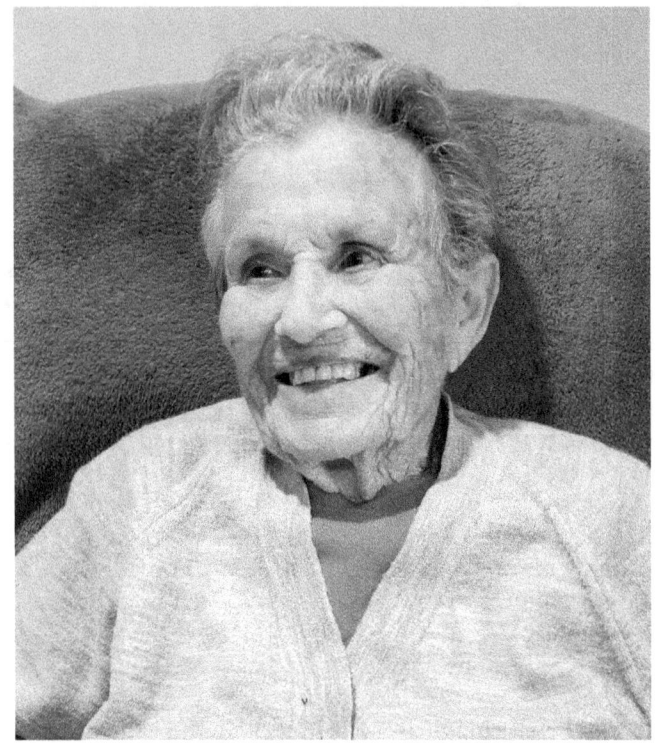

Anne John-Aitken. © 2020.

APPENDIX 1

Glossary

Ratings	Anyone under the rank of a Petty Officer
Matelot	Pronounced 'mate low', a sailor, naval rating
SPROG	A new entry
VAD's	Volunteer Aides
PIP's	Rank of an officer
Civvy St	When a person goes back to being a civilian
Gone for a Burton	A waste of time
Vicky verky	The other way

Incredible Memories

www.ingramcontent.com/pod-product-compliance
Lightning Source LLC
Chambersburg PA
CBHW070417010526
44118CB00014B/1794